MARKETING YOURSELF

JORDAN LE BEL
CORNELL UNIVERSITY

HAROLD SIMPKINS
JOHN MOLSON SCHOOL OF BUSINESS
CONCORDIA UNIVERSITY

Based on the *Marketing Yourself* online course
Winner of the Award for Excellence and Innovation
in Instructional Design in 2005 from the
Canadian Network for Innovation in Education

THOMSON

NELSON

Australia   Canada   Mexico   Singapore   Spain   United Kingdom   United States

Marketing Yourself
by Jordan Le Bel and Harold Simpkins

Associate Vice President, Editorial Director:
Evelyn Veitch

Acquisitions Editor:
Amie Plourde

Marketing Manager:
Ann Byford

Developmental Editor:
Joanne Sutherland

Photo Researcher and Permissions Coordinator:
Sandra Mark

Senior Content Production Manager:
Natalia Denesiuk Harris

Copy Editor and Proofreader:
Kelli Howey

Manufacturing Manager:
Joanne McNeil

Design Director:
Ken Phipps

Interior Design:
Glenn Toddun

Cover Design:
Jocelyn Sealy

Cover Image:
BelleMedia/Shutterstock

Marketing Yourself Logo:
Rachael Herbert

Compositor:
Doris Chan

Printer:
Thomson/West

Library and Archives Canada Cataloguing in Publication Data

Le Bel, Jordan, 1968–
  Marketing yourself / Jordan Le Bel, Harold Simpkins.

Includes bibliographical references.
Also available in electronic format.
ISBN 978-0-17-647183-5

1. Vocational guidance.
2. Marketing—Vocational guidance. 3. Career development.
I. Simpkins, Harold II. Title.

HF5415.35.L42 2008   650.14
C2007-905514-1

ISBN-13: 978-0-17-647183-5
ISBN-10: 0-17-647183-9

TABLE OF CONTENTS

Jordan L. Le Bel, Ph.D.

Jordan Le Bel is Associate Professor in the Department of Hospitality Facilities and Operations at the School of Hotel Administration (Cornell University), the worldwide leader in hospitality management research and education. Dr. Le Bel teaches introductory courses in food-service management as well as an advanced elective course on the design of pleasurable dining experiences. Prior to joining Cornell University, Le Bel was at the John Molson School of Business (Concordia University) in Montreal, where he taught courses in Experience Marketing, Consumer Behaviour, and Advertising and was the 2005 recipient of the Distinguished Teaching Award. Le Bel was born and raised in Montreal. He currently writes for *Commerce,* a French management monthly publication.

Dr. Le Bel conducts research in the areas of hedonic and aesthetic consumption. He is particularly interested in the definition of pleasure, its various dimensions, and its impact on decision making and behaviour. As a former chef, his expertise in the food industry frequently serves as the background for his research. For instance, using chocolate as a stimulus, he recently demonstrated that more intense pleasure does not necessarily translate into more consumption. He has presented his work at many professional and trade conferences such as the Association for Consumer Research, the Society for Consumer Psychology, the Marketing Science Institute, and the Canadian Institute of Food Science and Technology.

His work has been featured in *USA Today* and the *Washington Post;* on the *Today Show* (NBC) and CBS Radio; and across Canada in the *National Post,* on *Canada AM* (CTV), and on *This Morning Live* (Global). He has contributed to televised specials on chocolate (Discovery Channel, *Historia*), and recently authored the preface of the cookbook *Gastronomy and the Forest* (www.gastronomyandtheforest.com); the French version was the winner of the 2003 Best Cookbook in the World Award by Gourmand International. From 2002 to 2004, he was a regular contributor to the top-rated French television morning show *"Salut Bonjour!"* where he presented a segment on marketing and pleasure.

Prior to his academic career, Dr. Le Bel was an executive chef and a restaurant inspector for *Distinguished Restaurants of North America* and co-edited the book *Health and Pleasure at the Table* (1995). From 1992 to 1994, he was a lecturer at the Norwegian College of Hotel Management, where he taught courses on restaurant management and marketing.

Harold J. Simpkins

Professor Simpkins is Senior Lecturer at the John Molson School of Business (Concordia University), which he joined in 1983. Prior to entering academia he was vice-president of MacLaren McCann, one of Canada's largest advertising agencies. Before his agency career, Professor Simpkins was a product manager with a number of multinational food companies including Best Foods, now part of Unilever. Campaigns and programs he has developed have won a number of awards including the Canadian Award for Business Excellence in Marketing and the Retail Council of Canada's Marketing Communication Award.

In addition to Marketing Yourself, Professor Simpkins has developed and introduced the courses Business Communication and Integrated Marketing Communication. He also initiated and is the Academic Director of the Marketing Co-op Program, which has grown to become one of the largest program of its type at Concordia University. Additionally, Professor Simpkins created and launched the Marketing Cluster, a concentration of marketing courses for non-business students. It too has expanded to become the university's largest cluster.

Courses that Professor Simpkins teaches and has taught include Advertising, Retailing, Marketing Management, Integrated Marketing Communications, Business Communications, Contemporary Business Thinking, and Consumer Behaviour. In 2004, he was the recipient of the JMSB Distinguished Teaching Award.

His involvement with student activities focuses on coaching of JMSB teams in major interuniversity competitions, including the Commerce Games, Marketing Happening, *Défi Marketing,* and the *Concours de la relève publicitaire.* As an outgrowth of his coaching, Professor Simpkins has solicited businesses and not-for-profit organizations to provide real-life marketing problems to be used as the basis for in-class team projects. The resulting participants include Sotheby's, Bierbrier Brewing, Mega Bloks, the Concordia Institute for Cooperative Education, the JMSB Executive MBA Program, the Old Brewery Mission, the Canadian Human Rights Foundation, and the Lester B. Pearson School Board.

Professor Simpkins is President of Youth Employment Service, a non-profit organization that provides counsel to more than four thousand young Montreal job seekers, entrepreneurs, and artists annually.

ACKNOWLEDGMENTS

This book was truly a collaborative effort and we have been fortunate to have received the help and support of many talented and generous people.

Our thanks go first to Sachin Bhola and Lindsay Alexandre-Aimé, who assisted us in the development of the Marketing Yourself online course. This project would not have gotten off the ground without their outstanding efforts.

We'd also like to thank the many students who have given us input on the Marketing Yourself course, from those who took part in the focus groups we conducted prior to creating the course to those who have enrolled in Marketing Yourself and have given us a wealth of valuable, constructive suggestions.

We've had the pleasure of working with extremely committed and professional head teaching assistants whose help in managing the Marketing Yourself course freed up the time we needed to write this book. Merci to Jason Baxter, Sarah Beaumier, Aline Massouh, and Maude Lacoste. It has been a joy and privilege working with each of you. We are also grateful to all our other teaching assistants, including Tanya Saba, Michele Falcone, Shai Delson, Samantha Cleyn, Randy Bitensky, Ohad Reveh, Dilani Silva, Atul Sachdev, Tina Silverstein, Jennifer Nguyen, Noah Weinstein, and Dana Cook.

Our thanks also go to the individuals who accepted to be spotlighted in our Marketing Yourself in Action profiles. Your input has enriched the book and has added a very "real world" perspective.

We'd also like to recognize the support and guidance of our good friend Dr. Michel Bergier, former professor and chair of the Department of Marketing at the John Molson School of Business.

We want to thank the terrific group of people at eConcordia who have believed in the Marketing Yourself project from Day One and supported us throughout its evolution. Without the contributions of Andrew McAusland, Kaoru Matsui, Patrick Devey, Catherine Lahaise, Veronika Leisiuk, and Mylene Allard, the Marketing Yourself course and book would never have become a reality.

Finally, the support from the people at Thomson Nelson made it possible to create an end product that lives up to our hopes and expectations. Special thanks to Joanne Sutherland and the rest of the Nelson editorial team.

Appreciatively,

Harold Simpkins & Jordan Le Bel

Find a job you love and you'll never work another day in your life.
—*Confucius*

Students, colleagues, and book publishers have repeatedly told us that no one really reads book introductions. We truly hope that ours will be an exception. Marketing yourself and how you do it can have a profound effect on the rest of your life. The Chinese philosopher Confucius summed up this notion perfectly when he said, "Find a job you love and you'll never work another day in your life." With this in mind, our goal for this book is to help you identify and embark on a career that you'll love with the ultimate goal of making the work that you choose to do a joy.

Although we had been toying with the idea of writing a book such as this one for some time, the inspiration for *Marketing Yourself* came in a flash. As business school professors with more than 30 years of combined teaching experience, we had always assumed our students had fairly clear ideas about the careers they intended to pursue after graduating. We took it for granted they had done—or at least were planning to do—some basic research about the fields in which they were thinking of working. We assumed that they had developed career plans or at least had given serious thought to them. We were convinced they remembered and knew how to apply the material covered in the courses we and other marketing professors teach.

Over the years it became increasingly clear that our assumptions were not entirely valid. The evidence included the following:

- Many of our best students would show up at our offices just prior to graduation to ask us for advice on which careers to choose and to get tips on how to tweak their resumes and cover letters.

- When asked if they had researched any fields of interest and how their skills, knowledge, and personalities suited these fields, typically the answer was an embarrassed "no" or "not yet."

- In our advanced marketing courses, we were often surprised at how most students could not recall the most basic concepts that are taught in introductory marketing courses. So we began administering an anonymous test in the first classes of these courses. It asked students to provide short definitions for four of these concepts. More than 500 tests were completed and, on a scale of 100, the average grade was less than 20 percent.

Another piece of critical evidence fuelled our motivation to write this book. We both teach courses in advertising, and for years have kicked off the first class with the question *"How many of you would like to work in advertising after you graduate?"* On average, more than 90 percent of students answered in the affirmative. We used to leave it at that and assume that almost all of our students intended to pursue a career in advertising. Then, a few years ago, we began to probe further and added three more questions:

1. The median starting salary for newly graduating marketing majors is approximately $35 000. The median salary for new marketing graduates working for advertising agencies is about $23 000. How many of you still want to work in advertising?

   Fewer than 10 percent of those who had expressed an interest in working in advertising still wanted to work in the field.

2. The typical work week in entry-level marketing positions is between 35 and 45 hours. In advertising agencies, it's between 45 and 60 hours. How many of you now want to work in advertising?

   More than half of those with their hands still up now dropped out.

3. With a marketing major, the most likely position you'll qualify for will be in account service, meaning you'll be doing a fair amount of selling and spending most of your time managing relationships with clients who can be unpredictable and demanding. How many of you now want to work in advertising?

   By this time, there were usually one or two—and sometimes zero—students wanting to work in the field.

This little exercise helped us understand why so many students had come to our offices in a state of disillusionment after securing those hard-to-get job interviews with advertising agencies. Some had even been called back for the even-harder-to-get second interviews, only to feel insulted, shocked, and disappointed with the salary offers they received. "I can't live on the money they're prepared to pay. Plus, they expect me to work up to 60 hours a week. I'll have no social life. There's no way I'm going to work for an advertising agency. I don't have a clue about what I'm going to do now." These are typical of the comments we've heard. Our feeling about their reactions was, "If they had done their homework and researched the advertising industry, they might have chosen a completely different career path and wouldn't have gotten sidetracked on a path that didn't suit their needs and expectations." This led us to ask many of our other soon-to-be-graduating students about their career plans. Quite frankly, we were surprised that—of all people—virtually all the marketing majors we talked to hadn't even thought about applying the key concepts they had learned in the marketing courses they took to themselves and their careers! They hadn't analyzed and evaluated alternative career paths. Their career goals, when these students had any, were often unfocused and poorly articulated.

They had ill-defined strategies for achieving their goals, and very few of them had thought about what their next steps should be let alone set a timetable for taking them.

That's when the flash struck: before graduating neither of us had done any of the research we expected our students to have done. And we became marketing professors! If we hadn't made the connection between the theories and practices we spent so much time learning and ultimately teaching, how could we expect students to make the connection? The inspiration quickly followed: Why not teach students how to market themselves as potential employees, entrepreneurs, artists, and professionals? Why not teach students who have never taken a marketing course the fundamentals of marketing by showing them how these apply to themselves? Why not refresh the knowledge of these fundamentals among students who have taken marketing courses but who seem to have forgotten them? *Marketing Yourself* was born.

We decided to introduce *Marketing Yourself* as an online course. Prior to the launch, we conducted focus groups with current university students and those who had recently graduated. Focus-group participants were overwhelmingly supportive of the idea of the course and their input led us to many valuable insights for designing the course. We were particularly intrigued by the benefits that students saw in such a course. Here are two examples:

> *This course could help undergraduate students improve their chances of landing quality jobs. It offers real value: the course provides students with an incentive to really examine who they are and how to market themselves in a competitive job environment.*

> *I would expect this course to give me the confidence to approach potential employers.*

These comments motivated us to develop a course that, in addition to being academically rigorous, would deliver tangible benefits to students. It would not only provide students with valuable advice on how to approach potential employers, customers, and clients, but also teach them how to create marketing plans to help them select and launch their careers.

To help us ensure the course was focused on the ever-changing needs of the various fields our students might be entering, we created an advisory panel that included individuals with successful track records as employees, entrepreneurs, artists, and professionals. We also solicited the advice and guidance of professional career placement counsellors. In the summer of 2004, we beta-tested a fully developed version of Marketing Yourself with a group of 50 students at Concordia University's John Molson School of Business. The feedback they gave us was overwhelmingly positive. And their comments led to improvements to the course. In September 2004, Marketing Yourself was added to the Concordia University undergraduate curriculum. In May 2005, the course went on to win the Canadian Network for Innovation in Education's Award for

Excellence and Innovation in Instructional Design. (Find out more about the course at http://www.marketingyourself.ca/.) Development of the *Marketing Yourself* book began the following summer.

As we set out to write this book, we not only intended it to serve as a companion guide to the online Marketing Yourself course, but also wanted to make it stand alone as a page-turner—a book you would enjoy reading for both its instructional and inspirational value. As is the case with the online course, the *Marketing Yourself* book seeks to fulfill two objectives: first, to ensure you learn the fundamentals of marketing; and second, to encourage you to put these fundamental notions into practice by showing you how to apply them to yourself. To this end, we've cited several practical examples throughout the book. We have limited the number of theoretical models to a meaningful few. We've included a number of features that we hope you'll find interesting, such as the Marketing Yourself in Action vignettes at the opening of every chapter. Through these, you will meet former students of ours who have graciously accepted to share their experiences and thoughts on career planning. Another feature we've introduced is a collection of reality checks about the many myths surrounding the career planning process. We've included these to identify and dispel some of the misconceptions about the career planning process and to emphasize how marketing can improve the outcome of the process.

As with the online course, our overriding objective for this book is to help you develop a deeper understanding of what marketing actually is and to help you discover the full extent of its power. Throughout this book, you will be asked to see yourself as a product. Then, in keeping with marketing terminology, the fields in which you are interested in working will be identified as your markets. As you progress through this book, you'll have the opportunity to develop a personalized marketing plan with the goal of making your product—that is, yourself—as appealing as possible to your chosen markets. As part of this process, you'll identify your product's strengths and weaknesses, as well as any necessary product improvements, as they relate to your markets. You will set income and revenue goals. You will identify the cities, regions, or countries where you'll have the greatest potential for success. Finally, you'll create a program to communicate what you stand for, that you are available, and that you can satisfy your market's needs. At the conclusion of all of this you'll put together your own individual marketing plan, a document you can use as your career companion.

Just as marketing is much more than advertising and promotion, marketing yourself is much more than writing and sending out well-crafted resumes and cover letters. It begins with analyzing your target markets and developing an understanding of your prime prospects. It involves every aspect of your product: your knowledge, skills, and personality; how you behave; and how you price yourself. Those who understand this and apply it to their careers will have major advantages over those who will be competing for the same jobs or the same clients and who don't have the benefit of this understanding. Our hope is that by learning and applying the marketing concepts you'll be exploring in this book you'll get a head start on the career path you want to follow. To borrow Confucius's words, we'd be delighted if this book gets you on your way to never having to work another day in your life.

Welcome to Marketing Yourself.

Jordan L. Le Bel

School of Hotel Administration

Cornell University

Harold J. Simpkins

The John Molson School of Business

Concordia University

Visit www.marketingyourself.nelson.com for additional resources. You'll find online self-assessments, links to career-development websites, and more information about the Marketing Yourself online course.

MARKETING YOURSELF IN ACTION

What is YOUR passion?

Meet Darcy Raymond. Darcy is the vice-president of branding and fan experience for the Tampa Bay Devil Rays baseball organization.

Darcy's everyday preoccupations focus on developing and managing an outstanding multi-sensory baseball experience for Devil Rays fans. Specifically, Darcy leads all aspects of customer service, entertainment, and brand development.

Darcy didn't originally set out to work in marketing. In fact, he was a math major at Concordia University. Darcy says, however, he's glad that he started in a degree program he was not passionate about—it enabled him to discover what truly excites him. After one marketing class, he switched majors and has never looked back. His first job was with Procter & Gamble, where he discovered his passion for the process of learning about consumers, and from these insights developing marketing strategies and tactics.

Darcy credits his creative thinking abilities and leadership skills in enabling him to move forward in his career. He believes that his involvement in student organizations was the single most defining experience of his undergraduate education. He highly recommends that you get involved, too.

We asked Darcy what three tips he would like to share with readers of *Marketing Yourself*. Here are his thoughts:

1. *Identify the areas or things that make you passionate and experience them daily.* Immerse yourself in these things; follow your passion with your heart and your mind. Become an expert in your areas of passion by living them; surround yourself with other similar enthusiasts. When you identify and pursue your passion, getting out of bed to go to work in the morning will never become a disenchanting chore.

2. *Develop your leadership and teamwork skills.* Envision. Enable. Engage.

3. *Become a credible communicator.* This may become your greatest asset in your career. Great ideas are nothing if you cannot communicate and sell them. Learn how to write and speak effectively; understand the power of body language, tone, and vocabulary; and develop the ability to connect with people.

Today, marketing is everywhere. So much so that it is hard to imagine a world without television ads, telemarketers, events with company logos, and other marketing communications. But imagine yourself living four thousand years ago. Many of the things you now take for granted—televisions, computers, telephones, restaurants, supermarkets, clothing stores, cars, and trains—don't exist. You live in an isolated community comprising a few hundred people. Since it's located near a mountain, they've named it Mountain View. The houses in Mountain View are made of rocks and tree branches. They provide adequate protection except in severe cold and wet weather. Your clothes are made from the hides of animals you have captured. Just like your fellow citizens, you spend most of your time hunting, gathering, and cooking food. A good day is when you have had enough to eat. A bad day is when you go to bed hungry or sick. There are more bad days than good ones because there usually isn't enough food to go around. Economists would say you're living in a subsistence economy, meaning one that consumes everything it produces, where there are no surpluses.

Then after one bad day too many you say to yourself, "There has to be a better way to live and I'm going to try to find it." So you leave Mountain View, and after two weeks of walking you arrive at a community that's also close to a mountain. The locals call it Mountain Sights. Mountain Sights seems to be about the same size as Mountain View, with the same number of people. The language they speak is almost identical to yours. However, that's where the similarities end. The houses are made of logs that have been cut so they fit almost perfectly together. Outside each house are stacks of neatly cut firewood and huge clay pots filled with more corn, beans, and onions than you've ever seen before. In pens behind the houses are the biggest, healthiest-looking cattle, sheep, and chickens you've ever laid eyes on. There are fields with neatly planted rows of crops sprouting up in them. In the centre of Mountain Sights is an area about the size of ten houses and it's buzzing with trading activity. Not only are the citizens of Mountain Sights exchanging animals and crops with each other, but there are people from other communities here. They're trading spices, salt, and cloth for what the citizens of Mountain Sights have to offer. Then the realization hits you: this community and most of its residents produce more than they can consume. There are surpluses, and the citizens of Mountain Sights can trade these surpluses for goods they need and want but don't produce.

 Self Check

Have you spotted the key difference between these two communities? How does that difference relate to marketing?

In Mountain Sights, there were surpluses. When there are no surpluses, there is no need for marketing. Surpluses make marketing necessary.

You're amazed by the abundance in Mountain Sights and struck by how people there seem to be much happier and less stressed than those in your community. Curious, you introduce yourself to a middle-aged man who appears to be the owner of a large house. His name is Bud. You say to him, "There's something puzzling me. The place I come from is pretty similar to Mountain Sights, but we often go to bed hungry, we have scrawny animals and rickety houses, and we never have strangers who visit us offering spices, salt, and cloth. Why are you so rich and we so poor?" Bud replies, "Well, many years ago we lived the same way you do. Then one of the young women in the community discovered how to extract iron from the ground. It wasn't long after that her brother figured out how to make tools from iron. Let me show you some of them." He goes to a small enclosure behind his house and brings out a hoe, plough, shovel, saw, and axe. You're almost floored when he tells you work that used to take days without these tools takes mere hours with them. It comes as no surprise, then, when Bud tells you that because of the tools the Mountain Sights community can produce more than it can consume and, as a result, its people don't have to suffer through the day-in-day-out struggles for survival that your people constantly face.

Your mind races as you think about how much better off your community could be if it had these tools. So, you ask Bud to give you a set and to show you how to use them. Laughing, he asks, "Why should I give you the tools and the training? What's in it for me?" Since money hasn't been invented yet, you reply, "I'm smart, strong, and hardworking. If you give me the tools and show me how to use them, I'll work in your fields planting, weeding, and harvesting. I'll feed your animals and clean their pens. I'll milk your cows twice each day. I'll chop firewood and stack it for you. And I'll do all of this for 30 days." "Make it 45 days and you've got a deal," he counters. "Done!" you exclaim. You've just engaged in your first-ever act of marketing yourself.

Myth

I can't pursue the career that I really love because I'm not an expert in that area.

Reality Check

Most true experts are simply people with a passionate interest and desire to solve a problem they care about or who feel they can make a difference in some way, large or small. They don't necessarily start out with expert knowledge in a particular field.

DEFINITIONS OF MARKETING

Every form of marketing involves an exchange, but that's merely the beginning. For marketing to occur, both parties must see value in the exchange: the performance of goods and services that are exchanged must meet the buyer's expectations. Although no money changed hands in our earlier story, there was still an exchange: Bud purchased your labour and you purchased goods (the tools) and a service (the training). Bud expects that you will take good care of his crops and animals. You expect that Bud's tools and training will improve the productivity of your community. For a successful exchange to occur, however, both parties must also derive some satisfaction: if each of you meets or exceeds these expectations, both of you will be satisfied.

In its simplest form, **marketing** is a process that identifies needs and then offers the means to satisfy them. In our story, you identified that Bud needed help tending his land and livestock and you offered your intelligence, diligence, and muscle as the means of satisfying this need. As you'll discover throughout this book, marketing is in a constant state of evolution and as it evolves it becomes increasingly complex. To take account of this ever-increasing complexity, the American Marketing Association (http://www.ama.org) has formulated what has become a widely accepted definition of marketing:

> *Marketing is the process of planning and executing the conception, pricing, promotion and distribution of ideas, goods and services to create exchanges that satisfy individual and organizational objectives.*

Exhibit 1.1 illustrates this definition. Let's relate the key points of this definition to your exchange with Bud.

● **Your individual objective:** To own the tools and learn how to use them

marketing — planning and executing the conception, pricing, promotion, and distribution of ideas, goods, services, organizations, and events to create and maintain relationships that will satisfy individual and organizational objectives

EXHIBIT 1.1 Defining the Term "Marketing"

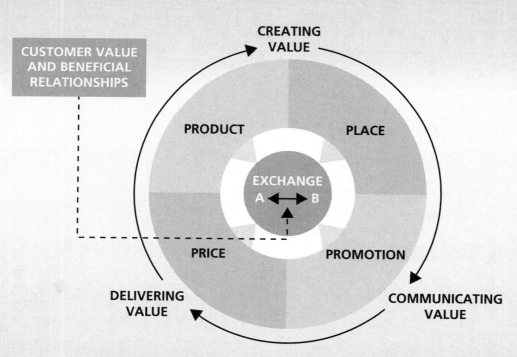

Source: From *Marketing* (with InfoTrac) 8th edition by LAMB/HAIR/MCDANIEL. 2006. Reproduced with permission of South-Western, a division of Thomson Learning: www.thomsonrights.com. Fax 800 730-2215.

- **Your services:** The 45 days of labour you will be providing to Bud
- **Your pricing:** The price you charged Bud was the five tools and the training
- **Your promotion:** You promoted yourself by telling Bud how smart, strong, and hardworking you are
- **Your distribution:** You travelled from Mountain View to Mountain Sights and delivered your service there
- **Your exchange:** You satisfied your objective by exchanging your labour for the tools and training

THE EVOLUTION OF MARKETING

Marketing as we know it began some three thousand years ago with the advent of ships and caravans to distribute goods that could be bartered or sold for money. Since then, it has evolved in four phases. Although these phases correspond loosely to separate chronological eras, they may also be thought of as approaches to marketing that can very well be present in one form or another in various industries even today. These four phases are illustrated in Exhibit 1.2; each one is then explained in more detail.

EXHIBIT 1.2   Four Phases in the Evolution of Marketing

ERA	Production	Sales	Marketing	Societal Marketing
PREVAILING ATTITUDE	"A good product will sell itself."	"Creative advertising and selling will overcome consumers' resistance and convince them to buy."	"The consumer rules! Find a need and fill it."	"A 'win' for society and the planet is a 'win' for the organization."
APPROXIMATE TIME PERIOD*	Prior to 1920s	Prior to 1950s	Since 1950s	Since 1990s

*In Canada and other highly industrialized economies.

Source: From *Contemporary Marketing* 1/E by BOONE/KURTZ. 2007.
Reproduced with permission of Nelson, a division of Thomson Learning:
www.thomsonrights.com. Fax 800 730-2215.

PHASE ONE: PRODUCTION ORIENTATION

> **production orientation —** focuses on the product, on what an organization can produce and control, as opposed to consumers' needs and desires

Production orientation began to come into its own during the mid-1800s, and while some companies and individuals still practise it today, its predominance started to fade in the 1930s. As the name implies, the focus here is on the product, on what an organization can produce and control, as opposed to consumers' needs and desires. The underlying assumption of the production orientation is that consumers will favour products that are easily available and affordable. At the same time, consumers are also motivated to seek products that offer the most in quality, performance, and innovative features. Consequently, under a production orientation, organizations focus on improving production and distribution efficiency and simultaneously improve their products (we will discuss various types of product improvements in more detail in Chapter 6). There are conditions under which a production orientation can lead to high levels of sales and profits. For instance, faster, more affordable technology or new and cheaper raw materials can facilitate continuous product improvements and thus support the effectiveness of a production orientation. Likewise, products that have little or no competition, or a situation when demand outstrips the capacity to fulfill it, are conditions that usually favour a production orientation. Examples include highly specialized professionals such as neurosurgeons and financial analysts, Ferrari automobiles, and gasoline producers.

However, as profitable as a production orientation can be, it can also lead companies and individuals to become too inward-looking and be slow to react to competition and new opportunities. The following examples illustrate how companies and people can be blindsided by competitors' offensives and changing consumer preferences when they adhere too strictly and for too long to a production orientation.

FORD

In the early 1900s, Ford pioneered the assembly line and standardized its products to keep production costs and selling prices to a minimum. As Henry Ford famously said, "You can buy a Ford in any colour as long as it's black." Ford's goal was to make its cars affordable to the greatest number of people possible, and the company not only achieved this objective but also established itself as the number-one car manufacturer in the world. So what was the key to General Motors later taking over the top spot? GM offered cars in a range of colours, and even though they added the cost of doing this to their selling prices, consumers were willing to pay more to get the colour of car they wanted.

PASSENGER RAILROADS

During the first half of the twentieth century in North America, if you wanted to travel long distances you took the train. Trains were the fastest way to get to your destination. The booming passenger railroad business was a glamour industry, and companies invested heavily in making rail travel faster and more comfortable. But as railways were pouring money into product improvements, the airline industry was just beginning to take off. Cross-country travel times were shrunk from days to hours. At the same time, governments were constructing more and more highways, making travelling by car more attractive. The railroad industry's response was to spend even more on making their products "better," but as travellers abandoned the railroads for airlines and cars in ever-increasing numbers most passenger railroad companies ended up spending themselves into bankruptcy.

NORMA DESMOND

If you haven't seen the 1950 movie *Sunset Boulevard*, you've missed out on one of the most striking examples of a production orientation. In *Sunset Boulevard*, Gloria Swanson plays Norma Desmond, a late-1920s silent film actress. Her once brilliant career has come to a sad end because, rather than adapting to the reality of talking movies, she convinced herself her fans would never want to be distracted from her alluring looks by having to listen to her voice. Needless to say, her career prospects didn't brighten up.

PHASE TWO: SALES ORIENTATION

By the 1930s, most companies in the Western world had more production capacity than ever before; some were facing overcapacity. They added new product lines. Competition intensified. The problem now wasn't how to manufacture enough goods to satisfy demand, it was how to beat competition and get more customers. So companies adopted the sales orientation and invested heavily in advertising, sales promotion, and personal selling. The product remained a key preoccupation, but firms realized that simply putting their product out there did not guarantee sales. The underlying assumption of the sales orientation is that consumers will not buy a firm's products unless the firm undertakes a large-scale sales and promotion effort. Under a sales orientation, firms seek to find the customers who would be most likely to buy their product. Firms attempt to sell what they make rather than making what they can sell; in other words, making what the market wants. A sales orientation is typically used for products that consumers are not actively seeking out. Examples include insurance, funeral prearrangement services, extended warranties, and magazine subscriptions.

While a sales orientation can be effective in "moving the merchandise," it can expose organizations and individuals to high levels of risk. It focuses on short-term sales transactions and not on long-term, profitable customer relationships. It assumes that customers who have been pushed into the decision to buy a product will like it—or that if they don't like it, their disappointment will be temporary and they'll buy it again in the future. These are dangerous assumptions: research shows that dissatisfied customers will not buy again and that, on average, they will tell ten others about their bad experiences.

> **sales orientation** — invests heavily in advertising, sales promotion, and personal selling

PHASE THREE: MARKETING ORIENTATION

The notion of marketing orientation began to take shape in the 1940s and gained wide acceptance by the 1960s. A marketing orientation implies that achieving organizational and individual goals starts with determining the needs and wants of target markets and delivering the desired satisfactions more effectively and efficiently than competitors do. Marketing-oriented organizations and individuals aim all of their efforts toward satisfying customers at a profit.

> **marketing orientation** — implies that achieving organizational and individual goals starts with determining the needs and wants of target markets and delivering the desired satisfactions more effectively and efficiently than competitors do

The differences between a marketing orientation and a sales orientation may seem subtle at first, but understanding these differences can lead to business-changing insights and truly big ideas. Compared to the sales orientation, a marketing orientation starts with current and potential customers, not the factory. Its focus is on customer needs and not with existing products. Under a marketing orientation, profits are achieved by satisfying—even delighting—customers, and not just through sales volume. Marketing orientation requires an outside-in versus an inside-out perspective: you start from the outside with customers' needs, wants, and desires and work backward to align the organization's functions and resources (the inside) to meet those needs better than your competitors.

One of the major challenges inherent in a marketing orientation is to identify those customer needs that are worth meeting. Although sophisticated marketing research and forecasting techniques have been developed to try to predict what customers truly want, these are far from being perfectly accurate. As evidence of this, consider the fact that the vast majority of new products fail. Uncovering unmet or poorly met needs requires a good sense of observation and the ability to transform observations into what is called "market intelligence." This, in fact, is central to the marketing concept, which emphasizes the fact that achieving organizational or individual goals depends on identifying customer needs and wants and satisfying these better than competitors can do.

With this concept, it is easy to see that marketing influences virtually all organizational functions and departments because all of them must ultimately focus on delivering satisfaction to one or more specific customer needs.

To get a better idea of the power that a marketing orientation can unleash, let's take a look at a few examples.

CREST TOOTHPASTE

Prior to Crest's introduction in the 1950s, North American toothpaste manufacturers relied on high levels of television advertising in a battle to take sales and market share away from each other. Their commercials all promised fresh breath and white teeth. Using marketing research with parents of young children, Procter & Gamble determined that the parents' main concern when it came to dental care was cavity prevention—not freshness and whiteness. So they developed a toothpaste that included stannous fluoride, a cavity-preventing ingredient. P&G gave it the Crest brand name, secured endorsements from the American and Canadian dental associations, and introduced its new product with advertisements featuring the simple promise "Crest fights cavities." The result? Crest became the number-one toothpaste brand almost overnight.

REVLON

In the late 1930s, Charles Revson launched Revlon with an investment of less than $100. By the mid-1940s, his company had become the industry leader. Asked what the key to his success was, he replied, "My competitors sell cosmetics. I sell hope." This is a classic example of the short-sightedness of a product orientation ("selling cosmetics") being overcome by the need-satisfaction focus of a marketing orientation ("selling hope").

CIRQUE DU SOLEIL

In 1984 Guy Laliberté launched Cirque du Soleil in Montreal, and to date its productions have been seen by almost 50 million people in 90 countries around the world. What's truly impressive is that the company has achieved this spectacular popularity in an industry that has been in steep decline for decades. The Cirque was aware of the increasing public discomfort with the use of wild animals by traditional circuses. It knew that the slapstick antics of the clowns and the traditional circus acts were becoming more passé with the passing of each day. But what contributed most to the Cirque's remarkable success was its understanding that in addition to the fun and thrills of the circus, customers wanted the intellectual sophistication and richness of the theatre at the same time. By offering both, Cirque du Soleil has breathed new life into an old and tired industry.

OPRAH WINFREY

Television stations and networks love talk shows. They're cheap to produce and celebrities clamour to appear on them at no charge so that they can promote their latest books, movies, music releases, and tours. Talk show hosts must be excellent interviewers and entertainers. Most importantly, they should appeal to large and growing audiences, because the greater the number of viewers, the more the stations and networks can charge for advertising. So why does Oprah Winfrey appeal to more viewers than any other North American talk show host? She's not just an interviewer and facilitator. She taps into and satisfies her audience's need for understanding and compassion. She supports causes that her audience identifies with and shares personal stories about the everyday struggles that she, despite being one of the most highly paid women in the world, deals with. She extends her need-satisfying offerings through her magazine and book club.

PHASE FOUR: SOCIETAL MARKETING ORIENTATION

Underlying the marketing orientation is the notion that organizations and individuals should determine the needs, wants, and interests of target markets and then aim all of their efforts to satisfy these at a profit. During the 1990s, concern for the environment and social responsibility became prevalent among consumers and marketers alike. Societal marketing orientation (also sometimes called *social marketing*) takes marketing orientation one step further by including the idea that satisfying customers should be done in ways that maintain or improve the well-being of both customers and society. The underlying idea is that what's good for corporations and individuals can also be good for society. Win–lose situations can be replaced by win–win situations. The challenge this represents for marketers is to find the appropriate balance between satisfying short-term customer wants and needs (and short-term profits) with the long-term welfare of society as a whole.

A societal marketing orientation should not be entered into blindly or half-heartedly. Organizations and individuals that adopt

> **societal marketing orientation —** (also sometimes called *social marketing*)—takes the marketing orientation one step further by including the idea that satisfying customers should be done in ways that maintain or improve the well-being of both customers and society

this orientation as a quick fix to create goodwill amongst their target customers usually end up *not* reaping the expected rewards. After all, consumers are usually quick to realize when an organization or individual is trying to pull the wool over their eyes, perhaps because many consumers have become distrustful of marketers. When organizations and individuals adopt a societal marketing orientation they must ensure that all decisions and actions, no matter how difficult or costly to implement, support their stated societal orientation and goals. Although consumers may forgive an honest mistake (especially if the organization or individual is quick and genuine in addressing the error), crass or deceiving practices are usually harmful to their perpetrators. For example, when it was reported that not all of the Body Shop's products were as wholesome as the company said they were and that, contrary to the Body Shop's claims, their purchasing practices did not always benefit the countries from which they sourced raw materials, the company's sales plummeted. Anita Roddick, the founder and president of the Body Shop, later won her case in court against a journalist who had fabricated some of these allegations, but the damage was already done. Learn more about societal marketing at http://www.social-marketing.com or http://www.sustainableproducts.com.

Many companies have become quite proficient at meeting the challenges that come with a societal marketing orientation, including the following four examples.

TOYOTA AND HONDA

Since the late 1990s, these companies have been making and selling hybrid vehicles that are powered by engines running on both gasoline and battery power. They do not pollute the atmosphere as much as regular cars and trucks, plus they get significantly better gas mileage. Because Toyota and Honda want them to appeal to as many people as possible, they have adopted an "affordable" pricing strategy—which, because it falls short of covering the costs of producing these vehicles, results in losses on the sales of these vehicles for both companies.

BEN & JERRY'S

A societal marketing pioneer, Ben & Jerry's ice cream is made only from natural ingredients that have been grown using environmentally and people-friendly methods. They support local Vermont farmers by buying all of their milk from them, and the company reinvests a substantial portion of its profits in this economically challenged state. Ben & Jerry's has been the leading brand of premium ice cream in North America for more than 20 years. Today, Ben & Jerry's is owned by the multinational company Unilever. Time will tell whether the new owner will retain the societal orientation espoused by the founders.

SUBWAY

While many quick-service restaurants have been criticized for featuring fatty, salty foods and for packaging them in polluting containers, Subway features freshly made, low-fat sandwiches wrapped in wax paper instead of Styrofoam boxes. In 2001, Subway overtook McDonald's as North America's largest quick-service restaurant chain.

EXHIBIT 1.3 **How Marketing Has Evolved**

	Production →	Sales →	Marketing →	Societal Marketing
	Sell what you can produce	Become better at selling	Understand customers and produce what you can sell	Consider the impact on society
FOCUS	Production and distribution efficiencies	Persuading customers to buy products	Understanding and satisfying customer needs, wants, and interests	Society's long-term well-being
SUCCESS IS...	Selling what you can produce, growing demand and profits through production and distribution efficiencies	Constantly increasing sales	Producing what consumers want, need, and desire; developing relationships with customers	Matching organizational and individual goals with those of society; accepting higher short-term costs in return for long-term profit
HOW?	Limit product choice; improve quality and add features	Provide more choices; advertise, promote, and sell to move the merchandise	Create satisfied and loyal customers; communicate and nurture brand associations	Create win–win situations between the organization and society
CHALLENGES/ DANGERS	Sustaining this approach amid growing competitive and technological developments; becoming complacent and being blind to changing environment	Short-term focus on sales can make the organization vulnerable to competition and changes in the marketplace; customers may come to resent being sold to	Staying ahead of customers' changing needs; uncovering unarticulated or hidden needs and motivations; meeting needs with the appropriate products	Avoiding knee-jerk reaction of abandoning this approach when results are slow to come; convincing customers that higher prices are worth it to them

BOB GELDOF, BONO, AND MICHAEL SCHUMACHER

These three individuals have established successful careers in the entertainment and sports industries. Bob Geldof and U2's Bono have done it as performing artists, and Michael Schumacher as the greatest Formula One driver in history. All three have expanded their personal marketing approaches to include societal components—Geldof through his initiation and support of Live Aid and Live 8, Bono through his work with environmental causes, and Schumacher through his $10-million donation to the 2005 tsunami victims. By lending a hand to worthy causes, these individuals have seen their popularity and appeal increase.

Myth

*Marketing is basically **advertising and selling**. It really doesn't apply to my search for a job or to my career.*

Reality Check

Marketing is all about satisfying customers' needs through a mix of **product, place, price, and promotion**. When you're in job-search mode, you're the product and your customers are your potential employers. By understanding your customers' needs you'll be in a better position to tailor your product (i.e., yourself) to them—even if it means improving it. You'll also be able to make better use of the resources available to you.

WHY MARKETING IS CRUCIAL TO YOU AND YOUR CAREER

Whether your goal is to become an employee, an entrepreneur, a professional, or an artist, adopting the marketing concept and marketing orientation can help you reach your objective faster than if you adopted a production or sales orientation or no orientation at all. Better still, if you're not sure of your career goal or haven't yet made a career choice, taking a marketing approach can help you decide on what it is that you would like to do. Let's explore some reasons why this is the case.

CAREER PLANNING IS BECOMING MORE COMPLEX

Looking back a generation or two ago, career planning was much simpler than it is today. Consider the following:

- Most people entered one career and stayed with it for their entire working lives.
- Choosing a career was easier as there were fewer career options.
- The nature of work was relatively stable and changes in how work was done evolved at a gradual, slow pace.
- Competition for jobs and customers came from local sources.
- Finding jobs and customers was simpler because the number of tools available to do so was relatively few. For the most part, only advertising and resumes and cover letters were employed.

Fast-forward to today, and we see the number of changes that have occurred is staggering. And the accelerating speed at which they're taking place is even more daunting. Now, for example:

- Most people will have multiple careers. Some will engage in more than one career simultaneously.
- The number of career options is growing exponentially to the point where the sheer number of choices has become overwhelming for many people.

- Technology is continuously and dramatically changing the nature of work and how it is done. With blinding speed, it's creating new markets and jobs while eliminating others almost overnight.

- Competition for jobs and customers is coming from anywhere in the world.

- The number of tools available to find jobs and customers is exploding. The toolbox now includes email, the Internet, sales promotion, formal and informal networking, public relations, personal selling, buzz marketing, and sampling.

In this dynamic and rapidly evolving environment, a product or sales orientation with its built-in limitations and blinders can restrict your view of the opportunities open to you and how to take advantage of them. On the other hand, a marketing orientation not only can open your mind to a full range of possibilities, but also can guide you in how to evaluate and take advantage of them.

THE PRINCIPLES OF MARKETING CAN HELP YOU CHOOSE A FULFILLING CAREER PATH AND SUCCEED IN IT

There are four broad career paths open to you: you can choose to become an employee, an entrepreneur, a professional, or an artist, or some combination of any of these. Let's examine how the principles of marketing can help you identify opportunities within each of these alternative routes and how adopting a marketing orientation can contribute to your success.

YOU AS AN EMPLOYEE

Deciding to become an employee means that you are choosing to work for a business or not-for-profit organization. Most people who select this career path think in terms of "finding a job." Typically, they prepare resumes, write cover letters, reply to "Employees Wanted" ads, and go to interviews. This is classic case of a sales orientation, or trying to "move the merchandise"—which in this case is you.

On the other hand, if you were to adopt a marketing orientation, you would adopt the following process:

- Identify the career option or options that interest you

- Assess the opportunities for you in these areas

- Determine the number of potential employers and their characteristics, needs, and problems

- As you are the product in this case, evaluate how you can satisfy these needs, solve their problems, and identify any requirements for product improvements

- Set your compensation goals, including salary and benefits

- Customize how you will promote yourself to potential employers based on their needs. Choose and use the promotion tools with the most potential to help you secure interviews.

FAVOURITES *job seeker*

http://www.careers-in-finance.com

This site provides detailed information about pursuing a career in commercial banking, corporate finance, financial planning, insurance, investment banking, money management, and real estate.

 *Myth*

Entrepreneurs are born, not made.

 *Reality Check*

Some entrepreneurs start out as such, though not all do. While entrepreneurs are probably born with a certain native intelligence, creativity, energy, and ability to handle risk, these attributes need to be shaped and built upon. The making of a successful entrepreneur is the result of the accumulation of relevant skills, experience, contacts, and self-development. Successful entrepreneurs sometimes begin their careers as employees where they can hone their skills and gain experience and confidence before they branch out on their own.

YOU AS AN ENTREPRENEUR

Choosing to become an entrepreneur means you will be working for yourself and will be producing goods and/or services you wish to sell to individuals or organizations. The rewards can be enormous. The risks can be even more so. Because you're so close to your product, it's easy to fall into the production or sales orientation trap and to lose sight of the threats and opportunities that await you. For example, while you may think the product you've come up with is the next best thing since the iPod, there may not be enough potential customers for it to make producing and selling it profitable. On the other hand, because of your proximity to your product, you may be blinded to the fact that there are large markets for it you never even considered.

However, if you adopt a marketing orientation, you would:

- Identify, qualify, and quantify the number of prime prospects for your product
- Determine their needs and how your product can satisfy these better than the alternatives currently available to them. Make any required product changes based on this determination.
- Set your profit goals and formulate a pricing strategy
- Use the appropriate marketing communication tools to make your prospects aware of your product and how it will satisfy their needs and solve their problems

 FAVOURITES *entrepreneur*

http://www.entrepreneur.com
http://www.inc.com

Two popular sites that offer useful tips, opportunities, and tools for entrepreneurs.

YOU AS A PROFESSIONAL

If you choose the career path of becoming a professional, you will be offering services that require highly developed skills and/or expert knowledge. You will be doing this on your own or in a group of other professionals. Professional careers include medicine, accounting, law, architecture, counselling, consulting, physiotherapy, and private instruction. As a professional, you are very much the product. The dual promise of high income and prestige is usually part and parcel of the choice of becoming a professional. It's deceptively simple to fall into the product orientation trap when it comes to professional careers and to look at the world from an inside-out (i.e., you) instead of an outside-in perspective. This approach could blind you to life-changing threats and opportunities. By adopting a marketing orientation, you would:

- Estimate the demand for professionals in your field for the next 10 to 15 years. Predict who will be the potential clients for your professional service and project how many there will be.

- Determine the nature and extent of the academic work and training you will be required to complete.

- Assess whether the professional field you have chosen suits your personality, aptitudes, basic skills, needs, wants, and passion. If not, identify if and how you need to change or if you should look at other options.

- Determine how you will satisfy potential clients better than your competitors.

- Establish your income objectives and formulate a fee strategy.

- Create a promotion strategy that will inform potential clients you are available to fulfill their needs and remedy their problems.

 FAVOURITES *professional*

http://money.cnn.com

This is the Internet home of magazines like *Fortune* and *Business 2.0*, which offer up-to-date information, tips, and ideas for business professionals.

 Myth

I can't support myself with a career in art.

 **Reality Check**

According to U.S.–based mixed media artist Luann Udell, you can make a living selling the art you want to make if you take the time to find your audience. She goes on to say that making modifications, temporary or otherwise, to make your art more marketable is good business sense—and does not constitute "selling out."

YOU AS AN ARTIST

Being an artist is very much like being an entrepreneur. You produce goods, such as paintings, or provide services, such as being part of a music group, and your products need to be sold. Being an artist is also similar to being a professional because, for the most part, the products you produce are unique to you. They wouldn't exist without you. A career in the arts gives you the opportunity to express your creativity and, in the process, to benefit financially. However, as those of you who are artists know only too well, the field is extremely competitive and making a living as an artist is extremely challenging. Adopting a marketing orientation can help you make your career as an artist the most fulfilling and rewarding it can be by guiding you to:

- Estimate the demand for the art you produce and assess whether there is sufficient demand to sustain you as a full-time artist.
- Identify and quantify the prospects for your products.
- Determine how your products will satisfy customer needs and identify any product changes that could improve the level of satisfaction they provide.
- Create a budget for yourself and use this as the basis for setting the prices you will charge.
- Use the appropriate marketing communication tools to encourage potential customers to take an interest in your art and, ultimately, to purchase it.
- Find the appropriate distribution outlets that will enhance your image and reach your target customer.

Whether your career path leads you to becoming an employee, entrepreneur, professional, or artist, you can adopt the principles and practices of a societal marketing orientation to create win–win situations for yourself, your clients, and society as a whole. You can achieve this, for example, by doing volunteer work, openly supporting causes that will make the world a better place, and donating a portion of your income or some of your products to charities.

MANY OF YOUR COMPETITORS WILL BE TAKING ADVANTAGE OF THE POWER OF MARKETING

Whether it's for jobs or clients, there will be plenty of other people and companies competing for space on your career path. And implicit in the marketing concept and in the marketing orientation is that to ensure success, the satisfaction provided by companies and individuals must surpass that offered by the competition. As those companies and individuals who practise marketing will be focusing on customer needs and on satisfying them better than their competitors, they will have significant advantages over those who don't.

More and more job seekers are becoming acutely aware that finding a position in the fields that attract them involves a lot more than sending out cover letters and resumes. Increasingly, entrepreneurs, professionals, and artists are discovering that finding customers and clients requires more than producing a great product and trying to sell it. These people are your competitors. Shouldn't you prepare yourself to compete with them on equal footing—at the very least?

APPLYING THE PRINCIPLES OF MARKETING WILL KEEP YOU AWARE, INFORMED, FLEXIBLE, AND OPEN TO NEW OPPORTUNITIES

When it comes to career planning, it's very easy to focus almost exclusively on yourself. As we now know, doing so can ultimately lead to falling into the product or sales orientation trap. The accompanying short-sightedness and inside-out perspective will more than likely put you on the road to missed opportunities.

The marketing concept puts the customer—not you—on centre stage. Once you adopt this perspective for your career plan, you'll see things in a whole new way. When you understand that customers will hire you or buy your products only if you satisfy their needs better than your competitors do, you'll become more aware of and interested in their needs and how they're changing. You'll be motivated to remain informed about your competitors and how to stay a step ahead of them. You'll appreciate the need to be open and flexible so that you can effectively respond to changes in your customers' needs and the behaviour of your competitors. And, because of this, you'll identify and create more opportunities for yourself than you would if you focused exclusively on yourself.

KEY TERMS

marketing — planning and executing the conception, pricing, promotion, and distribution of ideas, goods, services, organizations, and events to create and maintain relationships that will satisfy individual and organizational objectives

marketing orientation — implies that achieving organizational and individual goals starts with determining the needs and wants of target markets and delivering the desired satisfactions more effectively and efficiently than competitors do

production orientation — focuses on the product, on what an organization can produce and control, as opposed to consumers' needs and desires

sales orientation — invests heavily in advertising, sales promotion, and personal selling

societal marketing orientation (also sometimes called *social marketing*) — takes the marketing orientation one step further by including the idea that satisfying customers should be done in ways that maintain or improve the well-being of both customers and society

How Marketing-Savvy Have You Become?

1. For each of the four orientations below, identify two examples (organizations or individuals) that you believe are adhering to these orientations today.

Orientation	Examples
PRODUCTION	
SALES	
MARKETING	
SOCIETAL MARKETING	

2. How might each of these orientations apply to you and your career? What major risks and challenges does each orientation represent as applied to your career?

3. Charles Revson proclaimed that he sold hope, not cosmetics. Applying his way of thinking, what do the following companies sell: Nike, McDonald's, Disney, Gap, Apple, and Starbucks?

4. Now that you've read this chapter, do you believe that marketing can play an important role in your career? If so, why? If not, why not? What do you feel are the alternatives to applying the principles of marketing to your career

NOW WHAT?

As you embark on the journey of marketing yourself, pay closer attention to the effects of marketing around you. Try to identify and understand the various attempts by businesses and other organizations to market to you. What are they doing well? What are they not doing so well? What impresses you? What irks you? As you progress through the next chapters of this book, you'll be challenged to plan out your personal marketing efforts. Your day-to-day observations about marketing and the insights that follow from what you have observed will be of tremendous value as you prepare your course of action.

Why I wrote my own marketing plan

Meet Mike Owen. Mike graduated from Concordia University's John Molson School of Business in Montreal in 2002. Today, Mike is a highly successful real estate broker specializing in industrial property. His daily routine includes making and returning literally hundreds of telephone call and emails, travelling to and from sites, counselling clients on their real estate needs, and marketing buildings and land for sale or development. Although Mike realized long ago that he had an entrepreneurial inclination, it was by chance that he got into the business. One day, he met a real estate company recruiter at a job fair and then proceeded to research the industry, identify the key players in it, and focus his efforts on landing a job with a specific firm.

In fact, Mike did more than that: he actually put together an entire marketing plan for himself. With no experience but lots of ambition, he realized he needed to put his ideas and goals on paper. This first step helped him crystallize his ideas and identify the key steps he needed to take. Mike's plan did not sit on the shelf collecting dust: he made good use of it, referring to it regularly to evaluate his progress and make adjustments.

As is the case with Mike, even someone with strong initiative and drive can benefit from having a marketing plan. Otherwise good ideas can vanish into thin air and never materialize into anything concrete. Also, a plan focuses you and helps you to react—and in many instances proact—to changes in your environment.

We asked Mike what three tips he would like to share with readers of *Marketing Yourself*. Here are his thoughts:

1. *Identify and know your target market.* Make a list of companies or people you want to target. Then prepare a package that will interest these people or companies. Don't expect them to read between the lines: make it obvious why they should hire you.

2. *Don't rely on online job search sites.* Just because a company doesn't advertise on them doesn't mean they don't have an opening. Pick up the phone and call them. You might be surprised by the result.

3. *Get involved and hunt for experience.* There are many opportunities during your university years to get involved and to gain experience through internships, co-op programs, part-time jobs, or even volunteering. It's the kind of thing that gives you something to talk about during an interview and that sets you apart.

YOU WILL:

- know what a marketing plan is and what it contains

- know why marketing planning is so important to the success of organizations and individuals

- understand the key steps involved in creating a marketing plan

- understand what your personal marketing plan should include

Imagine yourself being in the following situation. You've completed your studies. If your goal is to find a job, you've crafted a professional, beautifully written resume with a cover letter to match. You have identified the companies, including the names and titles of specific individuals, to which you'll be sending them. You have their telephone numbers and email addresses so that you can follow up with them shortly after your mailing. You've honed your interview skills and have conducted mock interviews to sharpen them even further.

On the other hand, if your objective is to be an entrepreneur, professional, or artist, you've identified your potential customers and clients. You've lined up the financing to launch and sustain your business or practice. You've signed a lease on the space you'll need to produce your product or to service your clients and you've put an attractive sign on the front of the premises to announce your presence. You've arranged to be listed in the Yellow Pages, built an innovative website, and purchased ad space in your local newspaper.

If you had adopted the basic principles of marketing, this situation would be the culmination of the preparation and implementation of your marketing plan. Using an iceberg as an analogy, this anecdote represents the tip, the iceberg's smallest but most visible part. Could you have gotten to this point without going through the marketing planning process? Absolutely. Would you have maximized your chances of success and fulfillment? Not very likely. With that in mind, in this chapter you'll learn how marketing planning can help you define and achieve your career objectives.

THE MARKETING PLAN: ITS CONTENTS AND PURPOSE

Let's begin by defining what marketing planning is. Marketing planning is a structured process of researching and analyzing the marketing situation followed by:

- Formulating marketing objectives or goals

- Developing the strategies and tactics to achieve these goals

- Implementing, evaluating, and controlling the activities used to execute the strategies.

The essential steps of the marketing planning process are shown in Exhibit 2.1.

Marketing planning is neither an exact science nor is it purely an art. It's actually a combination of both. As you can see from Exhibit 2.1, marketing planning requires information gathering and an assessment of your marketing situation. Finding this information can involve scientific methods, and when the information needed is not readily available, a little ingenuity goes a long way to helping find it. Marketing planning also requires astuteness and creativity, particularly when it comes to devising successful strategies and tactics. Using poker as an analogy, not only do you need to get a good read of the situation, you also need to play your cards well in order to win.

The outcome of the marketing planning process is the marketing plan, a document of varying length. It essentially spells out

marketing planning process — the process of researching the marketing environment, establishing objectives, formulating strategies and tactics to achieve these objectives, and implementing and evaluating the impact of activities used to execute the strategies

marketing plan — document assembled at the outcome of the planning process that details each of its steps

EXHIBIT 2.1 The Marketing Planning Process

GATHER INFORMATION, RESEARCH, AND ANALYZE THE MARKETING SITUATION

▼

FORMULATE MARKETING OBJECTIVES

▼

SELECT ONE OR MORE TARGET MARKETS

▼

DEVELOP MARKETING STRATEGIES AND TACTICS

▼

PREPARE A MARKETING PLAN DOCUMENT

▼

IMPLEMENT MARKETING ACTIVITIES

▼

EVALUATE PROGRESS IN ACHIEVING OBJECTIVES

▼

MAKE STRATEGIC AND IMPLEMENTATION ADJUSTMENTS AS REQUIRED

where you are (your situation analysis), where you want to be (your objectives), and how you will get there (your strategy and tactics), as well as the evaluation methods and controls you intend to use to monitor your progress. As you begin to put your own marketing plan together, we suggest that you look at it as a living document, one that you'll use and adapt for years to come. In fact, after you've completed your marketing plan, you might come to the same conclusion that many people have reached: it is not so much the actual plan (namely, the final document) that matters but the process of planning itself. Planning teaches you to anticipate roadblocks and detours, think of contingencies (e.g., a Plan B), and also helps you to evaluate the consequences of various actions (e.g., if Y happens instead of X, then what?). Once you've completed your marketing plan, we're sure that the benefits of going through the planning process will be abundantly clear to you.

The marketing plan document typically includes seven sections (see Exhibit 2.2). A brief description of each component follows.

1. EXECUTIVE SUMMARY

The executive summary provides readers with an overview of the major points made in the marketing plan. Ideally one page or less in length, it presents a brief summary of the plan's goals and key recommendations and is written after you have completed your marketing plan. The executive summary forces you to identify and focus on the critical elements of your plan, thereby helping you to clarify your thinking on key issues.

EXHIBIT 2.2   Building a Marketing Plan

1. Executive Summary

2. Analysis of the Current Marketing Situation

3. Marketing Objectives

4. Target Market

5. Marketing Strategy

6. Marketing Tactics

7. Implementation and Control

2. ANALYSIS OF THE CURRENT MARKETING SITUATION

In this section, the market, trends within it, product performance, and competition are described. A key outcome of analyzing the current situation is to develop a deep understanding of customers. One of the section's main components is a SWOT analysis, which examines and assesses the company's, product's, or individual's internal strengths and weaknesses as well as external opportunities and threats. In Chapter 3, we will explain in more detail about how to conduct a situation analysis, and you will have the opportunity to take a number of self-assessment tests to help identify your own strengths and weaknesses.

3. MARKETING OBJECTIVES

Here, the specific goals that the company, product, or individual intends to achieve during the planning period are stated. For example, the objective for a company or product could be to increase sales by 20 percent in the next 12 months. An individual's goal could be to secure a position as an event planner with an annual salary of no less than $30 000 within three months of graduation. The more specific the marketing objectives are, the easier they are to understand, visualize, and act on. In Chapter 4, we will go over the process of setting goals and the characteristics that goals should possess.

4. TARGET MARKET

In this section, the market—current and potential customers, clients, and employers—is identified and quantified. Typically, companies like to talk in terms of "prime prospects"; that is, those individuals who are most likely to want and buy their products. The more precisely you define who your prime prospects are and the more you begin to think and feel like them, the greater your chances of converting them from prospects to actual customers or employers. For example, a manufacturer of diet soft drinks could define its market as the 120+ million North American females aged between 14 and 64. Using segmentation, the definition of the market to be targeted is then broken down into one or more groups that offer the highest sales and profit potential—for example, the 15+ million women between the ages of 25 and 45 who are actively controlling their weight through regular exercise and healthy eating. In Chapter 5, you will learn how to create a clear profile for your prime prospects.

5. MARKETING STRATEGY

The marketing strategy outlines the overall marketing logic that will be used to achieve the marketing objectives. It links each of the goals to the key strategies for each element of the marketing mix, also known as the "Four Ps" (see Exhibit 2.3).

For the overall strategy to be effective, these goals and substrategies should be formulated so that they address and respond to the threats and opportunities identified in the Analysis of the Current Marketing Situation section.

Many people find the concept of strategy difficult to understand, and yet in our daily lives we make strategic choices all the time. You've likely heard the expression, "All roads lead to Rome." Well, say you wanted to go to Rome and you were faced with the need to make a choice as to which of those many roads to take. When you pick any one of those roads, you have made a strategic choice: you have decided to travel on no other road but the one you have chosen. While your overall objective is to go to Rome, you may take road A, which offers great coastal scenery, or highway B, because it gets you there the fastest, or you may opt to use a succession of country roads because you feel that's where the most unexpected discoveries lie. Strategies, as we will see later, can change and be adapted to changes in the environment as needed, but all strategies imply an element of choice. Some choices will come easily and others will be more difficult and gut-wrenching, depending on the situation. A thorough situation analysis facilitates and simplifies the strategy development process, but by no means does it make it easy or guarantee success.

> **marketing strategy** — long-term plan of action designed to achieve the marketing objectives

> **marketing mix** — framework that spells out how marketing objectives will be achieved via strategies and tactics for four elements, the four Ps: product, price, promotion, place

EXHIBIT 2.3 **The Marketing Mix**

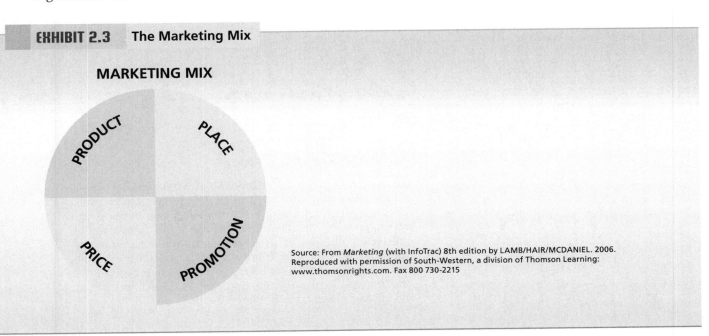

MARKETING MIX

PRODUCT PLACE PRICE PROMOTION

Source: From *Marketing* (with InfoTrac) 8th edition by LAMB/HAIR/MCDANIEL. 2006. Reproduced with permission of South-Western, a division of Thomson Learning: www.thomsonrights.com. Fax 800 730-2215

6. MARKETING TACTICS

The key element of the marketing tactics section is the series of activities that you will need to carry out in order to put the marketing strategy into action. These could include advertising, networking, media relations, packaging, product improvements, promotional pricing, and resume writing. Preparing and carrying out these activities for your own marketing plan can very much be manageable. But imagine doing the same for a company with a marketing department that employs hundreds of professionals. Everyone must be on the same page, activities must be coordinated, information and details must be conveyed in time, and so on. This is why the marketing tactics section of the marketing plan also includes the schedule and assignment of responsibility for the implementation of each of the activities. The costs associated with the implementation are identified and a budget is prepared.

7. IMPLEMENTATION AND CONTROL

Here the specific tasks and steps that will be taken to implement the marketing tactics are spelled out. Additionally, this section describes the controls that will be used to monitor progress toward the achievement of the marketing objectives and outlines how adjustments will be made to keep the marketing plan on track. Say, for instance, your tactic is to run an advertisement in your local newspaper to promote your landscaping services. Your implementation schedule might read something like the following:

- Call newspaper to inquire about the rates, type and format of artwork needed, and due date for publication in the first Saturday in May "At Home" section. Ask about possibility of placing the ad in top right corner on page 2 of the section. Also ask about rates if ad is repeated a few times.
- Find and brief a graphic artist to create and produce the ad.
- Get the required ad material to the newspaper on time.

Myth

I should start my job search three months before I graduate.

Reality Check

Job search is a process that should be started well before your last semester in school. You'll need time to prepare yourself for this process including doing internships and developing job search skills, including resume/cover letter writing and interview skills. Give yourself six months at a bare minimum. Note that in many fields there are hiring cycles. For example, educational institutions wishing to hire teachers typically hire one full year in advance. Starting your job search late can make the process more stressful than it needs to be.

TEMPLATES FOR YOUR MARKETING PLAN

To get you thinking in terms of the "big picture" for your marketing plan and to provide you with a framework into which you can fit the material that will be covered in subsequent chapters, we're providing you with two marketing plan templates. The first is for entrepreneurs, professionals, and artists. The second is for people who are or will be seeking jobs with a business or other organization.

ENTREPRENEURS, PROFESSIONALS, AND ARTISTS

If you choose the career path of an entrepreneur, professional, or artist, the templates for your marketing plan will be virtually identical to those used by businesses. For entrepreneurs and artists, the product could be a physical good, such as line of women's clothing or a piece of sculpture. The product could also be a service—for example, house painting, live music performances, and consulting. While you are the producer of the product and may be an integral component of it, the product is a separate entity and needs to be viewed as such. The primary focus of your marketing plan will be on your product, and, secondarily, on yourself. The steps and process that you should follow in preparing your plan are as follows.

1. EXECUTIVE SUMMARY

The executive summary, in a page or two at most, contains the essence of your marketing plan. Consider the following:

- What are the crucial elements of your plan?
- Can eventual partners, employees, bankers, and investors easily understand what you want to do?

2. ANALYSIS OF THE CURRENT MARKETING SITUATION

The goal here is to help you identify and comprehend the dynamics of the market in which you will be operating. As will be covered in detail in Chapter 3, the key questions that need to be addressed in this section are as follows:

- Which types of companies, organizations, and people make up the market? How many are there?
- What are the major market trends? Is the market declining or growing? What factors have a strong influence on how the market performs?
- Who are the key competitors in the market and how are they performing?
- What are your product's strengths and weaknesses?
- What are the key opportunities and threats that you should take into consideration when setting your objectives and developing your strategies?

3. MARKETING OBJECTIVES

Based on the foregoing analysis, your resources, your needs, and your ambition, the next step is to set revenue and market position objectives. These should be both challenging and attainable within the timeframe of your marketing plan.

- What are your sales goals in terms of dollars, units, hours billed, and number of customers or clients?
- What, if any, are your goals with respect to market share and market position?

4. TARGET MARKET

The clearer the picture that you have of your target market, the more potent your marketing strategy will be. In this section, you lay down the broad strokes.

- Who are your current and potential customers?
- What are their key characteristics, including geographic location, lifestyle, media usage, spending habits, and buying behaviour? What benefits do they seek?
- How many of them are there?

5. MARKETING STRATEGY

With your marketing objectives uppermost in mind, at this critical stage of your marketing plan you map out how you will go about achieving them. The marketing strategy is made up of two key elements: a detailed description of your target market and the marketing mix. It should answer the following questions:

- What market segments offer the best revenue and profit potential? Describe them in detail.
- How will you position your product to take maximum advantage of this potential?
- What will your marketing mix be? In your marketing mix you set objectives for each of the four Ps—Product, Place, Price, and Promotion—and then create strategies for each. These strategies outline how you will attain the product, place, price, and promotion goals.

6. MARKETING TACTICS

For each of the strategies that you have devised, you need to set out the activities that will be used to put them into action along with the associated costs, timing, and assignments of responsibility for making them happen. The marketing tactics section of your plan should answer these questions:

- **Product**—What changes, if any, will be made to your product?
- **Place**—Where will you make your product available to customers and how will you get it there?
- **Price**—What price changes, if any, will you be making?
- **Promotion**—What promotion tools will you be using to create awareness for your product and to persuade potential customers to buy it?

7. IMPLEMENTATION AND CONTROL

Here you list and describe the specific actions that will be taken to put the marketing tactics into action. Additionally, this is where you identify the controls that you will use to track the performance of your plan.

- How will the product, place, price, and promotion tactics be executed?

- What checkpoints will be used to monitor performance and how often will performance be measured? (e.g., sales, customer inquiries, surveys)

- When and how will your plan be adjusted?

Myth

Artists are not businesspeople.

Reality Check

Most successful artists have good business skills and those who don't can learn to master them through education, practice, and discipline. If they don't have them and don't have the desire to acquire them, artists always have the option of buying business skills from business agents, advertising and public relations agencies, and consultants.

JOB SEEKERS

If your career goal is to be an employee of a company or other organization, then you'll choose the path of a job seeker. In this case the product is you, and everything that you have to offer to satisfy the needs of potential employers. While the titles for the template for the job seeker's marketing plan are identical to the previous one, there are several important differences in the content.

1. EXECUTIVE SUMMARY

In less than two pages the executive summary should communicate the essence of your marketing plan to the person who will be implementing it—you. This serves to remind you, from time to time or when the going gets tough, of what you are trying to achieve and how.

2. ANALYSIS OF THE CURRENT MARKETING SITUATION

The market in which you will be operating comprises potential employers in your chosen industry. The objective here is to create an overview of the market and to develop an understanding of the market's dynamics and size. As will be covered in detail in Chapter 3, the key questions that need to be addressed in this section are as follows:

- Which types of companies and other organizations are there in the market?

- How many are there in the geographic area in which you would like to work?

- What are the major market trends? Is the market for jobs in the industry declining or growing? What factors have a strong influence on how the industry and market perform?

- Who will your key competitors be? How many of them are there?

- What are your product's strengths and weaknesses?

- What are the key opportunities and threats that you should take into consideration when setting your objectives and developing your strategies?

3. MARKETING OBJECTIVES

Based on the analysis of the marketing situation, the next step is to set well defined long-term and short-term career goals:

- Within three to five years, what type of work would you like to be doing? What specific job or position would you like to have?

- Assume that within one month of completing your marketing plan you have landed the job you want. What would it be?

4. TARGET MARKET

The objective here is to get a clear idea of the size and nature of your target market by answering the following questions:

- Who are the potential employers in your market?

- How many of them are there?

- What are their key characteristics, including geographic location, hiring trends, and size?

- How do they go about finding and hiring new employees to fill the type of position that you would like?

5. MARKETING STRATEGY

This is where you outline how you will go about achieving your marketing objectives. The marketing strategy is made up of two key elements: a detailed description of your target market and the marketing mix. It should answer the following questions:

- What market segments offer the best short-term and long-term employment potential? Describe them in detail.

- How will you position yourself (i.e., your product) to take maximum advantage of this potential?

- What will your marketing mix be? In your marketing mix you set objectives for each of the four Ps—Product, Place, Price, and Promotion—and then outline strategies for each. These strategies are how you will attain the product, place, price, and promotion goals.

6. MARKETING TACTICS

For each of the strategies that you have come up with, you need to set out the activities that you will use to put them into action along with the associated costs and timing. The marketing tactics section of your plan should answer these questions:

- **Product**—What changes, if any, will need to be made to your product?

- **Place**—In which geographic areas—countries and cities—do you want to work?
- **Price**—What is your income goal, including benefits, upon securing the job that you want? Within one year? Five years?
- **Promotion**—What promotion tools will you be using to create awareness for your product and to persuade potential employers to interview and hire you?

7. IMPLEMENTATION AND CONTROL

Here you list and describe the specific actions that you will take to put the marketing tactics into action. Additionally, this is where you identify the controls that you will use to track the performance of your plan.

- How will your product, place, price, and promotion tactics be executed?
- What checkpoints will you use to monitor performance and how often will performance be measured? (e.g., number of companies contacted by telephone and number of first and second interviews)
- When and how will your plan be adjusted?

 Myth

The most qualified person gets the job.

 Reality Check

Having the right qualifications is important. There is no getting around substance: you must have the goods. However, the person who lands the job is usually the one who makes the best impression and has the best fit with the organization's needs and culture. A strong resume will only open the door for you. You must still convince interviewers that you possess the right chemistry for their organizations and will solve their problems. This is where the marketing planning process will be useful: your research will help you know your own strengths and identify the organization's needs and situation. You'll also be able to respond more convincingly to anything an interviewer might throw your way.

KEY TERMS

controls — the mechanisms and measures that allow you to evaluate your progress and achievement of your objectives

implementation — concretely carrying out the actions you planned and setting a timetable for their completion

marketing mix — framework that spells out how marketing objectives will be achieved via strategies and tactics for four elements, the four Ps: product, price, promotion, place

marketing plan — document assembled at the outcome of the planning process that details each of its steps

marketing planning process — the process of researching the marketing environment, establishing objectives, formulating strategies and tactics to achieve these objectives, and implementing and evaluating the impact of activities used to execute the strategies

marketing strategy — long-term plan of action designed to achieve the marketing objectives

tactics — short- to mid-term activities that will be carried out to put the strategy into action

How Marketing-Savvy Have You Become?

1. The first step in the marketing planning process is to:
   a. Gather information, research, and analyze the marketing situation
   b. Identify your prime prospects
   c. Formulate marketing objectives
   d. Develop marketing strategies and tactics
   e. None of the above

2. What is the value of the executive summary in a marketing plan? Why is it written after the plan has been completed but is one of the first pages in the plan itself?

3. Many people believe that a well-crafted cover letter and professionally written resume is all they need to secure a job. Do you agree? If so, why? If not, why not?

4. What is the difference between a strategy and a tactic? Give concrete examples of strategies and tactics for the following:
   - Securing a job in the pharmaceutical industry
   - Introducing a personal shopping service for high-income individuals
   - Building a client base for a recently graduated psychologist
   - Creating demand for a professional fashion photographer's services

NOW WHAT?

At this point you may be thinking: Wow, there's so much that needs to be included in my marketing plan! Don't be overwhelmed. In the chapters to come, we'll take you step by step through the key concepts you need to understand to create your plan, and we'll provide you with the tools you'll require to complete each step. In the next chapter, we'll discuss the importance of conducting a thorough situation analysis and of knowing your product—in this case, yourself. You should now have a clear sense of what goes into a marketing plan and have an appreciation of the value of gathering key information about your chosen field. If you haven't already begun to do so, now is the perfect time to start looking for relevant data about the fields that you would like to work in.

How knowing the field and myself helped me land a great job

Meet Erica Horn. Erica is a market research analyst with a leading marketing research firm in Canada. She is responsible for all aspects involved in a research mandate, from designing questionnaires, to analyzing the data and writing reports in such a way that the intelligence gathered addresses the client's needs. Erica arrived at this position after a few twists and turns in the road. She obtained a Bachelor of Arts degree in humanistic studies and enjoyed the courses she took in anthropology, sociology, and art history. Upon graduation, she was hired by the alumni association of her university where she had a chance to work on the advertising for the association's magazine. She quickly developed a taste for the field of marketing. After nine months at this job, Erica decided to improve her career prospects in the marketing arena. She enrolled in a Master's of Science in Administration program with a concentration in marketing at one of Canada's leading business schools and graduated in 2004.

Upon graduation, Erica's career plan came into much clearer focus. Although she had never envisioned a career as a consultant or marketing researcher, her analysis of the marketing field led her to uncover a number of previously unforeseen opportunities. Ultimately, Erica concluded that she wanted to work in an environment in which she could have access to all types of clients and research mandates as opposed to working on the client side in one specific industry. Since Erica was not fluent in French, she found it difficult at first to find a Montreal-based research firm that would be willing to give her a chance. She used this to her advantage, showing employers she was a hard worker and in the process improved her French rapidly by taking intensive courses. Finally, she found a firm where her English fluency was considered a desirable asset to pursue mandates with English-speaking clients.

We asked Erica what three tips she would like to share with readers of *Marketing Yourself.* Here are her thoughts:

1. *You must like what you do or what you are planning to do.* This is important because happiness translates into eagerness and motivation. These traits are readily apparent to potential employers and clients.

2. *If you believe you have a particular weakness, work hard to improve upon that aspect of yourself.* Show initiative in dealing with your shortcomings and potential employers will respect you for that.

3. *Trust in the three Ps: planning, patience, persistence.* Plan and write out your career objectives and how you intend to land the job of your dreams. Be patient—not everything in life comes as quickly as we'd like, but don't settle for something that you think will not make you happy. Persist, don't give up, and make sure employers know you are motivated to achieve the goals you have set for yourself.

Put yourself in the position of a military commander on the verge of leading your troops into a major ground battle. The soldiers in your battalion are pumped up by a potent mix of fear and excitement. Caught up in the emotion, you order your soldiers to move forward into enemy territory. Within half an hour you're completely surrounded by hundreds of heavily armed enemy soldiers on foot and in tanks. As you hear the unmistakable clicking sound of the safety locks being removed on a terrifying number of rifles aimed at you and your troops, the optimist in you thinks: "Perfect, just perfect. We can attack in any direction!" Then the realist in you kicks in as you begin to realize that imminent defeat, or worse, is at hand. Just before ordering a complete surrender, you wonder what you should have done to have prevented this dangerous, woeful situation. As you and your soldiers lay down your arms and hope for kindness from the enemy, the answer comes burning through your sweaty skull: "Before moving into enemy territory, I should have conducted a situation analysis."

As is the case with military planning, situation analysis is essential to minimize potential failure and maximize potential success of marketing planning. That's why gathering information and research about the marketing situation and then performing an analysis of this situation are the first steps in creating a marketing plan. In this chapter, we will cover the steps in performing a thorough situation analysis, which typically includes a detailed examination of the external environment, the competitive dynamics in your chosen field, and the characteristics of the customers and employers that will ultimately influence the success of your marketing plan. To effectively market yourself, you need to develop thorough knowledge of your product (in most cases, yourself), including your strengths and weaknesses. Most of us rarely, if ever, take the time to look ourselves in the mirror and get to know ourselves better. That's why we'll be discussing the importance of self-assessment and psychological testing in this chapter. So, in addition to analyzing your chosen field, you'll be analyzing yourself with the goal of helping you to define and develop a powerful competitive advantage. [m.]

BY THE END OF THIS CHAPTER...

YOU WILL:

- know what a situation analysis is and how to conduct one

- understand the importance of knowing yourself and how this knowledge is crucial to your career plan

- know how to get started on your personal SWOT analysis to uncover your strengths, weaknesses, opportunities, and threats.

SITUATION ANALYSIS: ITS CONTENT AND PURPOSE

The fundamental reason for conducting a situation analysis is to acquire a "big picture" understanding of the marketing environment that you will be competing in. By understanding your markets and customers, you'll ultimately be able to align the elements of your marketing mix (the "four Ps") to better serve your target market and thus develop an advantage over your competitors. Exhibit 3.1 lists the key components (in red) typically covered when performing a situation analysis.

As you approach your situation analysis, you'll want to think about the following:

situation analysis — detailed research and analysis of the environment you will be competing in, designed to provide you with vital information to formulate other key portions of your marketing plan (such as objectives, strategies, and tactics)

EXHIBIT 3.1 **Components of a Situation Analysis**

- **Market and Industry Analysis**

- **Environmental Analysis**
  - Socio-cultural environment
  - Economic environment
  - Technological environment
  - Political and legal environment

- **Competition Analysis**

- **Customer Analysis**

- **SWOT Analysis**

Source: Adapted from *Contemporary Marketing* 1/E by BOONE/KURTZ. 2007. Reproduced with permission of Nelson, a division of Thomson Learning: www.thomsonrights.com. Fax 800 730-2215.

- **The markets and industries that you wish to enter:** What is going on in your chosen industry or field? What sales and hiring trends are you able to observe in these industries and fields?

- **The external environment:** This includes the identification and careful analysis of factors pertaining to the social-cultural environment, the economic environment, the technological environment, and the political-legal environment. Any one of those aspects could potentially influence your chosen field and, as a result, your own marketing efforts.

- **Your competition:** This entails identifying who your competitors are and an assessment of their strengths and weaknesses. This is often combined with an analysis of your product, including its differentiating attributes and how it compares to competing products. Who are your competitors? What are they known for? How do your customers or employers perceive your product and your competitors' products? These are critical questions.

- **Your current and potential customers:** Here, you want to identify, as precisely as possible, the key characteristics of your current and potential customers, including the benefits they seek in buying your product.

- **Your own strengths and weaknesses:** Once these basic components have been addressed, a situation analysis usually culminates with what is referred to as a SWOT analysis, which includes an analysis of your own strengths and weaknesses as well as the opportunities and threats present in the external environment.

Performing a systematic and thorough situation analysis can help you to uncover opportunities and potential threats you might otherwise overlook. Plus, a situation analysis will enable you to understand the dynamics involved in your chosen field, including the major issues facing the field and the key drivers of sales and profits in it. This knowledge will be valuable to you as you prepare to market yourself because it will help you to anticipate and meet the needs or solve the problems of your employers or customers.

Let's examine each step in performing your own situation analysis.

1. MARKET AND INDUSTRY ANALYSIS

The goal of this section is for you to develop an understanding of the structure and forces involved in your chosen industry. Michael Porter's five forces model provides a useful approach to address this issue. Porter proposed that industries can be analyzed by looking at "five forces" or rules that govern competition within them.[1] Here is a brief overview of these five forces:

1. **Threat of new entrants**—How difficult (or easy) is it for a new competitor to enter the industry? What are the barriers that might prevent a new competitor from entering it? If it is generally easy to enter the industry, then many new competitors might be expected to enter it, resulting in increased demand and prices for the raw materials necessary in that industry. If you are a job seeker looking to find employment with large organizations, then new entrants might be graduates about to enter the job market in that industry.

2. **Power of suppliers**—To what extent do suppliers have the ability to influence the cost, availability, and quality of materials that are needed in that industry? Some suppliers can have considerable bargaining power, often because they own proprietary technology or their products that cannot be found anywhere else.

3. **Power of buyers**—To what extent do customers in the industry have the ability to keep prices down or switch to another company? A number of factors can increase the power of buyers. A product that is very different from competitors typically reduces the power of buyers. If a single buyer represents a high percentage of a firm's business, that buyer will have more power. If the quality of the product is critical to buyers they will be less price sensitive, or even willing to pay a premium.

4. **Substitution**—Can buyers substitute another good or service for yours? If buyers can easily and quickly switch to another type of product for a comparable level of quality or performance, then substitution poses a very real threat.

5. **Rivalry amongst competitors**—How would you characterize the relationships among competitors? Friendly competition? Cut-throat, we'll-do-whatever-it-takes? This is a function of the number of competitors as well as the size and growth of the market. In a market that is not growing, competitors must survive and expand by stealing customers from other firms. The identity and strength of different brands can also be a factor here. In a competitive industry with strong brands, leaders will focus on protecting their brands' identities. Think of the ongoing cola war between Coke and Pepsi.

As you begin to define and research your chosen industry, you need to be wary of "marketing myopia." In 1960, publishing in the *Harvard Business Review*, Professor Theodore Levitt authored what has become a classic article in the marketing literature. In this now-famous piece, he examined what happens to industries that experience a failure to grow because of a limited view of their market. He called this phenomenon "marketing myopia." For example, Levitt argued that the decline suffered by the railway industry was due to the fact that companies in that industry assumed they were in the railroad business rather than the transportation business. These companies were product oriented instead of customer oriented and did not see changes coming in consumers' needs and transportation opportunities (i.e., passenger airlines). Such short-sightedness can cause you to miss opportunities that might otherwise be in plain sight. To safeguard against this, don't assume that your product will succeed forever. We'll address the importance of continuously updating and improving your product, namely yourself, in Chapter 6. Another important way you can prevent marketing myopia is to think broadly and far into the future. For instance, say you want to open your own catering company. You may think of your competitors as other caterers. That would not be a mistake. But you may also want to think of yourself as part of the entertainment business. In competing for your potential customers' entertainment dollar (and not simply catering dollar), whom will you be competing against? Simply adding that layer or perspective can help you see opportunities you might otherwise have overlooked.

At this point, you may already have a fairly clear idea of your areas of interest. Most entrepreneurs have specific products in mind that they would like to market and may already be producing them. Those who want to work as professionals probably already know if they want to be a lawyer, doctor, accountant, architect, psychologist, engineer, or university professor. People wanting to pursue a career in the arts most likely have chosen whether to be an actor, comedian, dancer, painter, sculptor, writer, musician, photographer, director, or producer. Knowing this, the next questions that should be addressed by each of these groups are as follows:

● **Entrepreneurs:** What market and industry will your product be competing in? In terms of annual unit or dollar sales, how large are these markets or industries? Who are the major competitors and how is the industry structured? If your product will be sold through intermediaries such as retailers, how many of them are there and what is their buying behaviour? What power structure is in place in your industry between those intermediaries and your competitors? For example, big-box stores such as Wal-Mart and the Home Depot usually have most of the power in their relationships with suppliers. Has the industry been growing, and what are the likely foreseeable future trends?

● **Professionals:** In terms of the number of practitioners and the total income earned by them, what is the size of the professional field that you wish to enter? What industry and market will you be competing in (e.g., independent or group practice, corporate or government practice)? During the past three years and projecting out to the next five years, what will demand be for the services you will provide? What key factors drive that demand? What are the fees typically charged by professionals in this field? How are those fees determined? What new skills and knowledge will be in demand in your field in the foreseeable future?

- **Artists:** What market and industry will you be competing in (e.g., television, cinema, live theatre, family entertainment, recorded music, or home decoration)? What have approximate sales levels been in this industry or market for the past three years and what are they likely to be five years from now? What factors drive the demand and prices in that industry? In most areas of the arts, the number of artists and the supply of their works far exceeds demand. What is the structure of the industry in your field—many producers/few customers, many producers/many customers, few producers/many customers, few producers/few customers? Will your product be sold through intermediaries such as galleries, theatres, stores, or clubs? How many of these are there? What might motivate them to distribute your product?

- **Job seekers:** For those of you planning to become employees of a business or other organization, your market and industry analyses may take a slightly different route. First, there are many of you who do not have a clear idea of the type of job or the kind of organization you would like to work in. You can use this step of the analysis to investigate various employment alternatives and then narrow down your options to the ones that are most appealing to you. Second, those of you who do have a fairly clear notion of where you would like to work can use this step to validate your career choice and to learn more about the industries and markets of interest to you. Following are some questions that you can use to guide you through this stage of your situation analysis: What field do you think you'd ultimately like to work in? Which companies and other organizations are in this field? How many of them are there in the geographical areas you would like to work in? What are their major challenges? What are the growth trends in this field? How many new employees are hired in a typical year? How many people typically compete for these positions? How do employers recruit new employees (e.g., through advertising, job fairs, consultants, internal postings, career centres)? What characteristics and skills are being demanded by employers? What are typical salaries in the industry for entry-level employees and for employees with backgrounds and experience comparable to yours?

Chapter 3 — Situation Analysis and Knowing Yourself

Myth

*Successful entrepreneurs are **big risk takers**.*

Reality Check

BusinessTown.com LLC reports that, like all prudent business-people, successful entrepreneurs know that taking big risks is a gamble. They are neither high nor low risk takers. **They prefer situations in which they can influence the outcome,** and they like challenges if they believe the odds are in their favour.

Dealing with these questions may appear daunting, but getting the answers to them may be easier than you think. In addition to the resources provided at the end of this chapter, here are some other information sources and information-gathering techniques that can help you in your quest for answers:

- Local, national, and international government agencies

- Local business associations

- Industry and professional associations

- Local and national media outlets, such as newspapers and television stations

- Business and trade publications, such as *Fortune, Forbes, Advertising Age, Marketing Magazine, Profit, Fast Company,* and *Business 2.0*

- Telephone directories such as the Yellow Pages. A fine arts student previously enrolled in our online Marketing Yourself course wanted to get an estimate of the size of the market for portrait painters, because she was interested in portrait painting as a career option. She did a search in the Montreal Yellow Pages for "Portrait Painters" and telephoned all six who were listed. Based on the answers to the questions she asked them about the number of paintings they sold and the prices they charged, she concluded that the market was indeed large enough to support her entry into it. What's more, she also got a good indication of the pricing structure in that field and who her major competitors would be.

- Formal and informal surveys with potential employers and customers

- People you know, and people who know people you know. Ask friends, relatives, former employers, teachers, and schoolmates for information about the industry or market that you're interested in. If these people can't provide you with answers, it's almost certain that one or more of them knows someone who can help you. Talking about your ideas, dreams, and ambitions is a good way to get the word out. You'd be surprised where help might come from as a result of doing this.

2. ENVIRONMENTAL ANALYSIS

Once you've begun to identify your desired markets and industry, you need to take a step back and look at the broader environment in which your market or industry operates. It is critical for you to develop a thorough understanding of the factors that affect the success of players in your chosen field. For example, there are external factors in the marketing environment that can shape the decisions and actions you will be taking in your marketing plan. For the most part, these factors are uncontrollable—meaning that you, as the marketer, have little or no influence over them. However, because they can represent opportunities and threats to your success, you need to be aware of them and their implications on your marketing decisions. These environmental analysis factors fall into the following broad categories: social and cultural, economic, technological, and political and legal.

> **environmental analysis** — part of the broader situation analysis, it includes a detailed analysis of the socio-cultural, economic, as well as political and legal environment in which you will compete

SOCIAL AND CULTURAL ENVIRONMENTS

What is going on in the society and culture at large? This question is undeniably broad. To begin to answer it, marketers typically first examine population growth and composition using demographic information that they then supplement with observations and information about trends in society. Demography is the statistical study of human populations in terms of size, growth, gender, marital status, location, age, ethnic background, occupation, and education. Demographics can exert powerful influences on product and employment markets. Consider, for example, one of the most important demographic shifts in recent history: the massive entry of women into the workforce starting in the 1940s with World War II and continuing well into the 1960s and '70s. This shift created unprecedented demands for products and services designed to meet women's nascent and growing needs for convenience. Dry cleaning, packaged cake mixes, disposable diapers, automatic clothes washers and dryers, and ready-to-eat packaged foods are just some of the products that enjoyed unprecedented growth because of this demographic shift. On the other hand, sales of products that were relatively inconvenient to use went into steep decline. Examples? Laundry starch, cloth diapers, sewing machines, and even oranges, the latter because of the introduction of frozen orange juice. These examples illustrate the profound impact that demographic changes can have on a variety of industries. Three of the most prominent demographic trends today are discussed below.

Aging of the Population

Most Western countries experienced a period known as the "baby boom" between 1946 and 1964, which was marked by an extremely high rate of birth. (For more information on this phenomenon, visit http://www.babyboomers.com.) Its impact was and continues to be enormous. By the early 1970s, the majority of North Americans were under 25 years of age. Their rallying cry was, "Don't trust anyone over 30." Today, the median age of the North American population is approximately 38; the youngest baby boomers are over 40, and the oldest are over 60. Now, "60 is the new 40" is their rallying cry!

EXHIBIT 3.2 Important Demographic Groups and Some Key Characteristics

Swing Generation	Baby Boomers	Generation X	Generation Y
Over 60 years old	*Born between 1946 and 1964*	*Born between 1965 and 1978*	*Born between 1979 and 1994*
Want to remain active; have high disposable income; love to eat out; require products and services adapted to certain physical limitations. Some still living alone in family home; others moving into assisted living communities that provide services and entertainment.	Seek convenience; want to remain active and healthy; prefer personalized products and services that appeal to their ego. Finished paying off their home, now buying second or retirement home (e.g., timeshare condos).	Like excitement; prefer "hip" products; like to indulge themselves; media-hungry and Internet-savvy. More likely to own a home (and still paying for it).	Like to be a star; want personalized products; and are beginning to "trade up" moving from less to more expensive product versions. Most still renting, not owning a home; many still living with their parents.

So, why is the population aging? The answer is simple: After the baby boom there was a steep decline in the number of babies being born. The net result is that there are far fewer people born between 1965 and 1978 (known as Generation X) and between 1979 and 1994 (known as Generation Y) than there are baby boomers. Exhibit 3.2 highlights some of the key aspects of these demographic groups that are relevant to marketing planning.

This aging phenomenon has broad and deep implications on markets and employment opportunities. Beyond increasing demand for more healthcare facilities and the fact that retirements of senior executives will be occurring in unprecedented numbers, what do you think the fallout will be for your chosen industry?

Increasing Multiculturalism

In several North American and European countries, there are actually more deaths than births every year. So not only are the populations of these countries getting older, they're also shrinking. Since the governments of these countries, as well as other countries with low population growth, do not want to expose their citizens to the negative economic consequences that can result from a declining or stagnant population, they admit immigrants in increasing numbers. It should come as no surprise, then, that the majority of people living in Toronto, for example, were not born in Canada.

This influx of immigrants is changing the demographic composition of the nations that open their borders. Just one or two generations ago, the predominant culture of these countries was European/Judeo-Christian. This is no longer the case. Demographic data confirms that Asians represent the fastest growing ethnic group in Canada. In the United States, Hispanics are the largest ethnic group. Suddenly, speaking a second language such as Chinese or Spanish can be a tremendous asset and competitive advantage if you or your organization intends to do business with these ethnic groups. People of African, Middle Eastern, and Caribbean origins are also constituting an increasing proportion of the demographic composition of many countries, including Canada and the United States.

These ethnic groups are of interest to marketers for many reasons, not the least of which is their sheer size and sales potential. For example, think of recently landed Asian immigrants who are likely to have left loved ones behind. The need to call home and keep in contact with friends and family represents a significant opportunity for telecommunication service providers. Importantly, these immigrants also bring with them their rich cultural heritage. Take a trip through Chinatown in Vancouver or Chicago and witness how Chinese and people of other Asian descent eat and shop differently. Food is merely one domain where differences may exist. How is the changing demographic composition influencing the markets you wish to enter? How is this affecting the qualifications required to work in these markets?

Decreasing Household Size and Changing Family Composition

The number of people per household is declining worldwide. For example, in 1966, there were almost four family members per Canadian household, while today there are barely three. So while population growth has been sluggish, household formation and demand for houses, apartments, and condominiums has been relatively strong. Some of the factors underlying these trends are:

- **Marriage**—The overall marriage rate is falling. This has resulted in an increase in the number of single people. Additionally, men and women are marrying later in life. During the 1970s, the median age for first marriage for Canadian women was 22. Today it's 32.

- **Births**—As more and more women work outside the home, they are not only delaying marriage, they're putting motherhood off—in some cases for good.

- **Divorces**—It's estimated that 30 percent of marriages in Canada and 44 percent of those in the United States end in divorce.

- **Income**—As incomes rise, people demand more living space and privacy. Consequently, the number of households in which three generations—children, parents, and grandparents—cohabitate declines as the latter increasingly live on their own.

How are these changes affecting the market for food products sold in grocery stores? What employment opportunities are they creating in the magazine industry? The leisure and travel industry?

ECONOMIC ENVIRONMENT

The next issue in the analysis of your external environment is to consider economic factors that influence the buying power of people in the fields you wish to enter. Many economic indicators are published regularly by regulatory and governmental agencies such as Statistics Canada, the Bank of Canada, the U.S. Federal Reserve Board, and the U.S. Department of Commerce. The key economic factors that influence buying power include:

- **Gross domestic product:** The GDP is the total value of goods and services produced in a country annually. Usually, the higher the GDP per capita, the greater the buying power of the country's citizens.

- **Inflation:** This refers to a general rise in prices for goods and services such as food, clothing, housing and furniture, and transportation. Official agencies report the rate of inflation periodically. For example, a basket of goods purchased at a grocery store that cost $100.00 in 2000 would cost $115.66 in 2006, representing an average annual rate of inflation of 2.45 percent. If wages do not increase to the same extent as prices, then buying power falls as people must divert a larger proportion of their income toward basic needs and have less discretionary income to spend on other things. Certain factors (e.g., natural disasters, political turmoil) can create inflationary pressure in many industries. Consider, for example, increases in the price of gasoline. They translate into a general increase in the prices of many goods and services so that manufacturers and distributors can offset their increased transportation costs.

- **Recession:** This is a period of economic activity during which income, production, and employment fall. This shrinks buying power, which in turn reduces demand for goods and services.

- **Real income:** This is income adjusted for inflation over time. Real income has been rising steadily in many parts of the world.

- **Disposable income:** This refers to income that is left after taxes have been paid.

- **Discretionary income:** This is what remains of disposable income after paying for basic necessities such as food, housing, transportation, and insurance. Discretionary income has not been increasing to the same extent as real income in most Western countries, thereby curtailing the growth of buying power. With stable or decreasing discretionary income, many consumers have begun to rely on credit in order to continue to afford luxuries, entertainment, and other goods and services such as home renovations and vacations. As a result, the level of debt has generally increased and so too has the rate of personal bankruptcies.

- **Employment and unemployment:** Unemployed people are those who do not have jobs and are actively looking for them. The higher a country's unemployment level, the lower the buying power of its people. To find the latest unemployment figures for Canada, visit www.statcan.ca. Notice how this key indicator is posted, along with others, on the front page.

Which of these economic factors will have an effect on the market for your product or yourself? What do you believe their effects will be?

TECHNOLOGICAL ENVIRONMENT

It wasn't that long ago that only a small minority of homes had Internet access, that only well-off businesspeople owned cellular phones, that the most popular games were board games like Monopoly, and that invasive surgery was the only way to examine certain parts of the human body. Advances in technology changed all that and more. And technology will likely be the most powerful force shaping markets for the foreseeable future. It will continue to dramatically affect every aspect of our lives, including how we entertain, inform, heal, educate, and employ ourselves. On one hand, it will eliminate markets and jobs—think of the gloomy prospects for photographic film and music CDs, photo-processing technicians, and music store managers. On the other hand, it will create an unprecedented number of opportunities for entrepreneurs, professionals, artists, and employees—think of the bright prospects for video games, intellectual property lawyers, music producers, special effects artists for movies, and computer engineers. The increasing rate of technological change will single-handedly result in most of you having multiple careers. How will technology affect the market that you'll be entering? To what extent will this create threats and opportunities? What can you do about it?

POLITICAL AND LEGAL ENVIRONMENT

Markets and marketing decisions are strongly influenced by the political and legal environments, which include laws, government agencies, professional and industry regulatory bodies, and pressure groups. Most countries have laws and regulations covering issues such as tariffs and duties, truth in advertising, consumer protection, environmental protection, competitive-pricing practices, tax collection and payment, product safety, and the rights and responsibilities of employers, employees, and consumers. Not respecting any of the various laws and regulations affecting your chosen industry can have serious implications, because ignorance of the law is not an acceptable defence.

Trade barriers are one example of regulations that can have significant impact on your chosen industry. As with any rules and regulations, these often change and you need to stay informed about any changes and their impact on your industry and your marketing decisions. For example, in an effort to protect their local textile industries, both Canada and the United States imposed quotas on textiles imported from China. On January 1, 2005, these quotas were lifted and cheaper textiles from China entered the North American market. As a result, many weaving mills across Canada, particularly in Quebec, went out of business and employment in the textile industry rapidly declined. Anticipating the consequences of changing trade barriers, many mills across Quebec decided to target new markets and in some cases to shut down entirely.

The political and legal environment also reflects the ongoing concerns of a society. Remember the financial woes of Nortel? The fall from grace of Enron and WorldCom executives in the United States, who misappropriated millions of dollars of investors' money? Whether in response to pressure groups or recent corporate scandals, companies and regulatory bodies are placing new emphasis on ethics and sound corporate governance. In an attempt to prevent further scandals and the misappropriation of funds by corporate executives, countries such as the United States have instituted special rules. For example, the Sarbanes-Oxley Act, passed in 2002, was designed to improve the accuracy and reliability of corporate disclosures so that investors could have more confidence in such financial data (for more information, visit www.sarbanes-oxleyfacts.com).

Chapter 3 — Situation Analysis and Knowing Yourself

In Canada, the Canadian Institute of Chartered Accountants establishes corporate governance guidelines. Find out more at www.jointcomgov.com.

What, if any, political and legal factors currently affect the market that you will be entering? How, specifically, will these factors influence your conduct and marketing decisions?

3. COMPETITIVE ANALYSIS

The fundamental reason why you need to analyze your competitive environment is that if you're going to outperform your competitors, you need to know what they're good at as well as how they can be topped. Your analysis of the competitive factors in the market you'll be entering should focus on the answers to the following questions:

- Who are your competitors? Here you need to think about your direct competitors, namely, people or organizations that market products similar to yours. Next, you also need to think broadly and consider who your indirect competitors are. For example, if you will be creating and selling sculptures, your indirect competitors could be manufacturers or retailers of decorative home accessories. Thinking broadly can lead you to redefine your market or industry and can uncover opportunities you might otherwise have overlooked.

- How many competitors are there? Which one(s) have the strongest influence on the market or industry?

- On what basis do competitors primarily compete? Product quality? Price? Location? Promotion?

- How do they typically react to threats and opportunities?

- What are your competitors' major strengths? Their major weaknesses?

- What does your target market think and believe about your competitors? (This answer will require some research, but the effort will be more than worth it!)

- How does your product stack up against the competition? What key features or benefits that customers will derive from your product can be used to differentiate yours in the eyes of your market?

4. CUSTOMER ANALYSIS

As you may recall from Chapter 1, a key feature of a marketing orientation is a focus on customers' needs. Therefore, it should come as no surprise that an important step in your situation analysis should be a customer analysis. In Chapter 5, we will discuss how to segment your market, but at this point what you need to do is to start thinking about where your sales, fees, or jobs will come from. Who will your customers be? What are their needs? How do they go about satisfying their needs? Your answers to these questions will go a long way to helping you develop a deep understanding of your market and the opportunities within it. As difficult as it may first appear, it is important to quantify your answers to these questions. In Chapter 5, we will further discuss how to paint a more complete picture of your customers. For now, attempt to answer the following questions as thoroughly as possible:

- Who are your customers? How many are there in your chosen field? If you are seeking employment with companies or non-profit organizations, who are they? How many are there?

- How do they approach the process of buying your product or hiring employees? Typically, customers must first recognize that they need your product. How does this happen? Can you influence this step in the process? Next, customers usually look for alternative ways to satisfy their needs. Which competitors do they think of first? Do they buy the first alternative they think of or do they have a reason to keep searching? If customers consider more than one alternative, how does yours fare in this process? How might you influence the outcome of the comparison? Typically, during this process customers will seek advice from colleagues, friends, or people in the know, also referred to as "opinion leaders." Who are the opinion leaders in your field of interest? Making sure that these people know of your product and speak well of it can have an enormous impact on your marketing efforts. Finally, customers may have chosen to buy your product, but in many cases they still need to locate and access it, and then make the final purchase arrangements. What can you do to facilitate this process?

- Where do customers typically buy your product? When do they typically purchase? Why do customers buy this product? What functional and/or psychological benefits does your product provide to customers? Alternatively, you may want to ask the reverse question: why don't they buy your products?

- What do customers do with your product? This may seem like a strange question but you need to consider how customers use and interact with your product or service. This could lead you to ideas for improving your product or for promoting it to potential customers.

INFORMATION AND INTELLIGENCE GATHERING

Don't be overwhelmed by the questions we have included as part of the situation analysis. They're meant to stimulate your thinking and highlight the importance of conducting a thorough examination of your chosen field. However, getting good answers to these questions requires reliable information. This is the perfect opportunity to make you aware of a very important issue. There are differences among data, information, and what is often referred to as "competitive or market intelligence." The distinctions may appear subtle at first, but they are significant. Data constitute the facts and figures you need to collect. From these you can extract information. For example, let's say you wish to determine which geographic region is "hot" in your chosen field. Well, if you have no idea whatsoever and you can't find the answer, then you could create an Excel spreadsheet that lists all your competitors or major players in your field on the left-hand column and then lists the location of each competitor's headquarters or major places of business in the column to the right. The entries in your spreadsheet will be your data. Now, say you fill 20 lines of data. You are still no closer to answering your initial question. You still need to summarize the data, looking for patterns and exceptions. You might, for instance, realize when looking at your 20 lines of data (using the "sort" or "pivot table" function comes in handy!) that 15 out of the 20, or 75 percent, of your competitors are located in the same geographic area. The facts and figures you have listed have just been transformed into information. You still need to turn this information into intelligence and figure out what it means for your marketing plan. Why are those competitors concentrated in the same area? What historical or political factors have contributed to this situation? How could this influence your decisions?

Competitive or market intelligence is the ongoing gathering of information and the search for patterns with the objective of predicting, anticipating, or improving reaction times to changes in the market. To stay up-to-date with changes in the marketing environment, many companies set up market intelligence departments that typically focus their efforts on finding answers to the following questions: 1) What are customers' current needs, how are they being met, and by whom? 2) What will customers' needs be in the future? 3) What are competitors up to? The goal of market intelligence is to find out about changes in the marketing environment so that appropriate decisions can be made and actions taken before your competitors make them. Establishing the information channels through which you can stay abreast of changes in the environment is crucial and can save you time. As you perform initial research to do your situation analysis, ask yourself how you can set up information pathways to help you monitor, on an ongoing basis, what is happening in your environment. Saving useful websites to your list of favourites is one possible mechanism. Other useful means include subscribing to industry or professional newsletters, initiating and maintaining regular contacts with people "in the know," and attending trade shows or conferences in your domain. A final piece of advice: create opportunities to observe and even talk with your competitors. The information that they can provide is priceless.

What other ways can you think of that will routinely feed you relevant and important information about your markets and industry?

 **Myth**

It all starts with knowing my customer.

 **Reality Check**

Actually, it starts with **knowing your product, namely yourself.** What are your values, what is your passion, what would you be happiest doing day after day? How do you handle risk? Do you prefer to work alone or in teams? The answers to these questions will help you identify areas that you'd like to work in and are available through introspection and through standardized self-assessment tests.

5. ASSESSING YOUR STRENGTHS, WEAKNESSES, OPPORTUNITIES, AND THREATS

We began this chapter with a discussion of situation analysis and provided a number of questions to spark your thinking. Focusing on your chosen field and gathering the relevant data and information is essential. However, as the above myth and reality check suggests, it is far more important to know yourself. So with that as a backdrop, let's move on to the key notion of SWOT analysis.

If the preparation of your marketing plan has been following the steps we've gone over so far, it should now be at a critical juncture. Your situation analysis has been completed and you're thinking about setting your objectives and determining the strategies you'll use to achieve these goals. The link between the completion of your situation analysis and objective setting is a SWOT analysis—an assessment of your strengths, weaknesses, opportunities, and threats. Its purpose is to help you achieve a strategic fit between your resources and capabilities and the external demands and possibilities of your chosen field. Strengths and weaknesses are often qualified as "internal," meaning that they relate to you. Opportunities and threats, on the other hand, relate to the external environment. Honest and thorough completion of a SWOT analysis is the first step to ensure you leverage your strengths and opportunities and think of ways to address the vulnerabilities and constraints that weaknesses and threats represent (see Exhibit 3.3).

Let's examine how each of the SWOT analysis elements can be addressed.

> **SWOT analysis** — a type of analysis designed to examine internal (strengths, weaknesses) and external (threats, opportunities) factors that can influence your ability to achieve your objectives

STRENGTHS

Strengths are those factors that make an organization or individual more competitive than others in the marketplace. In effect, strengths are the resources and capabilities that can be used to attain performance objectives. An example of a company's strengths could be that it can develop new products faster than its competitors. For example, Gillette has made a conscious decision to invest heavily in new product innovations and therefore introduces dramatically new

---

EXHIBIT 3.3   Elements and Examples of a SWOT Analysis

INTERNAL

STRENGTHS
- production costs
- marketing skills
- financial resources
- image
- technology

WEAKNESSES

EXTERNAL

OPPORTUNITIES
- social
- demographic
- economic
- technological
- political/legal
- competitive

THREATS

Source: From *Marketing* (with InfoTrac) 8th edition by LAMB/HAIR/MCDANIEL. 2006.
Reproduced with permission of South-Western, a division of
Thomson Learning: www.thomsonrights.com. Fax 800 730-2215.

---

products every two or three years, a competency that other players in the shaving industry have had difficulty replicating. Individual strengths can include being a team player, having specialized skills or knowledge, being fluent in several languages, and possessing a strong entrepreneurial spirit. In assessing your own strengths, try to determine which one(s) provide you with a unique, distinctive advantage that may be difficult to reproduce.

 Myth

*I should **never discuss any real weaknesses** in an interview, but rather offer up answers that are disguised strengths, such as "I'm a perfectionist and expend a lot of effort to make sure everything I do is the best it can be," or "I tend to take on more work than anyone else."*

☑ Reality Check

Employers will see through answers such as this and judge them as being shallow and evasive. These are not endearing characteristics. They know that everyone has weaknesses and **they're interested in hearing which ones you reveal** and what you intend to do about them. For example, you lack experience with a particular software, but you're working with it in your spare time to learn more about it; you're a bit shy speaking in front of people, but you believe that with practice you will overcome it; your written French is not as good as your spoken French, but (as Erica did) you're attending classes to improve it; or you haven't been taking enough time to read anything but business books in the past year, but you've just started reading a book on the history of China.

WEAKNESSES

Weaknesses are limitations that could keep organizations and individuals from achieving their objectives and thus make them vulnerable. Identifying and analyzing weaknesses is crucial because this will guide the decision as to whether to correct the weakness or to adapt to it. Consider the case of an independent sporting goods retailer who wishes to expand. Her analysis of the market and competition clearly indicates the big-box stores are taking an ever-increasing share of the market in mid- to large-size cities at the expense of independents. Relative to them she has a number of major weaknesses, including being a smaller outlet and having limited financial resources, less product selection, and weaker buying power from key suppliers such as Nike and Adidas. The latter limitation means that her retail prices will have to be higher than the big-box stores in order to cover her higher costs. Given her resources, correcting the weaknesses does not seem like a viable alternative. Ignoring the weaknesses will almost certainly lead to ever-decreasing sales and probably bankruptcy. If she chooses to adapt to her company's weaknesses, this could lead to her deciding to locate stores in smaller cities and towns, ones that do not have populations big enough to support a big-box store but that can support her more modestly sized outlets.

With individuals, especially recent graduates, a common weakness arises when, in order to enter a particular industry, they need previous experience in it. To many, this is perceived as a classic chicken-and-egg situation. (How can I get industry experience when no one in the industry will hire me in the first place?) This could lead them to conclude that their lack of experience doesn't qualify them for a job in this industry and to choose another one that doesn't require experience. Alternatively, they could decide to try to remedy this weakness by getting experience in a related industry as a step toward getting a job in their chosen field. If they discovered this weakness one or two years prior to graduation, they could try to secure part-time, seasonal, or volunteer work in this industry as a means of getting experience and later segue or move to the industry that truly attracts them.

OPPORTUNITIES

Opportunities are any relevant circumstances that can enable you to take advantage of your own strengths and/or foster superior performance. Opportunities are not internal and you do not necessarily control them, but by being aware of them, you can maximize your chances of being on the right side of the street at the right time. The number of opportunities open to organizations and individuals is infinite. The resources available to exploit them are limited. The focus here should be on identifying and analyzing those opportunities that match your resources and basic goals. (We will discuss goals and objectives in the next chapter.) Keep in mind that opportunities can be created by any and all of the environmental factors that are covered earlier in this chapter. Let's say that your basic goal is to be an entrepreneur in the restaurant business. You should look at trends, changes, and unmet needs in this market as a means of identifying opportunities you should consider exploiting. These could include growing preferences for foods from other countries, for healthier family meals, and for fancier, more adult fast food. If, on the other hand, your basic goal is to be a self-supporting musician—say, a keyboard player—you could look at trends and changes in music tastes to try to identify new or existing markets that are not yet being satisfied. Should your goal be to work for a company in the pharmaceutical industry as a salesperson, for example, you should research what the emerging trends are in the industry, particularly those in the areas of technology and legislation, and assess how these trends can support the demand for what you have to offer (i.e., your knowledge, skills, and personal characteristics) and, as much as possible, enhance your competitive position.

THREATS

As is the case with opportunities, threats are external to the organization and the individual and can come from any of the environmental factors discussed earlier. Threats include any unfavourable current or potential changes in the organization's or individual's environment that could jeopardize its ability to perform and compete. Threats can also be any change that suddenly turns one of your weaknesses into a liability, making impossible to adapt to it. On the economic front, for example, if interest rates were forecast to increase significantly this would be a threat to organizations in the real estate industry. If rates did indeed go up, the cost of mortgages and home ownership would escalate, thereby reducing demand for houses and all of the services associated with the sale of homes, including those offered by real estate agents, banks, title attorneys, and moving companies.

Demographic shifts can result in threats. Consider that for the past three decades in North America, the number of first marriages has been steadily declining. This represents a major threat to companies in the wedding industry, including dress manufacturers, tuxedo rental companies, and catering facilities, as well to individuals working in it, such as wedding planners, photographers, and invitation designers.

Competitors must always be regarded as threats for both the immediate and longer-term future. That's why a thorough analysis of existing and expected competition is essential. Relative to you or your product, what are your strengths and how can these be used to your disadvantage? What is the nature and scope of the threats your competitors represent? Remember, as with all threats, the greater the extent to which you expect competitive threats, as opposed to being surprised by them, the more effective your response is likely to be.

Finally, threats can lurk in the technological, political, and legal environments. Think of the effect that file sharing has had on the recorded music industry, that anti-smoking legislation is having on the tobacco industry, and that intellectual property laws and their enforcement have on the designer brand name fashion industry, particularly where counterfeiting is concerned.

 Myth

When choosing a career path, "What's the best thing for me to do?" is the most appropriate question I can ask.

Reality Check

It's unlikely that this question will lead you to the answers you're looking for. It is more likely to lead you to feeling overwhelmed with choices or feeling that you have to decide based only on what's practical. The question that is more likely to lead you to the answers you're looking for is: "What do I really want to do?" It's simple, but it's usually not easy.

GETTING TO KNOW YOURSELF

In addition to your own set of skills and talents, self-knowledge can be one of your greatest assets. Knowing yourself can help you make decisions and align your career choices in ways that will maximize your well-being and happiness. Many individuals tend to discount the importance of self-knowledge and as a result often end up in situations where they feel dissatisfied, overwhelmed, boxed in. When you take time to get to know yourself and take stock of the strengths, weaknesses, and personality traits that make you unique, you'll be less likely to make regrettable decisions.

The study of personality and personality traits started with *craniology* or *craniometry*, which is concerned with the analysis and measurement of human head physical features to predict such things as intelligence and the capacity for moral behaviour. Nowadays, the study of personality is much more sophisticated, featuring tests that employers use during the hiring process. In fact, the study of personality traits has spawned a thriving industry, with many proprietary tests costing in the hundreds of dollars. Finding out about yourself and making sense of the results of tests can be expensive, but the investment is usually well worth it. Perhaps the best known and most widely used personality test is the Myers-Briggs Type Indicator (MBTI), which was developed by Katharine Briggs and Isabel Briggs Myers in 1943. There are 16 personality types in this instrument that determine an individual's personality dispositions along four dimensions:

- **Introversion vs. Extraversion:** Being an extravert does not mean that someone is a wild, loud, and talkative individual. Rather, the MBTI uses this dimension to describe how people direct their energy and attention: inwards or outwards.

- **Intuition vs. Sensing:** This dimension refers to how people learn and acquire information. Sensors attend to the concrete, the facts, the details. Intuitors consider theories, future outcomes, and do not need hard facts and figures.

- **Feeling vs. Thinking:** This dimension is used to assess how you make decisions. Do you let your thinking or your feeling side dominate when you make choices and decisions? Thinkers are objective, while feelers often consider the impact of their decisions on others and their environment.

- **Perceiving vs. Judging:** How do you approach life in general? When going on a trip, for example, do you plan every little detail or do you feel comfortable just going where the road takes you? Perceivers tend to be spontaneous and flexible, while judgers prefer structure and predictability.

The Myers-Briggs Foundation, in an effort to protect the validity and credibility of its test, has tightly controlled its administration and availability. Further, it is generally considered a breach of ethics to administer the MBTI without proper feedback by a trained specialist. As a result, unless you pay to take the test, it is difficult to obtain your precise MBTI profile. Nonetheless, various providers enable you to get a close approximation of the MBTI. For an overview, visit www.personalitytype.com, then click on the "discover your type" tab. You can also learn more by visiting the official website of the Myers-Briggs Foundation at www.myersbriggs.org.

Intelligence testing is another area that can help you learn more about yourself and your own learning style. You have probably heard of tests like the SAT. Tests such as these are concerned with quantifying intelligence. On the other hand, noted researchers and scientists have argued that what matters is not how intelligent you are but what types of intelligence you possess. In 1983, Howard Gardner, a Harvard University professor, introduced the theory of

Chapter 3 — Situation Analysis and Knowing Yourself

multiple intelligences. He argued that what we typically call intelligence is not a single trait that can be adequately and accurately measured through a single number. Gardner proposed that there are nine types of intelligence:

1. **Visual/spatial intelligence** refers to the fact that some people learn best by visualizing and organizing things spatially. Charts, graphs, maps, pictures, and puzzles tend to appeal to people with visual/spatial intelligence.

2. **Verbal/linguisitic intelligence** is typically demonstrated by people in the language arts such as speaking, writing, reading, and listening. Such people are successful in traditional learning environments because their skills and intelligence fits with that traditional teaching style.

3. **Mathematical/logical intelligence** is present in people who have an aptitude for numbers, reasoning, and problem solving. These people also tend to do well in traditional classroom situations.

4. **Bodily/kinesthetic intelligence** leads some individuals to learn best through doing physical activities like sports, games, and hands-on tasks.

5. **Musical/rhythmic intelligence** is displayed by people who learn through songs and appreciate patterns and rhythms. These people typically enjoy learning a musical instrument or engaging in other forms of musical expressions.

6. **Intrapersonal intelligence** is present in people who are aware of and in touch with their own feelings and value-identity. They tend to be more intuitive and may appear somewhat shy or reserved.

7. **Interpersonal intelligence** manifests itself in individuals who are people oriented and like cooperative learning activities such as group projects. They're often labelled or described as outgoing and social. Together with intrapersonal intelligence, it forms the basis for what has more recently been called "emotional intelligence," which refers to the ability to read and react to one's and others' emotions.

8. **Naturalist intelligence** is used by people who can easily recognize and categorize natural objects and often have an ability to notice subtle differences in meanings that go unnoticed by others.

9. **Existentialist intelligence** refers to the ability displayed by some to ask and ponder fundamental questions about life, death, and the nature and role of humankind. Philosophy is a discipline in which individuals with this type of intelligence typically thrive.

Self-assessment and personality typing are not exact sciences. Results of personality and other psychological tests are meant to provide general guidance. Still, many organizations use tests such as these and often base their hiring decisions partly on their results. Again, the idea here is not to base your self-knowledge on the results these tests provide but rather to illuminate your introspection and increase your sense of self-knowledge. What matters here is the process of learning through these tests. This type of knowledge helps you to become more comfortable with yourself and to make decisions that are more likely to be in line with who you are. Another benefit is to be able to answer questions about yourself. If an interviewer asks you to describe yourself or to discuss your strengths and weaknesses (and most will ask you this!), you will be better prepared to answer the question convincingly.

There is a great number of personality and intelligence tests available out there (simply enter the topic "personality test" into a search engine such as Google and see for yourself what you come up with!). For your convenience, we have included a selection of tests in the adjacent MY Favourites feature. Once you have taken them (honestly!) try to summarize your findings and develop a sort of self-intelligence. What do these results, taken together, say about you? You might be surprised by what you find out.

KEY TERMS

environmental analysis — part of the broader situation analysis, it includes a detailed analysis of the socio-cultural, economic, as well as political and legal environment in which you will compete

situation analysis — detailed research and analysis of the environment you will be competing in, designed to provide you with vital information to formulate other key portions of your marketing plan (such as objectives, strategies, and tactics)

SWOT analysis — a type of analysis designed to examine internal (strengths, weaknesses) and external (threats, opportunities) factors that can influence your ability to achieve your objectives

How Marketing-Savvy Have You Become?

1. Why is a situation analysis so important to the marketing planning process?

2. Identify three key demographic trends that could have a powerful influence on demand for your product in the next five years. Why do you think this will be the case?

3. What are the differences among data, information, and intelligence?

4. Give two examples of recent technological changes in your chosen field and demonstrate how they have influenced the way customers in it go about buying or hiring.

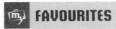 **FAVOURITES**

THE BIG FIVE PERSONALITY TEST
http://www.outofservice.com/bigfive/

Visit this website to take the Big Five personality test, which will return immediate feedback about your personality based on five dimensions: 1) openness to new experiences, 2) conscientiousness, 3) extraversion, 4) agreeableness, and 5) neuroticism.

PSYCHTESTS.COM
http://psychtests.com

This website provides you with a series of links to a variety of tests.

QUEENDOM.COM
http://queendom.com

This website provides you access to 225 different tests. Click on Tests & Profiles.

MONSTER.CA SELF-ASSESSMENT CENTRE
http://assessment.monster.ca/

This site provides a variety of self-assessment tests and articles on the subject. You can use these tools to evaluate yourself and/or your work. With the new feature "evalu8me," you can quickly take a self-assessment to determine how you see yourself and then find out (by invitation) how your co-workers see you.

WORKING RESOURCES
http://www.workingresources.com/quicksurveys/

A variety of tests with immediate and free results.

THE TEST CAFÉ
http://www.testcafe.com

This test super-site provides a variety of tests.

NOW WHAT?

Using the marketing plan template in Chapter 2 as a roadmap, and with your situation and self-analyses in place, the next step in preparing your marketing plan is to set objectives for yourself or your business. These objectives will ultimately lay the groundwork for the strategies and tactics you'll be using to put your marketing plan into action. Marketing objectives and goal setting are the two key topics we'll cover in the next chapter.

Note

1. Porter, M. (1985/1998). *Competitive Advantage: Creating and Sustaining Superior Performance.* New York: The Free Press.

MY SITUATION ANALYSIS TEMPLATE

To help you organize your thoughts and move ahead with your situation analysis, use this template.

I wish to be: ❏ an entrepreneur ❏ a professional ❏ an artist ❏ a job seeker

In the field of _____

1. Market and Industry Analysis

a. Briefly define and describe (2 sentences) the field or area you have chosen.

b. Identify and briefly describe the relevant **macroeconomic factors and trends** that will affect the number and types of opportunities in the career path you have chosen.

c. How large is the **market** represented by the area in which you would like to work? In a typical year, how large in terms of dollars spent (i.e., sales) is this market? Is the market growing or shrinking? How many people are employed in this market? How many new employees, entrepreneurs, professionals, and/or artists enter this market in a typical year? Who are the key organizations/individuals, if any, that exert high levels of control in that area?

d. Describe the **competitive forces** in your chosen field: How significant is the threat of new entrants? How would you assess the power of suppliers? Of buyers? What is the threat of substitution? What relationships and rivalries exist among competitors?

e. What are the particular **regions**—countries, provinces, states, cities—where the markets are stronger and more promising?

2. Environmental Analysis

Identify the key factors in each of the following areas that will affect the performance of the industry, market, or field you plan to enter:

- demographic and social environments
- economic environment
- technological environment
- political and legal environments

3. Competitive Analysis

a. Against whom will you be competing to get interviews, offers, and sales? Or to sell your product or services? Be as complete and thorough as possible.

b. Identify your direct competitors and describe them in terms of their strengths relative to yours. Do the same for your indirect competitors

c. What are your competitors' skills, education levels, grades, personality characteristics, and network memberships? **If you will be selling goods or services**, identify and describe your competitors' product quality, pricing, promotion, and distribution activities.

d. How is your product perceived by potential customers and employers relative to your competitors' products?

4. Customer Analysis

Describe **customer behaviour** in your market. How do your potential customers or clients go about hiring new people or buying the goods and services that you offer? When and where do they hire or buy? What benefits do they seek? If you are selling products or services, what is the decision-making process your prime prospects go through when it comes to buying your product?

If you are a job seeker, describe potential employers in the fields in which you would like to work in terms of industry size; hiring behaviour (i.e., how they go about recruiting new employees, in what numbers, and when); skill, knowledge, and other key characteristics sought in employees; and salary ranges for the types of jobs in which you're interested.

You may want to revisit this step after you've read Chapter 5.

5. SWOT Analysis

a. Which **strengths** do you possess that will make you attractive to potential employers, customers, and/or clients in your selected market? Some of these strengths should now be evident from the results of your self-assessment tests.

b. Which **weaknesses** will you need to address as you move to the next step of setting your personal marketing objectives?

c. What are the key **opportunities** you should explore as they relate to the field(s) in which you would like to work?

d. What **threats** do you need to be aware of and address prior to establishing your objectives?

Prior to performing your SWOT analysis, it's a good idea to revisit the results of your self-assessment tests. List the tests and the scores you obtained and then summarize, in a short paragraph, what these results say about you and what you have learned about yourself. Write this paragraph so that someone who doesn't know you, such as an interviewer or recruiter, could get a sense of what your personality is like by reading it. Summarizing the results of your tests will help you to identify and articulate your strengths and weaknesses. Then complete the template below.

	↓ To be leveraged ↓	↓ Develop contingencies to deal with ↓
Internal	Strengths 1. _____ 2. _____ 3. _____ 4. _____	Weaknesses 1. _____ 2. _____ 3. _____ 4. _____
External	Opportuities 1. _____ 2. _____ 3. _____ 4. _____	Threats 1. _____ 2. _____ 3. _____ 4. _____

Staying focused on your goal while facing the unexpected

Meet Julie-Anne Arsenault. Julie-Anne is an audience marketing manager for Microsoft Corporation, where she is responsible for event planning targeted at IT professionals in the U.S. Her scope of responsibility also includes field integration and ensuring the sales force is well informed of marketing campaigns in place and that their feedback is incorporated. Like many people, Julie-Anne did not have a clear idea of her career goal when she graduated. Upon graduation, as Julie-Anne puts it, "I was ready to take on the world. I was confident, motivated, and ready to deal with anything. But the situation I was not expecting to come up against was just how much I *didn't* know. My lack of knowledge compared to many of my colleagues was unsettling. This eventually changed and I routinely fell back on my strengths: being knowledge-hungry and a leader at heart. I persistently pushed myself and set increasingly higher personal goals."

In establishing her career goals, Julie-Anne built on her strengths and skills. She determined that she has always possessed a tendency to look for win–win situations when dealing with people. She also knew that she liked the process of selling and negotiating. She initially determined that she wanted to be a product or brand manager but realized she most likely would not be able to attain this type of position right after graduation. She also realized that becoming a product manager required a greater understanding of marketplace dynamics and customer relationship management than she possessed. A position as a territory manager at IBM enabled her to get on her way to achieving her objectives through intermediate steps and helped her gain a better understanding of customers and the marketplace.

We asked Julie-Anne what three tips she would like to share with readers of *Marketing Yourself.* Here are her thoughts:

1. *Know yourself and be yourself.* Know your strengths and find ways to capitalize on them. Do not try to be something you are not—this will rebound and cause discontent in the end. Take the time to get to know yourself and learn what your skills and aptitudes really are—these are your assets and selling points; play them up, and they will always work in your favour.

2. *Develop emotional intelligence.* Developing sound and rewarding relationships with your colleagues and your friends is based on this. This is even more important when selling, negotiating, and conducting business in order to find win–win situations. Emotional intelligence is something that is involved from the simplest of conversations to the most complex negotiations and greatly influences your success.

3. *Build your toolbox.* Participate in extracurricular activities, learn new skills, get out of your comfort zone, and continuously attempt to improve yourself to make sure you are a well-rounded individual.

To help you put objective setting into perspective, consider Tom's story. For 20 years, Tom owned and operated a television repair business. While he made house calls, most of his customers brought their broken televisions to his shop, which was located in a neighbourhood strip mall on the second floor above a shoe store. The income that Tom earned took care of the basics for his family and himself but left him with very little else. Meals were always eaten at home, never at restaurants. Out-of-town vacations were out of the question. Gifts for birthdays and other occasions were modest. Tom drove a 12-year-old car that was fighting a losing battle with rust. Making ends meet was a constant struggle. Then one day a salesman from one of the major television manufacturers dropped in to Tom's shop and, after introducing himself, asked, "When a customer brings in a television that's not worth repairing, what do you say to them?" "Well," said Tom, "I tell them that the cost of fixing their set will be more than the price of buying a new one and that they should replace rather than repair it." "When that happens," said the salesman, "You can create a win–win situation for both you and your customers by selling televisions in your shop. To prove my point, I'll deliver ten new sets to you tomorrow. Put a couple of them on display in the front of your store. At the end of 90 days pay me for the sets you've sold and, if you want, I'll take back the sets that you haven't sold. There's absolutely no risk." Tom agreed without hesitation.

The televisions actually sold quite well, and after 45 days Tom ordered more of them. Soon he was making more money selling television sets than repairing them. Life was becoming less of a struggle and thoughts of buying a new car danced in his head. That's when the salesman paid him a second visit. "I've been keeping track of your sales and you've done extremely well in a very short period of time," he declared. "I have a big idea for you. On the ground level of a small shopping mall just a few blocks from here is a retail store location that's just been vacated. Sure it's bigger than your shop and, yes, the rent will be higher than what you're now paying, but with an actual storefront and with the extra room, you could display so many more televisions in it your sales will skyrocket. Why even continue with the repair business? Use the whole space to sell and stock televisions." Tom took a few days to think about the idea, and within six weeks he was up and running with his new store.

He couldn't believe his good fortune. For eight consecutive months his income increased. He leased a new car and proudly used it to drive the family to their once-a-week restaurant outings. Visions of a beach vacation appeared with increasing frequency. Life was better than he had ever imagined it could be. And then he noticed a major construction project being started just across the street from the mall in which his store was located. In what seemed like almost no time, a new big-box home electronics retail store was built and opened. It carried a vastly superior variety of televisions than he did. It had viewing rooms

BY THE END OF THIS CHAPTER...

YOU WILL:

- understand the importance of setting objectives

- be able to recognize the characteristics of good objectives

- understand the process of setting marketing objectives

- understand the motivating power of values and needs

- understand the importance of identifying your own motivating values and needs

and offered "Don't pay a cent for two years" financing. Not only that, its prices were below what he was paying for televisions. In a panic, he called the salesman and asked how that could be. "Simple," was the reply. "The big-box store is part of a national chain that buys tens of thousands of televisions from us every year. Because of that, they get hefty volume discounts." "How can I get those discounts?" asked Tom. "Sorry, Tom, but your sales are not in their league. Never will be. So I can't offer you any discounts at all."

From the day the big-box store opened, Tom's sales went into steep decline. He cut his prices to try to compete, but his televisions were still more expensive than the big box's. Now not only were his sales declining, so were his profit margins and income. The store started to lose large amounts of money and there was no end in sight to the losses. Tom was almost broke when, with four years remaining on the store's lease and three on the car's, he closed shop and wondered how he was going to extricate himself from this horrible disaster. Tom's story is not as rare as you might think.

What happened to Tom? What could he have done to prevent this from happening to him? Do you think Tom had clearly thought out his objectives when he moved to the new store? If he had done so, might things have turned out better for him?

THE NATURE AND ROLE OF MARKETING OBJECTIVES

marketing objectives — short-term destinations along the path toward longer-term organizational or personal goals

Marketing objectives act as short-term destinations along the path toward longer-term organizational or personal goals. For example, in Tom's case, his long-term goal could have been to earn enough money to support his family comfortably by owning the most trusted and popular television repair shop in his neighbourhood and in the ones surrounding it. If this had been his goal, his annual marketing objectives would likely have included: to increase revenues and profits, to broaden his customer base, and to expand his product line to improve customer satisfaction. So when the television salesman came calling, Tom would have evaluated the attractiveness of selling (or not selling!) televisions using his long-term goal and marketing objectives as decision criteria. This could have set him on a different path. What might the alternative have been? Well, Tom could have decided to offer a narrow line of televisions and related items such as stands and basic home theatre sound systems for sale as a convenience for his customers, and to move to a more prominent retail location in the mall. But to effectively differentiate himself, he could have also continued to focus on repairs, to promote his repair services in local newspapers in the neighbourhoods surrounding his store, and to stay abreast of emerging television technology to ensure he could fix newer sets. Of course, Tom didn't have clear goals or objectives and he got swept up by someone else's—namely, the television salesman's. Two old but still relevant pieces of wisdom certainly apply here:

- If you don't control your destiny, someone else will.
- If you don't know where you're going, any road will take you there. But the road you end up on might not be the best one for you.

Marketing objectives provide direction and a means to control and evaluate your progress. The achievement of marketing objectives brings organizations and individuals closer to attaining their ultimate goals.

 Myth

*The first step in launching my career is to **check out what jobs are available**—in want ads, through friends, at placement centres, and so on.*

 Reality Check

While this may result in you landing a job, it's unlikely that you'll find the job that's right for you this way. Your first step should be to get to know yourself and come up with one or more ideas about what you'd like to do. Then spell out career goals based on the outcome of your soul-searching. By doing so, you'll be better able to **identify and seize job opportunities that will satisfy you.**

As this myth and Tom's story suggest, setting career goals is the first step in finding a satisfying job. Let's examine how you might go about setting your career goals.

ESTABLISHING YOUR GOALS

Goals come in all forms and sizes. Typically, goals are things that are meaningful to you and that you truly want to accomplish. Examples of goals might be: "I want to be a vice-president of an aircraft manufacturer by the time I'm 32" (a professional goal) or "I want to have a family, be a good dad, and make time for my children" (a personal goal). Virtually all large organizations have well-defined long-term goals and mission statements. While these may be reviewed from time to time, major changes occur very infrequently and, as a result, these organizations are in a position to focus on the next step of the marketing planning process—namely, setting marketing objectives.

Some of you may have already set fairly clear career goals and are ready to move on to your marketing objectives. These goals might read something like the following:

- To become a merchandiser with a major chain of clothing stores within five years of graduation.

- To become a social worker in a hospital or clinic within three years of getting my master's degree.

- To work as an independent film animator and to be a recognized talent in the movie industry within ten years of completing my education and training.

- To own my own vehicle leasing company within seven years of getting into the business.

> **goals** — meaningful things you truly want to accomplish

On the other hand, you may have just started thinking about your career goals. You're a year or two away from graduating or maybe you've just graduated and are not sure of what you want to do. You have an idea for starting a business that seems promising. You have artistic skills and a passion for your art and you're intrigued by the possibility of making art your life's work. It's time to set long-term goals for yourself. Your marketing objectives will follow. To set these goals, you need to determine what motivates you. In Chapter 3, you began the process of self-assessment and knowing yourself. The next step is to determine what your needs and priorities are.

IDENTIFYING AND PRIORITIZING YOUR NEEDS

Personal goal setting starts with a review of your situation analysis to identify the broad areas in which you might like to work and to narrow these down to a manageable few. Start by going over the results of the self-assessment tests that you took. Beyond what your self-assessment taught you about yourself, a useful exercise is to assess the strengths of the various needs that you have. Perhaps the best known method for analyzing and studying human needs was developed by Abraham Maslow (1908–1970). Maslow was a psychologist who, early in his career, noticed that some needs must be satisfied before others. For instance, if you are hungry you will mobilize your resources to procure food. But consider thirst. While you could survive many weeks without food, you could barely live a few days without water. So, in this sense, thirst is a stronger need than hunger. Now, the need for air is even more pressing than that for water, since you cannot live without it for more than a few minutes. This observation led Maslow to develop his now-famous "hierarchy of needs" (see Exhibit 4.1). You may already be familiar with it. Let's review some of its basic tenets and how they might relate to your career goals.

needs — the reason, purpose of underlying actions. May be physiological or psychological in nature

EXHIBIT 4.1   Maslow's Hierarchy of Needs

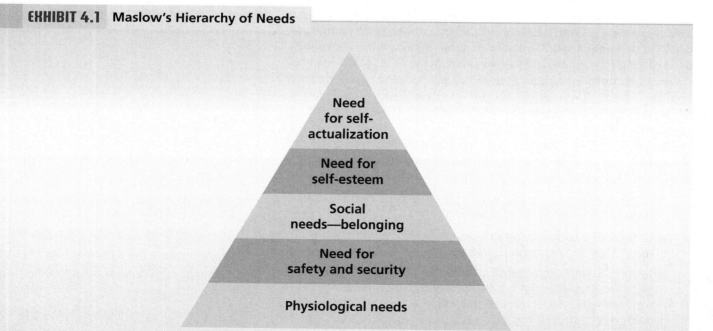

Need for self-actualization

Need for self-esteem

Social needs—belonging

Need for safety and security

Physiological needs

At the bottom of the hierarchy are physiological needs. Air, water, and food come to mind. Actually, it's a bit more complex than that; our body needs salt, sugar, protein, and minerals and vitamins. In fact, if we go without some of these for an extended period of time and develop a deficiency, our bodies will react by developing a craving for them in order to return to a normal, balanced state. We even need to maintain a certain pH and temperature. (We sweat when we are too hot and shiver when we are too cold. These are mechanisms designed to help us maintain or return to a more comfortable state.) One of the physiological needs is also the need to eliminate waste from our bodies. As this need becomes more pressing and urgent, our resources mobilize to satisfy it. Only then can we allocate our resources elsewhere. (When was the last time you "had to go" while driving on the highway? Hard to think of anything other than the next rest area, wasn't it?)

Safety and security needs come next. We typically seek safe, predictable, non-threatening environments. While we sometimes pursue the thrill of amusement park attractions or the exhilaration of extreme sports, we generally prefer safety, comfort, structure, and stability. After that are love and belonging needs. These are experienced when we begin to feel the need for connectedness to our friends and our families. Even our co-workers can provide a sense of belongingness. Think of all the products that are marketed as a means to help us stay connected, such as cell phones, instant messaging, email, and courier services. Self-esteem needs are next. Maslow divided self-esteem needs into two categories: lower self-esteem needs, which include the need for status, recognition, fame, and respect from others, and the higher-level needs for self-actualization, which include needs for self-respect, freedom, independence, competence, and achievement. As you can see, the satisfaction of lower self-esteem needs relies on external sources and/or other individuals. However, the satisfaction of higher self-esteem needs comes from within ourselves. Once needs for self-actualization are fulfilled, the feeling of achievement or contentment is almost impossible to undermine or take away. The lower-level needs (from physiological to self-esteem needs) are sometimes referred to as *deficit needs* because any deficit will be noticed and will trigger behaviours to correct it. However, if you meet these needs, then they no longer possess any motivating power—until the next time a deficit emerges.

The top of the hierarchy is the need for self-actualization, sometimes referred to as "being" needs. Maslow believed that only 2 percent of the population ever achieve self-actualization, which is really about achieving your full potential. Individuals who achieve self-actualization typically become autonomous, accepting of themselves and others, realistic, spontaneous, humble, enthusiastic, creative, and tend to look at situations as problems and solutions. Naturally, when lower or deficit needs are not met, you cannot devote resources toward achieving self-actualization.

Do you think Maslow's hierarchy is helpful? Some people discount the importance of needs or naively think that we are all motivated by the same things, such as money and status, and that everyone feels these needs in some equal measure. Such beliefs fail to appreciate the window that Maslow's hierarchy provides to better understand our needs and motivations as individuals. While we may

Chapter 4 — Setting Marketing Objectives

all be motivated by one or more of these needs in some way, their power and influence will vary greatly from one person to the next. To assess which needs exert more influence on you, begin by asking yourself the following questions:

- *Status*—To what extent is gaining the respect of friends, family, and the community important to you? If your need for status is high, this may lead you to consider a career in the professions such as dentistry, architecture, academia, or law. Status is often related to trust. In their book *What Canadians Think About Almost Everything*, Darrell Bricker and John Wright of the Ipsos-Reid marketing research firm listed the jobs Canadians indicated they trusted or mistrusted. Exhibit 4.2 is an excerpt from their list.

- *Security*—How important is it that you have assured employment with a steady income? The greater the importance you assign to this, the more likely you are to be attracted to careers in such fields as middle and senior management, engineering, and the civil service as well as to professions such as medicine and accounting. If security is not a priority, you may be attracted to riskier careers such as being an entrepreneur or artist.

- *Helping others*—Do you place a high value on directly contributing to the betterment of individuals, groups, or society as a whole? Careers in counselling, nursing, politics, training, and education have the potential to satisfy this need. You can also satisfy this need through volunteer work.

- *Affiliation*—How important is it for you to be recognized as a member of a particular organization such as a sports team or league, a specific corporation, academic institution, government department, artists' collective, or orchestra? The more important membership is, the easier it will be for you to narrow down your career options.

- *Power and authority*—To what extent do you need to control the work of others? The more you do, the more attractive are careers in fields such as coaching, management, administration, and business ownership as well as in artistic areas such as choreography and film directing.

EXHIBIT 4.2	Vocations That Canadians Trust (Or Don't)			
Firefighters	94%		Religious figures	35%
Pharmacists	91%		Journalists	31%
Nurses	87%		Lawyers	29%
Doctors	85%		Real estate agents	27%
Airplane pilots	81%		Trade union officials	21%
Teachers	79%		Chief executive officers	21%
Judges	53%		Local politicians	14%
Accountants	52%		Car salespeople	10%
Environmentalists	36%		National politicians	9%
Radio/television personalities	36%			

Source: Darrell Bricker and John Wright. (2005). *What Canadians Think.* Toronto: Doubleday Canada, p. 49.

Besides helping you to better understand your own motivation and to set your own goals, another benefit of Maslow's hierarchy is to help you identify which needs your product may be satisfying for your customers and to develop products for needs that you believe are not being met in today's marketplace. For instance, the success and popularity of Starbucks coffee shops may be in part attributable to the need for belongingness (a place where like-minded coffee lovers can gather) and the search for status or prestige (drinking and being seen drinking premium coffee). The combination of the two makes for a powerful motivation, one which will get you to willingly pay $4.75 for a Double Chocolate Chip Frappuccino®.

What other products can you think of that have been successfully marketed by appealing to some of Maslow's needs within their market? What about the iPod? Coca-Cola? Absolut Vodka? Nike footwear? Harley-Davidson motorcycles? Levi's jeans? Miss Sixty jeans? See Table 4.1 for some examples of products and marketing themes related to the different levels of Maslow's hierarchy of needs.

IDENTIFYING AND PRIORITIZING YOUR VALUES

Values are central beliefs that individuals, groups, and cultures hold "concerning preferable modes of conduct or end-states of existence along a continuum of relative importance."[1] From a broader perspective, values provide individuals with guidance in terms of what is considered appropriate behaviour and what is not within a given culture. At the individual level, some values are more impor-

> **values** — central beliefs that guide your actions and decisions. Values may be instrumental (modes of conduct; "to be or to act") or terminal (desired end states; "to have")

TABLE 4.1		Examples and Themes Related to Maslow's Hierarchy of Needs
PHYSIOLOGICAL NEEDS	Products	Vitamins, herbal supplements, medicines, food, exercise equipment, fitness clubs
	Marketing themes	Pepcid antacid—"Just one and heartburn's done" Puffs facial tissues—"A nose in need deserves Puffs indeed" Ocean Spray cranberry juice—"Crave the wave"
SAFETY NEEDS	Products	Cars and car accessories, burglar alarm systems, retirement investments, insurance, smoke and carbon-monoxide detectors, medicines
	Marketing themes	Volvo—"Protect the body. Ignite the soul." Blue Cross—"Protection doesn't get any better"
BELONGINGNESS	Products	Beauty aids, entertainment, clothing, cars
	Marketing themes	Old Navy—"Spring Break from coast to coast" Toyota—"Canada's Best Drives Start Here!"
ESTEEM NEEDS	Products	Clothing, cars, jewellery, hobbies, beauty spa services
	Marketing themes	Lexus automobiles—"The relentless pursuit of perfection" Jenn-Air kitchen appliances—"The sign of a great cook."
SELF-ACTUALIZATION	Products	Education, cultural events, sports, hobbies, luxury goods, technology, travel
	Marketing themes	Gatorade—"Is it in you?" Dodge cars and trucks—"Grab life by the horns"

Source: From *Contemporary Marketing* 1/E by BOONE/KURTZ. 2007.
Reproduced with permission of Nelson, a division of Thomson Learning:
www.thomsonrights.com. Fax 800 730-2215.

tant than others and the values we hold strongly guide us in our everyday choices and behaviours. The values you deem important can provide you with a sense of direction in your choice of career paths and can inspire and even facilitate your decision-making when you're faced with a dilemma. Values can empower you to be responsible and accountable. Identifying your core values can lead to a deeper understanding of yourself, what motivates you, and what will fulfill you.

Within the field of psychology, identifying human values has been a source of ongoing study. In fact, many value surveys exist, several of which are available (for a fee) on the Internet (e.g., http://www.psychometrics.com). In addition to the self-assessment or personality tests like the MBTI (discussed in Chapter 3), organizations routinely use values surveys to assess the value orientation of job candidates and to determine whether there is a fit with the organization. Milton Rokeach (1918–1988) developed what is arguably one of the most popular frameworks for identifying values. It's known as the Rokeach Value Survey or List of Values (LOV). In the late 1960s and early '70s, Rokeach created a nomenclature of values in which there were 18 "instrumental" values and 18 "terminal" values (see Table 4.2). Terminal values are ends in themselves, things you strive to have, such as self-respect. Instrumental values help you obtain terminal values. They are things you try to become.

TABLE 4.2   Rokeach's List of Terminal and Instrumental Values

Terminal Values "to have"	Instrumental Values "to be/to act"
• A comfortable life	• Ambitious
• An exciting life	• Broad-minded
• A sense of accomplishment	• Capable
• A world at peace	• Cheerful
• A world of beauty	• Clean
• Equality	• Courageous
• Family security	• Forgiving
• Freedom	• Helpful
• Happiness	• Honest
• Inner harmony	• Imaginative
• Mature love	• Independent
• National security	• Intellectual
• Pleasure	• Logical
• Salvation	• Loving
• Self-respect	• Obedient
• Social recognition	• Polite
• True friendship	• Responsible
• Wisdom	• Self-controlled

So, for example, if you value self-respect, you may rely on values of honesty and responsibility to help you achieve a high level of self-respect.

Consider the list of values in Table 4.2. At first glance, you may not think they're very useful when arranged in alphabetical order as they are. But try this exercise: on a piece of paper, make three columns—A, B, and C. Choosing from the lists of all 36 values in the table, in column A write down those that are absolutely necessary for you to have a satisfying life; that is, the values without which you would not be who you are or would have trouble accepting yourself. In column B, include the values that are important to you and which enhance your life; their removal from your life would not be tragic but might reduce your overall sense of well-being. In column C, include those that are of moderate importance to you and that are less important than those in column B. Now take a look at all three columns. Do you see a pattern? What does this pattern say about the person you are and what motivates you?

The values you hold strongly become central to your personal character. You've heard the expression "someone of character," which typically is a way to label or identify someone who upholds desirable values. Are there values that are more desirable than others? Greek philosophers thought so. For instance, in his book *The Republic,* Plato (circa 427–347 B.C.) identified a number of key or ideal values, including courage, justice, temperance, truthfulness, and wisdom. The values that are deemed desirable depend on the culture and the point in time. However, the notion that some values are of "higher order" or more desirable than others is still very present. Some surveys ask respondents to rank order various values. What matters in these exercises is not necessarily the final outcome or ranking (or the content of columns A, B, and C) but the soul searching and identity-building process that these exercises require (if you do them honestly and seriously!). Because your needs and values can change over time (e.g., as a result of important life events such as graduating from university or college, marriage, and having children), it's a good idea to revisit them from time to time to see how you evolved and make necessary changes in your goals and marketing objectives.

Here is another exercise to give you some insight about which needs and values you find more important. Imagine you have the chance to redesign the world we live in. What would that world look like, say, five years from now? A hundred years from now?

SETTING CAREER GOALS

Now that you have a better sense of your needs and values, it's time to begin setting the career goals that are meaningful and important to you. The ABC principle is a helpful framework that you can use to get you on your way.[2] It states that goals should be:

Actionable—You should be able to act on your goals and to develop a plan for achieving them.

Bounded—The progress toward achieving your goals should be measurable and time related.

Compelling—Your goals must be so important to you that you'll be motivated to work on achieving them.

Consider the goals that Lynn, Robert, Angela, and William have set for themselves. Within ten years of graduation, Lynn would like to be in charge of fundraising for a major not-for-profit organization. Robert would like to be a partner with a mid- to large-sized law firm within 15 years of obtaining his law degree. Angela wants to be a self-sufficient, self-employed graphic designer within two years of completing her studies in the field. William would like to own and operate a successful retail store selling high-end outdoor and camping gear within five years of receiving his business degree. All of these goals are actionable. Each individual can set out a plan to achieve them. They are time related, and Lynn, Robert, Angela, and William can establish benchmarks to measure their progress. Finally, because each individual identified their key needs and values and what they are passionate about, these goals are compelling and motivating. To help you move closer to defining your goals, answer the questions in Exhibit 4.3.

As you begin to get a clearer idea of your career goal, ask yourself: What is the main barrier between me and the attainment of my goal? Next, list some of the ways that you could overcome that barrier and achieve your goal. You'll find that there may be more than one way to achieve your goal and, should something get in your way, you needn't despair. Try to think around it. Exhibit 4.4 illustrates these notions. In the chapters to come, we will discuss the importance of marketing strategies and contingency planning (i.e., how to plan for unexpected bumps in the road).

Myth

Deciding on a goal is the best way to ensure that I will actually try to achieve it.

Reality Check

Research indicates that by **telling other people**—friends, family members, co-workers, and fellow students—what your goal is, **you will be up to six times more likely to pursue it** than if you keep it to yourself.

SETTING MARKETING OBJECTIVES

With a clearer idea of your career goals, you can now move forward and specify more precise and detailed marketing objectives that will take you closer to your goals. Companies typically state their marketing objectives in terms of annual sales, market share and position, and product development. For example:

- **Sales**—To sell two million Toyota vehicles in the United States to produce revenue of $60 billion.

- **Market share and position**—To increase the brand's share of the U.S. market by 3 percentage points and to move within 10 percentage points of the leading brand.

- **Product development**—To complete the development of and introduce one new car and three new trucks.

EXHIBIT 4.3   **Starting the Career Goal-Setting Process**

You've reviewed your situation analysis. You've gotten to know yourself better with your self-assessment test results and you've listed needs and values that you feel are important to you. If setting your career goals still appears out of reach, try to answer the following questions.

What is most important in your work? (check all that apply; add others if needed)

- ❑ freedom/control
- ❑ intellectual stimulation
- ❑ challenge
- ❑ predictability

- ❑ peace and quietness
- ❑ structure/stability/supervision
- ❑ variety/newness/constant change
- ❑ friendliness/human contact

What type of work would stimulate you intellectually?

What type of work would make it fun to get out of bed in the morning and make you look forward to your day? Go wild here. Work can be a source of fun and pleasure.

What are you able and willing to endure physically?

Where would you prefer to work? (check all that apply)

- ❑ at home
- ❑ alone, by myself
- ❑ in small teams
- ❑ in corporate environment

- ❑ indoors
- ❑ outdoors
- ❑ seated/sedentary
- ❑ standing/moving

What kind of atmosphere do you prefer?

- ❑ No friendships at work.
- ❑ I like to get to know my boss and my co-workers.
- ❑ I like to go out for a beer with my co-workers at the end of the day.
- ❑ Co-workers are like family; I like that.

For more ideas to get you started on the process of setting career goals, visit www.mygoals.com.

TABLE 4.4　Example of Goal Setting and Barriers

MY ANALYSIS	I like control, freedom, a comfortable living, but I'm single and don't plan to start a family for at least five to six years. I'm dynamic and energetic. I'm of Italian descent and while work is important, so are friends and family, and I like to have time for other leisure pursuits
MY GOAL	Within three years, I want to own and operate my own restaurant where I can keep some of my family's culinary tradition alive. This will mean that I want to have control over creative decisions
BARRIER	I don't have sufficient capital. The bank won't lend me money to open a restaurant. *Alternative 1:* Bring in financial partners. *Alternative 2:* Borrow money from friends or family.
BARRIER	Every location I want is too expensive. *Alternative 1:* Hire a real estate agent to help find a location. *Alternative 2:* Take over an existing but fledgling restaurant. *Alternative 3:* Select a less desirable location. Adapt the concept and give customers a reason to drive/walk to the location.
BARRIER	I'm not sure my cooking/management skills are sufficient to run a restaurant by myself. *Alternative 1:* Get a culinary degree part-time from a local hotel school. *Alternative 2:* Retain creative control but hire an assistant for managerial/operational tasks that could be delegated.
BARRIER	I'm not sure I want to stand on my feet for 12 hours per day and have no family life. *Alternative 1:* Bring in a partner who will complement your skills and work hours. *Alternative 2:* Scale down the concept to open only for lunch instead of lunch and dinner.

Increasingly, companies are expanding the scope of their marketing objectives statements to include the management of customer relationships. We will discuss the importance of customer relationship management in Chapter 6, but for now, continuing with our Toyota example, here are some possible objectives in this area:

- **Customer acquisition**—To increase Toyota's U.S. customer base by 300 000 people
- **Customer retention**—To reduce by 20 percent the number of customers who leave the Toyota brand for other marques
- **Customer satisfaction**—To be ranked no less than third in all major nationally recognized surveys of customer satisfaction
- **Channel relationships**—To make the brand more widely and conveniently available by opening 25 new dealerships in small- and medium-sized cities

Whether it's for a large corporation or an individual person, setting objectives is usually much easier than achieving them. The key to meeting and exceeding objectives is to set goals that are attainable. Doing so will provide the additional benefit of keeping frustration levels to a minimum. Attainable goals can best be described as:

- **Consistent**—Your objectives need to be consistent with your goals. For example, if your goal is to become a public relations manager within five years, a consistent objective would be to secure an entry-level position such as an administrative assistant, coordinator, or press release writer in the public relations industry within the next 12 months.

- **Reasonable**—Your objectives should be based on your or your organization's abilities and resources. If your goal is to own and operate your own business within ten years, reasonable objectives for the next 12 months would be to learn about the industry you'll be competing in by getting a job in it and to find a mentor who could guide you along the way to the attainment of your goal.

- **Challenging**—Your objectives should inspire you or your organization to perform at the highest levels. Rather than setting an objective to get a job in the financial services industry, you could stretch yourself by having the objective of securing a position with one of the top three financial services companies in the country.

- **Desirable**—To achieve a challenging objective, you or your organization must want it very badly. Yes there is the risk of major disappointment if you don't achieve it, but as advertising legend Leo Burnett so aptly put it, "When you reach for the stars, you may not quite get one, but you won't come up with a handful of mud either." Objectives that are fuelled by passion are the most satisfying of all to achieve and are often the ones that are most likely to be achieved.

- **Appropriate**—Objectives need to take into account market realities, competitive conditions, and the opportunities and threats that you identified in your situation analysis. For example, if your objective is to establish yourself as a self-sufficient real estate agent or broker within one year, this may not be entirely appropriate if the real estate market is in a state of collapse.

- **Measurable**—Your objectives should be specific and measurable. You'll be able to evaluate the extent to which you've achieved your objective if it's stated as "to have a salary of no less than $35 000 at the end of my first year on the job" as opposed to "to earn a good living."

- **Adaptable**—More likely than not you'll encounter forks in the road, roadblocks and other unforeseen circumstances on the way to achieving your goals. Prepare for the unexpected by making sure your objectives can be adapted to these. For example, if your objective is to work in an advertising agency as an art director, and during the first six months of your job search you discover that the market for people with your level of experience is very thin and there are almost no art director job availabilities open to you, you should have the flexibility to change your objective. In this case, you could set a new objective of finding a job that will help you gain the required experience so that within the next 18 to 24 months you'll be in a better position to secure the art director position.

EXAMPLES OF MARKETING OBJECTIVES

The nature of your marketing objectives will vary based on whether you intend to become an entrepreneur, professional, artist, or employee. Examples of marketing objectives for each of these career paths are provided separately.

ENTREPRENEURS

Marketing objectives for entrepreneurs will most likely include the kind of objectives that are set for companies—namely, sales, market share, market position, and product development—with a couple of major differences. Most people who are embarking on the entrepreneurial path are starting with few or no sales or customers. They typically require financing. The risks they're facing are daunting. Consider the following: Every year, more than one million people start a business in the United States. By the end of the first year of operation, 40 percent of them will be out of business. Within five years, 80 percent will have failed, and 80 percent of these will go under in the next five years, leaving only 16 percent still in business after ten years. For entrepreneurs, adaptable objectives are a must.

Myth

Entrepreneurs are pretty much totally independent.

Reality Check

According to BusinessTown.com LLC, entrepreneurs are far from independent and serve many masters including partners, investors, lenders, customers, suppliers, employees, and families. They can, however, make free choices of whether, when, and what they care to respond to. That said, it's extremely difficult to build a successful business singlehandedly.

First and foremost, entrepreneurs need a *business plan,* especially if they will be seeking financing. It should include:

- An executive summary
- A description of the company
- The market and competitors
- The marketing plan
- Product design and development plans
- Operations plans
- The management team
- Schedule of key dates
- Critical risks and problems
- The financial plan

As you can see, the marketing plan forms a part of the business plan and, in fact, it's an excellent starting point for the development of the business plan. With that in mind, here are some examples of marketing objectives for entrepreneurs.

SALES AND CUSTOMER RELATIONSHIPS

- To generate sales revenue that will result in the company breaking even at the end of the first 12 months in business (e.g., the specific measurable objective here could be to generate sales of $250 000 and to have the resulting profit cover all production operations and financing costs)
- To generate sufficient sales that will permit the owner or owners to earn a personal income of $40 000 each from the business during the year (e.g., to generate sales of $500 000 and a net profit of $80 000 to be divided equally between the two owners)
- To sell 300 units of the product at $1000 each
- To acquire 20 000 customers who will each buy the product for $5 an average of four times during the year to generate sales of $400 000
- To be ranked no less than equal to our largest competitor in terms of customer satisfaction
- To have the product carried by at least one major national chain of home improvement stores by the end of the year

MARKET SHARE AND POSITION

- To attain a share of 10 percent of the units sold within the national market by the end of the year
- To be among the top five brands based on dollar sales within 12 months
- To be the brand of first choice for at least 25 percent of the customers in the market by the end of the year

PRODUCT DEVELOPMENT

- To develop and introduce one new size (or flavour) of our product by the end of the first six months
- To add two new main courses and three dessert items to our restaurant's menu each month
- To expand the product line of our sporting goods store to include racquet sports equipment and clothing by the beginning of the third quarter of the year

PROFESSIONALS

Professionals who will be working independently will in effect be in business for themselves. Consequently, their marketing objectives are very similar to those for entrepreneurs. Examples follow. Objectives for professionals who will be working for business or other organizations, such as accountants and engineers, will be similar to those for employees.

SALES

- For a dentist: To generate fee income of $150 000 within the first 12 months after setting up practice
- For a consultant: To do $7000 in monthly billings by the end of the year
- For a massage therapist: To have $600 in weekly billings by the sixth month and to maintain that level for the balance of the year

CUSTOMER/CLIENT RELATIONSHIPS

- Dentist: To have a list of no fewer than 700 patients by the end of the year and to ensure that 90 percent of these become repeat patients
- Consultant: To have served at least 12 clients and to have no fewer than 20 proposals under consideration by current and potential clients. To be among the first three consultants that they call when expertise in my area is needed.
- Massage therapist: To have a base of 750 clients who will use my services once every two weeks on average

PRODUCT DEVELOPMENT

- Dentist: To add the most-up-to-date ceramic milling equipment to make crowns in-house by the end of the year
- Consultant: To expand my practice beyond tax planning and into corporate finance within nine months
- Message therapist: To offer products for sale such as massage oils and recordings of relaxing background sounds within six months

ARTISTS

If your career goal is to be an artist, your marketing objectives can take a number of forms. Should you decide to be a self-supporting independent artist, you could view yourself as an entrepreneur and focus on sales objectives. Alternatively, if you would like to work with a company on a full-time basis—for example, as an in-house graphic designer for a chain of retail stores—then you would set your objectives in the same way that an employee would. Then there's what we call the "hedge your bets" path.

Careers in the arts can be tremendously rewarding: you earn income by expressing your creativity and living out your passion. On the other hand, making enough money to be self-sufficient in the arts is extremely challenging as the supply of artists and their work typically exceeds demand. As is the case with entrepreneurs, the risks can be very high. This brings to mind the true story of a young man whose goal was to be a classical concert pianist. He excelled in music school and graduated first in his class with a master's degree. Music was his burning passion but throughout his education he knew that to earn a living as a concert pianist, he had to be one of the very few in the world capable of and chosen to perform with a major symphony orchestra. He was recognized by his teachers and people in the classical music milieu as being extremely talented, even gifted. But he and everyone else agreed that his playing was not at the level that would allow him to earn enough money to be self-sufficient as a classical pianist. He had no interest or desire to play anything other than classical music and performing any other type of music held no attraction for him. So he decided to go to medical school and became an emergency room physician. By doing so, he could work as a doctor as much as was needed to support himself, often as little as two weekends a month. This resulted in him having the time and financial resources to perform for little or no compensation and to pursue his dream career. The moral of the story is that by having a parallel career, artists can ensure their self-sufficiency.

However, the "hedge your bets" approach to pursuing a career in the arts has its critics. Many argue that it's a compromise, a cop-out because it cools the passion that fuels creativity. Others claim that struggle is a necessary rite of artistic passage. That said, you should have some idea of the extent to which you're willing to hedge your bets when setting your marketing objectives, as this will influence your decisions about having a parallel career and the resources that you will allocate to it.

A good way to start establishing your marketing objectives is to determine how much money you would like or need to earn within 12 months of launching your career as an artist. This will lead directly to your sales objective. Examples of marketing objectives for artists include the following.

SALES AND CUSTOMER RELATIONSHIPS

- To generate sufficient sales to generate an income that will enable me to be self-sufficient
- To attract a client/customer base of no fewer than 150 people or companies
- To have 30 percent of my sales come from repeat customers
- To create a database of one hundred potential new customers
- To give at least 50 performances

PRODUCT DEVELOPMENT

- To expand my repertoire from studio to include live performances
- To add an art consultation service for homeowners and businesses
- To produce an album featuring a new and unique Latin/ Middle-Eastern fusion musical style
- To add documentary film screenwriting to the services that I offer
- To broaden my photography portfolio to include food shots

Myth

Choosing to pursue a graduate degree in fine arts will be great for my personal development but will lead nowhere career-wise.

Reality Check

The *Harvard Business Review* (February 2004) listed the Master of Fine Arts as the new MBA. Writer Daniel H. Pink noted that graduate schools such as the Rhode Island School of Design, the School of the Art Institute of Chicago, and others in the U.S. were experiencing an influx of corporate recruiters searching for talent. It seems that many corporations are looking for creativity and innovation to set their products apart from those of their competitors.

EMPLOYEES/JOB SEEKERS

If your goal is to be an employee of a business or other type of organization such as a not-for-profit, government, or educational institution, your marketing objectives will most likely be to attain particular jobs or positions and to earn a certain amount of income and benefits. As with entrepreneurs, professionals, and artists, the starting point for setting your marketing objectives is your career goal. Examples of marketing objectives for those of you wanting to become employees are as follows.

JOBS/POSITIONS

- To secure a full-time teaching position with one of the top-ten-ranked high schools in the city where I live
- To be hired as a financial analyst by one of the country's leading brokerage firms
- To be part of a team of fundraisers for a prominent national not-for-profit organization
- To attain the position of research chemist with a major producer of petroleum or chemical products
- To be a junior economist with the federal government
- To break into the advertising business by securing any entry-level position available in the country

INCOME AND BENEFITS

- To earn a salary of no less than $32 000
- In addition to a base salary of no less than $35 000, to have a paid-for benefits package that includes health, dental, and life insurance as well as an annual vacation of three weeks

- To earn a base salary of $20 000 plus a 10 percent commission on sales I make and a car allowance
- To earn a salary of no less than $28 000 and to work four days per week (or flex-time)
- To earn whatever I'll be paid so that I can get my foot in the door of a particular company or industry

KEY TERMS

goals — meaningful things you truly want to accomplish

marketing objectives — short-term destinations along the path toward longer-term organizational or personal goals

needs — the reason, purpose of underlying actions. May be physiological or psychological in nature

values — central beliefs that guide your actions and decisions. Values may be instrumental (modes of conduct; "to be or to act") or terminal (desired end states; "to have")

FAVOURITES *job seeker*

ASSESSMENT.COM
http://www.assessment.com

This website introduces you to MAPP, the Motivational Appraisal of Personal Potential.

VALUES IN ACTION
http://www.viastrengths.org/register.aspx

This website introduces you to a values survey designed to help you identify what makes you happy.

How Marketing-Savvy Have You Become?

1. What is the difference between goals and marketing objectives?

2. What role do marketing objectives fulfill in career planning?

3. How does Maslow's hierarchy of needs facilitate the understanding of human behaviour and motivation?

4. Where did you learn the values that you now hold strongly? How likely do you think those values are to change in the future? Why might they change?

5. Identify and describe the values of three organizations or individuals that you admire

NOW WHAT?

The groundwork for your marketing plan has now been done. Your situation analysis is completed. You have established your goals and marketing objectives. The next step is to decide on the path that will help you reach your objectives; in other words, to create your marketing strategy. That's precisely what we'll be covering in the next chapter.

Notes
1. Rokeach, M. (1973). *The Nature of Human Values*. New York: The Free Press, p. 5.
2. Ciletti, D. (2004). *Marketing Yourself*. Mason, OH: South-Western/Thomson.

Here is a user-friendly template to help you set your career goals and summarize what you have learned so far about yourself. You may want to have your situation analysis nearby, including your SWOT analysis and the results of your self-assessment tests, so that you may refer to them as needed.

My most important **values** are (revisit Table 4.2 if needed):

My most important **needs** are:

My self-assessment revealed that I am:

My Goals

1. Within three years (or after graduating), what type of work would you like to be doing in the field(s) that you have identified as being attractive to you? (You may want to use a five-year outlook if you believe that is warranted or useful.)

2. Within 12 months (or after graduating), what type of work would you like to be doing in the area(s) that you have identified as being attractive to you?

3. What level of income would you like or need to earn immediately upon graduation? In the next 12 months? How much would you like to earn within three years? Make sure to properly research salaries in your field, given your level of education and experience (visit http://www.salary.com).

4. In which countries, provinces, states, or cities do you want to work? Make sure to identify the areas that are relevant in your field.

5. If you have any uncertainties about Questions 1 to 4, how can you clear these up? Make sure to address this question if you feel that you did not or cannot answer any of the previous four questions above.

Are My Career Goals:

Actionable: Can I map the steps to achieve them?	❏ Yes	❏ No
Bounded: Can I measure my progress with a clear time horizon?	❏ Yes	❏ No
Compelling: Will these goals get me charged up and out of bed in the morning?	❏ Yes	❏ No

Main Barriers

What might stand in the way of achieving my career goals?

1. _____

2. _____

3. _____

MARKETING OBJECTIVE-SETTING TEMPLATE

Now that you have outlined your career goals, you need to define your marketing objectives. This template is designed to help you get the process started.

I Plan on Becoming:

❑ an entrepreneur ❑ a professional ❑ an artist ❑ a job seeker

My Marketing Objectives

These will be stated in terms of the following (check all that apply and specify):

Entrepreneur

❑ sales

❑ customer acquisition/relationship

❑ market share/position

❑ growth/expansion

❑ other:

Professional

❑ sales

❑ customer acquisition/relationship

❑ product development/introduction

❑ other:

Artist

❑ sales

❑ customer acquisition/relationship

❑ product development/introduction

❑ other:

Job Seeker

❑ job/position

❑ income and benefits

❑ other

Are My Marketing Objectives:

consistent with my career goal?	❑ Yes	❑ No
consistent with my values?	❑ Yes	❑ No
consistent with my strengths?	❑ Yes	❑ No
realistic?	❑ Yes	❑ No
challenging?	❑ Yes	❑ No
important to me?	❑ Yes	❑ No
adaptable?	❑ Yes	❑ No
time-defined?	❑ Yes	❑ No
measurable?	❑ Yes	❑ No

Making the value of your offering visible to customers

Meet Harvey Schwartz. Harvey is the president and managing director of Engage Presentations, a consulting firm specializing in the strategic development and creation of presentations for the healthcare industry. Harvey is also a graduate of the Marketing Yourself online course, which he credits with helping him fine-tune the marketing strategy that he used to launch his second career.

A few years ago, Harvey was at a crossroads: either continue his career with a large pharmaceutical company or become his own boss and start his own consulting firm. With a strong background in healthcare marketing, Harvey decided to become an entrepreneur and offer his services to other firms. First, he cast a wide net and developed a broad service offering, with the goal of appealing to as many clients as possible. This soon led to a problem: while prospective clients found his proposal interesting, they could not easily grasp the offering and the benefits they would receive from using Harvey's services. By maintaining a dialogue with his prospective clients, Harvey was able to identify a specific area within his initial offering that was indeed of interest to them. He proceeded to focus his target marketing efforts and emphasized his ability to understand the communication challenges faced by healthcare companies and the needs of their audiences. Soon after repositioning himself, Harvey landed his first big contract, exceeding the revenue forecast he had set for that quarter. He used a portion of the proceeds to purchase a much-needed new laptop.

We asked Harvey what three tips he would like to share with readers of *Marketing Yourself.* Here are his thoughts

1. *Develop your communication skills.* You not only must be able to write and speak well but also must master the basic software programs necessary to build effective presentations. You must also be able to read an audience and identify its needs and barriers.

2. *Volunteer.* This is a very effective way to acquire valuable experience while honing your networking and communication skills.

3. *Treat everyone with respect.* As you navigate the paths toward your career goals, learn to treat everyone with respect and dignity. You never know when someone will cross your path again or might be able to help you in the future. Leave a positive impression wherever you go.

Why do some companies and individuals seem to move from success to success while others stumble and fail?

In many cases it's because of their marketing strategies—or lack thereof. In the late 1970s, when the market for typewriters began to decline because of the emergence of word-processing technology, many leading typewriter manufacturers such as Royal and Smith Corona failed to adapt and fell by the wayside. On the other hand, IBM expanded from being a maker of typewriters and became the leader in word-processing hardware and software including personal computers, printers, and operating systems. The decision to do this was a major contributor to IBM's growth throughout the 1980s and beyond.

As you learned in Chapter 3, at the end of the baby boom in the mid-1960s women began to change their roles as stay-at-home mothers to work outside the home. This phenomenon continued for decades and gave rise to a number of major industries including restaurants and frozen foods. Conversely, food products that were ingredients in recipes requiring several hours of preparation—for example, flour, pie fillings, yeast, lard, and corn starch—were now faced with the very real threat of significantly reduced demand. Baking soda could have been a sitting duck as this threat gained momentum, but the makers of the Arm & Hammer brand chose to enter new markets by developing new products and communicating to old and new users alike that in addition to being ideal for baking, Arm & Hammer baking soda could be used to keep refrigerators and freezers smelling fresh, to whiten teeth, and to make for a refreshing bath. The baking soda market and the Arm & Hammer brand achieved unprecedented and sustained growth.

The passenger airline industry has faced more than its share of ups and downs, and with these peaks and valleys many airlines have faltered while others have thrived. Eastern, Canadian, United, Swiss Air, Sabena, Pan American, Roots Air, and British Caledonian airlines have one thing in common—they're all out of business. By contrast, Southwest Airlines has more than just survived; its overall performance has soared. At the root of its success is Southwest's decision to focus its resources on the goal of providing long-distance transportation that is less expensive than travelling by car, bus, or rail. By doing so, it broadened the appeal of airline travel beyond businesspeople to include those who had never considered taking a plane. Unlike most of its competitors, throughout the past 20 years Southwest has generated consistently increasing revenue and profits.

Finally, consider Dell Inc. Since it went public in 1988, Dell has emerged as a major force in the computer market and now competes with Hewlett Packard for the number-one position overall. Its performance has eclipsed that of virtually all of its competitors, including much longer-established companies such as IBM and Apple. One of the keys to Dell's success is that it strives to provide the best value and latest computer and server technology to offices and individuals. However, what truly has set Dell apart is that it custom makes the products it sells

YOU WILL:

- know what target marketing is and what it involves
- know what segmentation is and how it can help you to develop a successful marketing plan for yourself
- know what makes market segments attractive and desirable
- know what positioning is and the bases along which products are typically positioned
- understand how consumers and organizations go about buying

and then delivers them directly to its customers. By not keeping huge quantities of computers and servers in inventory and by not distributing them through intermediaries such as retail stores, Dell has lower costs than many of its competitors. These, in turn, can be reflected in lower selling prices.

There are a few common themes in these four examples. Can you spot them? Did each of the relatively successful companies—IBM, Arm & Hammer, Southwest Airlines, and Dell—continue to target the same customers as their competitors on their roads to success? No. Did they expand their customer bases to include new ones? Yes. Was their success primarily a result of environmental factors, such as technology and the economy working out in their favour? No. Did they make conscious choices that steered them toward success, and did these choices involve the companies' products, promotion, price, place, or some combination of these? Yes. If you were able to spot these differences and correctly answer these questions, you're well on your way to understanding the notion of marketing strategy.

 Myth

*If I land a job that I thought was for me and after just one month on it realize that it's not, I should **stick it out for at least a year** so I won't look like a job-hopper.*

Reality Check

Life is too short to suffer for so long. Plus, doing something you don't like for up to a year can drain your motivation and energy and ultimately affect how attractive you'll be to potential employers. Learn from the experience and move on. When asked about it by potential employers, tell them the truth. **They'll be more likely to respect you for cutting your losses** early than for putting up with 12 months of agony.

As this Myth/Reality Check feature suggests, nothing can prevent the possibility you might end up in a job that is not for you. But a sound, well-thought-out marketing strategy can help to minimize the chances of this happening. And if it does happen, your marketing strategy can help you to react swiftly and move on in the direction that's right for you.

WHAT IS MARKETING STRATEGY ALL ABOUT?

It is widely held that the concept of strategy was conceived by the Greek military during the time of Socrates. To the Greek army leadership, strategy was the plan of action that would be put in place to surprise, defeat, and surpass the enemy. Over time, the meaning of strategy has evolved. In his 2005 book *Winning,* the former CEO of General Electric, Jack Welch, defined strategy as "an approximate course of action that you frequently revisit and redefine according to shifting market conditions."[1] Underlying both of these views is the idea that strategy involves making choices, usually about how you compete to achieve your objectives.

In the marketing arena, strategy refers to how individuals or organizations plan to achieve their marketing objectives. More specifically, marketing strategy is a two-step process:

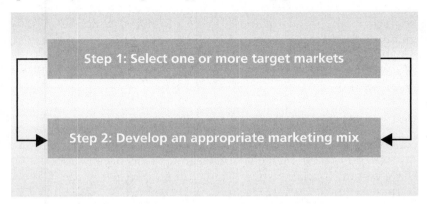

Step 1: Select one or more target markets

Step 2: Develop an appropriate marketing mix

Recall the four Ps from Chapter 2. A marketing mix is a unique blend of these four Ps—namely, the four key controllable marketing tools: product, price, place, and promotion. So, in effect, marketing strategy is the alignment of all the decisions involved in managing these four tools to satisfy one or more selected target markets. In this chapter, we'll discuss target market selection in depth. In the four chapters to follow, we'll cover each of the four Ps in detail.

IDENTIFYING POTENTIAL TARGET MARKETS

By now, you'll have realized that carefully identifying and focusing on your potential customers is one of the basic building blocks of successful marketing strategies. At first blush, it would seem logical to target everyone—all prospective customers and employers. That way, you would have the greatest market potential. However, the logic doesn't hold. Here are some reasons why:

- By targeting everyone, you would be assuming that every customer or employer has the same needs. There are precious few, if any, markets in which this is the case.

- It would be very unlikely that any organizations or individuals would have the resources, particularly financial, required to effectively target everyone.

- By targeting everyone, you would be giving in to the fallacy that satisfying everybody fairly well will lead to success. In fact, this approach will almost certainly result in failure. Why? Because potential customers or employers don't have the same needs—and even if they did, they wouldn't feel them with the same intensity and fulfill them the same way. You might get away with satisfying everyone fairly well for a while, but sooner than later competitors will start appealing to larger and larger chunks of your market and will try to satisfy them very—not fairly—well. Remember how Ford lost its market leadership position to General Motors when GM offered a choice of colours to car buyers while Ford's cars were available only in black?

Chapter 5 — Creating Your Marketing Strategies

The process of identifying your potential customers or employers begins with choosing a market that offers the most promise of achieving your marketing objectives. Then you narrow this choice down to those customers or employers whom you can satisfy very well with the resources you have available—these are usually referred to as your *prime prospects*. Next, you decide how you will position yourself in the minds of these prime prospects, which essentially amounts to teaching them to think of your product as a way to satisfy their needs that is different and more attractive than that of your competitors. The first step in this process is called *market segmentation*.

MARKET SEGMENTATION

> **market segmentation** — the process of dividing a market into distinct groups of customers (or organizations) that share certain characteristics and react in a similar way to a marketing offer

Market segmentation is the process of dividing a market into distinct groups or segments of customers or organizations that share certain characteristics. Then, you need to select one or more of these segments as a target to be reached with a specific marketing mix (i.e., the four Ps). A market segment is made up of customers or organizations that respond in a similar way to a marketing mix. The key question is how do you segment a market? In other words, how do you divide a broad market composed of heterogeneous individuals into groups of homogeneous people who will respond in a similar way to your marketing mix? On what basis do you group individuals together? There is no standard, fail-safe, or guaranteed way of doing this, but there are bases or variables that are commonly used by marketers. They're outlined in the following section. With these in mind, you try to identify patterns and select groups of individuals or organizations with similar characteristics and needs that you can satisfy.

The variables that are most widely used in dividing up consumer markets are as follows.

GEO-DEMOGRAPHIC VARIABLES

Geo-demographic variables include characteristics such as sex, age, marital status (including family or household composition: number of children, age of youngest and oldest child, other relatives living at home, etc.), income, education, and occupation. This information is typically cross-matched across specific geographic areas (e.g., countries, provinces, states, and cities). For example, a car brand such as BMW is targeted to people all over the world living in relatively large urban areas who tend to be male, are over the age of 35, have high levels of personal income, and are employed as professionals, senior managers, or business owners. Demographic information offers a critical advantage: it is often easy to access. For example, visit http://www.statcan.ca and you can easily quantify how many individuals match various demographic profiles in Canada. While demographic data is crucial, unto itself it is not sufficient to segment markets and act as the basis for your marketing strategy.

PSYCHOGRAPHIC DATA

> **psychographic data** — information concerned with consumers' lifestyles, usually described in terms of preferred activities, interests, and opinions

Psychographic data is concerned with people's lifestyles. A lifestyle is usually described in terms of preferred activities, interests, and opinions. Think of your own lifestyle. How might you define or describe it? It's a tough question, isn't it? Where do you begin? Sometimes, at the preliminary stages of market segmentation, it may be enough to assign descriptors that can roughly define your market's lifestyle. For example, athletic clothing is typically targeted to people who have or want to be seen as having a performance edge and who are or see themselves as being highly competitive and active. Of course, it is also possible to target a brand of athletic clothing to the fashion-conscious who see themselves as stylish and active. However, as you begin to paint a more complete picture of your market, you need to dig deeper. Fortunately, there are a number of proprietary systems that collect and report on consumer lifestyles. Many of these also offer the opportunity to obtain this information for specific geographic areas. Two of these deserve a brief mention.

The first psychographic classification system is called VALS™. It categorizes consumers based on their available resources and their primary psychological motivation. Here, resources are a function of both income and a combination of other traits—such as energy, self-confidence, novelty seeking, innovativeness, impulsiveness, and even vanity—that determines a person's propensity to consume goods and services. Primary motivation refers to what directs or governs people's activities. It is based on the underlying premise that people buy goods and services that reflect who they are and what gives meaning and direction to their lives. In a consumption context, people are motivated by ideals (including knowledge, principles), achievement (success), and self-expression (social/physical activities, variety, and risk seeking). When combined, these two dimensions—resources and primary motivation—form eight clusters (see Exhibit 5.1).

Consumers' VALS types are determined by the way they respond to the "VALS Questionnaire," a list of attitude statements and four demographics. A proprietary algorithm analyzes their responses and classifies them according to the VALS group they are most like and the VALS group they are second most like. For instance, upon taking the VALS questionnaire (http://www.sric-bi.com/VALS/), you might learn that you are most like an *Experiencer*, described as:

> *Motivated by self-expression. As young, enthusiastic, and impulsive consumers, Experiencers quickly become enthusiastic about new possibilities but are equally quick to cool. They seek variety and excitement, savouring the new, the offbeat, and the risky. Their energy finds an outlet in exercise, sports, outdoor recreation, and social activities. Experiencers are avid consumers and spend a comparatively high proportion of their income on fashion, entertainment, and socializing. Their purchases reflect the emphasis they place on looking good and having "cool" stuff.[2]*

Visit the VALS website to see more descriptions of the lifestyles associated with each group in Exhibit 5.1.

PRIZM is another popular lifestyle classification scheme. It also features geographic segmentation data and is referred to as a geo-clustering tool, which assigns consumers living in specific geographic areas to one of 14 social groups (see Exhibit 5.2). These 15 groups are then broken down into 66 different clusters with descriptive labels such as Minivan and Red Wine, Pools and Patios, and Cosmopolitan Elite. For instance, the Urban Uptown group is made up of five segments: Young Digerati, Money and Brains, Bohemian Mix, The Cosmopolitans, and American Dreams. The Young Digerati are described as tech-savvy singles and couples living in

EXHIBIT 5.1   The VALS Psychographic Classification

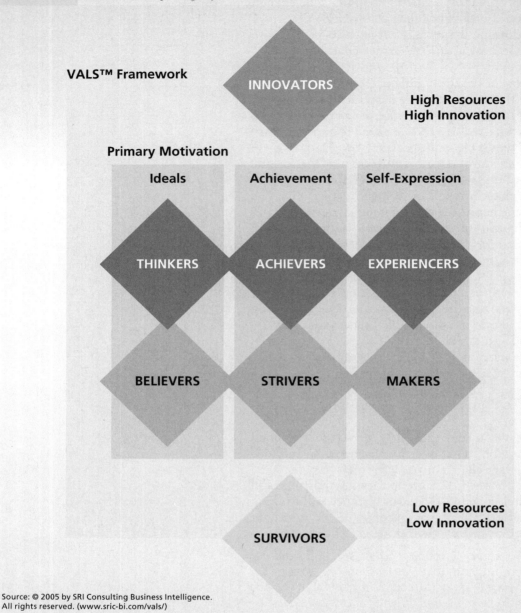

VALS™ Framework

INNOVATORS

**High Resources
High Innovation**

Primary Motivation

| Ideals | Achievement | Self-Expression |

THINKERS   **ACHIEVERS**   **EXPERIENCERS**

BELIEVERS   **STRIVERS**   **MAKERS**

**Low Resources
Low Innovation**

SURVIVORS

trendy condos in fashionable neighbourhoods. They're affluent and highly educated, and typically belong to a fitness club, shop at clothing boutiques as opposed to malls, and dine at casual restaurants. You can find out more about the various PRIZM lifestyles by visiting http://www.claritas.com, the site for the parent company that owns and provides this service. For a recent application of PRIZM to the Canadian market, visit http://www.environicsanalytics.ca.

As you might expect, age has a defining impact on lifestyle. Nowhere is this more obvious than in the teen market, which is attracting ever-increasing attention from marketers fuelled in part by the realization that it's a market worth more than $100 billion.[3] Think for a minute of how different a young teenager's lifestyle might be from your own, from your parents'. Related to age is the notion of life stage or life events. Your lifestyle is likely to change in significant ways as you progress through various stages

EXHIBIT 5.2   **The 15 PRIZM Groups**

Group U1—Urban Uptown	Group C1—2nd City Society
Group U2—Midtown Mix	Group C2—City Centers
Group U3—Urban Cores	Group C3—Micro-City Blues
Group S1—Elite Suburbs	Group T1—Landed Gentry
Group S2—The Affluentials	Group T2—Country Comfort
Group S3—Middleburbs	Group T3—Middle America
Group S4—Inner Suburbs	Group T4—Rustic Living

Source: Claritas website <http://www.claritas.com/claritas/Default.jsp?ci=3&si=4&pn=prizmne_segments>

of your life. These will be marked by important events such as gradation (Yes, you'll finally have a life and disposable income!), marriage (or divorce!), promotions (or, alas, termination), birth of your first child, and so on. For instance, newlywed couples tend to spend more on restaurants and entertainment. Other major events can also change lifestyle patterns. After September 11, 2001, consumers made remarkable changes to their spending patterns as if suddenly they appreciated the finality of their life and the importance of enjoying it. Many consumers began to spend on products, including leisure experiences, that brought them closer to their families. For example, after 9/11 the hotel industry experienced a severe downturn, with businesspeople travelling less and less. However, many hotel management companies saw this as an opportunity to pursue other markets such as managing timesharing condominiums. Visit Marriott Vacation Club International's website at http://www.vacationclub.com and see how images of happy families, typically with kids under 15, are used to appeal to affluent families who appreciate the no-hassle usage of a two-bedroom condominium in a sunny destination.

Are there global lifestyles; that is, lifestyles that can be found in every country, every culture? There are, but only a few. Think of brands like Coca-Cola, Nike, Absolut Vodka, and McDonald's. All have achieved remarkable global acceptance. Might they be tapping into a common lifestyle? Or, think about business executives all over the world. While they speak different languages, sometimes even dress differently, they tend to have similar preferences and needs when they travel. Global lifestyles can be useful if your product has a broad appeal across country borders. Promotion campaigns for global lifestyles can be designed around a central theme and then simply adapted by using different images and voiceover narrative for different countries. The "I'm lovin' it" campaign for McDonald's is an example.

MEDIA PREFERENCES

Media preferences constitutes another variable or type of characteristic used to analyze and divide the market. Media are the sources where customers get their news and entertainment. For example, Square Enix, the manufacturer of the Final Fantasy video game series, primarily targets people who source entertainment and product information on the Internet. Radio stations, newspaper publishers, television programming executives, and advertisers are all very interested in consumers' media preferences. Tracking studies routinely assess consumers' usage of various media. For example, the Newspaper Advertising Data Bank (NAD Bank, http://www.nadbank.com) tracks the newspaper-reading habits of various consumer categories. As you can imagine, the increasing popularity of the Internet has resulted in the erosion of newspaper readership among many younger consumers, who rely on the Internet as their primary source for news and entertainment. Understanding media preferences can help you to identify where to communicate your message and effectively reach your prime prospects.

PURCHASE BEHAVIOUR

Purchase behaviour refers to data that describe the purchase habits of customers. This might include usage rate (non-user; first-time user; repeat user; light, medium, and heavy users), frequency and timing of purchase (e.g., every week, every month, every two years), location of purchase (e.g., grocery store, convenience store, Internet), and brand loyalty. This type of information may be assessed for an entire product category (e.g., clothing), a specific product within a category (e.g., men's casual wear), or a specific brand (e.g., Dockers, Gap). The idea is to understand customer spending and shopping patterns so that marketing strategies can be planned and timed appropriately. In the context of grocery shopping, examples of purchase behaviour data might include the answers to questions such as the following (as you read these questions, ask yourself how you might use your own answers to improve the product selection and service at the grocery store you patronize):

- How often do you go grocery shopping?
- How far is the grocery store from your house? Do you drive, walk, or use public transportation to get there?
- How long do you usually spend in the store? What navigation patterns do you use?
- Do you bring a list of things to buy? What percentage of purchases are planned (e.g., buy a six-pack of Sprite), semi-planned (e.g., buy some meat and salad veggies for Saturday's BBQ), or impulsive?
- How many items do you buy?
- How much money do you spend in total? On meat? On fruits and vegetables? On dairy? On beverages? Frozen foods?

Segmenting users based on usage rate is a frequently used approach. For example, throughout the 1960s in the United States, the Shaefer brand of beer used the slogan: "Shaefer is the one beer to have when you're having more than one." The segment it was targeting? Heavy users. Keeping with another beer example, Alexander Keith's, a Canadian beer brand, uses the slogan: "Those who like it, like it a lot." In this case they are targeting heavy-using, loyal drinkers. Or consider the Mercedes-Benz advertising campaign that posed the question "What are you waiting for?" It was used to target potential younger customers with the goal of turning them into first-time users.

BENEFITS SOUGHT

Benefits sought refers to the most important or desirable benefits that the customer seeks from using your product. Here, a benefit is the consequence, functional or psychological, that purchasing or using the product will deliver. Functional benefits are the practical consequences of using the product—namely, what does it do for the customer? Psycho-social benefits are often less tangible or visible and refer to how your product makes the customer *feel* or be perceived by others. The point here is to focus on the key benefits that your product can deliver to your prime prospects. In the toothpaste market, different products can be developed and produced to deliver different benefits to different customers. The next time you're in the toothpaste aisle of your drugstore or supermarket, check out how certain brands promise to deliver whiter teeth, help you fight tartar buildup, give you fresher breath, come in a convenient no-mess pump dispenser, or have great cinnamon burst flavour. These are all examples of benefits.

Benefits are sometimes conveyed in an explicit manner, such as Domino's Pizza's "30-minute delivery guarantee." Other products, such as designer clothing and fragrances, rely more on visual cues to make the benefits implicit: the sexy feeling you get when you wear your Miss Sixty jeans or the feeling of desirability that comes with using Calvin Klein cologne. Some products primarily deliver functional benefits (e.g., gasoline), others provide mostly psychological benefits (e.g., cosmetics), and some products offer both types (e.g., cars). Here are some more examples:

- Fast-food drive-through windows—We've gotten used to them by now, but the key benefit they produce for customers is to save time: no need to park, go into the restaurant, and wait in line. Simply drive through, give your order, pay, and you're on your way.

- Just for Men hair colouring promises to cover grey hair. On the one hand, the functional benefit could simply be "no more grey hair." Well, that's only part of the answer. The appearance of grey hair is something many men wish to put off for as long as possible. Just for Men makes that possible. The psychological benefit? While it may be phrased in different ways, how about something like "renewed confidence that comes with a more youthful and no-more-grey-hair appearance" or "feeling young, sexy, and attractive again"?

- The BMW M6 Cabriolet model with its 500-horsepower engine can take you from 0 to 100 km/h in less than 5 seconds. Functional benefit? You can get to your destination in very little time. But imagine how you might feel stopping for a red light at a busy downtown intersection with the top of your M6 down. Pretty cool, right? Status, perceived power, the thrill or pleasure of driving—these are all examples of the many psycho-social benefits involved in driving an M6. These benefits by themselves may not prompt you to buy an M6, but with the car's other functional benefits, they might convince you to buy that model as opposed to one of BMW's competitors' vehicles. Think of other car manufacturers and how they communicate the psycho-social benefits of their products. For instance, Mazda's "Zoom Zoom" slogan is a throwback to childhood memories of fun times when playing with toy cars and making them go "zoom zoom" fast.

- Head & Shoulders shampoo targets people who want to get rid of dandruff. Here, a functional benefit might be "no more dandruff flakes on your dark-coloured suit" and the psychological benefit might be "no more embarrassment" or "the confidence to wear black sweaters again."

Identifying the key functional and psycho-social benefits that customers care about often requires marketers to use research methodologies that provide access to customers' inner thoughts and feelings to help them understand what using the product does for its customers. One-on-one interviews and focus groups are useful techniques to uncover such information. A keen sense of observation and the ability to extract insight from everyday situations can also be useful. Here's an exercise to get the point across.

❓ Self Check

Think of the goods (e.g., toothpaste or potato chips), services (e.g., hair styling or car repair), or experiences (e.g., movies, restaurant meals, or vacations) that you use or purchase. What key functional and psycho-social benefits do you derive from each one? What do these products do for you? How do they make you feel?

PUTTING IT TOGETHER

As we mentioned earlier, on its own each of the segmentation bases we've outlined is usually not sufficient to effectively segment a market. Additionally, the richer and more complete the picture you paint of your prime prospects, the better your chances of successfully influencing and satisfying them. The segmentation variables we've just covered are invaluable tools that can help you achieve this. The profiles of various types of snackers in Table 5.1 illustrate how the variables can be applied.

As you gather and piece together information about your own target market, your goal is to begin to think and feel like your customers. Remember the 2000 movie *What Women Want* with Mel Gibson and Helen Hunt? Gibson played an advertising executive whose career was on the line when he suddenly developed the ability to hear what women were actually thinking. In one scene, to think and feel (and literally behave!) like the women his advertising agency was targeting, he decided to try on lingerie, lipstick, and pantyhose. We are not inviting you to go to such lengths! The point is that you need to put yourself in your customers' shoes to see the world as they do.

TABLE 5.1 **Segments of Snackers**

	Nutritional Snackers	Weight Watchers	Guilty Snackers	Party Snackers	Indiscriminate Snackers	Economical Snackers
Percentage of snackers	22 percent	14 percent	9 percent	15 percent	15 percent	18 percent
Lifestyle characteristics	Self-assured, controlled	Outdoorsy, influential, venturesome	Highly anxious, isolated	Sociable	Hedonistic	Self-assured, price-oriented
Benefits sought	Nutritious, without artificial ingredients, natural	Low in calories, quick energy	Low in calories, good tasting	Good to serve guests, served with pride, go well with beverages	Good tasting, satisfies hunger	Low in price, best value
Consumption level of snacks	Light	Light	Heavy	Average	Heavy	Average
Types of snacks usually eaten	Fruits, vegetables, cheese	Yogurt, vegetables	Yogurt, cookies, crackers, candy	Nuts, potato chips, crackers, pretzels	Candy, ice cream, cookies, potato chips, pretzels, popcorn	No specific products
Demographics	Better educated, have younger children	Younger, single	Younger, or older, female, lower socio-economic status	Middle-aged, nonurban	Teenager	Have large family, better educated

Source: From *Marketing*, Third Canadian Edition by LAMB/HAIR/MCDANIEL/FARIA. 2005. Reproduced with permission of Nelson, a division of Thomson Learning: www.thomsonrights.com. Fax 800 730-2215.

For those of you who have chosen the job-seeking career path, you need to think slightly differently about these various types of customer information because your customers will be the businesses or other organizations you will be targeting. The variables you can use to segment these markets are as follows.

- **Demographics**—What is the industry (e.g., healthcare), company size (e.g., multi-billion dollar annual sales, number of employees), company ownership (e.g., publicly traded vs. privately owned), geographic location (e.g., Northeastern United States, Eastern Canada, Australia)?

- **Purchase behaviour**—What are the hiring approaches used by these businesses? Job fairs, school visits, advertising, websites, internal announcements and postings of openings, referrals, placement consultants?

- **Benefits sought**—What are these businesses looking for when they hire? Motivation, initiative, persistence, creativity, flexibility, sociability, language skills, job-related and soft skills, specialized knowledge, and general knowledge are all examples of benefits these companies might seek. You might be thinking "companies look for all of this, so can I tell the difference?" Job postings often include job descriptions that can give you an idea of the benefits these companies are seeking. Also, you can speak with people who work for those types of organizations. Ask around and try to find out more about the person who will be interviewing and about the types of people who thrive there. The answers to those questions will help give you a clearer idea of the benefits sought by the organization.

- **Organizational characteristics**—How would you describe how these organizations operate and what they value? Do they have a formal or informal culture? What are their ethics, values, vision, and concern for employees' well-being? Are they aggressive, methodical, fast- or slow-paced?

 Myth

*To maximize my chances of getting the job I want, I should email my resume to **as many potential employers as possible**.*

 *Reality Check*

Everyone else with a computer and an Internet connection can do and is doing the same thing. Mass emailing your resume is basically an exercise in spamming and it generally produces the same results as regular spam: it gets deleted without being read. **Think target market and not mass market.** Send your resume only to those people and organizations that can lead you to the job you really want. Protect your resume and treat it as something that has value. Your resume can make you more valuable in the eyes of hiring managers and recruiters if they don't see it plastered all over the Internet.

WHY SEGMENT?

Obtaining psychographic information for consumer markets can be costly. (Lifestyle information is rarely free!) Researching the various businesses you may wish to target will cost you time and possibly some money as well. So why bother? In the final analysis, we segment markets to increase the probability that the resources we expend on creating our marketing mixes will lead to success. So, if segmenting your market and tailoring your product, price, place, and promotion decisions to suit that market gets you no further ahead, then segmentation has little value. In reality, segmentation doesn't always work. For example, buyers of frozen orange juice can be divided into people who have blue eyes and those who have brown eyes. But eye colour has no influence whatsoever on the purchase of frozen orange juice. And if all frozen orange juice buyers purchased the same amount of the product weekly, if they believed all frozen orange juice brands are identical, and if they all wanted to pay the same price, marketers of frozen orange juice would not gain very much by segmenting the market.

So how do you know that your segmentation approach has led you closer to defining segments that are attractive and potentially viable to target? Check to see if the segments that you've identified meet the following criteria known as the three Ms:

- **M for Meaningful:** The market segment must be large or profitable enough to serve. A segment comprising 2000 people may be interesting to Lamborghini but would be of no economic interest or value to Honda. Will your segment generate sufficient sales or can it be grown to generate substantial sales? Are the segments large enough so that you can achieve your marketing objectives within them in the short and long terms? For example, certain segments of the market for high-technology products may be sizeable today but could have an uncertain future.

- **M for Measurable:** You must be able to quantify the size, purchasing power, and key characteristics (e.g., psychographic profiles) of the segment. Using the previous orange juice example, it would be very difficult to determine the number of blue and brown eyed people in a population, let alone obtain any demographics on them. On the other hand, quantitative information on the number of female university graduates—if those were part of your target segment—is readily available.

- **M for Marketable:** You must be able to effectively reach and serve the segment. While a segment comprising heavy-using left-handed males may be of interest to a cereal marketer, unless these males use the same media or shop at certain retailers they will be very hard to reach with any degree of efficiency. On the other hand, a marketer of left-handed hockey sticks would have little difficulty in serving its market as virtually all left-handed shooters buy their sticks in sporting goods stores.

Once you've assessed whether the potential segments in your market meet these criteria, the next step is to decide which and how many segments you or your company will serve. Remember that once you've chosen your segment(s), you must be able to design a marketing mix that will be effective in attracting and satisfying the needs of your segment(s). For example, if you were a small regional marketer of bath soaps, at most you may have the capacity to design and distribute a handful of different products. On the other hand, Procter & Gamble has the human and financial resources to create and distribute dozens of brands in just about every country in the world.

SELECTING TARGET MARKET SEGMENTS TO SERVE

First, let's define what a target market segment is. A target market segment consists of a set of buyers (e.g., customers or employers) who share common needs or characteristics that the company or individual decides to serve. To illustrate, a restaurant operator could choose to serve parents who want the healthiest food available for themselves and their children, who want the dining experience to last no more than 30 minutes, and who are prepared to pay a 20 percent premium over the prices of the fast-food alternatives (for an example, go to http://www.freshcity.com). Or a job seeker could decide to target all fashion retailers, manufacturers, and importers who might need a manager who has a strong sense of style, is consistently ahead of the fashion curve, and possesses the creative skills to design and display garments.

In selecting segments to target, two other issues should be considered. First, it is relevant to think about the market's structure. (This is where your situation analysis comes in handy!) You must determine whether the segments that you're considering are currently being targeted by one or more strong competitors. If so, those segments may not be so attractive. What is the strength of buyers or employers relative to sellers or job seekers? To put this question into perspective, consider the advertising agency business. If working in this industry segment is of interest to you, before you try to enter it you should be aware that there are many more highly qualified people looking for entry-level positions than there are jobs available. This high level of competition allows agencies to be very selective in whom they choose to interview and hire. Additionally, it gives them the power to offer relatively low salaries and to require more hours of work compared to most other service industries. Secondly, you need to consider your resources and objectives. Do you or your company have the skills and resources to succeed in the segment? If you don't have them, can they be acquired quickly? For example, you may have identified the luxury segment of the online travel industry to be large, growing, and structurally attractive. However, you have estimated that it will cost approximately $500 000 to develop the necessary booking software, build a competitive website, and promote the site online and offline. If this amount of money is beyond your means and if you cannot raise it before competition intensifies, then the segment should be abandoned. Another guiding question is: do the segment and the opportunities within it align with your long-term objectives? Continuing with the online travel example, if your long-term goal is to own and operate a high-end spa, will running an Internet-based travel business lead to attainment of that objective? If your answer is "no," you should drop the segment or at least put this idea on hold.

When it comes to choosing target markets, a decision can be made to include just about everyone. This is called undifferentiated or mass marketing. Alternatively, one could choose to focus on a very small group of customers or on just one or two potential employers. This is called micromarketing. Between these two extremes are differentiated marketing and concentrated marketing. Let's examine all four approaches.

UNDIFFERENTIATED OR MASS MARKETING

A word of caution: because undifferentiated or mass marketing implies that organizations or individuals ignore market segment differences and target the whole market with one offer, it is akin to the selling or production orientation discussed in Chapter 1. Remember the blind spots that these can create? That said, there are companies that achieve success through practising undifferentiated marketing. When it comes to customer needs, they focus on similarities and not differences. They develop one product and one marketing program designed to appeal to the largest number of buyers and rely on mass advertising and distribution. Undifferentiated marketing is best suited for basic commodities such as salt, sugar, lumber,

and garden soil. The major threat encountered by mass marketers is the difficulty they come up against competing with firms that are better at satisfying the needs of specific segments. As examples of this, today there are companies producing flavoured salts, fair trade coffee, blemish-free lumber, and fertilizer-enriched garden soil with easy-pouring bags for consumers who seek convenience and ease of use.

DIFFERENTIATED MARKETING

When organizations or individuals use differentiated or segmented marketing, they decide to target several market segments and they create a different marketing mix for each. Some examples:

- The Ford Motor Company now offers vehicles targeted to a broad range of segments, each with its own individual marketing program. The company's products include the Ford Focus, Explorer, and F150 pickup truck as well as the Lincoln, Volvo, Jaguar, and Land Rover brands.

- Harlequin Enterprises targets various segments of female readers with books branded under its mainstream Harlequin banner (Intrigue, Blaze, Medical Romance, and American Romance) as well as offerings under the more risqué Silhouette banner (Intimate Moments, Desire, and Bombshell). The company even produces large-print versions of its publications for older customers.

- Yum Brands Inc. appeals to several segments of the fast-food market with its KFC, Taco Bell, Pizza Hut, A&W, and Long John Silver's restaurant chains.

- L'Oréal offers a variety of beauty and skincare products under brands designed to target a wide range of segments throughout the world. The company's brands include Lancôme, Giorgio Armani, Garnier, Maybelline, Ralph Lauren, Cacharel, Redken, and Biotherm.

Underlying the decision to produce many different offerings is an organization's goal of maximizing sales and market position within each segment with the ultimate objective of generating more total sales than if the organization used undifferentiated marketing. From the standpoint of profit, one of the basic tenets of differentiated marketing is that because it attempts to satisfy customers very well, these customers will be willing to pay a price premium over offerings that are marketed in an undifferentiated fashion, which tend to satisfy customers only fairly well. These higher prices can lead to higher profits. However, differentiated marketing usually increases the cost of doing business since producing, promoting, and distributing a wider array of offerings is typically more expensive than doing so for one or two.

CONCENTRATED MARKETING

Concentrated marketing is also known as niche marketing, and it is most frequently used by organizations and individuals with limited resources. Here, achieving a large share of a small number of submarkets is the goal as opposed to obtaining small shares of a number of large markets. Examples of firms employing niche marketing include:

Chapter 5 — Creating Your Marketing Strategies

- Forensic Technology Inc., which produces hardware and software that is used to identify the guns from which bullets have been fired. Their target market comprises law enforcement agencies around the world.
- The Red Line Synthetic Oil Corporation, which sells motor oils, gear oils, and cooling system additives primarily targeted to the car racing market.
- The Body Shop, which offers cosmetics and skincare products targeted to women who are willing to pay a premium price for a health and beauty brand with a social conscience.
- Château Lafitte, Château Pétrus, Opus One, and Sassicaia, which all are examples of fine wines—selling for more than $100 per bottle—that target people who can afford this amount, have a taste for the best things in life, and possess the patience and means to age the wine before drinking it.

A key advantage to the practice of concentrated marketing is that because niches are small, they tend to attract fewer competitors than larger markets. Additionally, firms and individuals can market more effectively and efficiently than if they used differentiated marketing. They can fine-tune their marketing mixes to provide high levels of satisfaction to clearly defined segments that can be served well and offer the highest levels of profit potential.

There are two significant risks implicit in concentrated marketing. The first is that as niches grow, they attract increasing levels of competition. For example, in the late 1990s, only one brand of energy drink was available in most countries, Red Bull. Today, there are hundreds of brands, many of which are produced by the major global soft drink manufacturers. Second, concentrated marketing can lead to a focus on the organization's or individual's product and not the market. Recall the kinds of disasters that can result from a myopic product orientation.

MICROMARKETING

Micromarketing occurs when organizations or individuals customize their offers to suit the needs and tastes of specific individual customers or locations. It includes local marketing and individual marketing. With local marketing, brands and promotions are tailored to the needs and wants of local customer groups such as cities, neighbourhoods, and, increasingly, specific stores or chains. For example, when a company such as 3M sponsors the training of hockey coaches and supports individual amateur teams, it is engaging in micromarketing. When a snack food manufacturer like Frito-Lay conducts a Super Bowl promotion with a particular supermarket chain (for example, Safeway), it too is practising local marketing. This type of marketing can go a long way toward strengthening relationships between a company or brand and its customers. However, because of the many details that need to be tended to under local marketing, it can be very costly and extremely challenging to manage. Individual marketing or one-to-one marketing involves customizing products and programs to the needs of individual customers. When it is done on a broad level, it is sometimes referred to as "mass customization," which may appear like a contradiction in terms, but implies customizing your offering not just for a lucky few customers but for a large number of customers. The growing popularity of individual marketing has largely come about as a result of advances in technology. Companies whose customers are other businesses frequently use individual marketing to tailor their offerings to individual customers. For example, advertising agencies create separate teams, departments, and even divisions to service the needs of each of their large clients. Those whose customers are consumers, such as Amazon, use past and current purchase behaviour information as the basis to make customized book recommendations to shoppers. In Europe, BMW has a division called Individual, which builds and finishes BMW vehicles to customers' individual tastes. Want a purple 745i luxury sedan with yellow leather interior and a fully equipped office in the backseat area with refrigerator and bar? No problem! Provided, of course, that you're willing to pay a big premium to have your automotive dream fulfilled. While individual marketing can deliver the ultimate in customer satisfaction, it can be extremely costly to implement, particularly because of the absence of economies of scale.

RELATING TARGET MARKETING TO CAREER PLANNING

So far in our discussion of target marketing we've focused mainly on businesses and other organizations. Now let's examine how it applies to job seekers. Assume that you have always wanted to work in sports management with a top-level North American professional football, baseball, hockey, or basketball team. Following is an overview of how the four target-marketing strategies could relate to your job search process.

> target marketing — a marketing approach designed to focus on key groups of consumers and tailor the marketing mix to their needs and want

- **Undifferentiated marketing**—Here, you would prepare one resume and cover letter and send it out to all the teams in the National Football League, Major League Baseball, National Hockey League, and National Basketball Association. In your letter you would give a general description of your qualifications and how they could benefit the team. Your resume would be designed to appeal to every team and, as a result, may not include details about experiences you had or courses that you took in one specific sport—say, baseball.

- **Differentiated marketing**—Pursuing this strategy will require more work on your part. You be the judge as to whether you think the extra effort will be worth it. First and foremost, you'd start by getting to know the main characteristics of the four leagues and the general needs that the teams in each league have, focusing on needs that you can satisfy. Based on your identification of these needs, you would then prepare and send out four different cover letters and resumes—one to NFL teams, one to MLB teams, one to NHL teams, and another to NBA teams—in which you would highlight why you are the ideal candidate for vacancies they may have. Your resume/cover letter packages will be addressed to individuals who have hiring authority or who influence it. You'll have obtained their names and coordinates through extensive research.

- **Concentrated marketing**—Two things will likely occur to you with this approach. The amount of work that you'll have to do to research the four leagues/120 teams and to send out the cover letter/resume packages is daunting. Your marketing instincts tell you that your chances of success would be much better if you learned more about the individual teams' needs as well as their problems and opportunities. This will require even more work and you just don't have the time to do it. Plus, you're not sure if you would like to live outside of the Northeastern United States or Eastern Canada. So you decide to segment your target market on two bases. First, to make your workload more manageable, you drop MLB and the NBA from your target market, leaving you to concentrate on your two favourite sports, football and hockey. Then you segment geographically and include only those teams in New York, Boston, Philadelphia, Toronto, Ottawa, and Montreal. This leaves you with a target market of 11 teams. You then research each team's needs in depth and prepare 11 separate cover letter/resume packages addressed to the person who can make the decision to hire or interview you. Your packages highlight how your skills, knowledge, and experience can be put to work immediately to satisfy their team's needs. You let recipients know that you will be following up with each of them to arrange an interview, and you do this on a regular basis. This concentrated approach verges on individual marketing.

- **Individual marketing**—After all of your research, you decide that all along what you really wanted was to work for your favourite team—the Toronto Maple Leafs. So you dig deeper to learn what their needs, problems, and opportunities are. Through friends, relatives, co-workers, and schoolmates you create a network of contacts—journalists, Maple Leafs employees, former prospects and players, and suppliers—who you can approach to give you insight about the team's situation. You determine that you have many of the qualifications they need except one—event planning. You enroll in an event-planning course and you join a volunteer group that needs help with planning events. You find out the name of the person who is responsible for hiring people in your area and arrange a half-hour information meeting to get to know the team better and to open the door to your candidacy. You highlight your relevant qualifications, including the fact that you are enrolled in an event-planning course. During the meeting you ask if the team offers internships as a way to get to know prospective employees. The answer is yes, so you then ask how you can apply for an internship. Based on the reply, you create a customized application package and personally deliver it to the interviewer's office within 48 hours. You follow up with him or her weekly.

In this example, undifferentiated marketing appears to be the easiest and simplest approach, but it will most likely be a hit-and-miss affair—with the emphasis on miss. There are many competitors for jobs in sports management and a general approach is unlikely to get you noticed, let alone contacted for an interview. Differentiated marketing would appear to be a big step forward and could bring you closer to your goal. It would be appropriate if you had the time and energy to implement it. Concentrated marketing would reduce the number of potential employers, but it could move you up the hiring ladder faster because of your sharper focus on the employers' needs and how you could satisfy them. And if you feel that you'd be disloyal by working for any other team than your favourite, be it the Yankees, Patriots, Senators, 76ers, Canadiens, or Blue Jays, individual marketing is the only way to go!

POSITIONING

After you've chosen your target marketing strategy, the next step is to create a **positioning** strategy. In simple terms, positioning is about teaching your customers to think of your product as a means of satisfying one or more of their needs in a way that competitors cannot. Let's examine the key elements of that definition.

> **positioning** — teaching your customers to think (or feel) about your product as a solution to a need (broadly defined) and in a way that is superior to the competition's offering

- "Teaching" takes time, patience, and clarity, which means that you or your organization must be clear on the position you wish to own.

- "Your customers" implies you've clearly identified who your customers are.

- "To think of your product as a means of" forces you to articulate how you want customers to think and feel about your product. Your analysis of "benefits sought" will come in handy here.

- "Satisfying one or more needs" implies you have identified those needs.

- "In a way that competitors cannot do" underscores the fact that a market position is always defined relative to your competitors.

The fundamental idea behind positioning is that you need to stand for something. If you try to be everything to everyone, you'll likely end up meaning nothing to anyone. If you aren't clear on what it is you or your product stands for, how can your customers be clear on what you stand for? Positioning is all about owning "mindspace" and ingraining in your customers' minds what you or your product represent. Examples of products and brands with clear, memorable, and compelling positions are:

- Google—The simplest, most extensive, and uncluttered way to search the Internet.

- Axe—Fragrances that boost men's sex appeal to the point where women will fight over them.

- Hummer—Over the top, macho vehicles and proud of it.

- Sharon Stone—The most alluring 50-something Hollywood actress.

Myth

No one will hire me because I lack experience, have low grades, have gaps in my work history, and so on.

Reality Check

People overcome all kinds of challenges to find the work they will like. How you handle adversity is a good indicator of your ability to persevere. If you don't have experience you can get it by volunteering or in work related to the jobs you'd like to do. If you have low grades, highlight other qualifications in your resume and interviews. Overcome doubts about gaps in your work history by focusing on your skills. Remember, for most entry-level jobs employers are looking for general qualifications such as communication skills, interpersonal capabilities, and enthusiasm. Most importantly, **a positive attitude is something employers truly value** and they know that it can't be taught.

One useful way to begin to think about your market position is to list your main competitors and then to define the position they currently own in the market. Is there a gap somewhere? Could you fit into that gap and "own" that position? As you attempt to identify the position you would like to own in the market and in customers' minds, you need to consider the competitive environment in which you're operating. Whose toes will you step on as you attempt to own that position? How are your competitors likely to react?

Take the graph in Exhibit 5.3, for example. It's what is known as a positioning map, showing the positions that various car makers have in consumers' minds. Notice the vacant space in the "sporty-classy" quadrant? Such a vacancy could represent a window of opportunity to either introduce a new car or to reposition an existing model so that it can own that vacant space. To create such a graph, you first need to identify the axes along which products in that industry can be positioned. Price and quality are not the only two that can be used here. Understanding the product benefits that customers care about can lead you in the right direction to choose axes that would yield valuable insight into the market. There are no absolutely correct or incorrect answers when going through this process. The idea is to develop an overview and understanding of the market that will allow you to identify opportunities that may have been overlooked by your competitors.

Once you have adopted a position, you need to make sure that you have the resources and willpower to stay the course. When faced by competitive attacks, some organizations exhibit a "knee jerk" reaction, cave in, retreat, and reposition. This usually ends up confusing consumers and results in a phenomenon called "concept drift." Quite literally, your concept is "adrift" in the sea of competing offers. To help you determine how you might position yourself or your product, consider the following bases upon which businesses typically position their offerings.

EXHIBIT 5.3   Positioning Map for the Car Industry

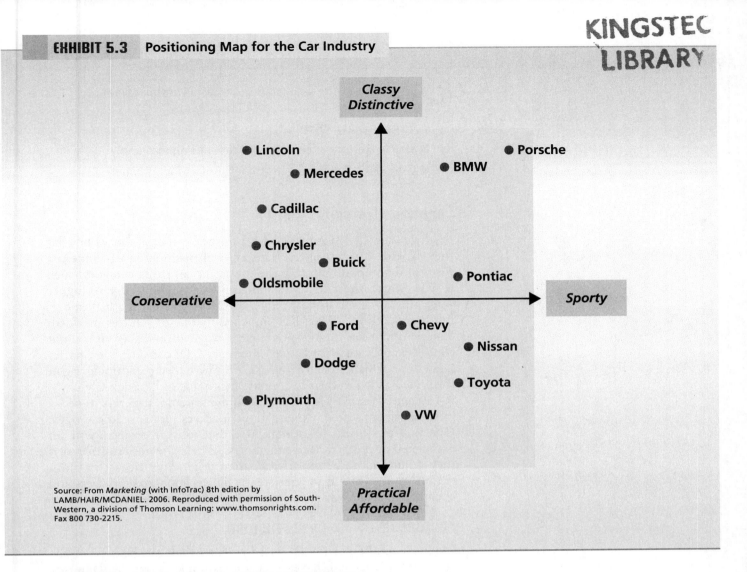

Classy Distinctive

● Lincoln   ● Porsche

● Mercedes   ● BMW

● Cadillac

● Chrysler

● Buick

● Oldsmobile   ● Pontiac

Conservative ←————————————————→ **Sporty**

● Ford   ● Chevy

● Nissan

● Dodge

● Toyota

● Plymouth

● VW

Practical Affordable

Source: From *Marketing* (with InfoTrac) 8th edition by LAMB/HAIR/MCDANIEL. 2006. Reproduced with permission of South-Western, a division of Thomson Learning: www.thomsonrights.com. Fax 800 730-2215.

POSITIONING BY PRODUCT ATTRIBUTES OR BENEFITS

Here, the product's features—or the benefits that customers will derive from using the product—are at the heart of the position. For this positioning approach to be effective, these features and benefits must be what the target market needs or cares deeply about. And, if the attribute or benefit is superior to that offered by competition, the positioning will be even stronger. For example, a wine producer may pride itself on making products that contain fewer sulphites than any other wine or wines that are created from organically grown grapes. If wine drinkers are not concerned about sulphite content or grape-growing methods, this would not be a promising positioning dimension. On the other hand, if the low sulphite content resulted in the wines being preferred for either their flavour or other reasons (e.g., physiological reactions), then this could be the basis for a compelling positioning.

As a second example, assume that you can speak and write five languages. This impressive range of fluency would have particular appeal to a potential employer who needs multilingual workers. But what if you were seeking employment in an industry in which knowing many languages is considered unimportant? You could use this attribute to demonstrate that you are a fast learner, are adaptable, and can grasp complex topics.

> **benefits** — the positive consequences of using a product; benefits may be functional or psycho-social

Some examples of products that are positioned by attribute or benefit are as follows:

- Buckley's Mixture—Outstanding effectiveness in relieving cold symptoms ("It tastes awful but it works")
- Volvo—Safety ("For life")
- BMW—Performance ("The ultimate driving machine")
- Campbell's Soup—Great-tasting comfort food ("Mmm Mmm good")

POSITIONING BY PRICE/QUALITY

Products can be positioned based on price and/or the value that they provide for customers. This type of positioning can take the form of a company offering the lowest prices in its category, such as Wal-Mart. Alternatively, a company may acknowledge its higher price but use this to its advantage: "L'Oréal might cost a little more, but I'm worth it." When Kia launched its line of vehicles in North America, its price/quality positioning was expressed as "It's about time everyone can afford a well-made car." Or consider the Charles Shaw line of wines, selling for $1.99. The enormous popularity of the wine has led to the affectionate nickname of "2 Buck Chuck."

Potential employees or professionals could use this type of positioning by offering their target markets more for the money. One way to do this is to guarantee that jobs or projects will get completed at pre-arranged timetables, salaries, or fees regardless if they require more hours of work than originally forecast to finish them. Another way is to consistently deliver more to employers and clients than what was promised and what they expect.

POSITIONING BY USE OR APPLICATION

Products can be positioned based on how they can be used or the applications they can have. A classic example is Arm & Hammer baking soda. As fewer and fewer people made bread, pies, and cakes from scratch at home, the market for baking soda declined steeply. Instead of giving up on the product, Arm & Hammer repositioned it as a deodorizer for refrigerators and freezers, a tooth whitener, and an enhancement to a soothing bath. To increase overall demand, Florida orange producers repositioned orange juice as being "not just for breakfast anymore." Kellogg's initiated an advertising campaign to teach young adults that it was acceptable to eat cereals for dinner.

This type of positioning can be applied to individuals too. Think of retired athletes who have become commentators or actors. Many personal fitness trainers have expanded their usages and applications to include nutritional and lifestyle counselling, thereby giving them a real competitive advantage. Employees who regularly perform tasks beyond their job descriptions—for example, taking part in organizing social events—position themselves based on use or application and become the "go to" person in that organization.

POSITIONING BY PRODUCT CLASS

Here, the objective is to position the product within a particular product category. For example, Tylenol is positioned in the pain relief category, Absolut Vodka is in the premium spirits category, and Gap is in the affordable, casual fashion category. Products can stretch their positioning so that they encompass expanded categories. These companies pretty much "own" the category, meaning that they are often the first name that most people will think of if you simply mention the product category. The Southwest Airlines example in the introduction to this chapter illustrates how a company positioned its product not just as air travel but as one in the long-distance travel category, which includes not only airplanes but also cars, buses, and trains. BMW's products are not confined to the sports car or luxury car categories but are positioned in a category that the company created: sports luxury. In product class positioning, arguments are often used to position the product at the top of the class. Think of advertisements for cars that claim "rated number one in its class by J.D. Power."

Adopting product class positioning forces marketers to understand what class or category of products will be triggered or thought of when their customers identify a need that they want to fulfill. When visiting websites for apparel, athletic gear, or other products, have you ever wondered which tab to click because you're simply not sure where the company might have categorized or located the product you're searching for? In a hardware or grocery store you have visited for the first time, have you ever spent time looking at the overhead signs trying to figure out in which aisle your desired product is located? This is what happens when companies don't categorize products in the same class or category that their customers themselves use.

Product class positioning can also be employed by individuals and professionals. For example, a lawyer could position himself or herself as a mediator. So, rather than representing clients only in confrontational situations, he or she could help parties with opposing interests resolve their conflicts without resorting to expensive and risky litigation. A family doctor could position himself or herself as someone who can be relied on not only for medical advice but also for psychological counselling. A marketing manager could take on the position of speech writer for a company's CEO. A job applicant could adopt the position of problem solver as opposed to management trainee.

POSITIONING BY COMPETITOR

While positioning against competitors is inherent in any positioning strategy, some products often go head-to-head with their main competitor. If you choose to do so, you want to make sure you can deliver on the promise you are making to customers. Some examples:

- 7UP—To get users to consider the brand when choosing a soft drink, 7UP was positioned against market leaders Coke and Pepsi as the Uncola.

- Avis—This brand positioned itself against the number-one car rental company Hertz with the attitude and slogan, "We're number two so we try harder."

- Burger King—Positioning itself against McDonald's, the leading fast-food chain where product standardization is the rule, Burger King promised customers that they could have their hamburgers dressed to their individual tastes with the slogan, "Have it your way."

Chapter 5 — Creating Your Marketing Strategies

- Visa poked fun at American Express with an ad campaign that invited customers to take their Visa cards with them to selected retail outlets. Their commercials ended with the catch phrase, "And they don't take American Express."
- The butter substitute known as "I Can't Believe It's Not Butter" is a good example of a product positioned directly against its direct competitor.

Positioning by competitor is frequently used by professionals and employees. For example, a dentist could position himself or herself as providing the gentlest, most pain-free treatment. Competitive positioning for a financial adviser could take the form of promising to be the only one to review clients' financial situations every three months and to recommend adjustments to their plans based on these assessments. An employee can position himself or herself competitively by:

- producing the most thorough work
- consistently completing projects ahead of schedule
- paying the most attention to detail
- being the most reliable during times of stress
- behaving the most professionally and politely with customers

BUYER BEHAVIOUR: WHY AND HOW CONSUMERS AND ORGANIZATIONS BUY

Effective marketing starts with an understanding of your customers or clients, especially the reasons why they buy (or don't buy!) your product. As a starting point to begin the understanding process, a colleague of ours, Dr. Michel Bergier, has summarized buyer behaviour in two simple and crystal-clear observations:

- Consumers buy products to solve a problem or to feel good.
- Organizations, particularly companies, buy products to make money or save money.

With these insights in mind, let's take a closer look at consumer and organizational buying behaviour.

CONSUMER BUYING BEHAVIOUR

If your target market is made up of consumers, understanding them should begin with the question, "What problem can my product solve for them, or how can it make them feel good?" Determining their purchase motivations can go a long way in leading you to the answer. Table 5.2 lists some common motivations that may lead consumers to consider or purchase your products.

Typically, when consumers recognize that they have a problem or experience the need to feel good, they go through a four-step decision-making process. Understanding the problems that consumers are looking to solve, the positive feelings that they want to experience, and the process that they go through to do so is fundamental to being able to satisfy their needs. Here is a breakdown of that process:

TABLE 5.2   Consumers' Purchase Motivations

MOTIVATION	ORIGIN
Problem removal	Prospect experiences a problem (e.g., a headache) and seeks a product to remove it (e.g., an analgesic).
Problem avoidance	Prospect anticipates a future problem (e.g., loss of income because of illness) and seeks a product to prevent occurrence (e.g., disability insurance).
Incomplete satisfaction	Prospect is not satisfied with current product (e.g., his or her doctor) and seeks a better one.
Mixed approach–avoidance	Prospect likes some things about product (e.g., the food and prices at a particular restaurant) but not others (e.g., distance from home) and tries to find a product to resolve this conflict (e.g., a similar restaurant closer to home).
Normal depletion	Prospect is out of stock or close to it (e.g., running out of milk) and seeks to maintain normal inventory (e.g., have a new container on hand before current one is completely empty).
Sensory gratification	Prospect seeks physical gratification (e.g., quenched thirst) or enjoyment (e.g., delicious taste).
Intellectual stimulation	Prospect seeks psychological gratification (e.g., peace of mind) or to explore or master a situation (e.g., sense of accomplishment)
Social approval	Prospect sees an opportunity for social rewards (e.g., elevated status) or personal recognition (e.g., being admired) through use of the product.

Source: "Table 5.2: Consumers' Purchase Motivations" adapted from *Advertising and Promotion Management* by John R. Rossiter and Larry Percy. Published 1987 by McGraw-Hill.

● *Information/alternative search*—Here, consumers look for information about how to solve the problem or how to enhance their well-being. At this stage, customers may rely on their own memory and perform an "internal search" for information or alternatives they may already know. Sometimes this might be sufficient. (That's why many companies advertise heavily—it's so you will think of them first and stop your search there.) Otherwise, they might go on to consult various sources such as family, friends, co-workers, authority figures, or third-party neutral sources (e.g., *Consumer Reports*), the Internet, the media, and advertising. Typically the more important or ego-involving the purchase, the more effort consumers will expend to search for information and alternatives—unless, of course, they've already "fallen in love" with one particular alternative, in which case they are likely to try to rationalize or defend their choice. This step might lead to a list of alternatives that will then be considered or evaluated. From the marketer's perspective, it is important to find out which sources will be consulted and whether his or her product makes it in the list to be considered.

- *Evaluation of alternatives*—With the information they've gathered at hand or in mind, consumers then evaluate the alternative solutions or means of feeling good available to them. The previous experiences that they have had with brands can be a major influence. So too can word-of-mouth. From this evaluation, they may decide to buy a specific product or brand, to forgo buying, to postpone their purchase, or to narrow down their list and keep searching for more information that will enable them to feel more confident about their purchase. Here, it is important to understand how the selection is made. Do customers compare brands one by one? If so, along which attribute (e.g., price, size, colour)? Asking consumers can identify clues as to how that process works (e.g., What made you decide to come and purchase your television here? Why are you buying that one? Have you considered other models and stores? Which ones?).

- *Purchase*—Having decided which brand or product to buy, consumers then need to purchase it. This may appear to be an obvious, no-explanation-needed step, but it warrants special consideration. Say a consumer has decided on a particular product or brand. Then what? The customer still needs to locate the product, physically pick it up, pay for it, and then take it home or wherever else it will be used. Paying close attention to each of these details can lead marketers to take specific actions to improve customer satisfaction with their products and the shopping experience. For instance, think of how Amazon.com simplifies navigation on its website and facilitates purchases by storing account and customer credit card information. It also offers gift-wrapping and delivery to the recipient of the gift.

- *Post-purchase behaviour and satisfaction*—Major purchases are usually made to solve a big problem (e.g., the breakdown of a refrigerator) or to feel extraordinarily good (e.g., a two-week oceanfront getaway to escape the stress and strain of everyday life). Very often, after making a major purchase consumers may experience serious doubts and even guilt. (Shouldn't I have gotten the refrigerator with the automatic ice-making feature? Should I really have committed to spending $3000 for that trip to Costa Rica?) This phenomenon is called *cognitive dissonance*, and it can result in consumers transferring their negative feelings onto the product and brand that they just bought. Marketers can take a number of actions to minimize or eliminate cognitive dissonance. For example, immediately after the sale is made, they can reassure customers about their purchase decisions. This can be done by reiterating how worry-free the warranty is on the refrigerator or by providing purchasers with testimonials from satisfied customers. Marketers can send letters or make phone calls to congratulate customers for having made a wise purchase decision and at the same time double check that everything is working as it should be. After-purchase service and follow-up questionnaires can be used to assess and enhance customers' satisfaction.

ORGANIZATIONAL BUYING BEHAVIOUR

Whether you're an entrepreneur selling to retailers, a professional offering your services to educational institutions, or someone looking for a position with a major corporation, understanding how organizations buy should begin with the question: "How can I make money or save money for my potential customers, clients, or employers?" Even if your goal is to work in the not-for-profit sector, this question is applicable. At one time or another most not-for-profit organizations need to raise funds, and because of their limited financial resources it's crucial to their survival that they practise vigilant cost control. With this in mind, let's examine how organizations go about purchasing the goods and services they need.

Organizations go about buying differently than do consumers in two fundamental ways. First, virtually all major organizational buying decisions, including hiring, are influenced and made by several people and not just one person, as is usually the case with consumer purchases. Second, the criteria employed by organizations in evaluating products, people, and suppliers are simpler and often more rational than those used by consumers. Let's take a closer look at each of these differences.

THE ORGANIZATION BUYING CENTRE

A buying centre includes all of the people in an organization who participate in the buying decision. They play one or more of the following roles.

- *Users* are members of the organization who will actually use the product, and in many cases they initiate the buying process and help set the specifications. For example, in the hiring process, users would be the supervisor or manager to whom the new employee will report.

- *Influencers* help in defining the specifications and provide information for evaluating alternatives. Using the hiring example, influencers could be human resources specialists who prepare job descriptions and administer psychological tests to screen applicants.

- *Buyers* are the people who make the actual purchase. In hiring situations, buyers are the ones who make the job offer and negotiate the terms of employment. In large organizations, these functions are typically the responsibility of a human resources manager.

- *Deciders* have the power—formal or informal—to select suppliers or approve purchase decisions. Major hiring decisions—for example, those for senior executives—often require the approval of the organization's chief executive officer.

- *Gatekeepers* control the flow of information to other members of the buying centre. Receptionists, administrative assistants, and human resources personnel can have a powerful influence on whether an applicant's phone calls are taken, emails are answered, and resume/cover letter packages get into the hands of the appropriate buying centre participant.

Whether you're selling a product or yourself to an organization, your chances of success will be strengthened if you understand how their buying centres work, who belongs to them, and what their needs and wants are.

THE EVALUATIVE CRITERIA USED BY ORGANIZATIONS

Organizational buyers evaluate products, people, and suppliers on three key criteria. In order of importance, they are:

- *Quality:* Here, quality refers to how well the product (including prospective employees) will perform in helping the organization make money or save money. It also includes the reputation of the supplier's salespeople and the company that they represent.

- *Service:* Organizations require satisfactory service. This could include the seller conducting a pre-purchase evaluation of the organization's needs, installing the purchased product, training employees on how to use the product, and regularly maintaining the product.

- *Price:* Organizations usually want to buy at the lowest prices. However, in pushing for the lowest prices or salaries, they must be careful not to put suppliers or prospective employees into a position in which product or service quality will be compromised.

How does your product fare on these three dimensions? Is your product positioned to convey your superiority on all or any one of these criteria?

WHAT IS YOUR TARGET MARKETING STRATEGY?

It is now time for you to specify your target marketing strategy. Use the following template to walk yourself through the critical steps in spelling out your strategy.

TAKING STOCK

We've covered an enormous amount of material in this chapter. Although you may feel a bit overwhelmed by its sheer volume, don't be alarmed. This is a perfect time to take stock of everything you've accomplished so far and to look ahead at what's coming. Exhibit 5.4 puts this in perspective for you and outlines the entire strategic marketing process, from situation analysis to implementation and control. Notice the tab, "You are here." It's impressive just how far you've come, isn't it?

Step 1: Market Segmentation

Attempt to divide the market based on one or a combination of the variables in the table below. List up to four possible segments and attempt to describe them thoroughly. (If you think it's necessary, you can investigate more than four segments.) Give each segment an evocative nickname that captures, in your mind, its key characteristics. What patterns can you see?

If you're a job seeker and will be targeting organizations of various sizes, attempt to describe your potential target segments in terms of location, size, company structure, organizational culture, decision styles, and the benefits sought by decision makers.

	Segment 1	Segment 2	Segment 3	Segment 4
Nickname				
Geo-demographics				
Psychographics				
Media preferences				
Purchase behaviour				
Benefits sought				
Decision process: Where is the customer in the decision process? What is motivating the customer?				

Step 2: Selecting Market Segments to Serve

Now, evaluate each segment. After evaluating how meaningful, measurable, and marketable each segment might be, attempt to evaluate its overall desirability and from that identify which one(s) appear the most desirable for you to target. Here, you need to be opportunistic and objective. Leave feelings aside and try to focus on the opportunity that each segment offers you to achieve your career goals.

	Segment 1	Segment 2	Segment 3	Segment 4
Nickname				
Meaningful: Can the segment generate interesting sales?	Short term? Long term?	Short term? Long term?	Short term? Long term?	Short term? Long term?
Measurable: Can you readily obtain more data on this segment if needed?	❏ Yes ❏ No	❏ Yes ❏ No	❏ Yes ❏ No	❏ Yes ❏ No
Marketable: Can you reach this segment? Give some thought as to how.	❏ Yes ❏ No	❏ Yes ❏ No	❏ Yes ❏ No	❏ Yes ❏ No
How desirable: Will this segment allow me to reach my goals?	0 = not at all 10 = extremely good opportunity for me	0 = not at all 10 = extremely good opportunity for me	0 = not at all 10 = extremely good opportunity for me	0 = not at all 10 = extremely good opportunity for me

Based on your analysis so far, identify the segments that provide you with the best opportunity to reach your marketing objectives (if you believe it to be relevant, you can rank order more than two segments):

- Primary or best segment: _____

- Secondary or second-best segment: _____

You should now be able to "think and feel" like your target customers; otherwise, seek out additional information to complete the picture of your prime prospects.

Step 3: Targeting Strategy

Which approach will you use to reach the segments you've identified as more desirable? Consider the pros and cons of each one.

- Undifferentiated marketing   ❑ Yes   ❑ No
- Differentiated marketing   ❑ Yes   ❑ No
- Concentrated marketing   ❑ Yes   ❑ No
- Individualized marketing   ❑ Yes   ❑ No

Step 4: Positioning Strategy

Here, you need to draw upon your situation analysis (namely, your competitive analysis), the results of your self-assessment tests, and your understanding of the segment(s) you have identified as more desirable. How do you want each segment to think about your product? What key bases will you use to position yourself? Consider the appropriateness of the following bases to position yourself.

	Primary Segment	Secondary Segment
Nickname		
Attributes	Appropriate for this segment? ❑ Yes ❑ No Which attribute(s):	Appropriate for this segment? ❑ Yes ❑ No Which attribute(s):
Benefits	Appropriate for this segment? ❑ Yes ❑ No Which benefit(s):	Appropriate for this segment? ❑ Yes ❑ No Which benefit(s):
Price	Appropriate for this segment? ❑ Yes ❑ No	Appropriate for this segment? ❑ Yes ❑ No
Quality	Appropriate for this segment? ❑ Yes ❑ No	Appropriate for this segment? ❑ Yes ❑ No
User	Appropriate for this segment? ❑ Yes ❑ No	Appropriate for this segment? ❑ Yes ❑ No
Usage or application	Appropriate for this segment? ❑ Yes ❑ No What usage specifically?	Appropriate for this segment? ❑ Yes ❑ No What usage specifically?
Competition	Appropriate for this segment? ❑ Yes ❑ No	Appropriate for this segment? ❑ Yes ❑ No
Product class	Appropriate for this segment? ❑ Yes ❑ No	Appropriate for this segment? ❑ Yes ❑ No

EXHIBIT 5.4   The Strategic Marketing Process Applied to Your Career

SITUATION ANALYSIS

- Market and industry analysis
- Environmental analysis
- Competitive analysis
- Customer analysis
- SWOT analysis

CAREER GOALS

- Your needs and your values
- Are your goals Actionable, Bounded, Compelling?

MARKETING OBJECTIVES

Entrepreneur	Professional	Artist	Job Seeker
❑ Sales	❑ Sales	❑ Sales	❑ Job/position
❑ Customer acquisition/ relationship	❑ Customer acquisition/ relationship	❑ Customer acquisition/ relationship	❑ Income and benefits
❑ Market share/position	❑ Product development/ introduction	❑ Product development/ introduction	
❑ Growth/expansion			

MARKETING STRATEGY

- Market segmentation
- Choose segments to target
  - Undifferentiated or mass marketing
  - Differentiated marketing
  - Concentrated marketing
  - Micro or individual marketing
- Positioning: How will you teach your customer(s) to think about your product as a solution superior to that of your competitors?

You are here ⟶

MARKETING MIX DECISIONS

- Objectives, strategies, and tactics
  - Product (Chapter 6)   – Place (Chapter 8)
  - Price (Chapter 7)   – Promotion (Chapter 9)

IMPLEMENTATION AND CONTROL (CHAPTER 10)

- How will you carry out your plan?
- How will you know you have been successful?
- How will you approach benchmarking and self-feedback?

KEY TERMS

benefits — the positive consequences of using a product; benefits may be functional or psycho-social

market segmentation — the process of dividing a market into distinct groups of customers (or organizations) that share certain characteristics and react in a similar way to a marketing offer

positioning — teaching your customers to think (or feel) about your product as a solution to a need (broadly defined) and in a way that is superior to the competition's offering

psychographic data — information concerned with consumers' lifestyles, usually described in terms of preferred activities, interests, and opinions

target marketing — a marketing approach designed to focus on key groups of consumers and tailor the marketing mix to their needs and wants

How Marketing-Savvy Have You Become?

1. In your own words, describe the four target marketing approaches.

2. What is positioning and why is it so important? Provide an example of a company or brand that positions itself along each of the positioning bases below.

   Price

   Competitor

   Use/application

   User

3. Why is it important to understand where and how consumers obtain information when trying to solve a problem?

4. After consumers identify a problem or a need, what steps do they typically go through to solve that problem or fulfill that need?

NOW WHAT?

Let's take a quick look at where we've been and where we're heading. We first discussed the importance and structure of the situation analysis. Hopefully this helped you to articulate your career goals based on your own personal values and needs. The next step was to set the marketing objectives that could help you achieve your career goals. Then, in this chapter, we've explored the notion of marketing strategy and the first step in creating one: selecting one or more target markets. In the next chapters, we'll concentrate on the second step in creating a marketing strategy: developing a marketing mix—namely, the unique blend of product, place, price, and promotion tools that will be employed to satisfy your target markets—and to do so better than the competition does.

Notes

1. Welch, J. (2005). *Winning*. New York: Harper Business, p. 166.
2. www.sric-bi.com/VALS/presurvey.shtml
3. Moses, E. (2000). *The $100 Billion Allowance: How to Get Your Share of the Global Teen Market*. New York: Wiley & Sons.

Finding happiness through a career realignment

Meet Marc-Olivier Bossé. At 23, Marc-Olivier already has an impressive list of career achievements. He is one of the top-ranked figure skaters in Canada. Having won medals and championships since the age of 12, Marc-Olivier has travelled all over the world representing Canada and honing his skills. He's competed in Japan, Croatia, France, and the U.S. But at the 2006 Canadian Championships, when a bad cold and a number of unexpected circumstances led to a disappointing finish, Marc-Olivier decided that it was time to take a cold, hard look at his situation.

Despite his passion for his sport, he concluded that his chances at a medal-winning performance were slim. A new, highly controversial judging system had just been introduced, and figure skating was now going through a major transition. In addition, the demands of Marc-Olivier's training regimen, his full-time schooling, and a part-time job were starting to take their toll. He was no longer having fun and the pleasure from skating had been replaced by the stress of pleasing everyone else, from the judges to the fans to his coaches. Marc-Olivier decided it was time to look elsewhere for fulfillment. Unlike other skaters at his level, he always choreographed his own routines and this had won him praise and attention from international-level coaches. In spring 2006, Marc-Olivier decided to withdraw from the competitive arena and become a figure skating coach and choreographer.

On April 8, 2006, in front of a packed house, Marc-Olivier bid farewell to thousands of fans with a groundbreaking performance. It featured moves not permitted in competition, including a back-flip and never seen before moves such as his unique "hydroglide."

After this memorable performance, he decided to pursue his coaching certification and obtain a bachelor's degree in sports psychology, so that he could help his students face the fears, challenges, and disappointments that are everyday fare in his sport. The results so far? Judges, coaches, and skaters are now well aware of his unique style of choreography and offers are coming in to work on special events.

We asked Marc-Olivier what three tips he would like to share with readers of *Marketing Yourself*. Here are his thoughts

1. *Always innovate.* Whatever form innovation may take in your career, moving forward is what it's all about. Do things better, more elegantly, more efficiently. Don't stop because of what others may say or think. Most of all, don't cling to praise. Seek criticism and look for ways to improve yourself.

2. *Learn to negotiate.* It can feel awkward at first, but setting and negotiating the right price for yourself will make you happier and will establish your worth in the marketplace.

3. *Identify what makes you happy.* Persistence is one thing; hanging on when you've outgrown a challenge or a situation eventually eats away at your motivation (and sanity!).

When the word "product" comes up, physical goods such as canned soup, cameras, shoes, clothes, cars, and gasoline typically spring to mind. But consider the case of coffee, one of the world's most widely used and enjoyed products.

Until the late 1800s, coffee was essentially a physical good. Beans were roasted by coffee producers and shipped in bulk to stores, where they were scooped into bags according to the amounts that individual customers wanted to purchase. Just before the turn of the century, one U.S. producer realized that when it came to selling coffee, retailers had all the power. They could switch suppliers any time they wanted and their customers wouldn't know the difference. This made it easy for retailers to pit coffee suppliers against each other to extract the lowest prices. To tilt the balance of power in his favour, this producer came up with three groundbreaking ideas. The first was to give his coffee a name—Maxwell House—and by doing so he effectively "branded" his product. The second was to advertise the brand to consumers. The third was to pre-package his coffee in conveniently sized bags, with the Maxwell House name prominently featured on each bag, of course. This made things easier for retailers because now coffee was a self-serve product. No more scooping, weighing, and bagging. Most importantly, though, if a retailer decided to stop buying his coffee, he had a strong argument for the retailer to reconsider. Because it was being advertised, consumers were insisting on the Maxwell House brand—and if a particular retailer didn't carry it, consumers would switch stores in order to buy it. So now coffee was more than just a physical good: as a product, it was also a brand and a recognizable package that instilled desire and a willingness to purchase.

A major breakthrough in the coffee market came in the mid-1900s with the introduction of instant coffee. As a result of this new product development, coffee was now easier and quicker to make. After decades of slow or no growth, industry sales soared.

Throughout the second half of the twentieth century, continuous product improvement was the name of the game as producers introduced better tasting instant coffee and more varieties of coffee. Then came Starbucks. This Seattle-based company took coffee to new heights (and not just in its astronomical pricing!) by turning its consumption into an experience. By creating comfortable environments, adding new

BY THE END OF THIS CHAPTER...

YOU WILL:

- know what products are made up of and some key similarities and differences between goods and services

- have a clear sense of the notion of product lifecycle and the consumer adoption process

- understand branding, including brand loyalty and its role in product strategy

- understand the importance of continuous product improvement

- know the basic idea and importance of customer relationship management

- have a clear sense of the role of packaging in product strategy

coffee choices, and providing the services of its baristas, Starbucks and its competitors have taken the basic product—coffee—light years beyond being just a physical good. They've added a service component and an experience to the basic core product thereby augmenting it, and, in the process, have gotten more people drinking more coffee and paying more money for it. So what was once a simple commodity has evolved into a dynamic, multi-faceted, and increasingly popular and profitable product.

We'll be covering plenty of ground in this chapter, including concepts that can help you make your product (including yourself, of course) more attractive to your target market and to make it more competitive. Ultimately, you want your product to stand out and to be highly regarded by members of your target market. The goal of this chapter is to help you create a product strategy that turns your product into a strong brand, one that will be sought after by your potential customers, clients, or employers. ⓜ

WHAT ARE PRODUCTS?

First, let's remind ourselves what products are. In marketing language, *product*, one of the four Ps, refers to any offering that is the object of a transaction. More precisely, according to Philip Kotler, one of the world's foremost marketing academics, a product is anything that can be offered to a market for attention, acquisition, use, or consumption that might satisfy a need or a want. A product can take on many forms, including one or more of the following:

- A physical good—for example, a refrigerator, soft drink, or pair of jeans
- A service—a travel agency, bank, or lawyer
- A retail store—a supermarket, automobile dealership, or online bookseller
- An organization—a not-for-profit organization, trade association, or union
- A place—a country, region, or city
- An idea—a political, social, or charitable cause
- A person—an entertainer, professional athlete, job seeker, or you!
- An experience—a stay at Universal Studios, a safari in Kenya, a spa vacation, or an event such as the Just for Laughs comedy festival held in Montreal every summer

CORE AND AUGMENTED PRODUCTS

An organization's or person's core product is the basic benefit or key feature at the heart of what it offers to its customers. The core product usually flows from an organization's or individual's core competency—that is, the one thing it is exceptionally good at doing and that competitors can't easily duplicate or imitate. For example, Porsche makes some of the most sought-after and best-performing sports cars in the world. Oprah Winfrey is one of North America's most popular and respected talk show hosts. Core products focus on the problem or feeling that is at the heart of the customer's purchase decision. With Porsche, it could be the need for a sense of excitement, accomplishment, and status. Oprah provides engaging entertainment that makes weekday afternoons enjoyable and inspiring. Try to replicate Porsche's core product: It would take enormous financial resources to gather the necessary knowledge and competencies. Try to imitate Oprah's caring and connection with her audience. The magic touch that is uniquely hers would probably elude most of us.

However, customers often don't buy just the core product; they buy an entire bundle of benefits or features that constitute the augmented product. Organizations and individuals can add features and benefits to their core products to make them more competitive and desirable. Porsche offers special wheels and aerodynamic body add-ons to make their cars faster and even more exclusive. Oprah broadens and deepens her connection with her target market through her magazine and book club. The challenge, of course, is to pinpoint what benefits or features should be added to your core product. Here, our discussion of positioning in Chapter 5 comes in handy. Augmenting your core product should be done with a thorough knowledge of the competitive landscape and the strengths and weaknesses of your major competitors as well as a clear understanding of your customers' needs and wants. What feature or benefits would enhance your customers' satisfaction and trump competitors' efforts? Table 6.1 provides you with some examples of core and augmented aspects of everyday products to energize your own thoughts on this matter.

> **core product** — the basic benefit or key feature at the heart of what an organization offers to its customers

> **augmented product** — the entire bundle of benefits or features in the core product

FAVOURITES *artist*

CANEHDIAN
http://www.canehdian.com

For musicians, this site offers links to relevant industry resources.

STYLE CAREER.COM
http://www.stylecareer.com

This site offers tips and advice on how to promote yourself in the fashion and image industry.

? Self Check

What is your core product? What is your core competence? (The results of your self-assessment tests should be useful here.)

How can you augment your core product so that you stand out from competition in the marketplace?

TABLE 6.1   Sample Core and Augmented Products

PRODUCT/BRAND	CORE	AUGMENTED
Kleenex	Paper tissue	Tissue with a medicated layer that kills cold and flu viruses.
Hair salon	Haircuts	A scalp massage to make worries float away; extensive art collection for purchase (on loan from local artist).
Briggs & Riley	Luggage	Lifetime warranty: replaced or repaired at no cost if it ever gets damaged. Unique design solution to fit the lifestyle and travel needs of today's busy businessperson.
Dentist	Fillings, cleanings, dental surgery	Door-to-door limo service; foot massage while you wait.

THE GOODS–SERVICES CONTINUUM

Goods are tangible products that customers can touch, see, hear, smell, and taste. Your computer is a good. Goods can be stockpiled and inventoried for later use or sale. The production of goods can be controlled and necessary checks can be implemented to ensure their quality. On the other hand, services are intangible. One way to distinguish goods from services is to think of them as being on a continuum, as shown in Exhibit 6.1, with pure goods being on one extreme and pure services at the other. A box of cookies is an example of a pure product. So is a motorcycle. However, motorcycle dealers offer repair and maintenance services, and these would fall into the pure service category. A dinner at your favourite restaurant is a combination of pure goods and services. The food and drinks are goods, while the waiters and chefs deliver pure services. The food and drinks are tangible features, but the chef's and waitstaff's efforts and how they make you feel are more intangible aspects of service. Most hairstyling salons offer pure services. Many of them also sell grooming products, which are pure goods. Consultants are at the pure service extreme. They strictly provide advice, and although they might write and deliver a report (tangible) the core of their offering is an intangible service. All of this is to say that most products and services are a blend of the tangible and intangible elements.

Services are different from goods in a number of significant ways. Here are some of the major characteristics that distinguish them.

- **Services are intangible:** Services do not have physical features per se that customers can see, hear, smell, taste, or touch prior to purchase. Service providers, whether they be

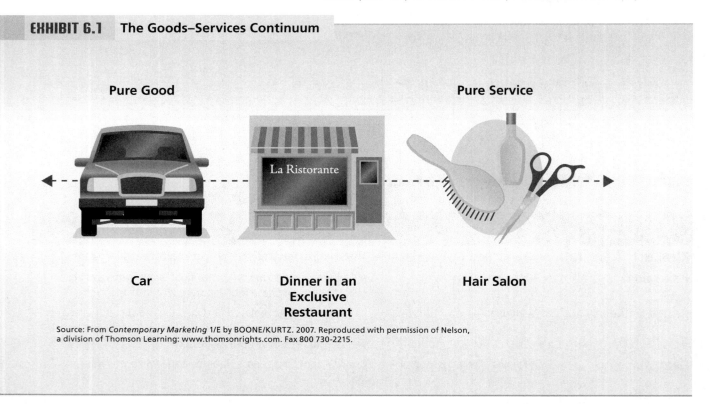

EXHIBIT 6.1 **The Goods–Services Continuum**

Pure Good

Pure Service

La Ristorante

Car

Dinner in an Exclusive Restaurant

Hair Salon

Source: From *Contemporary Marketing* 1/E by BOONE/KURTZ. 2007. Reproduced with permission of Nelson, a division of Thomson Learning: www.thomsonrights.com. Fax 800 730-2215.

dentists, advertising agencies, psychologists, interior designers, event planners, or financial advisers, ask their customers to buy on a promise of satisfaction, and such promises are certainly intangible. This is one of the reasons why reputation, often created and reinforced by positive word of mouth, is a key element of the marketing mix for service providers.

- **In the delivery of services, production and consumption are inseparable:** In order to deliver the service, the service provider needs the customer to be present and to participate in the delivery of the service. Consider something as simple as a haircut. The barber or stylist cannot get to work until the customer is actually present or seated in the chair. Further, the stylist typically solicits and relies on input from clients before beginning to cut their hair. Now imagine something more complex, such as a kitchen renovation. Designers and contractors will typically rely on customers' input at all stages of the project. Advertising campaigns are almost always the result of close collaboration between advertisers and advertising agencies. Clear communication is key, and it's in the service provider's best interests to make sure this occurs.

- **Variability comes with the delivery of services:** The fact that a service is produced as it is being consumed implies a certain amount of variability from one service occasion to the next. While checks can be implemented in a factory to ensure that every pen, alarm clock, or computer functions as it should when it gets to customers, the same can't be done every time with services. With a service, one customer can have an excellent experience and another customer may have a very negative one. Or, as a customer, you may receive outstanding service one day, but poor service the next. Why? Because both providers and customers are humans, and their feelings and behaviours are not identical day in, day out. If you've ever worked in a service setting—as a waiter, for example—you know how difficult it can be to "put on a happy face" and provide good service when you're having an off day or are not feeling well. Because the quality of services largely depends on the individual people providing and receiving them, service encounters (i.e., the moment when provider and customer come together) are difficult to standardize. However, many organizations are making progress in changing this. For example, Disney carefully screens and recruits its theme park employees. They are then trained as "cast members" to put on a show and treat park visitors as guests. While a portion of the service encounter is scripted and employees or "cast members" are highly trained on how to deal with customers, there always remains a portion of variability in any service.

- **Services are perishable:** Services cannot be stored or stockpiled. This presents a number of unique challenges to service providers. In seasonal businesses such as income tax return preparation and outdoor construction, companies need the flexibility to have adequate staffing levels during times of peak demand and to reduce them when demand falls. In non-seasonal businesses such as consulting, public relations, and architecture, companies need a steady stream of work from their clients in order to cover their major cost—staffing. If orders decline, their basic choice is to keep the same staffing level, even though employees' time may not be fully utilized, or to cut staff. Perishability also places the burden on service managers to carefully manage their capacity. For example, on a plane or in a movie theatre, the lost revenue from an unsold and unoccupied seat is lost forever.

WHERE ARE YOU ON THE GOODS—SERVICES CONTINUUM?

Where do you fit on the goods–services continuum? The answer depends in large part on the basic career path you're currently on or considering. Let's examine a few options.

ARTISTS

If you'll be creating visual and performance art, your creations should be considered pure goods. If in addition to creating art you advise your clients on the amount and type of art they should purchase, how to get the most out of it (installation), and how to care for the art they've purchased (Note: this may be a way to augment your core product), then you'll be combining pure goods with a pure service. If you focus exclusively on counselling clients, you'll be providing a pure service.

PROFESSIONALS

For the most part, professionals provide pure services. However, if along with your service you'll be selling goods, then you'll be a goods provider as well. Examples would include being a personal trainer selling nutritional supplements, a country club golf professional selling clubs and clothing, and a technology consultant selling computer hardware or software.

ENTREPRENEURS

Entrepreneurs can fit anywhere on the spectrum depending on which goods and services they offer and the extent to which they offer each.

EMPLOYEES

If you're an employee in the corporate, government, or not-for-profit sectors, or are planning to be one, you should look at yourself as a service and your current or potential employers as customers or clients. The work you will be doing for them is intangible, inseparable, perishable, and not easily standardized. Your employer (i.e., customer) has or will play an important role in the nature, quantity, and quality of work that you do. Consequently, you are or will be providing a pure service, and the principles of service marketing will be the most applicable to you.

CLASSIFYING PRODUCTS FOR CONSUMER AND BUSINESS MARKETS

Products are typically classified as either consumer products (also called B2C products, for business-to-consumer) and business or

B2B (business-to-business) products. B2C products are destined for use by ultimate consumers—for example, frozen pizza. B2B products contribute directly or indirectly to the production of other products for sale—for example, the packaging material (cardboard, plastic film) needed by the producer of your frozen pizza. Many products are offered to both the consumer and business markets. Examples include the cheese, pepperoni, tomato sauce, and mushrooms that consumers can purchase to make their own pizza or that manufacturers of frozen pizza buy as ingredients for their finished products.

Artists primarily produce B2C products, although their products can be sold to businesses for inclusion in their clients' products. For example, an artist could be commissioned to paint the exterior of an office building or theatre. Entrepreneurs' products could be classified as B2B, B2C, or both, depending on the goods and services that they choose to offer. Professionals can serve either consumer or business markets or both. For example, a psychologist could relegate his or her practice to individuals (B2C). He or she could focus on helping companies pre-screen potential employees (B2B). Or do both. So, if your goal is to be an employee, which will you most likely be: a B2C or B2B product? The answer is a B2B product, since you will be offering yourself or your service to a company or other organization that will incorporate your work into its output.

These two broad categories of products can be subdivided into more specific categories. As you'll see, knowing which category your product is in can be an important first step in creating your product strategy.

THE THREE TYPES OF BUSINESS-TO-CONSUMER PRODUCTS

One of the most widely used consumer product classification systems focuses on the buyer's perception of a need for the product and the ease with which products can be procured to fulfill that need. For instance, unsought products are marketed to consumers who may not yet realize any need for them. Examples of these are the services provided by plumbers and criminal defence lawyers. Customers for their services usually don't think about buying them before there's a clogged drain or an arrest. That's why plumbers and criminal defence lawyers have some of the biggest and most prominent advertisements in the Yellow Pages. They want their messages to stand out in the medium that many people refer to immediately when their unsought products turn into sought-after products!

Consumer products typically fit into one or more of the following categories: convenience products, shopping products, and specialty products.

Convenience products are goods and services that consumers purchase frequently, immediately, and with little effort. Convenience goods include canned soup, laundry detergent, and candy bars. Examples of convenience services are, as the name so aptly implies, convenience stores, quick oil change facilities, and dry cleaning. Marketers subdivide convenience products into impulse items,

unsought products — products marketed to consumers who may not yet realize any need for them

convenience products — goods and services that consumers purchase frequently, immediately, and with little effort

impulse products — products that are purchased on the spur of the moment

staples — convenience products that consumers constantly replenish so they'll always have them on hand

emergency products — products purchased in response to unexpected and urgent needs

shopping products — products that consumers buy only after comparing competing offerings on such criteria as price, quality, style, colour, and fit

specialty products — products that offer unique features and benefits that result in consumers placing high value on them and their brands

staples, or emergency items. Impulse products are purchased on the spur of the moment, such as potato chips and beer at a sporting event. Staples are convenience products that consumers constantly replenish so that they'll always have them on hand. Examples include facial tissues, deodorant, and gasoline. Emergency products are bought in response to unexpected and urgent needs. Towing services, roofing services, cough medicine, and upset stomach remedies are examples. Since consumers expend little effort in their decisions to purchase convenience products, marketers need to make exchanges as simple as possible (for example, by selling their products in vending machines) and ensure that their products are highly visible and widely available.

Shopping products differ from convenience products in that consumers buy them only after comparing competing offerings on such criteria as price, quality, style, colour, and fit. They usually cost more than their convenience counterparts and include goods and services such as clothing, home furnishings, major appliances, insurance, auto repairs, and landscaping. Shopping products are differentiated on a number of features including physical attributes, pricing, places of purchase, styling, warranties, and after-sales service. A brand's or a store's reputation can have a strong influence on the consumer's decision to buy a particular shopping product, as can the performance of the outlet's salespeople.

Specialty products offer unique features and benefits that result in consumers placing high value on them and their brands. Examples of specialty goods are Dom Perignon champagne, Rolex watches, Bentley automobiles, Godiva chocolates, and Hugo Boss clothing. Examples of specialty services include high-end cosmetic surgery, personal executive coaching, and estate planning. Purchasers of specialty products know what they want and are willing to pay whatever is required to get it. They begin shopping with complete information and refuse to accept substitutes. Customers are often willing to go out of their way to buy specialty products and, as a result, they can often be sold by just a few retail outlets. Highly personalized service and image-enhancing advertising and promotion are employed extensively with this category of products.

APPLYING THE CONSUMER PRODUCTS CLASSIFICATION SYSTEM TO MARKETING STRATEGY

You've probably already noticed that many products do not neatly fit into one single category. Clothing provides a perfect illustration. For example, a new coat could be a shopping product for one person and a specialty product for someone else. Or an everyday outfit for school could be a shopping product, but a prom dress or suit becomes a specialty product. These subtleties underscore the importance of considering the purchase from the customer's perspective. What need is being fulfilled? How is it being fulfilled? Asking yourself these questions can lead to useful insights about branding, promotion, pricing, and distribution decisions. Table 6.2 lists some of the marketing mix decisions typically associated with each type of B2C products.

TABLE 6.2   Consumer Products and Typical Marketing Mix Decisions

	Convenience Products	Shopping Products	Specialty Products
CONSUMER FACTORS			
Planning time involved in purchase	Very little	Considerable	Extensive
Purchase frequency	Frequent	Less frequent	Infrequent
Importance of convenient location	Critical	Important	Unimportant
Comparison of price and quality	Very little	Considerable	Very little
MARKETING MIX FACTORS			
Price	Low	Relatively high	High
Importance of seller's image	Unimportant	Very important	Important
Distribution channel length	Long	Relatively short	Very short
Number of sales outlets	Many	Few	Very few; often one per market area
Promotion	Advertising and promotion by producer	Personal selling and advertising by both producer and retailer	Personal selling and advertising by both producer and retailer

Source: From *Contemporary Marketing* 1/E by BOONE/KURTZ. 2007. Reproduced with permission of Nelson, a division of Thomson Learning: www.thomsonrights.com. Fax 800 730-2215.

THE SIX TYPES OF BUSINESS-TO-BUSINESS PRODUCTS

The classification of business-to-business products is based on product uses rather than the buyer's personal needs or purchase behaviour. B2B products typically fall into one of the following six categories:

- **Installations:** These are specialty products and include major capital investments for new plants, heavy machinery, and telecommunications systems.

- **Accessory equipment:** Products in this category cost less and last for shorter periods of time than do installations. They are considered to be capital investments, so their costs are depreciated over several years. Examples include power tools, computers, printers, and office furniture.

- **Component parts and materials:** These are finished business products of one producer that become part of the final products of another producer. For example, GE makes jet engines that are purchased by aircraft manufacturers for inclusion in their airplanes. Intel makes micro-processors that are bought by computer makers for inclusion in their final products.

- **Raw materials:** Raw materials also become part of the buyers' final products, but unlike component parts and materials, they are not finished products. Typically, they are natural resources and farm products and include copper, steel, lumber, beef, butter, soybeans, and flour.

Chapter 6 — Creating Your Product Strategy

- **Supplies:** Supplies constitute the regular expense items that an organization uses in its daily operations and which do not become part of its final products. Supplies fall into three subcategories:

  – Maintenance items—for example, abrasives, light bulbs, lubricating oils, and cleansers

  – Repair items—such as screws, clamps, solder, and roofing tiles

  – Operating supplies—including ink cartridges, photocopy paper, electrical power, and shipping cartons

- **Business services:** Accounting, legal, advertising, office cleaning, consulting, and marketing research.

If you already are or are considering becoming an employee, you are or will be in effect providing a business service. You'll also be providing a business service if you work as an independent accountant, consultant, or sales trainer. Business services include the intangible products that organizations buy to facilitate their production and operating processes. Insurance, advertising, telemarketing, office cleaning, Internet service providers, and legal advice fall into this category.

When it comes to hiring employees, the organization's purchase decision process is usually complex and typically involves thorough analyses of the applicants as well as lengthy negotiations on price (i.e., salary), benefits, and other terms of engagement. The more prospective employees know about how they can save money or make money for their potential employers, the stronger their bargaining position will be.

Table 6.3 summarizes the impact on marketing strategy of the business classification system.

 Myth

Good grades and a degree guarantee that I will get a good job.

 Reality Check

You'll need much more than these to get the job you want. While employers do look for academic success, they would rather see a B average plus a combination of leadership activities, community service, technical skills, and relevant internships or part-time jobs than an A average with very few or none of these.

QUALITY AND CUSTOMER SATISFACTION

Regardless of how a product is classified, nothing turns off customers and employers more than products that do not deliver what they promise or that break down or wear out prematurely. On the

TABLE 6.3   Business Products and Typical Marketing Mix Decisions

FACTOR	Installations	Accessory Equipment	Component Parts and Materials	Raw Equipment	Supplies	Business Services
ORGANIZATIONAL FACTORS						
Planning time	Extensive	Less extensive	Less extensive	Varies	Very little	Varies
Purchase frequency	Infrequent	More frequent	Frequent	Infrequent	Frequent	Varies
Comparison of price and quality	Quality very important	Quality and price important	Quality important	Quality important	Price important	Varies
MARKETING MIX FACTORS						
Price	High	Relatively high	Low to high	Low to high	Low	Varies
Distribution channel length	Very short	Relatively short	Short	Short	Long	Varies
Promotion method	Personal selling by producer	Advertising	Personal selling	Personal selling	Advertising by producer	Varies

Source: From *Contemporary Marketing* 1/E by BOONE/KURTZ. 2007. Reproduced with permission of Nelson, a division of Thomson Learning: www.thomsonrights.com. Fax 800 730-2215.

other hand, nothing engenders customer loyalty more than products that consistently deliver more than they promise. For manufacturers of goods, service providers, not-for-profit organizations, even individuals, product errors, defects, and mistakes all have costly consequences. Since the 1950s, thanks to the pioneering efforts of scholars and management specialists like W. Edwards Deming, Philip Crosby, and Joseph Juran, programs have been developed to ensure that products perform as they should. In the first wave of such quality initiatives, the focus was on quality control—implementing the necessary inspection checks to make sure that no defective product ever left the factory. Then came quality assurance, where the basic idea was to identify and solve, even before they occur, potential problems or breakdowns that could jeopardize quality. Finally, total quality management or TQM focuses on continually improving products and processes with the goal of achieving ever-increasing levels of customer satisfaction. ISO, the International Organization for Standardization (http://www.iso.org), defines TQM as "a management approach of an organization, centred on quality, based on the participation of all its members and aiming at long-term success through customer satisfaction, and benefits to all members of the organization and to society."[1] The basic premise of TQM is that a product designed, manufacturered, and delivered under this approach is cheaper to produce because costly errors and mistakes have been designed out of the system.

Central to the TQM approach is the importance of defining quality as the customer perceives it and then aligning the efforts of marketers, engineers, front-line staff— virtually every employee—to achieve the targeted level of quality. Many of the tools and techniques at the heart of TQM were first developed and applied in engineering and manufacturing contexts. In a manufacturing context, the goal is to build a production system that results in zero defects. Statistical methods are used to monitor the occurrence of problems

quality control — implementing the necessary inspection checks to make sure that no defective product ever leaves the factory

quality assurance — intended to identify and solve, even before they occur, potential problems or breakdowns that could jeopardize quality

total quality management (TQM) — continually improving products and processes with the goal of achieving ever-increasing levels of customer satisfaction

Chapter 6 — Creating Your Product Strategy

so management can take action when appropriate. The same ideas and concepts can also be applied to the domain of services. In a service context, TQM specialists speak of zero defection,[2] the idea being to satisfy existing customers and discouraging them from defecting to a competitor. Exhibit 6.2 shows the defection rates for various service industries. High defection rates can have a disastrous impact on a firm's profits as it must expend considerable marketing dollars to acquire new customers to replace the ones that defect.

To achieve zero defects or zero defections, firms must focus on achieving high levels of *customer satisfaction*. In fact, by now you'll have picked up on the fact that customer satisfaction is central to the marketing concept. As Exhibit 6.3 illustrates, in its most basic form customer satisfaction can be defined as a confirmation or disconfirmation of expectations. Customers purchase goods and services with certain expectations in mind, and as they consume those products or services, their expectations are either confirmed or disconfirmed by their perception of the product or service's performance. When perceptions of quality exceed their expectations, satisfaction results. When perceptions of quality fall below expectations, dissatisfaction follows. Satisfied customers are likely to return and repurchase and to spread positive word-of-mouth. Dissatisfied customers, not surprisingly, tend to spread negative word-of-mouth and in some cases to seek redress from the manufacturer or service provider.

As you can see in Exhibit 6.3, expectations and perceived quality are two central concepts in the definition of customer satisfaction. Expectations are set in part by marketers by advertising, promotions, brand names, distribution, and product packaging. In fact, all elements of the marketing mix directly or indirectly influence customers' expectations. Expectations may also be created by word-of-mouth and by opinion leaders (i.e., individuals who influence the

customer satisfaction — a confirmation or disconfirmation of expectations

expectations — set in part by marketers by advertising, promotions, brand names, distribution, and product packaging

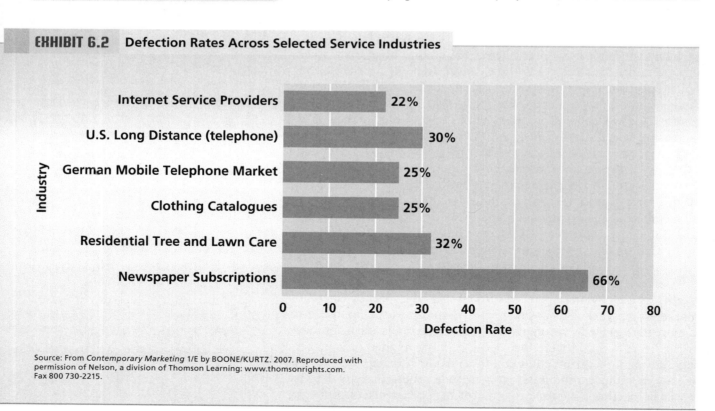

EXHIBIT 6.2 Defection Rates Across Selected Service Industries

Industry / Defection Rate

- Internet Service Providers — 22%
- U.S. Long Distance (telephone) — 30%
- German Mobile Telephone Market — 25%
- Clothing Catalogues — 25%
- Residential Tree and Lawn Care — 32%
- Newspaper Subscriptions — 66%

Source: From *Contemporary Marketing* 1/E by BOONE/KURTZ. 2007. Reproduced with permission of Nelson, a division of Thomson Learning: www.thomsonrights.com. Fax 800 730-2215.

EXHIBIT 6.3 **The Dis/Confirmation Model of Customer Satisfaction**

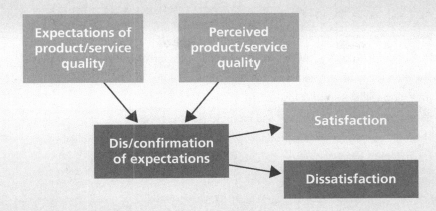

purchases of other people by virtue of their recognized expertise in a specific field). Customers may not always know or even be clear on what exactly they expect, hence the need to maintain open and clear communication with them. Sometimes, just asking simple questions such as, "How did you hear about us?" or "What made you buy this model?" can produce surprisingly useful insights into the expectations that customers have of your product or service.

Perceived quality must be defined from the customer's perspective and then translated into operational specifications. For example, a customer might expect a "powerful car that handles well at an affordable price" or "good fun food in a friendly atmosphere." Then the manufacturer or service provider must translate those expectations into product or service specifications that engineers and restaurant staff can understand and implement.

Consumer research has unveiled some of the key dimensions that consumers use to evaluate product and service quality. Table 6.4 lists some of these. Understanding the key dimensions upon which consumers base their evaluations of product and service quality is crucial as it helps organizations and individuals to prioritize their actions and to decide where to allocate resources.

Despite all the dimensions and research contained in Table 6.4, the perception of quality can frequently rest on a seemingly minor detail such as the colour of an employee's attire, the layout of the aisles in a supermarket, or the ease of opening the package (ever struggled with a video game wrapper?). By learning to think and feel like their prime prospects, marketers can view the experience their product provides from their customer's perspective and then take steps to address those elements that can enhance or jeopardize satisfaction. Think, for instance, of how UPS turned the apparently boring colour of its employees' uniforms (brown) into the tongue-in-cheek humorous slogan "What can brown do for you?" Or of how grocery stores can help their customers find what they are looking for and navigate their way through the store through helpful signage.

TABLE 6.4   Dimensions of Quality

DIMENSIONS OF PRODUCT QUALITY

1.	**Performance:**	Performance on the core characteristics of the product
2.	**Features:**	Number of features that supplement the core characteristics
3.	**Reliability:**	The probability of malfunctioning or breaking down
4.	**Durability:**	How long will the product last?
5.	**Serviceability:**	Ease of repair, speed, courtesy and promptness of personnel
6.	**Aesthetics:**	The look, sound, feel of the product
7.	**Conformance to specifications:**	The extent to which the product meets production benchmarks

Source: Garvin, D. A. (1988). *Managing Quality: The Strategic and Competitive Edge.* New York: The Free Press.

DIMENSIONS OF SERVICE QUALITY

1.	**Tangibles:**	Includes the physical facilities, equipment, furniture, fixtures, the appearance of employees, communication material
2.	**Reliability:**	The ability of the service provider to perform dependably and give consistent service from one occasion to the next
3.	**Responsiveness:**	The probability of malfunctioning or breaking down
4.	**Assurance:**	Employees' knowledge, courtesy, ability to inspire trust.
5.	**Empathy:**	The service provider's ability to care and provide individualized attention

Source: Parasuraman, A., V. A. Zeithaml, and L. L. Berry. (1988). "SERVQUAL: A Multiple-Item Scale for Measuring Consumer Perceptions of Service Quality." *Journal of Retailing,* vol. 64, 12–36.

Have you noticed a conspicuously absent component in the model of customer satisfaction in Exhibit 6.3? Recently, consumer researchers have been investigating the role of customers' moods and emotions. Their emotional frames of mind as they approach the purchase and consumption of goods and services can greatly influence their perceptions of quality and their ultimate satisfaction. Additionally, customers' emotional responses during the actual consumption experience or usage of the product can also affect their evaluations. The influence of emotions can be positive or negative. For example, as you go out to celebrate after you receive an A grade on an exam or a job promotion, you might be more forgiving of a service provider's small mistakes. On the other hand, think how the frustration of opening your video game wrapper can put you in a bad mood which, in turn, could predispose you to negatively evaluating it.

As an artist, entrepreneur, or professional, you should try to identify those aspects of quality that influence your clients' satisfaction. What aspects can be irritants and decrease their satisfaction? What aspects can enhance their satisfaction? The dimensions listed in Table 6.4 can help you to answer these questions. If you are an employee, the concept of product quality is equally important. Many employers have clear job descriptions that make quality evaluation clear-cut. Make sure you understand all the components of a job description and ask for clarifications if needed. And, just as in any other business context, learn to identify the irritants that can decrease your current or potential employers' satisfaction with your services and those which can improve it.

THE PRODUCT LIFECYCLE AND ITS RELATIONSHIP TO MARKETING STRATEGY PLANNING

Products, like people, pass through stages as they age. Products pass through four such stages: introduction, growth, maturity, and decline. This progression is referred to as the product lifecycle and is shown in Exhibit 6.4.

The product lifecycle concept applies to products or product categories and not to individual brands. For example, digital video recorders are currently in the introductory stage but are quickly moving into the growth stage. MP3 players are in the growth stage, while CD players are in the decline phase. Sugar, salt, and flour are in the maturity stage. Lifecycle lengths vary from product to product, and products move through the four lifecycle stages at different rates. Fads, for example, have very short lifecycles. Bio-diesel automotive fuel seems to be stuck in the introductory stage.

Entrepreneurs, professionals, and artists should have a clear idea of where their products are situated on the product lifecycle curve. This will give them a jump-start in creating their marketing strategies. Employees should know where their current and prospective employers' products are situated. This will help them assess the long-term prospects for their employers and themselves.

> **product lifecycle** — the various stages a product goes through as it ages; typically marked by different levels of sales

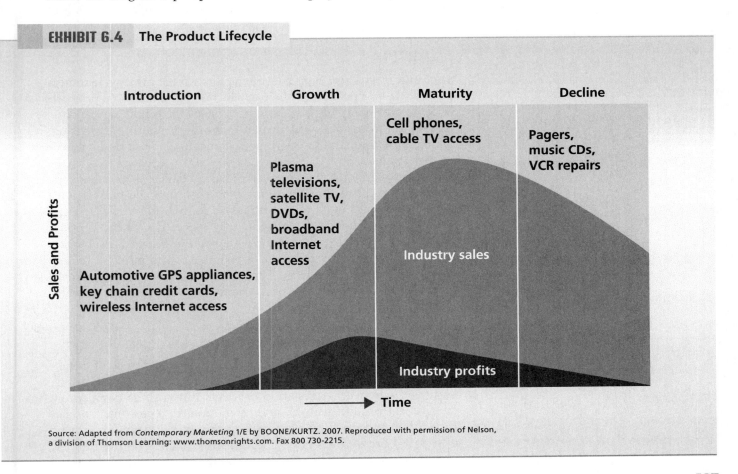

EXHIBIT 6.4 **The Product Lifecycle**

Introduction | Growth | Maturity | Decline

Cell phones, cable TV access

Pagers, music CDs, VCR repairs

Plasma televisions, satellite TV, DVDs, broadband Internet access

Sales and Profits

Automotive GPS appliances, key chain credit cards, wireless Internet access

Industry sales

Industry profits

Time

Source: Adapted from *Contemporary Marketing* 1/E by BOONE/KURTZ. 2007. Reproduced with permission of Nelson, a division of Thomson Learning: www.thomsonrights.com. Fax 800 730-2215.

Chapter 6 — Creating Your Product Strategy

Additionally, because profitability is linked to lifecycle stage, this knowledge could be valuable when it comes to salary negotiation. Another benefit of the product lifecycle concept is that it challenges individuals and organizations to ask the basic question: "What next?" That is, as a marketer, you need to anticipate the next life-cycle stage and manage your marketing mix accordingly. With that in mind, let's now take a look at each of the four product lifecycle stages and how they impact decisions regarding your marketing mix.

1. INTRODUCTION

At the introductory stage, organizations and individuals focus their marketing efforts on stimulating demand for their new product. Since the product is unknown to potential customers, promotion is used to create knowledge about its features, benefits, and availability. Promotion may also be used to persuade distribution channel members such as retailers to carry the product. The primary goal is to make potential customers aware of the product's existence and to develop acceptance and desire for the product. Prices may be set at low levels so that the market is penetrated quickly. Marketers of mass-produced food and personal care products commonly take this approach. Alternatively, if there is a customer segment that wants the latest product as soon as it's introduced and is willing to pay a premium for being among the first to own it, prices are set at high levels. This is often the case with high-tech products and luxury automobiles. The introductory stage is characterized by low sales and profits. In fact, losses are often incurred here as a result of high marketing expenses.

introductory stage — period when organizations and individuals focus their marketing efforts on stimulating demand for their new product

2. GROWTH

Sales and profits rise rapidly at the growth stage as new customers make their first purchases and early buyers repurchase the product. Prices typically fall at this phase because of the economies of scale that result from increased demand. Word-of-mouth, advertising, direct marketing, and sales promotion encourage hesitant buyers to try the product.

With the growth stage come a number of challenges for marketers. Their success attracts competitors who rush into the market with similar offerings. Toyota had the market for hybrid vehicles to itself with the Prius during the introductory stage, but as the product progressed to the growth stage, Honda and Ford entered the market and other manufacturers began developing hybrid models. To stay competitive at the growth stage, marketers may have to lower prices, increase spending on promotion, and make product improvements.

growth stage — period when new customers make their first purchases and early buyers repurchase the product

3. MATURITY STAGE

Sales and profits continue to grow during the early phase of the maturity stage, but then reach a plateau as the number of potential customers declines. Competition intensifies on many fronts. Differences between competing products diminish as competitors discover the product features and promotions that customers prefer. Production capacity and supplies begin to exceed demand, putting downward pressure on prices. Sales increases come at the expense of competition and, as a result, companies and individuals increase

maturity stage — period when sales and profits continue to grow but then reach a plateau as the number of potential customers declines

their promotional expenses with the objective of differentiating their products. Branding takes on an increasingly important role as product differences become negligible or non-existent. Products are often redesigned at this stage to extend their lifecycles and to keep customers interested in them. Think of toothpastes, mouthwashes, and chewing gum. New and improved versions of these products are introduced on a constant basis.

4. DECLINE STAGE

At the decline stage new product introductions or changes in customer preferences result in declining industry sales. The decline stage of an existing product often coincides with the growth stage for a new entry. Computer-generated presentations have replaced overhead slides and projectors, MP3 players are replacing CD players, and online travel sites are taking business away from traditional travel agencies at an ever-increasing rate.

decline stage — period when innovations or changes in customer preferences result in declining industry sales

Shifting demographics can also be a powerful factor. For example, because of the baby bust of the 1970s and 1980s, the number of first marriages in North America has been dropping. This has pushed the wedding dress and tuxedo rental markets into a state of steep decline.

While industry profits drop during the decline stage, the profits of individual companies can stabilize and even grow as competitors drop out of the market and promotion expenses are cut back dramatically.

A product's stage in its lifecycle will influence marketing strategy decisions. Exhibit 6.5 lists some of the common marketing mix decisions that are made as products pass through different lifecycle stages.

EXTENDING THE PRODUCT LIFECYCLE

Extending the length of each stage of the product lifecycle, particularly the growth and maturity stages, is an objective that many marketers pursue actively. Five commonly used ways of achieving this are as follows:

- **Increasing frequency of use:** Employed primarily at the maturity stage, marketers can attempt to get customers to use their products more often. "Orange juice, it's not just for breakfast anymore" and "Show your cheddar more warmth, take it out of the fridge more often" are two advertising slogans that illustrate this approach.

- **Increasing the number of users:** Marketers can try to increase the size of the overall market by attracting customers who have yet to use the product. In the U.S., air travel was primarily the domain of businesspeople until Southwest Airlines implemented its strategy of making air travel less expensive than travelling by bus, car, and passenger train. Their goal? To make air travel affordable and attractive to a whole new target market: leisure travellers who had previously never considered flying.

- **Finding new uses:** This is an excellent strategy for extending a product's lifecycle and has been successfully used in many industries. SUVs were conceived primarily as products for industrial and hard-core recreational use. As the product

EXHIBIT 6.5 The Product Lifecycle and Marketing Mix Decisions

	Product Life Cycle Stage			
Marketing Mix Strategy	**Introductory**	**Growth**	**Maturity**	**Decline**
Product Strategy	Limited number of models; frequent product modifications	Expanded number of models; frequent product modifications	Large number of models	Elimination of unprofitable models and brands
Distribution Strategy	Distribution usually limited, depending on product; intensive efforts and high margins often needed to attract wholesalers and retailers	Expanded number of dealers; intensive efforts to establish long-term relationships with wholesalers and retailers	Expanded number of dealers; margins declining; intensive efforts to retain distributors and shelf space	Unprofitable outlets phased out
Promotion Strategy	Develop product awareness; stimulate primary demand; use intensive personal selling to distributors; use sampling and couponing for consumers	Stimulate selective demand; advertise brand aggressively	Stimulate selective demand; advertise brand aggressively; promote heavily to retain dealers and customers	Phase out all promotion
Pricing Strategy	Prices are usually high to recover development costs	Prices begin to fall toward end of growth stage as result of competitive pressure	Prices continue to fall	Prices stabilize at relatively low level; small price rises are possible if competition is negligible

Sales (vertical axis) — *Time* (horizontal axis)

Source: From *Marketing* (with InfoTrac) 8th edition by LAMB/HAIR/MCDANIEL. 2006. Reproduced with permission of South-Western, a division of Thomson Learning: www.thomsonrights.com. Fax 800 730-2215

entered the late maturity lifecycle stage, the automotive industry repositioned SUVs as vehicles that impart a sense of security and road superiority to urban dwellers. Finding a new use (and new users as well) returned the product to the growth stage. Interestingly, it is estimated that fewer than 10 percent of today's SUV owners ever take their vehicles off-road.

● **Changing package sizes or product quality:** This strategy has been used extensively by marketers of consumer food, health, and beauty products as a means to extend product lifecycles. The candy bar industry introduced bite-sized versions of their products to be given away as Hallowe'en treats. They launched larger, thicker, chocolate bars to appeal to chocolate lovers with big appetites. Mouthwash marketers have added product features such as tooth-whitening and plaque-control ingredients. By introducing pocket- and purse-sized packages, they have expanded mouthwash usage to out-of-home situations.

● **Redefining the market:** An effective and often dramatic way to extend a product lifecycle is to redefine and, in the process, enlarge the market that the product serves. General

Electric, for example, has a policy whereby when one of its products achieves a market share of 40 percent, the market for that product must be redefined to one in which it has no more than 10 percent. So, for example, if its aircraft jet engine business were to hit the 40 percent mark, its market would have to be redefined to include other users of turbine engines, which could include ships and power-generating plants.

CAN THE PRODUCT LIFECYCLE CONCEPT BE APPLIED TO YOU AND YOUR CAREER?

If you are or plan to be an entrepreneur, artist, or professional, the answer is an unequivocal yes. The goods and services that you are or will be producing can all be viewed from the product lifecycle perspective. Let's take a look at the field of dentistry as an example. In the 1960s and 1970s, it appeared that the profession was doomed to enter the decline stage. Decay-preventing toothpastes such as Crest which were introduced in the 1950s dramatically reduced the number of cavities in the population. Improved diets and better overall dental care, including flossing, accelerated this phenomenon. Demand for fillings, a major component of a general dentist's revenue, declined steeply. But for as close as dental services came to entering the decline stage, it never quite happened. Dentists shifted their primary focus from filling cavities to performing cosmetic work, including whitening and replacing damaged teeth with crowns and implants. These services have become a growing source of billing for dentists, as many baby boomers are now at a stage in their lives where their teeth have become discoloured and in need of major restoration.

If you are or have plans to become an employee, the product lifecycle concept can also apply to your situation, although the fit is not as snug as it would be if you were actually producing a product. Still, in this case, you're the product and the four stages can relate to you and you alone as you progress through your career. The beginning of your career is the introduction stage. Your income is low and demand for you is likely to be limited. Product improvement in terms of gaining experience and learning new skills moves you into the growth stage. You take on more responsibility and move higher up the organization chart. Your income rises and you become much more in demand. Continuous product improvement brings you into the maturity stage. You now are at the top of your game and are a senior executive, maybe even chief executive officer with the salary and perks that come with the position. Growth opportunities are much fewer and you may have actually reached the peak of your career. While not on the immediate horizon, the decline stage in which you gradually cut back on your activities in anticipation of retiring is certainly looming out there. If you wanted to extend your lifecycle, you could apply a number of the strategies we've just covered. You could increase the number of users by joining the boards of other organizations and doing volunteer work. You could find new uses by gaining the knowledge and experience required to work in another industry and then switch fields. You could move on to work for a larger company in the field you are now in by improving your management skills. Or you could redefine the industry or market that you work in to create bigger opportunities. For example, the hotel industry can be redefined as the travel and tourism industry, the restaurant industry as the hospitality industry, the pharmaceutical industry as the healthcare industry, the sports industry as the entertainment industry, the cement industry as the construction industry. The possibilities are limitless.

THE CONSUMER ADOPTION PROCESS

Consumers typically don't jump out of bed one morning and decide to buy a product they've never heard of. In the case of impulse products, the decision to buy a new product (e.g., Dentyne gum's newest flavour) may be taken almost instantaneously without any intervening steps. In most other cases, however, consumers tend to go through five stages as they decide to adopt a new product. These stages can extend over several days or weeks or can occur rather quickly.

The five stages that consumers go through—from first learning about a new product to trying it and deciding whether to buy it regularly or to reject it—make up the consumer adoption process. In Chapter 5, you learned about the decision process, going from problem or need identification to actual purchase and post-purchase behaviour. The consumer adoption process describes the stages involved when consumers are dealing with an entirely new product. The stages of the process are as follows:

- **Awareness:** Consumers first learn about the product but they lack full information about it.
- **Interest:** Potential buyers begin to search for information about the product—for example, online, in magazine articles, from friends or salespeople.
- **Evaluation:** Consumers consider the benefits and features of the product.
- **Trial:** Consumers make a trial purchase and evaluate the product's usefulness and how its performance compares to their expectations and fulfills their needs.
- **Adoption/rejection:** If the trial purchase results in a satisfactory experience, consumers decide to use the product regularly. If not, they do not buy it again.

In order to move potential customers to the adoption stage, it is essential that marketers understand the adoption process. A wide array of tactics is available to help them move consumers from one stage to the next. For example, if a marketer recognizes that a large number of consumers are at the interest stage, then he or she can stimulate sales by moving these consumers through the evaluation and trial stages. One way this can be achieved is through sampling and couponing. Samples of hair care products are often sent to households through the mail to encourage trial, and these samples are usually accompanied by cents-off coupons to trigger purchase. Which stage are your prime prospects at? How can you move them closer to adoption?

While the adoption process focuses on individuals and the steps they go through in making purchase decisions, the diffusion process concentrates on all members of a community or social system. Consumer innovators are people who purchase new products as

consumer adoption process — the process through which consumers eventually adopt or reject a product, from becoming aware of the product's existence, to interest, evaluation, trial, and eventually adoption

diffusion process — concentrates on all members of a community or social system in making purchase decisions

consumer innovators — people who purchase new products as soon as they reach the market

soon as they reach the market. Think of the people you know who are always the first to own the latest in technology, gaming, or fashion. As a general rule, innovators tend to have higher incomes, higher levels of education, greater social mobility, and more favourable attitudes toward risk. In the diffusion process, innovators are followed by early adopters, who often look to the innovators for advice. These early adopters are followed by the early majority, which is followed by the late majority. Finally, the last group of customers to buy a new product (by which time it may no longer be considered "new") are called the laggards. These groups and their approximate proportions of the population are shown in Exhibit 6.6.

Beyond the characteristics of individual consumers that might make them more likely to adopt new product innovations, there are characteristics of products that can facilitate the adoption process. Complexity, or the level of difficulty in understanding and using a new product, can impact the adoption rate. A more complex product tends to have a slower rate of adoption. Compatibility, or the degree to which a new product is consistent with customers' values, knowledge, past experiences, and needs, also influences adoption. A new product must also have a clear and meaningful relative advantage over substitutes and competing products. Observability refers to the extent to which the benefits of a new product can be observed by potential customers. Fashion shows, product demonstrations, and "infomercials" all focus on demonstrating product benefits and making the benefits observable to viewers. Finally, a new product stands better chances of being adopted if it possesses trialability: Can it be tried on a limited basis? Samples of a new product mailed to your home are designed to facilitate trial and accelerate adoption. Car dealerships that offer incentives to test-drive a new model are also focusing on trialability.

early adopters — people who often look to the innovators for advice in making purchase decisions

early majority — people who follow the early adopters in making purchase decisions

late majority — people who follow the early majority in making purchase decisions

laggards — people who are among the last to adopt new products

complexity — the level of difficulty in understanding and using a new product

compatibility — the degree to which a new product is consistent with customers' values, knowledge, past experiences, and needs; also influences adoption

EXHIBIT 6.6 **The Diffusion of Innovations Curve**

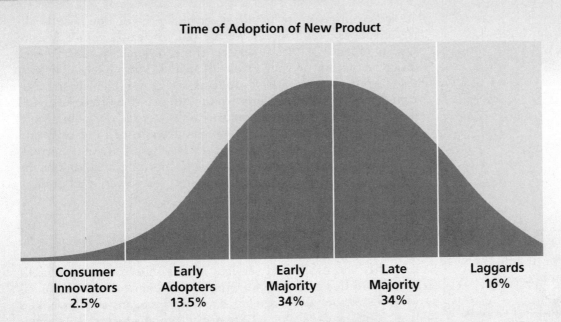

Time of Adoption of New Product

| Consumer Innovators 2.5% | Early Adopters 13.5% | Early Majority 34% | Late Majority 34% | Laggards 16% |

Source: From *Contemporary Marketing* 1/E by BOONE/KURTZ. 2007. Reproduced with permission of Nelson, a division of Thomson Learning: www.thomsonrights.com. Fax 800 730-2215.

relative advantage — a new product's clear and meaningful advantage over substitutes and competing products

observability — the extent to which the benefits of a new product can be observed by potential customers

trialability — a product's ability to be tried on a limited basis

To help strengthen your understanding of the diffusion process and its influence on marketing strategy, consider cellular phones. If you already own one, in which category of ownership and usage were you when you bought your first cell phone? How about your parents? Your grandparents? If you were the marketing manager for a cell phone company, would your advertising messages be the same to each of the five categories of adopters? If not, how would these messages be different? What combination of benefits and features do you think would best appeal to each group? These are essential questions that marketers of new products must address when making marketing mix decisions.

 Myth

As soon as it's evident that the job I'm doing is unsatisfying, I should resign.

 **Reality Check**

Even if you can afford to live without a steady income for a while, **unemployed candidates are a lot less attractive** to employers than people who already have jobs. Stick it out until you find a new job. Let the prospect of change be your motivation. Use that period of time to work on your product strategy and on product improvements so that you may be ready for the next stage or big challenge that comes your way.

BRANDING AND ITS ROLE IN PRODUCT AND MARKETING STRATEGY

Think of your favourite breakfast cereal. Or, if you don't eat breakfast cereal, think of your favourite pair of jeans, your favourite make of watch. Or pick a service: think of your favourite quick-service restaurant or your favourite airline. More likely than not, these favourites are branded products. Moreover, chances are that when these products came into your mind, you visualized the actual product itself. Perhaps you conjured up the crunch of your favourite cereal or imagined the cartoon characters used to identify and promote it. Maybe you thought of the last time you ate the cereal, your daily breakfast ritual, and how your mornings wouldn't be the same without it. Those associations reflect the power of a brand.

WHAT IS A BRAND?

brand — any combination of characteristics that uniquely identifies the product of one seller

According to the American Marketing Association, a brand is "a name, term, symbol, or design, or a combination of them, intended to identify the goods and services of one seller or group of sellers and to differentiate them from those of competition." Included in the AMA's definition are logos and even slogans such as Nike's "Just do it" and Allstate's "Are you in good hands?" In today's competitive, cluttered world where differences between products are increasingly becoming negligible or non-existent, brands play a key strategic role. Quite often, in fact, the only difference between products is the brand. Think McDonald's and Burger King, Coke and Pepsi, Shell and Sunoco, Duracell and Energizer. Blindfolded, without the red-haired clown, the distinctive logo on the can or signage, or the pink bunny, very few customers would be able to identify differences in quality among those products. The brand name, logo, advertising messages, and any other distinctive signs make all the difference.

For customers, brands facilitate the decision-making process. How? Largely by reducing the uncertainty associated with the purchase. Many purchases are fraught with risk: *financial risk* (the money involved), functional risk (Will the product break down when I need it most?), *physical risk* (to your or someone else's body), *psychological risk* (Will those jeans make me feel as sexy as I think they will?), *social risk* (how others will perceive you), and *time risk* (in terms of the time involved in the purchase and how much time the product or service might save you—or cost you). The trust and safety implicitly conveyed by a brand reduce the amount of perceived risk associated with a purchase. Also implicit in a brand is the promise of a predictable consumption experience. McDonald's is not just about hamburgers and fries, it's also the promise of a fun experience for the kids with in-store playgrounds or the promise of speedy drive-through orders. A brand also offers benefits to marketers by facilitating the identification of the product and the communication of its key benefits. Typically, a brand also generates more repeat sales as consumers, once satisfied by a brand, are often likely to simply repurchase it the next time and thus minimize the amount of effort and uncertainty in the decision process. Also, a strong brand can facilitate the introduction of new products under the brand's name. Think, for instance, of the success of Arm & Hammer's room deodorizers and toothpaste. Without the Arm & Hammer brand, these new products might not have fared nearly as well as they did when first introduced. Succinctly put, a strong brand is the answer to the customer's question, "Where can I get more of that?" If yours is a brand that consistently is the answer to that question, then you have managed to build a truly strong and desirable brand.

BRAND EQUITY

Brand equity is the added value that a brand name gives to a product. For instance, if you were to buy Coca-Cola—the company, that is, beyond the factories, the office furniture, and all the other physical assets—how much might you pay for the name Coca-Cola itself? Be prepared to write a pretty large amount on the cheque! According to an Interbrand survey[3] (http://www.interbrand.com), Coca-Cola is the world's most valuable brand, evaluated at more than US$67 billion, with Microsoft following in the number-two spot at a little under US$60 billion.

According to researcher Kevin Lane Keller,[4] brand equity rests on the positive associations that consumers develop about the brand. These associations can be product-specific and pertain to the actual product, its packaging, its price, or other elements of the marketing mix. Associations may be non-product-related and pertain to the mental imagery associated with the type of consumers who use this product or situations in which this product is typically used (e.g., what type of person drives a Corvette?). This emphasis on the associations that consumers have in mind underscores the importance of managing a *brand's identity*. What does the brand stand for? Over time, advertising, promotions, the type of imagery created, where the product is sold, its price, and other marketing mix elements contribute to shaping the identity of a brand in the mind of consumers. When brand managers contemplate marketing strategy decisions, they frequently find themselves asking the question, "Is this consistent with what we want our brand to be?" This is another way of asking how decisions will strengthen our brand identity.

Brands with higher equity confer financial advantages on individuals and organizations because customers are often willing to pay more for them. At the corporate level, brand equity has been linked to higher profits and stock prices. In your opinion, which of these brands has the higher level of equity? Which one(s) have the clearest and most distinctive identity?

The New York Yankees or the Minnesota Twins

Nike or Reebok

NASCAR or Formula One

Heineken or Corona

American Express or MasterCard

Microsoft or Apple

Global advertising agency Young & Rubicam has developed a brand equity system called the Brand Asset Evaluator. According to Y&R's system, firms build brand equity sequentially by focusing on four aspects:

- **Differentiation:** The brand's ability to stand apart from its competitors. A brand such as L'Oréal stands out in people's minds as a symbol and provider of beauty.

- **Relevance:** The real and perceived appropriateness of the brand to a big consumer segment. Google's customer or user base is in the hundreds of millions of people.

- **Esteem:** A combination of perceived quality and consumer perceptions about the growing or declining popularity of a brand. A rise in perceived quality or public opinion about a brand enhances the brand's esteem and vice versa. Brands with high esteem include Ben & Jerry's, Starbucks, Lexus, and Intel.

- **Knowledge:** The extent of consumers' awareness of the brand and the understanding of what the brand represents. Knowledge implies that consumers feel an intimate relationship with the brand. Examples include Disney, Campbell's Soup, and Band-Aid.

BRAND LOYALTY AND COMMITMENT

As organizations and individuals move through these stages and build brand equity, they usually find that customers' *loyalty* also increases. In the past, loyalty was often thought to be a simple matter of purchase pattern: A brand achieved high levels of loyalty if consumers' purchase patterns revealed a high frequency of repeated purchases of that brand. Consequently, loyalty and frequency programs were put in place to provide consumers with incentives to purchase more frequently. Under these programs, consumers receive discounts, alerts on sales or new products, and other incentives to buy more frequently. Some coffee shops or video rental stores give you a free beverage or free rental after every 10 or so purchases. Canadian Tire money was introduced in 1958 by Canadian Tire. More than 90 percent of customers eventually redeem their Canadian Tire dollars, thereby enticing them to revisit the company's stores often.[5]

Organizations and individuals are discovering that there is more to loyalty than mere repeat purchase. **Brand commitment** occurs when a customer experiences such a deeply rooted and emotional connection with a brand that he or she is willing to exert extraordinary effort to buy this brand. Think about your favourite brand of deodorant or peanut butter. What might happen if one day you noticed a new brand on the shelves? Would you still buy your favourite? What might happen if one day the store was out of your favourite brand? Would you go to another store? Wait until you could buy your favourite? If the answer is yes, then that is brand commitment.

> **brand commitment** — when a customer experiences such a deeply rooted and emotional connection with a brand that he or she is willing to exert extraordinary effort to buy the brand

 **Self Check**

Think of brands that have your commitment. What has made you committed to these brands? Consider how the elements listed below might have contributed (or not) to your commitment. Can you think of other reasons?

Packaging

Quality

Advertising

Retail store

Spokesperson (sexy or trustworthy?)

Cute character (e.g., Pillsbury's Doughboy)

Peer pressure

Salesperson

Exceptional service or product quality as well as meaningful marketing communications all contribute to brand commitment. Committed consumers often become **brand advocates** or **brand ambassadors**, consumers who will spread positive word-of-mouth every chance they get, adding to and becoming part of the buzz around that brand. Identifying those committed consumers and making sure they have a reason to talk up the brand is becoming an important marketing objective. In fact, many marketing consultants offer services that are designed to tap into the power of word-of-mouth and the ability of brand ambassadors to generate it. For example, BzzAgents (http://www.bzzagent.com) are recruited for their ability to spread word-of-mouth within their circle of friends and acquaintances. For more on buzz marketing, visit http://www.buzzmarketing.com.

> **brand advocates or brand ambassadors** — consumers who spread positive word-of-mouth, adding to and becoming part of the buzz around a brand

CUSTOMER RELATIONSHIP MANAGEMENT

> CRM — customer relationship management, a business philosophy that focuses on the long-term value of a customer and attempts to nurture relationships with consumers

In many cases there is a considerable upside potential for organizations and individuals to form and nurture long-term relationships with customers. Customer relationship management or CRM is a company-wide strategy that focuses on optimizing customer satisfaction and profitability by developing long-term relationships with customers. The basic idea of CRM is to transform a new customer into a brand advocate or ambassador. CRM is based on the notion that it costs less to keep an existing customer than it costs to acquire a new one. Also at the heart of CRM is the recognition of both a customer's long-term financial value (repeat purchase and higher spending propensity) and marketing value (word-of-mouth contribution).

CRM requires organizations and individuals to learn from each interaction with their customers, whether those interactions are in person or via a website, a toll-free number, or third-party vendors. Then, with information about customers and their preferences in hand, they can enhance the purchase and consumption experience. Achieving a more meaningful relationship with customers may be done by a combination of the following: providing individualized attention, upselling or encouraging customers to spend more, offering them other items that fit their lifestyles, and improving the product or service based on customer feedback. To illustrate, consider your latest visit to Amazon. If you were a repeat customer, then chances are you were greeted by name and offered recommendations for books or other items that match your lifestyle and purchasing profile. To achieve this level of personalization, Amazon mobilizes many business functions, which work toward the goal of continuously strengthening relationships with customers.

Hilton's "OnQ" (pronounced "On Cue") is another good example of CRM at work. OnQ was introduced in May 2003 at a cost of more than US$50 million. The system was designed to enable and empower Hilton's 200 000 employees to reliably deliver the Hilton experience across its 2100 hotels and different brands (which include Hilton Hotels, Hampton Inn, Homewood Suites by Hilton, Embassy Suites, Doubletree, Hilton Garden Inn, and Conrad Hotels). The system was designed to link major business functions that require customer information so that when an employee finds out important information about a customer (e.g., birth date, favourite ice cream flavour) he or she can enter it in the system, making it instantaneously available to all employees who might interact with that customer.

Another example of CRM is Air Canada's Aeroplan membership program. While most airlines' reward programs are no more than loyalty or frequency programs, Aeroplan has reinvented itself as an experiential brand. Members routinely get updates about their status via personalized booklets designed to strengthen their relationship and provide them with opportunities to enjoy their rewards. With a distinctive look and feel, Aeroplan's one-on-one communication with its members establishes the brand's identity as hip, customer-centric, and pleasure-oriented. Some of the noteworthy rewards (among the more than 300 available) include romantic weekend escapes, widescreen plasma TVs, and BOSE sound systems.

DEVELOPMENT STRATEGIES

To ensure growth, product development should be an ongoing endeavour. An organization's or individual's strategy for product development depends on their existing product mix and the match between the products they now offer and their overall marketing objectives. Exhibit 6.7 identifies the four fundamental development strategies, which we discuss next.

MARKET PENETRATION

The goal of market penetration is to increase market share by increasing the sale of existing products in existing markets. To achieve this, companies attempt to get existing target segments to buy more and/or more frequently. For example, if Campbell's Soup were to start a major campaign for its line of cream soups using advertising and sending coupons and recipe ideas to existing customers, it would be using a market penetration strategy. Under a market penetration strategy, an employee could take on more responsibilities in his or her job, a professional could offer reduced prices to encourage clients to use his or her services more frequently, and an artist could increase the exposure of his or her works by having more galleries exhibiting them.

MARKET DEVELOPMENT

With this strategy the objective is to attract new customers (i.e., find new markets) to existing products. Segmentation comes into play here. For example, using geographic segmentation an entrepreneur could introduce his or her products in cities, regions, or countries in which they have not been available. Tim Hortons did just this by expanding from Canada to the United States. An employee could telecommute to different company offices. A professional could expand his or her market by offering and selling services worldwide on the Internet. An artist could do the same for his or her products. The *Marketing Yourself* e-book could be sold abroad to other markets.

EXHIBIT 6.7 **Four Fundamental Development Strategies**

	Existing Product	New Product
Existing Market	**MARKET PENETRATION** ↑ share	**PRODUCT DEVELOPMENT** ↑ products
New Market	**MARKET DEVELOPMENT** ↑ customers	**PRODUCT DIVERSIFICATION** ↑ products & markets

PRODUCT DEVELOPMENT

This strategy entails the introduction of new products into markets where the organization or individual already has an established position. Coca-Cola continuously adds new soft drink flavours to its Coke-branded line. The company has also expanded its line to include bottled water and fruit drinks. An employee could undertake the necessary product development to evolve from being a process engineer into a general manager with his or her employer. A professional such as a personal fitness trainer could add nutrition and lifestyle counselling to his or her product mix. A musician could add arranging and vocals to his or her repertoire.

PRODUCT DIVERSIFICATION

Under this strategy, completely new products are introduced into new markets. Classic examples include Apple's introduction of the iPod, Nike's launch of athletic clothing, Sony's entry into the laptop computer market, and McDonald's entry into the market for Tex-Mex food with its Chipotle chain of restaurants. Because of the uncertainties inherent with both new products and new markets, this is the riskiest of the four strategies. On the other hand, it can also have the biggest impact on sales and growth. An employee could decide to change fields completely—say, from customer service to project management—and develop the new competencies that would be necessary to make the switch a success. A professional such as a lawyer could choose to become a corporate executive and begin the change process by enrolling in an MBA program. An artist such as a photographer could add framing to his or her product mix.

As you can appreciate, product improvement can be a critical component of development strategies for organizations and individuals alike. But what is meant by the words "new product"? There are basically six categories of new products:

1. Discontinuous or dramatic innovations (sometimes also called new-to-the-world products) are products that are entirely new, never heard of, and that often change the way consumers behave, interact, or view things. The telephone and the television are examples of discontinuous innovations.

2. New product lines are products that a company or individual did not start out to make. For instance, the line of Arm & Hammer room deodorizers and air fresheners is an example of a new product line for that company.

3. Additions to existing product lines include products that supplement the initial basic product line of the company. For example, Cascade's dishwasher tablets are an addition to its line of existing dishwasher liquids.

4. Continuous product improvements are routine revisions to existing products. Hellmann's squeezable bottles are an example of a continuous product improvement. Note here that the same mayonnaise in a new bottle would be a continuous improvement, but a new flavoured mayonnaise would be an addition to the existing line of mayonnaise.

5. Repositioned products are existing products that are being targeted to a new market or for a new use or situation.

Recently, France's Poulain chocolate undertook a massive campaign to teach 30-something consumers to think about its upscale dark chocolate as a dessert alternative and not merely as a snack food.

6. Lower-priced products are products that provide performance comparable to other competing products and/or brands but at a lower price. Multi-function printers that combine scanning, faxing, and copying functions in addition to printing are lower priced than the combined price of all those devices purchased separately.

 Myth

My college or university major should be **directly related to** my career.

 *Reality Check*

This doesn't have to be the case. You can choose a major in a subject you love and make sure you get relevant experience from internships, part-time jobs, and volunteer work that match your career goals. For example, you'd be surprised at the number of successful businesspeople who have degrees in liberal arts. And if at some point you decide that you really do need a business education, you can always take an MBA full- or part-time.

PACKAGING

Product strategy needs to address questions about packaging. As is the case with brands, a product's package can have a powerful influence on buyers' purchase decisions. For goods, packaging fulfills three basic functions:

- **Protection against damage, spoilage, and pilferage:** It must offer physical protection for the merchandise at all stages of handling between manufacturing and customer purchase.

- **Assistance in marketing the product:** In large supermarkets, drugstores, and mass merchandise outlets such as Wal-Mart, tens of thousands of items compete for the attention of shoppers. To set their products apart and catch the customer's eye, if only for a tiny fraction of a second, marketers use combinations of graphic design, colour, shape, sizes, and typefaces. Packaging can also be used to make products more convenient for shoppers to use. Think of squeeze bottles, microwavable containers, and re-sealable bags.

- **Cost effectiveness:** Packaging must perform its various functions at a reasonable cost as customers prefer not to pay a significant portion of the purchase price for something that will ultimately be discarded. (An exception to this rule is for the packaging of luxury goods, which are proudly displayed in the home or in retail outlets. These include designer fragrances and upscale liquor brands.) Changes in packaging can result in lower production and distribution costs and, ultimately, in lower prices. For example, the switch from glass to aluminium and plastic dramatically reduced breakage and the resulting downtime in the manufacturing of soft drinks and juices. And because aluminium and plastic are a fraction of the weight of glass, the change resulted in a dramatic reduction in the cost of transporting soft drinks and juices from the factory to distributors and retail outlets.

Packaging can also play a crucial role in the product strategies for services and individuals. You'll recall that services are intangible. Packaging can add a sense of tangibility and, in the process, enhanced customer confidence to services. For example, the business cards, letterheads, envelopes, and presentation folders used by service providers such as financial advisers, real estate agents, and graphic designers can be used to impart strong visual and tactile imagery. The appearance of service employees (including style of dress) is also a component of the service's packaging and influences how customers will relate to and interact with employees.

The packaging of individuals is made up of two key elements: appearance and etiquette. For example, how you dress can go a long way toward creating a powerful first impression and leaving a lasting one. (Consider that most decisions not to hire a potential employee are made in less than 15 seconds after meeting him or her.) With that in mind, here are a number of helpful tips that can put you on the road to dressing for success.

- If you're unsure how to dress, visit the company's plant, office, and/or employee parking lot prior to your interview or sales call (not on a Friday) and check out how employees are dressed.

- Solid colours are usually a safe bet. If you want to add your own personal twist and splash of colour, don't make it distracting or overbearing.

- Be mindful of temperature. You know your own body and reactions under stress: If you are likely to get nervous and perspire, don't dress with too many layers.

- When in doubt, it is much better to be slightly overdressed than underdressed. In most instances, modest apparel works better than flashy or revealing clothing.

- Use perfume, cologne, and makeup sparingly. Better yet, don't use fragrances at all; you never know if the person you'll be meeting is allergic to them.

- Limit the amount of jewellery you'll be wearing and avoid "noisy" bracelets.

- If you are going for an important interview or sales call, make sure to try on your outfit at least one day BEFORE the interview or call. Check for loose threads, missing buttons, and stains. Make sure what you're wearing is properly ironed or pressed.

- If your outfit is too tight or too loose, put it back in the closet and save it for another occasion.

When it comes to etiquette, note that out of two equally qualified candidates, the odds favour the one with better manners. This applies not only to your superiors, but also to your colleagues and your subordinates. A professional, polite, and courteous demeanour can make all the difference. It indicates that you are attuned to people in your environment and sends positive cues about your social skills—an important tool in any industry. Importantly, etiquette is not just a matter of knowing which fork to use at a business luncheon; it's everyday behaviour that conveys your awareness and consideration for those around you. Etiquette includes how you handle yourself on the telephone, in written correspondence, in person, and in meetings. All of this is part of your packaging. Want to assess and improve your etiquette? Check out the information in Exhibits 6.8, 6.9, and 6.10.

EXHIBIT 6.8 Telephone Manners: Hello, Goodbye, and In Between

You've probably never thought about how you answer the phone—it's just second nature. But in business, the way you speak on the phone not only creates an impression for callers but can actually make or break a sale, a deal, or a relationship. So it is important to be aware of how others perceive your phone etiquette. Here are a few tips from the experts to make your telephone conversations proceed smoothly:

1. When you answer the phone, state your name and the name of your firm clearly. Ask how you can help the caller. If you are answering another person's line, state his or her name, then identify yourself.

2. If you are calling someone, state your name and ask to speak with the person you want to contact. If an assistant offers to take a message, politely leave a brief message indicating the reason for your call.

3. Be an active listener during a phone conversation. The other person can't see you nod your head or smile, so be sure to offer an occasional "I understand" or "Yes" or "Let me see if I can help you." This way, the other person is reassured that you are listening.

4. Toward the end of the call, try to recap the important points such as "I'll see you at the conference on Friday," or "I will get back to you on Tuesday morning," or "I understand your problem with this product, and I will correct it for you." Even if the conversation has become a bit strained, try to end it on a positive note. Thank the person for his or her time, regardless of who called whom.

5. When you are talking with someone about business matters, be considerate of the other person's time—it is a workday, and he or she probably has many other things to handle. Make your call informative and short without being abrupt or rude.

Telephone etiquette plays a large role in customer service activities as well as other strategies involved in bringing services to the marketplace. A friendly voice, a pleasant attitude, and a willingness to be helpful can go a long way toward cementing marketing relationships over the phone lines.

Sources: "Business Telephone Etiquette for Success," PageWise, http://nyessortment.com/businesstelepho.rtli.htm, accessed April 2, 2004; Marilyn Ledgerwood, "Telephone Etiquette," PageWise, http://mtessortment.com/telephoneetique.rbpa.htm, accessed April 2, 2004; "Telephone Manners," http://www.salary.com/advice/layouthtmls/advl_display_nocat_Serv83_Parl176.html, accessed April 2, 2004.

EXHIBIT 6.9 **How to Run a Business Meeting**

Despite the prevalence of electronic communications in business, meetings will never go away. There is probably no more efficient way to deliver information to, or get agreement from, a group than a well-run meeting. Here are a few tips for making your meetings successful.

If you're running the meeting

1. Set appropriate goals. The best meetings are short (under an hour), so if you have a lot to accomplish you might want to have more than one meeting to cover everything.

2. Distribute an agenda with time frames before the meeting. An agenda not only lets you plan your time—and ensures that you get to all the necessary points—but also lets the attendees know what to expect so they can prepare. Stick to the agenda and time frames, and start and finish at the designated times.

3. Keep attendees informed. In addition to the agenda, participants need to know why their presence is necessary and how they will benefit from attending. Make sure you let them know so you can ensure their cooperation.

If you're attending the meeting

1. Let the meeting organizer know whether you will attend. If attendance will be poor, the meeting might have to be rescheduled.

2. Come early and come prepared. Don't be late, and bring information you will be asked to share as well as something to take notes with.

3. Avoid interrupting when others are speaking, either by speaking yourself or by having your phone or pager go off. Hold or forward your calls so you can listen attentively throughout the meeting.

4. Keep your questions and comments brief and to the point. This guarantees you'll be heard when you do speak, and it helps the meeting end on time.

5. Maintain your cool. Don't allow yourself to become angry or upset at other participants, and don't fidget or lose your concentration. It distracts others, particularly those who are speaking.

6. Be prepared to stay for the entire meeting. Leaving early is disruptive and rude.

7. Follow up after the meeting, promptly completing any tasks you've been assigned.

Meetings are an important part of any successful business career. Understanding how to facilitate a well-run meeting and understanding how to participate properly in a meeting led by someone else are important skills to obtain. The tips presented here will help you start your career with a better understanding of how best to handle meeting situations successfully.

Sources: Jared Sandberg, "A Survival Guide for Office Meetings: Bring Your Own Toys," *The Wall Street Journal*, May 19, 2004, p. B1; "Three Easy Steps to a Well-Run Meeting," *Strategic Communications*, http://www.strategiccomm.com, accessed April 17, 2004; Gary M. Smith, "Eleven Commandments for Business Meeting Etiquette," *Society for Technical Communication*, http://www.stc.org, accessed April 17, 2004; Vadim Kotelnikov and Ten3 East-West, "Effective Meetings," *The Business e-Coach*, http://www.1000ventures.com, accessed April 17, 2004; John Eckberg, "Mind Your Meeting Etiquette," *The Cincinnati Enquirer*, http://www.enquirer.com, December 23, 2003.

EXHIBIT 6.10 **More Useful Etiquette Tips**

- A firm handshake communicates confidence and sincerity. Make sure that yours is appropriately firm by practising it with friends or relatives. Establish eye contact and maintain it for the duration of the handshake.

- Return emails and phone messages promptly. Speak clearly when leaving a voicemail and state your return number twice.

- If you would like to send someone a special thank you, send him or her a personal note or card by regular mail. This will show that you mean it and will make you stand out from the crowd. Hardly anyone sends handwritten correspondence these days, so yours will certainly get noticed and remembered.

- If you are expecting calls on your personal telephone from employers or customers, make sure that your personal voicemail greeting is appropriate. The same goes for your personal email address.

- If you're not sure what cutlery to use at a restaurant or dinner party, start with the knives, forks, and spoons that are farthest on the outside and work your way inward as the meal progresses. Without being obvious, observe how the hosts are conducting themselves at the table and follow their lead.

- Consume alcohol at business functions moderately or not at all. Its effect on your judgment and behaviour is unlikely to be positive.

SOME FINAL (AND SOMEWHAT RANDOM) THOUGHTS ON PRODUCT STRATEGY

Over the many years that we've been teaching and working in marketing, we've had thousands of assignments handed in to us. Eight—we repeat, eight—have been handed in early and we can still remember the names of every student who submitted theirs before the due date. This and similar experiences got us thinking about how organizations and people can truly stand out. We humbly submit our short-list of suggestions.

- Make it a policy to deliver before the due date or deadline.

- Always deliver a little more than you were asked for or what you promised. Hardly anyone does this and it's not that difficult to do.

- Don't arrive at the office at the same time as everyone else. Get there a little earlier and leave a little later. Senior executives will notice that you're not like all of the others who can't wait to vacate the premises.

- Don't hold on to bad news until the very last minute. The best surprise is no surprise.

- Everything you are against weakens you. Everything you are for empowers you. Focus your time and energy on positive issues and activities.

- Stand for something.

- Make the world a better place. Both you and your organization will be better off for it.

FAVOURITES *professional*

CANADIAN PSYCHOLOGICAL ASSOCIATION
http://www.cpa.ca

The website of the Canadian Psychological Association.

WORKPLACE.CA
http://www.workplace.ca

Provides useful resources for human resources professionals involved in training, leadership development, and management consultancy.

MY Product Objectives

- What is my core product?

- What is my augmented product?

- What key quality dimensions will my customers use to evaluate my product?

- What do I want my product to be known for and remembered as?

- What skills and talents will I need to attain my marketing objectives?

MY Product Strategy: How Will I Achieve My Product Objectives?

- How will I acquire those skills and talents?

- What will be MY brand identity? What will my brand stand for?

- What role will I reserve in my product strategy to
  - a) TQM?
  - b) CRM?
  - c) product improvements?

MY Product Tactics: How Will I Execute My Product Strategy?

- What specific activities will enable me to put my strategy into action?

- When will I perform those activities?

	artist	*employee*	*entrepreneur*	*professional*
	To get you thinking about your product strategy, here are some examples of product strategy statements along with the objectives that led to them and the tactics that will be employed to execute them.			
MY PRODUCT OBJECTIVES	By graduation, complete a collection of works that will appeal to the needs and tastes of my target market	Become proficient in business French	Create a design and content for a magazine that attracts readers and advertisers who will view it as an authoritative and entertaining source of information about skiing and snowboarding	Establish myself as the hippest, best mannered dentist in this and neighbouring areas; be known for performing dental work that is as painless as possible
MY PRODUCT STRATEGY	Create 15 new works of different sizes and themes	Create opportunities to learn and practise French	Use successful on- and offline industry magazines as benchmarks. Improve on these by being more involving, user-friendly, and provocative, keeping in mind that their advertisers will likely be my advertisers.	Continuously hone my chairside manners; routinely update the artwork and décor in the clinic with hip music; have the latest equipment that minimizes pain
MY PRODUCT TACTICS	1) Identify three themes that I am comfortable painting and that will likely resonate with my target market 2) Produce the works	1) Register for French courses 2) Watch French newscasts 3) Get a part-time job in a French environment	1) Identify content that makes the magazine more appealing than the benchmarks. 2) Engage a designer and writer with proven abilities to inform and entertain members of the target market. 3) Prepare two/three designs and test them on small groups of target market members; expose the winning version to potential advertisers for feedback.	1) Purchase the newest drill on the market 2) Improve my freezing technique 3) Have professional designer decorate the clinic 4) Solicit up-and-coming artist to leave work on consignment to improve décor 5) Subscribe to hip magazines for the waiting room.

KEY TERMS

augmented product — the entire bundle of benefits or features in the core product

brand — any combination of characteristics that uniquely identifies the product of one seller

brand advocates or brand ambassadors — consumers who spread positive word-of-mouth, adding to and becoming part of the buzz around a brand

brand commitment — when a customer experiences such a deeply rooted and emotional connection with a brand that he or she is willing to exert extraordinary effort to buy the brand

compatibility — the degree to which a new product is consistent with customers' values, knowledge, past experiences, and needs; also influences adoption

complexity — the level of difficulty in understanding and using a new product

consumer adoption process — the process through which consumers eventually adopt or reject a product, from becoming aware of the product's existence, to interest, evaluation, trial, and eventually adoption

consumer innovators — people who purchase new products as soon as they reach the market

convenience products — goods and services that consumers purchase frequently, immediately, and with little effort

core product — the basic benefit or key feature at the heart of what an organization offers to its customers

CRM — customer relationship management, a business philosophy that focuses on the long-term value of a customer and attempts to nurture relationships with consumers

customer satisfaction — a confirmation or disconfirmation of expectations

decline stage — period when innovations or changes in customer preferences result in declining industry sales

diffusion process — concentrates on all members of a community or social system in making purchase decisions

early adopters — people who often look to the innovators for advice in making purchase decisions

early majority — people who follow the early adopters in making purchase decisions

emergency products — products purchased in response to unexpected and urgent needs

expectations — set in part by marketers by advertising, promotions, brand names, distribution, and product packaging

growth stage — period when new customers make their first purchases and early buyers repurchase the product

impulse products — products that are purchased on the spur of the moment

introductory stage — period when organizations and individuals focus their marketing efforts on stimulating demand for their new product

laggards — people who are among the last to adopt new products

late majority — people who follow the early majority in making purchase decisions

maturity stage — period when sales and profits continue to grow but then reach a plateau as the number of potential customers declines

observability — the extent to which the benefits of a new product can be observed by potential customers

product lifecycle — the various stages a product goes through as it ages; typically marked by different levels of sales

quality assurance — intended to identify and solve, even before they occur, potential problems or breakdowns that could jeopardize quality

quality control — implementing the necessary inspection checks to make sure that no defective product ever leaves the factory

relative advantage — a new product's clear and meaningful advantage over substitutes and competing products

shopping products — products that consumers buy only after comparing competing offerings on such criteria as price, quality, style, colour, and fit

specialty products — products that offer unique features and benefits that result in consumers placing high value on them and their brands

staples — convenience products that consumers constantly replenish so they'll always have them on hand

total quality management (TQM) — continually improving products and processes with the goal of achieving ever-increasing levels of customer satisfaction

trialability — a product's ability to be tried on a limited basis

unsought products — products marketed to consumers who may not yet realize any need for them

How Marketing-Savvy Have You Become?

1. Implicit in the notion of total quality management is that organizations and individuals perceive quality not as they see it but as their potential customers, clients, and employers see it. What does "quality" mean to your potential customers, clients, and/or employers?

2. The importance of branding for goods and services is evident. What are the potential benefits of branding to individuals, whether they're artists, professionals, employees, or potential employees?

3. Choose three brands that have your loyalty. For each one, identify the logical and emotional reasons why you're loyal to them.

4. Now identify three brands in the same product categories as your answer to question 3 that you would **not** consider buying. What are your logical and emotional reasons for this?

5. Completing projects and assignments a little ahead of schedule and delivering just a bit more than what was expected seem like easy and obvious ways to stand out, get noticed, and create loyalty. Why do you think that almost no organizations or individuals do this? If you intend on delivering before the due date and exceeding what's expected of you, what barriers will you have to overcome to consistently do this? What strategies will you use to overcome them?

NOW WHAT?

You've taken that all-important first step in creating your marketing mix by setting product objectives and strategies. The second crucial step is to establish your pricing (including salary) objectives and the strategies that you'll use to achieve them. Pricing is what we'll cover in the next chapter.

NOTES
1. From www.iso.org.
2. Reichheld, F. F., and W. E. Jr. Sasser. (1990). "Zero Defections: Quality Comes to Services," *Harvard Business Review* (September–October), 105–11.
3. Published in *Newsweek,* August 1, 2005.
4. Keller, K. L. (1993). "Conceptualizing, Measuring, and Managing Customer-Based Brand Equity." *Journal of Marketing Research,* vol. 57 (January), 1–22.
5. Vaandering, E. (2002). "Hey, Big Spender," *Marketing Magazine,* January 14.

Hard work and well-aligned strategies helped me succeed

Meet Mark Gentile. Mark is an independent contractor providing personal training and health services to individuals in fitness centres as well as in their own homes. Having worked as a personal trainer part-time while going to school, he enjoyed the freedom it gave him and the opportunity to think independently. Mark likes to teach and to interact with others. Expressing his creativity is also important. A consulting job for a well-known upscale fitness centre led to an invitation to join as a personal trainer, and Mark seized the opportunity. He recalls the tough beginning: "The biggest obstacle was the difficulty of starting out. The hours were long and the payoffs didn't always match the hours I put in. But as my reputation and word-of-mouth grew, so did the rewards."

To reach his goal of becoming a successful independent personal trainer/businessman, Mark lined up some interesting marketing objectives and strategies. For instance, so as not to compete head-on with other trainers who possessed formal education in physiology or kinesiology, Mark decided to focus on his marketing and service know-how. Thus, he set out his product objective: to become known as a flexible and customer-oriented trainer. He used a strategy he refers to as the ABCD concept: going Above and Beyond the Call of Duty. Did he make mistakes? Sure. One of his early mistakes was the lack of a clear price objective, which led to an ineffective strategy. Mark soon realized he was not charging enough and admits that he should have done more research into the going rates to figure out what clients were willing to pay for a more flexible service such as his. In sum, his pricing strategy needed to be more closely aligned with his product strategy.

We asked Mark what three tips he would like to share with readers of *Marketing Yourself*. Here are his thoughts:

1. *Do your own SWOT analysis.* Know yourself and what opportunities are out there. Opportunities typically do not materialize out of thin air. Research them.

2. *Try to meet and network with as many people as you can.* Talk to friends, family members, professors, co-workers, bosses, neighbours, even strangers! You never know where your next lead, sales, or contact might come from.

3. *Be positive.* Positive people give off positive energy and others can sense that. Positive energy attracts other positive people. You don't have to be the poster-child of unbridled optimism, but a positive attitude makes everything else you have to do a whole lot easier.

YOU WILL:

- know what constitutes price

- understand the relationships between price and the other elements of the marketing mix

- know how to set your price objectives and strategies

- understand basic pricing strategies including pricing yourself as an employee

- understand how to negotiate prices and salaries

What's the price of a single-serving size can or bottle of cola?

There are many answers to this seemingly mundane question. In supermarkets, no-name or private label cola can typically be purchased in cases of 24 cans or bottles for as little as $4.00, or 17 cents per can. Brand-name cola such as Coke and Pepsi sell for about $1.00 more per case, or 24 cents per unit. In this instance, the brand commands a 25 percent price premium. When you're selling billions of cans each year, that 7-cent difference delivers tens of millions of additional dollars to the bottom line. Convenience stores price brand-name colas in the $1.00 range, and in vending machines they're often priced at $1.50 per can. One of the major cola manufacturers actually tested selling its cans and bottles in vending machines that adjusted prices upward as the outdoor temperature increased! Public outcries of price gouging put a speedy end to that experiment.

Of course, a can or bottle of cola can sell for plenty more than $1.00. In movie theatres and professional sports venues the equivalent of a single-sized serving sells for $2.50 on average. Depending on the status of the bar, restaurant, or hotel, it can be priced at up to $5.00 or more. Need proof? Order a Coke from room service the next time you stay at a Ritz-Carlton property.

So how is it that the price of a product can range from 17 cents to $5.00—a spread of almost 3000 percent? Real and perceived product differences affect pricing. So does the situation and the environment (how badly do you want that soda on a hot day sitting in the bleachers watching a baseball game?). As you might have guessed from Chapter 6, branding and brand equity also affect pricing. That's why some people are willing to pay more for Coke and Pepsi than for store brands. The addition of a service to the product—for example, bringing a cola to your hotel room—can have a dramatic impact on pricing. Providing convenience and the availability of competing products—or lack thereof—can also affect pricing. This is the case in theatres and sports arenas.

So, what's the price of a single-serving size can or bottle of cola? There really is no one single price. It depends on the product, place, and promotion as well as on market conditions.

Compared to developing and implementing product and promotion strategies, pricing strategies are relatively simple. In most cases all that has to be done is to decide on a price and communicate it to the market. While the effects of product and promotion decisions can take weeks, months, or even years to be felt, the impact of pricing decisions is often immediate and dramatic. For example, most people will switch gas stations based on price differences of tenths of a cent per litre. So if you decide to price your gasoline at two tenths of a cent over your competitors, your sales will almost certainly suffer. Price it at two tenths of a cent less and they'll skyrocket. Despite the short-term impact of pricing decisions, they frequently have long-term repercussions. Set too high a price for a new product and its diffusion could be extended by months or years. Set the price too low and customers may question the quality of your product or service. If you too eagerly accept a low salary, employers may see you as someone who will settle for less than what the market bears. This decision could result in you earning less than the employer is willing to pay for the duration of your employment at his or her company.

In the general marketplace for goods and services, price is the amount of money that customers exchange to obtain a desired product. In the job market, price is usually salary. It's the amount of compensation (including benefits such as paid vacation, health insurance, and stock options) that an employer is willing to give in exchange for your skills, knowledge, and the results of your work.

Myth

*Employers almost always low-ball candidates when beginning to talk about salary. Therefore I should start negotiating by **asking for a very high amount.***

Reality Check

Experienced negotiators realize that **the goal of a successful salary negotiation is to conclude with a win–win solution.** Employers spend considerable amounts of time and money scouting and evaluating candidates. They don't want their efforts to go to waste by missing out on desirable candidates because of systematic low-balling. Employers need your talent. You need their salary and the opportunity to work for them. Instead of asking for an unrealistically high salary, do your research to find out the going rate for the position for someone with your profile. Then if you are convinced you're worth more than the going rate, develop convincing arguments to persuade your potential employer to pay more by showcasing your unique capabilities and how you will add value to the organization.

SETTING PRICE OBJECTIVES

Up until the 1980s, pricing in the automotive industry followed a time-tested process. The designers would conceive a new car. Based on the design, the engineers would decide on the mechanical specifications and components for it. The accountants would then determine what these specifications and components would cost. With the finance people, they would then determine the selling price of the vehicle, usually by applying a standard mark-up to the cost. So, for example, if the cost of producing the car was estimated to be $15 000 and the standard mark-up was 30 percent, then the selling price was set at $19 500. If the company's salespeople felt that this price was too high for the target market, they would tell the engineers to delete certain features, such as magnesium wheels and power door locks and windows, to reduce the cost and ultimately get the price down to, say, $18 250. Then off to the dealerships the cars would go. What's missing from this scenario? If you concluded "the customer," you're absolutely right.

Since the 1980s, automotive manufacturers have increasingly based their pricing processes by focusing on their customers' needs, wants, and budgets. Through research they determine the features that customers in various market segments desire in new vehicles. They then ask them what they would be prepared to pay for vehicles with these features. Next, the designers, engineers, and accountants determine if the desired vehicles can be produced at a cost that would allow the company to make its required profit at the selling price that customers are willing to pay. If it can, the project is a go. If it can't, either the project is cancelled or the vehicle is modified based on back-and-forth dialogues between the company and the customers. If you see a marketing orientation in action in this scenario, congratulations on your 20/20 vision!

Now let's take a look at some typical pricing objectives for those who will be selling products (i.e., professionals, artists, entrepreneurs, businesses, and other organizations) and for people who are or intend to become employees.

PRICING OBJECTIVES FOR PROFESSIONALS, ARTISTS, COMPANIES, AND OTHER ORGANIZATIONS

The pricing objectives for these individuals and enterprises generally fall into one or more of the following major categories: profitability, volume, and prestige. Table 7.1 gives you an overview of how these pricing objectives relate to a person's or organization's overall goals.

PROFITABILITY OBJECTIVES

Businesses, professionals, and artists usually set prices with profits uppermost in mind. (Recall that the marketing concept is all about satisfying customer needs at a profit.) Not-for-profit organizations

---

TABLE 7.1 Pricing Objectives

OBJECTIVE	PURPOSE	EXAMPLE
Profitability objectives	Profit maximization Target return	Low introductory interest rates on credit cards with higher standard rates after six months
Volume objectives	Sales maximization Market share	Dell's low-priced PCs increase market share and sales of services
Marketing competition objectives	Value pricing	Per-song charges for music downloads
Prestige objectives	Lifestyle Image	Designer fashions such as Giorgio Armani and watches by Piaget

Source: From *Contemporary Marketing* 1/E by BOONE/KURTZ. 2007. Reproduced with permission of Nelson, a division of Thomson Learning: www.thomsonrights.com. Fax 800 730-2215.

must set prices too. These include contribution levels from fundraising efforts, which need to be high enough to cover expenses and to provide a financial cushion to be used when unforeseen needs or expenses arise. With this in mind, setting prices is both an art and a science. The key to successful pricing strategy is to strike a balance between desired profits and the customer's perception of value.

Because the marketing landscape (including the technological, economic, competitive, demographic, and social environments) is constantly changing, marketers need to continually evaluate and adjust prices. For example, as new computer monitor and television screen technology is introduced, the prices of existing monitors and screens needs to be decreased to move them through the distribution channel and to make room for the new products. Once the new monitors and screens are widely available in stores, competition will intensify and this will invariably have the effect of driving prices down. A marketer of products such as these will have to decide whether to keep its prices above the ever-decreasing average market prices, at the same level, or below them.

Profits are a function of two things: revenue and expenses.

> Profits = Revenue − Expenses

> profits — whatever is left from revenues after all expenses have been paid

Revenue is determined by the product's selling price and the number of units sold:

> Total revenue = Price × Quantity sold

To increase profits, you could decide to increase your price. However, a price designed to maximize profits rises to the point at which further increases will result in disproportionate decreases in the number of units sold. A 15 percent price hike that results in only a 12 percent reduction in volume sold will result in a net revenue gain of 3 percent. On the other hand, if the same increase results in a 17 percent sales decrease, total revenue will decline by 2 percent.

As an alternative to profit maximization, marketers can set target return objectives. These objectives are stated as percentages of sales or investment—for example, to make an 8 percent profit or to achieve a 12 percent return on investment. Objectives framed as target returns or percentage of profitability serve as tools for evaluating performance and satisfy desires to generate "fair" profits as judged by managers, owners, and the public.

VOLUME OBJECTIVES

Some organizations and individuals believe that from a competitive standpoint, increased unit sales are more important in the long run than are short-term profits. As a result, they continue to expand sales as long as their total profits do not fall below the minimum return acceptable to management. During its early years, one of Amazon's major goals was to establish the company as a leading retailer of books. Amazon achieved this goal by pioneering and expanding the online marketing channel. A key to its ultimate success was to gain broad consumer acceptance and ever-increasing revenues by pricing its products competitively against those found at bricks-and-mortar stores, even if this meant forgoing profits. The objective was to achieve volume by getting increasing numbers of people to the website buying more books. The number of units sold, the conversion rate of browsers into buyers, and the number of transactions completed are examples of measures used to monitor a volume-oriented objective.

Another volume-related pricing objective relates to market share. The goal here is to attain and hold a particular share of the market or position within that market. For example, the major domestic brands of beer are typically priced with this objective in mind.

PRESTIGE OBJECTIVES

The goal of prestige pricing is to establish a high price to create and maintain an image of quality and exclusivity with particular appeal to status-conscious customers. Although profit and sales volume considerations play secondary roles with this strategy, prestige pricing can result in extremely high profit margins. For example, the typical cost of the ingredients in a $100 designer fragrance is less than $5. When using prestige pricing, firms must strictly control the other elements of the marketing mix to ensure that the high price is not compromised by distributors or retailers. For instance, if your store sells Chanel and Hugo Boss suits, the designer will actually tell you when you can have a sale and by how much you can discount their garments at the end of the season. They're also likely to dictate how you must display their clothing so as to match their upscale image.

In addition to Rolex, Prada, Tiffany, Louis Vuitton, and Montblanc, can you think of five brands that use a prestige pricing strategy? Based on your observations, how have they managed to maintain their prestige pricing over time?

PRICING OBJECTIVES FOR EMPLOYEES

When it comes to setting pricing, including salary objectives, many people take the "I'll see what the market bears" approach. Market conditions can have an enormous influence on your salary; however, they're not the only factors. For example, the product that you have to offer, including your education level, skill set, previous experience, and attitude, plays a significant role as do your values and goals. In the job market, the main component of your price is salary. Benefits such as vacation, health insurance, and pension plans are another component. Your price—salary plus benefits—is the amount of compensation an employer is willing to give in exchange for your work.

Employers have expectations about what a product such as yours is worth. And as is the case with the pricing for most products, salary levels fluctuate. The economic climate, demand, competition, and the states of the industry and the organization all have some impact on the salary that you can expect. Most employers are expert buyers when it comes to talent. They estimate the bottom-line contribution of a position, conduct research on the job market, and set a salary range. The top of the range is reserved for experienced employees. Entry-level employees start at the lower end of the range.

In their research, employers typically examine:

- Salary ranges for their industry and in similar industries
- Geographical variations—for example, salaries are typically higher in New York, Toronto, London, and Hong Kong because of the relatively high cost of living in these major cities
- The unemployment rate and the availability of qualified applicants
- The economic outlook
- The desirability of the organization as an employer

Let's put this into perspective by using an example of someone starting her career and setting salary objectives. Janet has decided that she wants to work in the advertising business after graduation, specifically in media planning. Her goal is to be in a middle-management position with a leading global agency in Chicago, London, or New York within five years. Current salaries for this type of position in these cities are in the $80 000 to $90 000 range, and this is in line with Janet's five-year salary objective.

With graduation day six months away, Janet initiates her own research in earnest. While demand for entry-level media planning positions is strong, so is competition for them. The economy is performing well and forecasts are for this situation to continue. In her hometown, Vancouver, she discovers that typical starting salaries in media planning are between $20 000 and $22 000, more than 30 percent below what she could earn in other industries. However, she learns that after working two to three years in the agency business and getting promoted once or twice, salary levels catch up to those for comparable jobs in other fields.

Janet was put off by the low starting salary level. To determine whether she could make ends meet on such a starting salary, she prepared a monthly budget using the template on page 160.

Her heart sank. She'd never realized all the expenses she'd have to face when living on her own. Moreover, she realized that her monthly expenses far exceeded the take-home pay she would earn during her first two years in media planning. Decision time! Should she rethink her career choice, or find ways to cut expenses? After a week of soul searching, Janet concluded that the short-term pain of a lower salary was worth the long-term gain of having a job she wanted and was passionate about and that would put her on the path to earning her targeted income. She decided to put off buying a car, moving out from her parents' house, and taking an expensive vacation until she could afford these things. Janet's short-term pricing objective immediately fell into place: to set a price that will make her competitive with other recent graduates applying for media planning positions with major global advertising agencies in Vancouver.

MY MONTHLY BUDGET	
Expenses	**Amount**
Housing (rent or mortgage payment)	$
Utilities (gas, electricity)	
Cable or satellite TV	
Internet access	
Security/alarm system	
Phone (including cell phone)	
Car payments (including monthly payments, gas, maintenance)	
Insurance (car, personal property)	
Education loan repayments	
Food (groceries, take out, deliveries, eating out)	
Clothing	
Transportation (taxi, public transport)	
Entertainment (clubbing, movies, etc.)	
Gym membership	
Vacations (e.g., weekend getaways, holiday vacations)	
Savings	
Property & school taxes (if applicable)	
Other debt payments	
Total Monthly Expenses:	**$**

DETERMINING SALARY RANGES

As noted earlier, salary ranges depend on a number of factors including supply and demand and the levels of education, experience, skills, and responsibilities required of the position. Knowing the salary range for positions that interest you means you have some understanding of your worth in the employment marketplace. Research is needed, but where do you look? Fortunately, there are many sources of salary range information. Here are some key ones.

- **Career placement offices:** Most educational institutions have these. They provide access to a vast number of publications and employer surveys related specifically to salary ranges in virtually every career field.

- **Job listings and employers:** Many organizations provide salary range information in their advertisements for job openings. Human resources departments may supply this information if asked. Potential employers may be willing to reveal what their salary ranges are during information interviews.

- **Associations:** Industry associations frequently conduct employment surveys and salary range questions are often included in these. The results of these surveys can be found on association websites.

- **Your contacts:** If you don't know someone who works in the field you're interested in, it's more than likely you know someone who knows someone who does. Think of your parents, their friends, relatives, your friends, your friends' parents, former classmates, teachers, and employers. You might be surprised at how quickly you can get in touch with someone who has an idea of salary ranges in your chosen area.

- **The Internet:** Here you'll find a wealth of information about salary ranges. Monster.ca, JobBoom.com, and Working.com are three of the most helpful sites. Many government agencies provide salary data online. And, of course, you can check out other web sources using your favourite search engine.

FAVOURITES *job seeker*

SALARY.COM
http://www.salary.com

Salary information for various professions and geographic areas

COMMISSIONS VS. SALARY

Most payment packages comprise 100 percent salary. On the other hand, a number of positions exist that are compensated on the basis of 100 percent commission. These are typically sales positions in such areas as real estate, financial services, technology, media, and automobiles. The downside of this type of compensation is the uncertainty of your income stream. If, for whatever reason, sales drop, so will your earnings. The upside, of course, is that there is no hard cap on the amount of money you can earn under a 100 percent commission arrangement. And, yes, we do have former students who have reported earnings of more than $500 000 annually within ten years of graduation. Oh, and we also have those who tried working on a 100 percent commission basis and quickly bolted to the security of a 100 percent salaried position.

People who enjoy working on a purely commission basis seem to share a number of key characteristics. They love to sell. They don't mind cold-calling and are not bothered by the seemingly endless stream of rejections. In fact, most are motivated by rejections to make more calls. They despise routine. They are willing to work extraordinarily long hours to close a sale. Risk is like adrenaline to them. It energizes them. Winning is their biggest reward. These types of people thrive on compensation packages that are based exclusively on commission and feel boxed in by salary-based arrangements. A little introspection and analysis of the self-assessment tests you've taken should help you determine if you're in this group and the extent to which being paid only on commission appeals to you.

Between the extremes of pure salary and commission compensation packages are those that offer a base salary plus performance-based commission. This provides some income stability with the benefit of upside earning potential. If you plan to work in sales and would be happy with a relatively low salary but with the opportunity to enhance your earnings based on the results you produce, this may be an alternative you should explore with potential employers.

OTHER COMPENSATION PACKAGE ELEMENTS

When setting your price objectives (and eventually negotiating your compensation package), there are several other components besides base salary and commission that you may want to consider, including:

- **Hours of work:** Is it important for you to have a fixed schedule of work with predictable starting and leaving times? On the other hand, are you the type of person who will take whatever amount of time is required to get the job done? If you prefer a fixed schedule, you should make this clear to potential employers and also ask about how overtime is paid. Is working on a flexible schedule something you would like to do? If so, this should be included in your price objectives.

- **Frequency of salary reviews and promotion:** This will determine how quickly your income can rise and how fast you can progress within an organization. Is regular and frequent progress in these areas important to you? If it is, include it in your price objectives.

- **Vacations:** How important to you is vacation time, and when do you like to take vacations? Would you be willing to take unpaid vacations if an employer offered these? As part of your price, you should have some idea of the length, timing, and extent to which vacation time will be paid for.

- **Insurance and pensions:** To what extent are employee-paid health, dental, life insurance, and pension plans priorities for you? If they are a high priority, they should be included in your price objectives. While you may think you are in perfect health, what happens when you need new glasses? Or if you have an accident and break a tooth? We don't like to think about things like these, but health, dental, and life insurance should be considerations when you set your price objectives as an employee.

- **Stock options:** These offer you the opportunity to purchase shares in your employer's business at some future date at a set price. For example, assume that the employer's shares are trading at $5 today and the employer gives you 10 000 options to purchase shares at $5 starting 12 months from now. A year goes by and the shares are trading at $10. You could hold on to your options in the hope that the price of the shares goes even higher, or you could exercise your option to buy them at $5 and then immediately sell them for $10, thereby making a $50 000 profit. (Of course, if the company's shares never trade above $5, your options will be worthless.) Companies that include stock options in their compensation packages are often in their start-up or growth phases and expect employees to be paid less in base salary than for comparable jobs elsewhere. Does this type of compromise interest you?

- **Education and training:** Some employers help their employees pay for education and training in whole or in part. If you intend to continue your education while being employed, employer support should be included in your price objectives. Many employers will also set aside "professional development" funds for you to attend a workshop or conference.

- **Expense account/car allowance:** Certain jobs—in sales, for example—may come with allowances for a car and/or expenses such as meals. While these allowances are not a source of income per se, they can contribute to lowering your own monthly expenses.

- **Signing bonus:** This amount is negotiated by both parties and usually serves as an incentive for a potential employee who has a uniquely desirable profile to commit and accept an offer. This bonus typically takes the form of a one-time lump-sum payment.

- **Moving expenses:** A moving allowance (usually with a preset maximum) is designed to help offset the cost of relocation. Some employers will require that you reimburse such an allowance if you quit after a minimum period of time (e.g., one year).

 Myth

*Lowering my salary demands will **make me a more attractive job candidate.***

 *Reality Check*

If you lower your reasonable salary demands, **it may make you appear to be desperate for the job**. This will likely result in you not getting the job offer. Even if you got the offer and accepted it, you would probably not be happy in your job or with your employer because you would feel you're being paid less than you're worth.

PRICING STRATEGIES

After price objectives have been established, the next step is to create a pricing strategy. As we did in our discussion of price objectives, we'll be looking at pricing strategy from two basic perspectives: that of entrepreneurs, artists, and professionals and that of employees. When we discuss pricing strategies for employees, we'll be focusing mainly on negotiation. For those of you who have chosen to be entrepreneurs, artists, or professionals, our coverage of negotiation shouldn't be overlooked, because at some point in your careers you'll likely be hiring employees and will be negotiating terms of employment with them. All you have to do is imagine yourself being on the other side of the negotiation table.

PRICING STRATEGIES FOR PROFESSIONALS, ARTISTS, COMPANIES, AND OTHER ORGANIZATIONS

The pricing strategies that individuals and organizations use to price their goods and services are an extension of the marketing objectives they have put in place to accomplish their overall individual and organizational goals. For example, prices could be set above the market (*price skimming*), at the market level (*competitive pricing*), or below the market (*penetration pricing*).

Price skimming (also referred to as market-plus pricing) involves setting a relatively high price compared to competitive or substitute products. It's typically used as a market-entry price for products with little or no competition or products that are perceived to have unique and distinctive advantages. When supply begins to exceed demand or when competition catches up, the initial high price is reduced. A classic example of the application of this strategy was evident with the introduction of plasma screen televisions. When they were launched in 1999, the average retail price for a 42-inch unit was $20 000. As more and more competitors entered the market, prices fell, and within six years 42-inch plasma units were available for under $2000. With skimming, one of the key underlying assumptions is that customer innovators and early adopters are willing to pay a significant premium to be among the first to own or use the product.

A skimming pricing strategy offers significant benefits. The high profit margins it creates can allow a manufacturer to quickly recover its research and development costs. This is frequently the case with producers of pharmaceutical and high-technology products. This strategy also permits marketers to control demand in the introductory stages of a product's lifecycle and then increase production capacity to match growing demand.

As with any strategy with high prices at its core, skimming has one serious disadvantage: it attracts competition. Potential competitors see innovative firms enjoying large financial returns and decide to enter the market. The new supply they bring to the market usually forces prices—and profit margins—down. This certainly has been the case with digital cameras, cellular telephones, and laptop computers.

A penetration pricing strategy uses low prices as a major marketing tool. Here, marketers price their products lower than competing or substitute products when they enter new markets in which there are several competing brands. Once the product achieves some market recognition through initial purchases stimulated by its low price, the price may be increased to the level of competing brands or substitute products. The introduction of the Lexus brand of automobiles is an interesting example of penetration pricing. Prior to its North American launch, the luxury segment was dominated by Mercedes-Benz and BMW. Using penetration pricing, Lexus quickly became the leading luxury brand, and once it attained this position, it raised its prices to match those for competing Mercedes-Benz and BMW models. Lexus's pricing strategy was successful in attracting a critical mass of buyers and moving this unknown brand through the brand-recognition stage to the brand-preference stage.

> **price skimming** — a pricing strategy that involves setting relatively high prices compared to your competitors; often used to enter a market for products with little or no competition

> **penetration pricing strategy** — a strategy whereby low prices are used as a major marketing tool to enter a new market

Penetration pricing works best for products in markets in which there are large numbers of highly price-sensitive customers. (And, yes, high income earners are known to pay very close attention to price when it comes to purchasing big-ticket items.) It's also appropriate in situations in which large-scale operations and long production runs result in economies of scale in both manufacturing and marketing. Finally, penetration pricing can be used to pre-empt competition as it can result in a product capturing a large, even dominant, market share before competitors enter the market.

Under competitive pricing (also known as *pricing parity* and *status quo pricing*) the goal is to reduce the emphasis on price by matching competitors' prices and to concentrate marketing efforts on the other three elements of the marketing mix. While price can be a dramatic means of achieving a competitive advantage, this could be short-lived as price is by far the easiest marketing variable for competitors to match. In industries with fairly similar products such as energy, basic foods, personal computers, and dry cleaning, competitors must match each other's prices and price reductions to maintain market share and to remain competitive. For example, advertising agencies all charge approximately the same fees for their services. They differentiate themselves primarily on the basis of creativity. Dentists' fees tend to be very similar. They differentiate themselves in several ways including convenience (office hours and availability in case of emergency) and fear minimization (chairside manner).

Competitive pricing should be used with caution, especially when reducing prices to become more competitive. A price reduction affects not only the first organization or individual who drops prices, but also can have dramatic financial consequences for the whole industry if the price cuts are matched by competition. Unless the lower prices can attract new customers and expand the overall market, all competitors will experience a revenue decline and industry revenues will fall. That said, organizations and individuals may have little choice but to reduce prices before competitors do so before them.

Once competitors are routinely matching each other on price, to attract customers and create a distinctive competence the three other elements of the marketing mix need to be emphasized. For example, gasoline retailers use location, and many have convenience-store facilities to offer consumers one-stop shopping. Some supermarkets have self-service checkouts to speed up grocery bagging and payment. Computer companies such as Dell make choosing and buying personal PCs and peripherals simpler through their state-of-the-art websites. And many dry cleaners offer repair and alteration services to make caring for their garments easier for customers.

competitive pricing (also known as pricing parity and status quo pricing) — reducing the emphasis on price by matching competitors' prices and concentrating marketing efforts on the other three elements of the marketing mix

Myth

I should set whatever price I think my art is worth and see if it sells.

Reality Check

Begin the pricing process by determining your costs including supplies, overhead such as rent and the value of your labour, and then your profit margin. **To command high prices, you will need to constantly promote your name and your work.** You'll need to establish a network of galleries, wholesalers, exhibit spaces, and private customers. To ensure that people will continue to be willing to pay the prices you're charging, you'll have to follow through with schedules, meet deadlines, take orders, prepare invoices, and make sure you get paid.

PRICING TACTICS

Once the broad pricing strategy has been set, marketers still have some leeway to fine tune their price by using various pricing tactics. Here are some of the most popular ones.

Value pricing emphasizes the benefits a product delivers in comparison to the price and quality levels of competing offerings. Private-label brands such as President's Choice are an example. Note that prices do not necessarily need to be lower than those of competition. "L'Oréal might cost a little more, but I'm worth it" is a perfect example of this notion.

While value-pricing strategies work best for relatively low-priced products, they can be successfully applied to those in expensive price categories. The retail price of the BMW M5 sports sedan is approximately $100 000. Compared to virtually all mid-sized four-door cars, this price is over the top. However, the M5 is not an alternative to these vehicles. Thanks to its 500 horsepower V10 engine and race car–inspired engineering, its performance equals and in many cases exceeds that of $175 000 Porsches, $225 000 Aston Martins, and $300 000 Ferraris. Plus, it has ample room for four adults and two more doors!

With psychological pricing, the underlying belief is that certain prices or price ranges make products appealing. The most commonly used psychological pricing tactic is odd pricing, where prices are set at odd numbers just below round numbers. The assumption is that buyers perceive a price of, say, $4.99 or $999 as being distinctively different, even lower, than $5.00 or $1000. Gasoline retailers are probably the most conspicuous and consistent users of odd pricing.

With flexible pricing, different customers pay different prices for the same product. Flexible pricing is often used with price-sensitive customers. It gives salespeople and resellers the discretionary power to adjust prices to close a sale. Profit margins tend to fluctuate more when this tactic is used. Flexible pricing can also be used to tailor prices to different types of customers. For example, first-time buyers could be offered a lower price to encourage them to try a product

value pricing — emphasizes the benefits a product delivers in comparison to the price and quality levels of competing offerings

psychological pricing — based on the belief that certain prices or price ranges make products appealing

odd pricing — the most commonly used psychological pricing tactic, where prices are set at odd numbers just below round numbers

flexible pricing — different customers pay different prices for the same product

and loyal customers could be given discounts to reward them for their loyalty.

Product line pricing is a tactic whereby several items within a product line are offered at specific price points. A maker of office chairs could offer three models at $300, $550, and $900 with no products priced at levels in between. Hotels practise product line pricing when they set rates at different levels based on room sizes and amenities. Clothing manufacturers do it when they offer different collections of garments at various prices. Ralph Lauren sets separate price points for its Chaps, Polo, and Black Label lines.

With single-price pricing, a retailer or professional sells all its goods and services at the same price. Dollar stores typically use single-price pricing. In effect, this removes the element of price in the consumer's decision process and typically eliminates price-based comparison shopping. A professional might use single-price pricing when he or she sells customer service training seminars at the same price regardless of circumstances or the client's profile.

Bundling involves selling two or more items combined in a single package at a set price. The best example of bundling is the typical fast-food "trio" or "value meal" that usually includes a sandwich, fries, and a soft drink. Services such as hotels also use bundling when they sell weekend packages that include, for example, a room, welcome cocktails, and dinner and breakfast for two, all for a single price. Unbundling is the opposite practice as it limits the number of goods or services that come with the basic offer. To stay with the previous example, some hotels charge for parking instead of bundling it with the price of a room.

With promotional pricing, prices are temporarily reduced from regular prices. Promotional pricing can be used to achieve a number of objectives, including the following:

- To get customers to try the product for the first time: For example, new subscribers to magazines are typically offered prices that are deeply discounted from those for renewing subscribers.

- To increase product consumption: Offering a buy-one-get-the-second-at-half-price deal for a case of 12 cans of soft drinks could result in customers drinking more of the product simply because they have more of it in their refrigerators.

- To offset competitive efforts: Here, marketers try to load customers up with their products to discourage them from buying their competitors' products. For example, when the makers of Edge shave gel learned that Gillette was planning to launch a competing gel product, they initiated a buy-one-get-one-free campaign. The goal was to get two cans of Edge in their customers' bathrooms; since it takes four months on average to use one can, they effectively took their customers out of the market for eight months, thereby blunting Gillette's introduction.

- To liquidate seasonal merchandise: Think of Boxing Day sales.

You're probably now thinking about the price you might charge for your product. At this juncture, it is probably useful to bring in two more concepts that might enlighten your thinking on the subject. Hopefully, your customer analysis has led you to think and feel as your customers do. Now you need to ask yourself how

product line pricing — a tactic whereby several items within a product line are offered at specific price points

single-price pricing — occurs when a retailer or professional sells all its goods and services at the same price

bundling — combining two or more items in a single package at a set price

unbundling — the practice opposite to bundling; limits the number of goods or services that come with a basic offer

promotional pricing — temporarily reducing regular prices

floor price — a price below which the quality will become suspicious and the customer might decide to look elsewhere

ceiling price — the maximum price at which a customer will decide to either postpone the buying decision or seek ways to fulfill needs with substitute products

price elasticity — the fact that different customers will react differently to changes in price

 FAVOURITES

INDUSTRY CANADA
http://strategis.ic.gc.ca/

Industry Canada's website, offering a wealth of resources and advice for job seekers, professionals, artists, and entrepreneurs.

your customers think and feel about price. A customer's floor price is a price below which the quality will become suspicious and the customer might decide to look elsewhere, whereas the ceiling price is the maximum price at which a customer will decide to either postpone the buying decision or seek ways to fulfill needs with substitute products. Price elasticity refers to the fact that different customers will react differently to changes in price. A customer who is price elastic will be very sensitive to any variations in price and will adjust behaviour accordingly. A customer who is price inelastic, on the other hand, will exhibit little change in buying patterns due to price changes. What are your customers' floor and ceiling prices? To what extent are they price sensitive?

NEGOTIATION TACTICS FOR EMPLOYEES

The first step in formulating your pricing strategy as a current or prospective employee is to establish your worth to employers by determining the salary range for positions that interest you. Next, you should set your price objectives including your income and other compensation goals. That's the easy part. For most people, the hard part is negotiating the price that will be in line with your objective. As you'll see, it doesn't have to be so difficult.

The ideal outcome for all salary negotiations is win–win. Your needs are met and so are those of the employer. You both walk away with a positive feeling. Negotiation is a cooperative exercise, and in a good negotiation everyone wins something. In their book *The Only Negotiating Guide You'll Ever Need*, Peter B. Stark and Jane Flaherty provide three helpful guidelines for conducting negotiations that result in win–win situations. They are:

- **Avoid narrowing down the negotiation to one issue:** Focusing on just one issue sets the scene for a win–lose outcome. Yes, salary will likely be the most important issue in your negotiations, but by bringing up other price elements such as vacations, performance reviews, and education allowances you provide the opportunity to juggle the deal points to create a win–win outcome.

- **Realize that your counterpart does not have the same needs and wants as you do:** Failing to do this means you'll be negotiating with the idea that your gain is your counterpart's loss. And vice versa. Prospective employers are not very likely to be looking to hire the candidate with the lowest salary expectations. In addition to the qualifications that you bring to the table, they may be evaluating you on the basis of your creativity and your willingness to work beyond a nine-to-five schedule, to travel extensively, and to roll up your sleeves and do what has to be done even though it's not part of your official job description.

- **Don't assume that you know your counterpart's needs:** When they're in negotiation mode, employers, and for that matter buyers, have implicit and explicit needs. Explicit needs can be satisfied by price and product attributes, for example. Implicit needs involve the employers personally and include such things as feelings of trust; being "right," liked, and respected; a sense of safety and security; and a sense of importance. Explicit needs are often verbalized ("Our ideal candidate has a bachelor's degree in the social sciences and possesses excellent analytical and writing skills"). Implicit needs are not verbalized, but they frequently determine the outcome of a negotiation. How do you get to understand your counterpart's implicit needs and have a better chance of bringing the negotiation to a win–win conclusion? Ask questions and listen closely to the responses. Trust your intuition.

THE IMPORTANCE OF NONVERBAL BEHAVIOUR IN NEGOTIATIONS

Research suggests that as much as 90 percent of the meaning transmitted between two people in face-to-face communications is through nonverbal channels. It's been said that employers decide whether to *not* hire someone or to proceed with the interview with an open mind within less than 15 seconds of meeting a candidate. As a result, in many interviews the employer merely "goes through the motions" to get the meeting over with as quickly and politely as possible. What drives their hasty decisions? Non-verbal behaviour, including body language.

Because most nonverbal behaviour and its resultant communication are unconscious, psychologists claim that it is perceived as being more honest than verbal behaviour, which is more likely to occur at a conscious level. In fact, the perception of unconscious behaviour is an unconscious phenomenon itself. Intuition is rooted in these unnoticed and unfiltered perceptions. Understanding nonverbal behaviour and your responses to it can have a significant impact on the outcome of a negotiation. However, achieving this understanding is not easy. It comes with keen observation, experience, and time.

In his book *Nonverbal Selling Power,* Gerhard Gschwandtner suggests conducting a "body scan" to make sure you are catching the nonverbal signals your counterpart is sending. His formula is to divide the body into five zones: face and head, body, arms, hands, and legs.

FACE AND HEAD

Following are some of the signs to look for. Remember, your counterpart is most likely looking at these very same signs from you!

- **Broken eye contact:** A person who is trying to hide something will tend to avoid or break eye contact when speaking less truthfully
- **Looking past you:** A counterpart who is bored may gaze past you or glance around the room
- **Piercing eye contact:** Someone who is angry with you or feels superior may practise piercing eye contact
- **Steady eye contact:** Maintaining good eye contact usually indicates that a person is being honest and trustworthy
- **Head turned slightly:** A counterpart who is evaluating what you are saying may turn his or her head to one side as if wanting to hear you better
- **Tilted head:** This may indicate that your counterpart is uncertain about what you are saying
- **Nodding:** Someone in agreement with you will usually nod his or her head as you are speaking.
- **Smiling:** A person who is confident and is in agreement will typically smile at you.

 FAVOURITES

ABOUT PERSONAL GROWTH
http://www.about-personal-growth.com
Useful self-help material. Click on the tab 'communication' to find out more about nonverbal communication.

BODY

If your counterpart starts to lean closer to you, you are probably making progress. However, when you say or do things your counterpart disagrees with, he or she will tend to position his or her body away from you. When a counterpart moves side to side, shifting their weight back and forth, this suggests insecurity, nervousness, or doubt.

ARMS

Generally speaking, the more open the position of your counterpart's arms, the more receptive he or she is to the negotiation process. Arms folded tightly across the chest are a sign that he or she is not receptive to what you are communicating. If your counterpart moves away from the table and throws an arm over the back of the chair, it may signal a need for dominance or a negative reaction to something being discussed.

As the negotiation moves on, the arms are one of the best indicators of changes in the nonverbal communication process. For example, at the beginning of the negotiation, your counterpart's arms may be resting openly at the table where you are both sitting. Then when you mention that you would like to have three weeks of paid vacation, your counterpart might take his or her arms off the table and cross them over the chest. This is likely an indication that what you have just said was not well received. If this occurs, you may need to clarify your request or ask your counterpart if he or she has a concern about the three weeks of paid vacation.

HANDS

Unto themselves, hand gestures won't give you a complete picture of what your counterpart is thinking. However, combined with other aspects of body language, they can be very revealing. Look out for these signs.

- **Open palms:** These are generally considered to convey a positive nonverbal message. They indicate that a person has nothing to hide.
- **Hands crossed behind the head:** A sign that your counterpart may have a need for dominance or superiority.
- **"Steepling" of the fingers:** Touching the fingers on one hand to the matching fingers on the opposite hand may be a show of dominance or may indicate that your counterpart has a need to control the negotiation.
- **Hand-wringing:** This is generally an indicator of apprehension, nervousness, or a lack of confidence.
- **Self-touching gestures:** Involuntary touching of the nose, ear, chin, head, or clothing usually indicates general nervousness or insecurity.

LEGS

Believe it or not, crossing your legs can have a disastrous effect on negotiations. In *How to Read a Person Like a Book,* authors Gerard I. Nierenberg and Henry H. Calero reported on a study of sales transactions. They found that out of 2000 videotaped transactions, not one sale was made by people who had their legs crossed. If you want your counterpart to perceive you as cooperative and trustworthy, it's best not to cross your legs. With your legs uncrossed, feet placed flat on the floor, and body tilted slightly toward your counterpart, you will have a much better chance of sending an open, positive signal.

One of the best ways to ensure that your nonverbal behaviour is communicating what you want to get across is to practise. Conduct mock interviews with friends acting as employers. Get their feedback on your body language. Better yet, have someone videotape you during one or more of these interviews to determine how you can improve your nonverbal behaviour. Practise making these improvements until you feel that you're doing the best you can. This alone could give you an enormous advantage over your competitors.

 Myth

Money is the prime motivating factor for entrepreneurs.

 Reality Check

Successful entrepreneurs are primarily driven by the quest for responsibility, achievement, and results rather than by money. **They thrive on a sense of achievement** and out-performing competition. By virtue of their accomplishments they may earn plenty of money, but this is more a by-product of the entrepreneurship process than a driving force behind it.

TALKING PRICE

The most crucial and often the most tension-packed point of any negotiation arrives when the subject turns to price. You and your counterpart have come to the conclusion that there's a fit between what you have to offer and what your counterpart needs. If you agree on price, it's highly likely that a win–win outcome will be the result. If not, a lose–lose outcome is a virtual certainty. Your goal is to get the highest possible price. Your counterpart's is to get the lowest. Let the fun begin!

The first big step in price negotiations is when one of the participants states a price that he or she is willing to accept or pay. As a prospective employee, you would like the employer to table his or her price first. After all, it might be a lot higher than what you were going to ask for. The employer, on the other hand, will typically want you to name your price first. It could very well be lower than what he or she was expecting to pay. In most negotiations, the party with the least power is the one who tables his or her price first. And in most prospective employee–employer negotiations, the employer has the most power. Why? Because they have more knowledge about the position and the responsibilities that go along with it, they have more alternatives, and in most instances they have more time to decide than the applicant. This is why it is so important for prospective employees to gather as much knowledge as possible before entering into salary negotiations, especially about industry salary ranges.

So the employer finally asks you, "What salary do you expect?" Based on your price objectives and equipped with the information that you gathered about salary ranges, you have a number of choices including the following:

- If this is your first job in this field, tabling a number in the low end of the mid-range so that you have room to negotiate down to somewhere in the low range.

- If you have experience in the field, starting with a number in the upper end of the high range.

- Tabling a salary amount at what you believe the employer is willing to pay. You could preface this with, "The more I got to know about this organization, the more I wanted to work here. I really don't want to make salary a major issue."

- You can also attempt to bring your future employer to table a number first: "Oh well, it's hard to put a dollar figure. But I thought about the going market value for someone like me with my qualifications. What do you think that is worth?" Such an answer can stall and win you some time to think of your next answer. (Your future employer will almost certainly know that trick and ask you again to put an actual dollar value on your desired salary.) This will not leave you much negotiating room, but it may help you land the job faster.

Ideally, you and your counterpart will quickly settle on a number that both of you are comfortable with and then move on to negotiating the other terms of employment. On the other hand, if it's clear that you are far apart on the salary issue, your choices include the following:

- Reject the offer outright or ask for time to think about it.

- Accept the salary offer with a commitment from the employer to review your performance within a certain period, say three or six months, and to adjust it to an agreed-upon amount if the review is satisfactory.

- Accept the salary and negotiate more favourable non-salary items such as paid vacation and sick days, education and car allowances, hours of work, and scheduling.

Salary negotiations can be extremely stressful. Potential employers will pick up on any overt or subtle signs of stress on your part: sweating, blushing, stammering, trembling, excessive blinking, and speeded-up speech. Needless to say, this could work against you. Eliminating stress is all but impossible to do, but you can take steps to minimize it and its effects on you. Acquiring knowledge about the organization you'll be negotiating with, the industry in which it operates, and its salary ranges will remove uncertainty and add to your level of confidence. Rehearsing your answers to the types of questions you are likely to be asked during a salary negotiation will make it easier for you to respond in a calm and credible manner. Rehearsing with friends, schoolmates, or co-workers is good. Doing it with someone who has been on the employer side of the table in negotiations is better. Getting eight hours of sleep the night before and working out the day of the negotiation will help put you at your best physically and mentally.

THE OFFER LETTER

Once you've agreed to the terms of employment, get the offer in writing from the employer. Most employers will readily provide you with one. If an employer refuses, this may be a sign that he or she is not fully committed to the agreement that you made. Proceed with caution.

The basic contents of an offer letter are as follows:

- The job or position title
- The base salary
- Other financial compensation such as commissions, bonuses, stock options, and profit-sharing
- Non-financial items including paid vacation; sick days; medical, dental, and life insurance; pension plan; and education allowances
- Timing and frequency of salary and performance reviews

Should you sign the first offer letter you receive? Many offer letters will sometimes include a limit date by which you must accept or reject the offer. Take your time. Ask yourself whether there might be anything else you would want. Nothing prevents you from making a counter-offer: either asking for a slightly larger base salary or asking for some of those other compensation elements described earlier (e.g., a moving allowance).

WAYS TO INCREASE YOUR VALUE (AND PRICE) TO EMPLOYERS

If you're still in school, there are a number of things you can do to maximize your value to potential employers once you graduate, including the following:

- **Gain work experience:** Work experience is proof that you can keep commitments and work with others. Part-time or summer jobs in areas that relate to your career choice are the best.
- **Intern:** The ideal internships are those that will give you experience in the field that you want to work in after graduation. Plus, you'll have relevant experience to communicate on your resume and in job interviews. Many colleges and universities have co-op programs which can help you secure internships.
- **Volunteer:** Doing volunteer work not only can give you valuable experience in many areas including teamwork, fund-raising, event management, and budgeting, but also makes a powerful statement on your resume. By volunteering, you express strong values and the desire and willingness to act on them.
- **Network:** Interning, volunteering, and working at part-time or summer jobs give you the opportunity to meet people who can help you find the job you want upon graduation. Keep in touch with them and, when you can, help them.
- **Make a good impression:** Every step of the hiring process is critical. Convey a professional image in your cover letter and resume, first telephone conversation, appearance and behaviour at initial interviews, nonverbal communication, and conduct after you've been hired.

Restate your career goal:

Restate your marketing objective:

MY Price Objectives

How much you would like to be earning

- within the next year?

- within the next three to five years?

MY Price Strategy: How Will I Achieve My Price Objectives?

How should you price your product now to give you the best chance to reach your objectives?

- Above market

- At market

- Below market

For Employees

What other compensation elements might you want to cover during negotiations?

MY Price Tactics: How Will I Execute My Price Strategy?

How will you convince your target market that you are worth the price you are asking?

How, specifically, will you communicate your price to customers?

What pricing tactics will you use?

	artist	*employee*	*entrepreneur*	*professional*
MY PRICE OBJECTIVES	Within one year of graduation, earn at least $15 000 from the sales of my works.	Earn $35 000 upon graduation.	To generate the bulk of the magazine's $250 000 revenue from advertisers while creating revenue-generating opportunities from readers.	Gross $325 000 in the first year of opening my dental clinic. This covers my fixed costs and pays for an assistant, leaving me with enough to live well for the first year of operation.
MY PRICE STRATEGY	Practise psychological pricing. Establish a base price of $500 and sell no piece for less than that.	Ensure that I maximize my value to potential employers by completing at least one internship in my field and by building my network of industry contacts.	Research what advertisers are currently paying for space in existing magazines. 1) During the six months after launch, charge slightly less than them to penetrate the market then increase prices to market levels. 2) Identify affiliate and pay-per-click programs that will generate revenue every time readers purchase from the affiliate or click on a link or banner.	1) Price my dental services slightly below established dentists in the area to give customers an incentive to try out my services. 2) Give customers a gift when they open an account, come for a regular check-up, and/or refer a new patient.
MY PRICE TACTICS	1) Augment the core product by packaging each work so as to give a perception of higher value. 2) Begin closing each sale with a "suggested retail price" with built-in room for negotiation.	1) Practise and refine my salary negotiation skills with people who have industry experience. 2) Research benefit packages offered in the industry and put together my benefits "wish list."	Create advertising rate card. Sign up for appropriate affiliate and pay-per-click programs.	Regular cleaning: $85 In-chair whitening: $145, etc. Free personal dental hygiene kit when opening account. Free toothbrush and floss with each regular visit.

KEY TERMS

bundling — combining two or more items in a single package at a set price

ceiling price — the maximum price at which a customer will decide to either postpone the buying decision or seek ways to fulfill needs with substitute products

competitive pricing (also known as pricing parity and status quo pricing) — reducing the emphasis on price by matching competitors' prices and concentrating marketing efforts on the other three elements of the marketing mix

flexible pricing — different customers pay different prices for the same product

floor price — a price below which the quality will become suspicious and the customer might decide to look elsewhere

odd pricing — the most commonly used psychological pricing tactic, where prices are set at odd numbers just below round numbers

penetration pricing strategy — a strategy whereby low prices are used as a major marketing tool to enter a new market

price elasticity — the fact that different customers will react differently to changes in price

price skimming — a pricing strategy that involves setting relatively high prices compared to your competitors; often used to enter a market for products with little or no competition

product line pricing — a tactic whereby several items within a product line are offered at specific price points

profits — whatever is left from revenues after all expenses have been paid

promotional pricing — temporarily reducing regular prices

psychological pricing — based on the belief that certain prices or price ranges make products appealing

single-price pricing — occurs when a retailer or professional sells all its goods and services at the same price

unbundling — the practice opposite to bundling; limits the number of goods or services that come with a basic offer

value pricing — emphasizes the benefits a product delivers in comparison to the price and quality levels of competing offerings

How Marketing-Savvy Have You Become?

1. Put yourself in the following position: Your career objective is to work in management consulting with a focus on conducting and analyzing the research that is frequently part of consulting projects. You have a large family and network of friends in the city where you live and do not want to move. You're involved in a number of community activities that take up a lot of your spare time and you enjoy these tremendously. Whatever leisure time you would have left over after working an eight-hour day, you'd like to spend with your boyfriend or girlfriend. You don't live in a major national business centre and job opportunities in management consulting do not come up very often. However, partly as a result of the excellent personal marketing plan that you created, one of the few international consulting firms in your city has offered you the type of position you've been wanting at a salary level that satisfies you. Everything seems perfect until your prospective employer says: "While the position will be primarily research-based, we need to be able to rely on you to handle periodic overloads from our other offices in this country. That will involve working late hours and weekends from time to time as well as travelling to their locations. Expect to be out of town 90 days a year on average for at least the first three years after starting here." What would your response be?

2. You're a sculptor and have created two identical pieces that you have put up for sale, using word-of-mouth to communicate their availability. In short order you get a call from a former client who meets with you and when she sees the piece, falls in love with it. "How much?" she asks. When you answer $900, she takes out her chequebook and pays you the asking price. Several months go by until you receive a call about the second piece. The potential customer is actually a friend of the person to whom you sold the first piece, and when you tell him the price is $900, he replies, "The most I'm willing to pay is $800." On one hand, you'd really like to sell the piece and could use the $800. On the other, you're concerned about how the first customer will react if she finds out that you charged her friend $100 less. What choices do you have in this situation? Which one would you act on?

3. You've just completed a degree in photography and have received outstanding grades in all of your courses. Your professors have consistently praised you on your creativity and the outstanding quality of your work. You're planning to launch

your own business that will concentrate on photographing special occasions, particularly weddings, anniversaries, and other celebrations. What are the opportunities and risks represented by the skimming, penetration, and competitive pricing approaches?

4. You are an interior designer for office spaces, and your business has done well since you launched it two years ago. All of your clients have been local businesses and the average fee that you've received from them is $500 per individual office. One of your former clients is married to a vice-president of a large national company; she calls to arrange a meeting with you, during which she tells you that she will be in charge of a project to redesign all of the 200 offices in her building. It will start sometime within the next 18 months. She also tells you that she would like you to quote on the project once she gets the go-ahead for it. Then she asks you to quote on redesigning four offices to be redone immediately. When you quote your regular $500 fee, she seems shocked and says, "Our business relationship could expand way beyond four offices. I'll soon be in charge of redoing 200 more. Five hundred dollars is way beyond what I would expect to pay for the four offices we have to do now and certainly for the upcoming 200. Three hundred dollars is more in our ballpark." What alternative responses would be appropriate here? Which one do you favour? Why?

NOW WHAT?

You've taken the second step in creating your marketing mix by setting objectives and strategies for price. This is probably the first time you've had to take a cold hard look at what you think you are worth in the marketplace. Next, you need to address the third P in the marketing mix: place. Whether you're an artist, entrepreneur, professional, or job seeker, you need to determine where you want to be and where you want your product to be. That's what we'll do in the next chapter.

Developing a sense of place

Meet Kim Tien Huynh. Kim Tien has always been goal-driven. She recalls reading an article in 1998 that predicted by 2004–2005 China would experience strong demand for qualified business professionals. That article inspired her—and since she was always up for a challenge, she set her sights on China.

While attending the John Molson School of Business, where she majored in marketing, Kim Tien joined the marketing co-op program, through which she got to work at Shell Canada, Bank of Montreal, and Imperial Tobacco. She supplemented this experience with various summer jobs in promotions, working on the Pepsi Taste Patrol and similar events. Upon graduation, she found her first job through Jobboom.com as a marketing coordinator with a high-tech company. Her dream of going to China had not faded: after taking classes in Mandarin, she left for China at the beginning of the summer of 2005. Her ultimate goal was to end up in Shanghai, as her research indicated there were many jobs for qualified foreigners in that city. So, Kim Tien left her full-time job, family, boyfriend, and friends to pursue her dream.

Her arrival in Shanghai was a rude awakening. In regular emails to her friends (and former professors!) she documented her attempts at finding a job, securing lodging, and making friends. Something as seemingly simple as finding an apartment became a fun, if at times frustrating, adventure. She learned the importance of "being at the right place at the right time," as finding a job in Shanghai is more often than not a matter of making contacts and being seen by the right people. She managed to find work at an insurance company but never really felt like it was the right place for her. So, she decided to go on a backpacking pilgrimage across the province of Yunnan. This "time out" helped her realize that what she was good at was not necessarily making her happy. However, when she got back to Shanghai, she couldn't help experiencing that "home sweet home" feeling. Although she still enjoyed the corporate marketing environment, she now realized that she likes and needs to interact with people—and she was more convinced than ever that her future, whatever that might be, was in China.

We asked Kim Tien what three tips she would like to share with readers of *Marketing Yourself*. Here are her thoughts:

1. *Part-time work and volunteering add a lot to your resume.* I volunteered for Tennis Canada for seven years and it was terrific experience. I watched world-class tennis, and most importantly I met great people who helped me to extend my network of contacts.

2. *Live your life fully; enjoy the here and now.* Don't worry about things you can't control. Don't waste your time stressing out. Seize opportunities as they come and enjoy every minute.

3. *Learn to be comfortable wherever you are.* Life puts you where you need to be and takes care of you, but you have to learn to be comfortable in the place where you end up—whether backpacking in the rain or schmoozing your way through a room.

What happens when you graduate from a leading university in your field but you don't want to end up in the hustle and bustle of a big city? You do as the new graduate in the following anecdote did: pack up and move to the Norwegian countryside!

At age 24, I not only had received an associate degree from l'Institut de tourisme et d'hôtellerie du Québec, but also had completed a master's of science in hospitality marketing at Cornell University. I was faced with a tough decision. Attractive job offers were coming in from hotel operators and educational institutions located in places such as New York, Chicago, and Los Angeles. Two of them stood out: one from a renowned school in Lausanne, Switzerland, the other from a lesser known school on the western coast of Norway. In the end, I decided to pack up and visit all the companies and educational institutions that had extended the offers. All the places I went to were very nice; every organization had an enticing compensation package; and everyone I met was friendly. By the time I reached the Norwegian School of Hotel Administration, my last stop, I was getting tired and had become stressed out by the impending decision I had to make. After spending three short days in beautiful Stavanger, however, I fell in love with its people, landscape, and lifestyle. The thought of living in Norway on the edge of the North Sea appealed to me. My immediate supervisor would be a dedicated older woman, herself a foreigner. I knew I could work well with her and learn from her. I ended up working there for two years, away from the hectic pace that would have awaited me had I accepted any one of the other offers I had received.

Despite my privileged situation, the first six months were difficult. When I first visited Norway, it was in mid-June with close to 24 hours of daylight, which was incredibly energizing. Little was I prepared for winter, with its virtually perpetual darkness. Learning the language had proven more difficult than I had anticipated, and this limited my social interactions. Toward the end of my first year, I was chatting with a friend and found myself asking, "What am I doing here?" She countered, "Every period of life has its own richness; look harder to find it." Although her advice wasn't what I wanted to hear, she was right. I had totally neglected to appreciate that my employer had given me freedom to do what I wanted to do. It was a unique chance that few junior educators would have been afforded anywhere else. So I began to develop new courses and seminars that ended up serving me well beyond that first job. I also realized that I had neglected to take advantage of my location, so I decided to travel across Norway and the rest of Scandinavia. At the end of my two years, I had travelled extensively and sampled the many delights of Norway and its neighbouring countries. I had also carved out a niche for myself and my reputation was beginning to spread; I knew it was time to move on. On May 12, 1994, when the plane took off for France, where my next job awaited me, I was sad to leave friends and colleagues behind. But I knew that I was ready to move on and that another place, another challenge awaited me. Oh, just in case you haven't figured it out: I'm Jordan Le Bel, the co-author of this book!

YOU WILL:

- know what constitutes place in the marketing mix

- understand the relationships between place and the other elements of the marketing mix

- know how to set your place objectives

- understand basic place strategies

PLACE AND THE MARKETING MIX

place — one of the four Ps of marketing; concerned with issues of distribution, channel management, and location selection

Place, or distribution, is concerned with getting your product to your customers and making it available when they want it. One aspect of this third P in the marketing mix is the physical movement of goods, which in some cases can involve rather elaborate logistics. Say you are a small producer of gourmet cheeses located in a rural area. You'd most likely need to engage one or more intermediaries who will sell and distribute your products to various retailers and restaurants. You could also allow customers to purchase directly from your website. This would require you to use the services of a courier company and to purchase the packaging material necessary to ensure that your cheeses arrive fresh at customers' doors. Another aspect of place is concerned with the appropriateness of various locations and distribution approaches for your particular product. A new artist, for instance, may not mind leaving some of his or her work on consignment at a local restaurant, hoping to sell some paintings. However, an accomplished painter would prefer to deal with established galleries, perhaps even giving one gallery exclusivity to sell his or her work.

As we did with product and price, we'll be looking at place from the perspective of entrepreneurs, artists, professionals, and employees. The two key components of place are as follows:

- **Distribution:** Moving goods and services from producers to consumers
- **Marketing channel:** Also called a distribution channel, this is a set of interdependent organizations that facilitate the transfer of ownership as products move from the producer to the end user.

As you will discover in our discussion of place, its role is quite different for goods, services, and people.

MARKETING CHANNELS AND MARKETING STRATEGY

marketing channel — a set of intermediaries organized to ensure the movement of goods from producer to end-consumers

Marketing channels play key roles in the marketing strategies of organizations and individuals because these channels provide the means by which organizations and individuals make their products available to buyers and users. Channels fulfill four important functions. First, they make the exchange process easier by reducing the number of marketplace contacts necessary to make a sale. To illustrate, let's say you just saw a commercial for McCain Rising Crust Pizza that triggered your taste buds to the point that you had to have one *now*. You go to the nearest food store, say, Wal-Mart, where you'll find the complete line of McCain pizzas. Wal-Mart forms part of the channel that brings you, a potential buyer, and McCain, the manufacturer, together to complete the exchange process. Now imagine a world without retailers like Wal-Mart. Try to imagine the complexity, for McCain and consumers alike, to do business. McCain produces hundreds of products and varieties. How would it get these products to the millions of consumers who want to buy them? A carefully planned and executed distribution strategy enables McCain, via Wal-Mart and other retailers, to satisfy the demand for its products.

Second, marketing channels adjust for discrepancies in the market's assortment of products through a process called sorting.

Single producers tend to maximize the quantities they make of a limited line of goods. For example, Kimberly-Clark manufactures household and personal paper products, most of which are marketed under the Kleenex brand. A single buyer, 7-Eleven for instance, needs a limited quantity of a wide selection of merchandise. In addition to Kleenex paper products, it needs an enormous range of other products. Sorting alleviates the discrepancies such as the one between Kimberly-Clark and 7-Eleven by channelling products to suit both the buyer's (7-Eleven, in this case) and the producer's (Kimberly-Clark) needs.

The third function of marketing channels involves standardizing exchange transactions by setting expectations for products and the transfer process itself. This can include delivery schedules, purchase quantities, and payment terms. Standardization helps make transactions efficient and fair. The online travel industry, which includes Expedia, Travelocity, Priceline, and CheapTickets, is an example of a channel that standardizes the transactions for airline tickets, hotels, car rentals, and vacation packages.

The last channel function is to facilitate searches by both buyers and sellers. Buyers look for specific products to fill their needs, while sellers attempt to learn what buyers want. Channels bring buyers and sellers together to complete the exchange process. eBay is a perfect example of a channel member that does this.

TYPES OF MARKETING CHANNELS

The first step in choosing a marketing channel is to determine which type of channel will best meet the seller's goals and the distribution needs of customers. Exhibit 8.1 provides an overview of the major channels available to marketers of consumer and business products.

Most, but not all, channel options involve at least one marketing intermediary. Marketing intermediaries, also called middlemen, are organizations or individuals that operate between producers and end users. Examples include wholesalers and retailers. A short marketing channel is made up of few intermediaries, while a long one has many. Business products tend to move through short channels because of the relatively small number of business purchasers. Service providers market primarily through short channels because

> **marketing intermediaries —** organizations along the distribution channel that ensure the movement of goods from producer to end-consumers; can include import agents, wholesalers, brokers, retailers, and others

EXHIBIT 8.1   Overview of Marketing Channels

CONSUMER CHANNELS	BUSINESS CHANNELS	ALTERNATIVE CHANNELS
• Direct • Retail • Wholesaler • Agent/broker	• Direct • Industrial • Agent/broker • Agent/broker industrial	• Multiple • Nontraditional • Strategic alliances

Source: From *Marketing* (with InfoTrac) 8th edition by LAMB/HAIR/MCDANIEL. 2006. Reproduced with permission of South-Western, a division of Thomson Learning: www.thomsonrights.com. Fax 800 730-2215.

> **direct channel** — channel that
> carries products directly from a
> producer to the business user or
> consumer

> **direct selling** — a marketing
> strategy in which the producer
> establishes direct sales contact
> with the product's final users

their product is intangible and because of their need to maintain personal relationships within their channels. Consumer products, such as clothing, tend to move through long channels from manufacturer, to importer, to distributor, to retailer. Following is a brief description of the major types of channels.

DIRECT SELLING

A direct channel carries products directly from a producer to the business user or consumer. This channel forms part of a direct selling marketing strategy in which the producer establishes direct sales contact with the product's final users. Professionals—for example, doctors, lawyers, accountants, and psychologists—typically sell their products directly to their customers. So might artists, although many of them move their products through agents and retailers.

Direct selling plays a major role in business-to-business marketing as many companies sell to other firms through their own dedicated sales forces. Direct selling is also a factor in consumer markets. Companies such as Avon, Tupperware, and Dell use it as a key component of their marketing strategies.

CHANNELS USING INTERMEDIARIES

Despite its simplicity, direct selling is not appropriate for all products. Some products are intended for sale in different geographic areas or countries that have an enormous number of potential end users. Other categories of products rely on repeat purchase. Producers of these may choose more efficient and less expensive alternatives to direct selling. Five of these alternatives are as follows:

- **Producer to retailer to consumer:** Large producers such as Kraft and Colgate Palmolive sell directly to large retailers such as Safeway and Loblaws, which in turn sell to consumers. (They use longer channels to sell to smaller retailers.) Some artists sell their works through galleries. Professionals such as personal fitness trainers, massage therapists, and nutritionists frequently sell their services through health clubs.

- **Producer to wholesaler to retailer to consumer:** This is the traditional channel for consumer goods. Wholesalers carry goods from thousands of small producers with limited product lines and sell them to local retailers.

- **Producer to wholesaler to business user:** This type of channel is created when similar characteristics in organizational markets attract marketing intermediaries to operate between producers and business users.

- **Producer to agent to wholesaler to retailer to consumer:** In markets served by many small companies, an agent performs the basic function of bringing the buyer and seller together. The agent represents a producer by seeking markets for its products or a wholesaler by locating a supply source.

- **Producer to broker to wholesaler to business user:** Brokers serve the business market when small producers attempt to market their products through large wholesalers.

You can imagine that within longer channels, there often takes place a visible struggle between manufacturers and intermediaries to keep control over price and other marketing decisions. Manufacturers can retain some price control in various ways. Printing "Suggested Retail Price" on a package is one way to prevent retailers from charging more or less for the product. Manufacturers may also enter exclusivity arrangements with some wholesalers and retailers. They could decide to sell directly to consumers. (However, this may incur the risk of antagonizing retailers and lost sales.) Developing strong brands is one way manufacturers can keep some control over intermediaries, as wholesalers and retailers may be keen on making these brands available to their customers.

CHANNEL STRATEGY DECISIONS

Organizations and individuals face several strategic decisions in choosing channels and intermediaries for their products. Selecting a specific channel is the most basic of these. They must also make decisions about the desired level of distribution intensity.

SELECTING A MARKETING CHANNEL

A variety of factors come into play here: market factors, product factors, and organizational factors. Table 8.1 breaks these factors down and illustrates their influence on channel decisions.

The factors listed in Table 8.1 provide a good opportunity to emphasize, as we did in Chapter 5, the inter-relatedness of the four Ps of the marketing mix and their sensitivity to environmental and competitive factors. Nowhere is this more evident than when facing place-related decisions. As you develop your distribution strategy,

TABLE 8.1 Factors Influencing Marketing Channel Strategies		
	Characteristics of Short Channels	**Characteristics of Long Channels**
MARKET FACTORS	Business users	Consumers
	Geographically concentrated	Geographically dispersed
	Extensive technical knowledge and regular servicing required	Little technical knowledge and regular servicing not required
	Large orders	Small orders
PRODUCT FACTORS	Perishable	Durable
	Complex	Standardized
	Expensive	Inexpensive
ORGANIZATIONAL FACTORS	Manufacturer has adequate resources to perform channel functions	Manufacturer lacks adequate resources to perform channel functions
	Broad product line	Limited product line
	Channel control important	Channel control not important

Source: From *Contemporary Marketing* 1/E by BOONE/KURTZ. 2007. Reproduced with permission of Nelson, a division of Thomson Learning: www.thomsonrights.com. Fax 800 730-2215

distribution intensity — the number of intermediaries through which a producer distributes its products in a particular market

you may decide that you need to be where the competition is, as do most coffee shops. You may have a perishable product like fresh flowers that must handled quickly and with extreme care. You may have chosen to use a prestige pricing strategy and therefore need to carefully select retailers and locations that are consistent with your desired image. Your new product may have a high adoption rate, which will require you to blanket the geographic area in which it's sold before competitors introduce a new version or substitute product. All these factors impact your distribution decisions.

Distribution intensity refers to the number of intermediaries through which a producer distributes its products in a particular market. It varies along a continuum of three general categories: intensive distribution, selective distribution, and exclusive distribution. The optimal outcome of distribution intensity decisions is to achieve a level of market coverage that is in line with the goals of the organization or individual, the type of product, and the consumer segments in the target market.

Start-ups and small businesses must also take production capacity as well as human and financial resources into consideration when making decisions about channels and distribution intensity. While broad-scale distribution can result in high sales, the enterprise needs to be able to produce and deliver its products in the quantities ordered and on time. Getting an order from the Home Depot for 100 000 of your products for delivery in 30 days might be cause for celebration. But if you can produce only 5000 units per month, you're going to have one big, unhappy customer who may never buy from you again if you fail to deliver on time. Less intensive distribution may be in order here. The services provided by intermediaries are not free of charge. However, if you don't have a sales force or if the costs associated with hiring one are beyond your means, intermediaries may be the solution.

intensive distribution — a strategy that aims to have a product distributed through all available channels in a trade area

Intensive distribution is a strategy that aims to have a product distributed through all available channels in a trade area. It is particularly suitable for products with wide appeal across broad groups of consumers. Bottled water, candy bars, dry cleaners, and gasoline are examples.

selective distribution strategy —strategy where organizations and individuals choose a limited number of outlets in a market area to sell its products

Under a selective distribution strategy, organizations and individuals choose a limited number of outlets in a market area to sell its products. This alternative can enhance the product's image and minimize price-cutting among retailers. Examples include luxury fragrance brands such as Yves Saint Laurent, which are sold exclusively in major department stores, and premium sound systems such as Bang & Olufsen, which are distributed through high-end specialty retailers. Selective distribution may be a viable alternative for individuals and organizations with limited resources. Once sales and profits reach levels that can support increased production capacity, distribution intensity could be increased.

exclusive distribution — strategy where a producer may decide to give the exclusive rights to a wholesaler or retailer to sell its products in a geographic region or country

With exclusive distribution, a producer may decide to give the exclusive rights to a wholesaler or retailer to sell its products in a geographic region or country. On one hand, this will make its products harder to find. On the other, this may make the product seem more valuable. Swiss-based manufacturers of top-of-the-line watch brands such as Blancpain, Piaget, and Vacheron Constantin distribute their products through only one retail store in many cities. Artists frequently make their works available in one gallery or studio.

Myth

Successful people first decide the type of work they would like to do and use that decision to determine where to live.

Reality Check

Many if not most people choose location first and then look to establish careers in those locations. A 2002 survey of 4000 recent college graduates reported in the *Wall Street Journal* found that **75 percent of the graduates identified location as more important** than the availability of jobs when choosing a place to live.

RETAIL LOCATIONS

If you'll be selling goods and services directly to your final customers, having one or more retail locations may be part of your strategy. Your career plan may actually require you to have a retail outlet. This would be the case if your goal is to own and operate a restaurant, a fashion outlet, or a health food store. It could also be the case if you intend to provide services such as counselling, income tax filing, and dentistry directly to customers. For services and professionals, distribution decisions typically focus on location, so let's begin there.

LOCATION

First and foremost, where a retail outlet is located can have an enormous impact on the traffic that will be drawn to it. Being in a major shopping mall or on a busy downtown street will expose an outlet to thousands of potential customers annually. Being in the right place in a mall or at street level—say, next to a major department store—will result in even more exposure. This in turn could result in a significant reduction in promotion expenditures as less advertising will be needed to make people aware of your store's existence. Location also affects how organizations and individuals are perceived. Locating a clothing store in an exclusive neighbour-hood can lend an aura of exclusivity about the merchandise and the store itself.

Convenience is a feature of your location you should not over-look. Why? Because unless you give them a very compelling reason (e.g., if yours is a very desirable specialty product), your customers will typically expend only a modest amount of effort to find you and shop at your outlet. If getting to your store or website is too complicated or time-consuming, your customers will likely find a more convenient way of fulfilling their needs. This is precisely why, as part of its distribution strategy, Starbucks has often opened coffee shops on every corner of busy intersections in cities such as New York. The company realized that many potential customers were unlikely to cross the street and go out of their way to get their coffee fix.

As you've probably figured out by now, location has an enormous impact on real estate expenses whether they are rental or purchase costs. So while the exposure and image benefits of a prime location may be very desirable, it's crucial to determine if they're really necessary and affordable.

SIZE

The decision of how big a retail outlet should be is based on two main factors: function and aesthetics. The store needs to be large enough to display merchandise to its best advantage, to allow customers to shop in comfort, to have storage space for replacement inventory, to accommodate a check-out counter or other payment facility, to allow for any necessary changing rooms or waiting areas, and to help create an ambience that complements the products and brand. The bigger the space, the higher the purchase price or rental costs. Plus, heating, air conditioning, and lighting expenses increase with outlet size. As a result, a balance needs to be struck between space requirements and the financial resources available to pay for them.

Professionals also need to consider size carefully. Recall that in our discussion of service quality, we pointed out the intangibility of services and how customers often use other cues such as the ambience of where the service is delivered to evaluate its quality. If you're a professional you need to consider how much space you'll need and where the line of visibility (i.e., the portion that customers see and the portion that serves as a back office, which clients typically do not see) will be. Your back office needs to be large enough to store files as well as other material and equipment. A roomy, well-lit, and tastefully furnished office will likely suggest to potential clients that you are successful and well-established. If a large office space is prohibitively expensive (especially during your first few years in business), you may want to consider other ways to convey professionalism—such as the first impressions created by your lobby or receptionist, your décor, and the certificates, diplomas, and awards hanging on the walls.

RENT

Most retail spaces are rented, and usually rental rates are expressed as an annual amount per square foot. For example, assume a store size of 25 feet by 40 feet, or 1000 square feet in total. In a neighbourhood strip mall, rent could be as low as $10 per square foot or $10 000 per year, depending on the location within the mall and the amount of frontage or size of display windows. At the other extreme, rents in major regional shopping malls can be as much as $200 per square foot or $200 000 annually—or more. The price of visibility and prestige! When faced with a rental decision, it is useful to do a quick reverse calculation and ask yourself how much in gross sales or revenues you need to generate in order to cover your monthly rental expenses. Consider the advertisements for two retail spaces in New York City shown in Table 8.2. The 200-square-foot kiosk in Times Square will be exposed to hundreds of thousands of people who walk by every week. But at $17 000 per month, how many ice cream cones will you need to sell just to make your rent payment? Or consider the larger 2000-square-foot space with 20 feet of very desirable frontage in SoHo. How many pairs of shoes, paintings, or neckties will you have to sell or how many haircuts or spa therapy treatments would you need to deliver in order to make $14 000 in rent payments every month?

Landlords quote rents on both a net and gross basis. Net refers to the basic monthly cost of occupying a space. Gross includes what are referred to as common area expenses, including your space's share of property taxes; security; parking lot maintenance; heat, light, and power for non-rented spaces; and insurance. Gross rents can be up to 50 percent more than net rents, so it's important to be clear on which one is being quoted. Most leases are for terms of between three and five years. Before signing one, do your best to make sure that the space you're renting fits in with your medium- and long-term plans.

OTHER CONSIDERATIONS

Here are some important questions that need to be answered after you have come to terms on location, size, and rent.

- Lease renewal or termination—When signing a lease, make sure to have a provision for early termination. What happens if business slows down and you can't make ends meet? You want to be able to exit the lease without burdensome financial penalties. Likewise, if all goes well, you may want to have the right of first refusal or the opportunity to renew at your lease's end before the landlord offers the space to someone else.

- How much construction will be required to get the space to the condition that will be needed? How much will this cost? To what extent will you and the landlord share in any construction costs?

- Does the space come with heating, air conditioning, and ventilation equipment? If not, how much will this cost to install and who will pay for the installation?

- How much will fixtures such as display racks, desks, storage cabinets, counters, and shelving cost?

TABLE 8.2 **Two Retail Spaces in New York City**

Times Square	SOHO
Kiosk retail space in the center of Times Square on Broadway	2000 square feet with 20' frontage. $14 000 monthly rental. All uses considered. Landmark district. Beautiful store in move in condition. High ceilings with original tin, new tiled bathroom, finished original wood floor, skylight and kitchenette. Escalations are 4% compounded annually plus increases in real estate taxes. 1000 sf storage basement included.
200 sq. ft.—$17 000 per month	
Best for currency exchange, ice cream store, news/magazines stand or any other business serving tourists. Will consider food (no cooking).	
Source: http://www.aboveny.com	Source: www.findnyoffice.com

Chapter 8 — Creating Your Place Strategy

- How much will equipment such as computers, cash registers, and printers cost?

- Is there access to the outlet for handicapped people? Will modifications and additions need to be made to the store's interior to accommodate their needs?

- Does the space have employee washrooms? If these are needed and are not in the space, how much will they cost to install and who will pay for them?

- Does the space have the required number of electrical outlets and water faucets? If not, how much will installation cost and at whose expense will it be?

- Is there adequate parking for customers and employees? Can your suppliers make deliveries pretty easily?

- Are there any municipal zoning laws that may prohibit or hinder the operation of a business such as yours in the space? You also need to look into laws regarding signage. Most municipalities and malls have very strict codes for the size, colour, and type of sign you can put outside your store.

- Are there any regulations concerning your hours of operations? Here municipal, provincial, and state regulations must be taken into consideration. Mall owners may also impose or restrict hours of operation.

- If you are renting in a mall, you may want to negotiate a clause that limits businesses that are similar to yours from coming into the mall. If you're a clothing store you may not be able to prevent another clothing store from opening, but if you're an accountant or spa, landlords may give you exclusivity.

As you can see, selecting a location and building out a retail outlet can be a complex and expensive process. Before making the final decision on a particular store, talk to the owners or managers of nearby outlets to get their assessments of the quantity and quality of traffic. Observe the flow of traffic during peak and non-peak hours. Speak with other tenants in the building in which you are considering locating your outlet to see if there are any red flags you should be aware of, such as maintenance and security lapses. Finally, consider using the services of your own real estate agent to help you negotiate lease terms and conditions, an interior designer to ensure that the space will be as functional and aesthetically pleasing as it needs to be, and a lawyer to advise you about any potentially troublesome clauses in the lease of which you should be aware.

PLACE AND EMPLOYEES

Up to this point, our discussion of place has focused on the strategic and tactical issues facing businesses, professionals, and artists. When it comes to place strategy as it relates to employees, two of the key questions that need to be addressed are: Where are the opportunities in your field of interest? and What types of organizations are most suitable to your needs and wants?

Myth

The recruitment tool most commonly used by employers is ads in major daily newspapers.

Reality Check

Doing your research includes checking out more than the big newspapers. Increasingly, **employers are using websites and bulletin boards to announce job opportunities.** Make sure to check them out. Not only will you get a feel for what is offered and how much a particular job pays, but you never know what you might find. Kim Tien, spotlighted in this chapter's opening vignette, found her first job on www.jobboom.com.

WHERE ARE THE OPPORTUNITIES?

You may be perfectly satisfied with where you are living now and there may be abundant job opportunities there in your field of interest. So for the time being, a change of place may not be part of your career plan. On the other hand, what if where you're living now doesn't have an abundance of opportunities in your chosen field? For example, your objective could be to become a securities analyst in one of the world's major financial centres, to work as a designer with an international clothing manufacturer, to be an engineer at a leading software developer, or to conduct research at a government laboratory. If opportunities in these areas do not exist where you live, to pursue your career goal you'll likely have to move—in other words, create a new place strategy.

To help you develop your place strategy, here are some suggestions.

- If you don't know where the opportunities in your area are, do the necessary research to find out.

- If you've never been to the countries or cities where the opportunities are, consider doing a school term in one of them as part of an exchange program. Alternatively, take a vacation in one or more of them.

- Get a clear idea of the economics of living in another place. The cost of living in many cities is extremely expensive. New York, London, Paris, San Francisco, Vancouver, Boston, and Hong Kong are examples. Can you earn enough to cover rent and other expenses? If not, what are the alternatives? (For example, finding a roommate.)

- If you are thinking about working in another country, determine the legal requirements for being permitted to work there and begin taking the necessary steps to conform to these.

- If you conclude that it may not be economically or legally feasible for you to work in the country or city of your choice at this time, think about working in an area that is considered a stepping stone to your ultimate destination. In the field of advertising, Chicago, Miami, and Toronto are regarded as stepping stones to New York. In software engineering and design, Montreal and Boston are seen by some employers as steps along the way to Silicon Valley.

WHAT TYPES OF ORGANIZATIONS?

Ideally, the company or organization in which you'll be employed will have a size, structure, and culture that fits in with your needs, skills, personality, and working style. Some people prefer to work in environments with relatively few fellow employees. Others like the presence of many co-workers. Some of us like formalized structures where codes of behaviour are clearly spelled out and conformity to them is expected and rewarded. Many large corporations have this type of structure and have cultures that encourage employees to socialize with each other, often to the exclusion of other people. Some organizational structures and cultures are not well defined and the emphasis is more on getting the job done right, on budget, and on time rather than on how the job gets done. In these organizations, employees are expected to manage their time on their own and, for the most part, have the flexibility to work on their own schedules. While the structure and culture may appear to be loose, there is little or no tolerance for falling short on quality, missing deadlines, or exceeding budgets. This type of culture will appeal to people who are highly self-disciplined and enjoy a high degree of independence.

Some organizations are rooted in teamwork while others are characterized by people working independently. Some have well-defined long-term business strategies where everyone seemingly works single-mindedly to execute them. Others have poorly defined or ever-changing strategies and seem to operate in a constant state of chaos. In some organizations, chaos occupies a large portion of the cultural makeup because of the very nature of the businesses they are in. Working in professional sports, the media, entertainment, hospitality, event planning, consulting, emergency medicine, law, and public relations usually involves dealing with chaos on a regular basis because of unexpected client emergencies, uncontrollable events, and seemingly unrealistic deadlines. As one of our ad agency copywriter acquaintances somewhat jadedly expressed it, "Advertising is all about boredom punctuated by moments of panic." If unpredictable schedules, frequent and daunting challenges, and seemingly impossible due dates appeal to you, these types of organizations may be attractive to you.

An effective way to determine in which types of organizational structure and culture you will be your happiest and most productive is to do the self-assessment tests available on the Marketing Yourself website and take the time to apply the results to yourself.

SAMPLE PLACE OBJECTIVES, STRATEGIES, AND TACTICS

	artist	*employee*	*entrepreneur*	*professional*
MY PLACE OBJECTIVES	Expose 30 000 potential customers to my photographs	Investigate Toronto, Boston, and London as possible places for employment and living	Since the product (i.e., a magazine) is online, the place component would deal with how the magazine will be found by potential readers. This then becomes a promotion issue.	Within five years, open two more dental clinics, each with two chairs. In each one, rent out one of the chairs to an associate.
MY PLACE STRATEGY	Place my photographs in selected upscale locations to appeal to the type of clientele most likely to be interested in them	Visit Toronto and Boston. Read about London and talk to contacts who have experienced life in these cities		Choose locations far enough from my first clinic so as not to cannibalize on my existing business and yet close enough for me to be able to manage all three locations. Ideally, location should be in a neighbourhood with high-income families.
MY PLACE TACTICS	1) Lend or rent my photographs to upscale bars and clubs 2) Place them in lobbies of mid-size companies with reputation for innovation 3) Showcase my work on the Internet and offer it for sale via a professionally designed website	1) Determine the cost of living in these cities by checking out newspaper classified ads for living accommodations 2) Investigate work and immigration permits and requirements		Retain the services of a commercial real estate broker to help me scout good locations and negotiate leases; engage the services of a designer to prepare cost estimates for preparing spaces for my needs.

MY Place Objectives

Where, geographically speaking, would you like to work

- upon graduation?

- in the next three to five years?

In what type of environment (e.g., organizational culture) would you like to be?

How will your place strategy contribute to or enhance other elements of your marketing mix?

If you are or will be a professional, artist, or entrepreneur selling goods or services, what will be your distribution objectives?

MY Place Strategy: How Will I Achieve My Place Objectives?

Would studying or working abroad, for example, help you attain your place objectives?

How many outlets will you have to open to achieve your place objective? Where will they be located? When will they be opened?

What type of channel strategy will you employ? What intermediaries will you use, if any?

MY Place Tactics: How Will I Execute My Place Strategy?

If studying or working abroad is part of your strategy, what will you do make sure this happens? When will you do it?

If your strategy calls for opening retail outlets, how will you go about doing this?

If your strategy calls for getting distribution through a number of retailers, how will you get them to carry and display your product?

KEY TERMS

direct channel — channel that carries products directly from a producer to the business user or consumer

direct selling — a marketing strategy in which the producer establishes direct sales contact with the product's final users

distribution intensity — the number of intermediaries through which a producer distributes its products in a particular market

exclusive distribution — strategy where a producer may decide to give the exclusive rights to a wholesaler or retailer to sell its products in a geographic region or country

intensive distribution — a strategy that aims to have a product distributed through all available channels in a trade area

marketing channel — a set of intermediaries organized to ensure the movement of goods from producer to end-consumers

marketing intermediaries — organizations along the distribution channel that ensure the movement of goods from producer to end-consumers; can include import agents, wholesalers, brokers, retailers, and others

place — one of the four Ps of marketing; concerned with issues of distribution, channel management, and location selection

selective distribution strategy — strategy where organizations and individuals choose a limited number of outlets in a market area to sell its products

How Marketing-Savvy Have You Become?

1. In your own words, describe the relationships between place and the other three elements of the marketing mix.

2. You've decided to open a retail store, and after researching several potential locations find that it seems landlords are all offering the same terms and conditions. You visit one final location, and when the subject of rent comes up in your conversation with the landlord, she says— unlike the others—that she will build out the space to your specifications, install an air conditioner, and give you three months' free rent. Monthly rent will be approximately the same as for the other spaces you looked at. As this seems too good to be true, what other factors can you use to evaluate her offer before agreeing to it?

3. What is an intermediary? What intermediaries would a musical artist likely have to deal with to make his or her CD available for sale to potential customers?

4. Placement consultants, frequently referred to as headhunters, are a type of intermediary used by employers and potential employees. As someone looking for a job, what are the key advantages and disadvantages of using the services of a placement consultant?

NOW WHAT?

Having discussed product and price in previous chapters, we've now addressed the third element in creating your marketing mix by setting objectives and strategies for place. The next important step is to establish your promotion goals and the strategies that you'll put in place to achieve them. Promotion—including advertising, public relations, direct marketing, sales promotion, personal selling, and online marketing—is what we'll be covering in the next chapter.

When promotion is your daily bread

Meet Peter J. Loyello. P. J. is the vice president of communications and broadcasting for the Major League Baseball team the Florida Marlins, which he joined in February 2002 after serving seven seasons with the Montreal Expos. With more than 15 years of experience in building strong brands, P. J. oversees the efforts of six departments including media relations, broadcasting, community affairs, community foundation, in-game entertainment, and creative services. He also serves as the team's official spokesperson for business and baseball-related issues.

P. J. was always interested in sports, and started his career in professional baseball in 1993. During the last semester of his bachelor of commerce studies, P. J. contacted the Ottawa Lynx, which at the time was the Expos' new Triple A farm team. He followed up with phone calls and visited Ottawa repeatedly in his attempts to arrange an interview with the team's general manager. His persistence paid off. He was hired as director of public relations for the Lynx's inaugural season and was then named director of baseball operations for the 1994 season prior to joining the Expos in February 1995.

Throughout his career, P. J. has deepened his understanding of marketing communications. As P. J. discovered early in his career, although it's a private business, baseball is very public, and everything a team's organization does is openly scrutinized and covered by the media. As head of public relations, P. J. must keep his cool and accept the occasional knock or criticism. He believes that it's imperative to learn from one's mistakes, to never let emotions overwhelm the message, to stay cool, and to focus on the key message.

P. J. is also a firm believer in the importance of community involvement. He serves on the board of directors of the Marlins' Community Foundation, and under his leadership the Marlins distributed more than $1 million to various community projects in 2004. P. J. also shares his expertise in the development of Concordia University's sports administration program, where he's been a frequent guest lecturer.

We asked P. J. what three tips he would like to share with readers of *Marketing Yourself*. Here are his thoughts:

1. *Build and maintain your list of contacts.* Know the companies and the people who you would like to work for. You'll waste valuable time if you put off doing network building until after you've graduated, and this will make it much harder to get the interviews that you want.

2. *Make sure your cover letter and resume convey your brand's top qualities.* What value are you offering? How will your cover letter and resume stand out from others?

3. *Be prepared to show potential employers why they should hire you.* Create a "you should hire me because..." statement. Work on it early and know the reasons thoroughly so you can deliver them convincingly. Who knows when the phone is going to ring and you'll be given 30 seconds to audition for your dream job?

This is a story about two independent businesspeople.

Samantha and Michael Brock are 36- and 38-year-old siblings. Both have degrees in business: Samantha majored in accounting and Michael in marketing. They've always enjoyed working in construction, they both like to be their own boss, and for the past ten years each has been a general contractor specializing in home renovations, especially kitchens and bathrooms. Their prices are virtually identical and the quality of their work is excellent. They operate in two different cities with populations of approximately 500 000 each, and while these cities are quite a distance from each other, they are very similar demographically. Over the years, Samantha and Michael have been communicating less and less because they've been so busy with their businesses and their growing families. It's gotten to the point where in most years they get together only at Christmas and occasionally on their parents' wedding anniversary.

Of the two, Samantha is more conservative and this disposition is evident in many aspects of her business. Her business cards are as basic and inexpensive as it gets: plain white with equally plain black lettering. Her five trucks are painted white and, as with her business cards, they feature the name and telephone number of her company in plain black type—S. Brock Construction Inc. 555-675-2376. She and her construction crews dress for work in whatever clothing they feel is appropriate. Samantha has no website and does no advertising. She believes that a good quality product speaks for itself and that the resulting word-of-mouth referrals are an effective and economical way to grow the business. This seems to have been the case with S. Brock Construction Inc. With no marketing communications support (and its associated costs) Samantha's business has grown steadily from year to year and the income she earns from it provides for a comfortable lifestyle for her and her family.

Michael is more outgoing than Samantha and this trait permeates every aspect of his business. Prior to starting his company, he noticed that almost all of the contractors in his city were named after their owners. So to set himself apart, he decided to create a brand name for his company: Picture Perfect Renovations. He developed a signature line for the brand: "Beautiful kitchens and bathrooms. On schedule and on budget." Then Michael hired a local graphic artist to design a logo as well as business cards and truck signage. The off-white and medium blue colour combination that she recommended along with a stylized illustration of a cozy house in a picture frame that she included as part of the logo gave the cards and trucks a look that immediately communicated style, professionalism, and trust. Michael liked it so much that he ordered polo shirts, t-shirts, and caps in the colour scheme featuring the Picture Perfect Renovations logo. He then created a website, www.PicturePerfectRenovations. com, with his signature logo and colour scheme. The site not only described his business, it also showcased before-and-after photos of

YOU WILL:

- know what integrated marketing communications is and how you can use it to promote your product or business

- understand the relationships between promotion and the other three Ps (i.e., product, price, and place)

- know the strengths and weaknesses of the major integrated marketing communications tools—advertising, sales promotion, public relations, direct marketing, the Internet, and personal selling

- know how to set promotion objectives and formulate promotion strategies for your product or your business

- understand the importance of having a clear, competitive, and compelling message, and how to create one

renovations his company had done accompanied by testimonials from customers. Visitors considering a renovation were invited to register on the site and Michael or one of his people would get back to each of them to discuss their needs and arrange for a consultation. He exchanged links with interior designers and architects. He fed them clients and they did the same for him. His site designer included a section on the website that listed plumbers and electricians who could be contacted in case of emergency. He exchanged links with them too. Michael even arranged to have the company's phone number to be 555-737-3328, or 555-PER-FECT.

He had postcards designed featuring his logo, signature line, and company colours. At the end of each project, he would print between 100 and 200 of them with the following text on the back: "We've just completed another Picture Perfect renovation at xxxx Street (i.e., the address where the renovation was done). For the kitchen or bathroom of your dreams, visit us at www.PicturePerfectRenovations.com or call us at 555-PER-FECT for a no-obligation consultation." He would sign each one and then have his two children deliver them to homes in the neighbourhood surrounding the house where the project had just been completed. Invariably, he would get at least two inquiries within the next month from each round of distribution.

Michael was a member of his city's chamber of commerce. His company provided services at discounted prices to community organizations such as religious groups and daycare centres whose buildings needed minor repairs. Michael contacted radio stations in his area and offered to be the renovation expert on phone-in shows during spring, the prime renovation season. They readily accepted. He advertised in the local newspapers and wrote (or had written for him!) periodic articles on home renovation that the papers published at no charge. In all of his ads and media appearances, he made sure the company's phone number and web address were prominently mentioned.

After the family Christmas dinner last year, Samantha and Michael got to talking about their businesses. Samantha mentioned that she was thinking about replacing three of her five trucks and Michael suggested that she visit the dealership where he bought his vehicles. "In the past five years I think I've bought almost forty trucks from her and I get a big volume discount. I'm sure she'll extend it to you," he said to Samantha.

"My gosh, how many trucks does your business own?" she asked with a fair amount of surprise.

"Well, I have 35 on job sites right now and two are in the shop for repairs," he replied.

"Wow!" exclaimed Samantha.

"Hey, between you and me, Sam, my sales this year will top ten million dollars and should grow by 20 percent next year," Michael confided.

"I'll be lucky to hit two million and I'm not growing anywhere near as quickly as you are. What's behind your success, Mike?" asked Samantha.

Michael went on to explain how he integrated advertising, direct marketing, public relations, personal selling, and the Internet to build his business. He told Samantha that it took time, money, and effort to do it but that it paid off handsomely. For the first time ever it dawned on her that it wasn't just about product, price, and place: promotion could play an enormous role in growing and sustaining her business. Moreover, she was also coming to realize that it wasn't all about advertising, as she had thought up until now.

"Hey Mike, how long would it take you to teach me how to use marketing communications to grow my business the way you've grown yours?" she inquired.

"Oh, about as long as it would take you to teach me how to do my personal income tax returns," he replied.

"So we have a deal, right?" answered Samantha.

"Sure, but let's not wait until next Christmas to make it happen. Why don't we get together early in the new year? Business will be kind of slow and the deadline for filing income tax returns will be four months away," Michael replied.

Myth

If I build a better mousetrap the world will beat a path to my door. In other words, **a superior product will sell itself.**

☑ Reality Check

No matter how good your product is, **if no one knows about it and where to buy it, customers will be few and far between.**

AN OVERVIEW OF PROMOTION

If you asked a thousand members of the general population what marketing is, an overwhelming majority would say that marketing is selling or advertising. This is not surprising, as selling and advertising are the most visible and talked about aspects of marketing. However, as you know by now, marketing also includes the other three Ps—product, price, and place. Selling and advertising are just two components of the fourth P—*promotion*.

Promotion is all about the communication of information between buyers and sellers with the ultimate goal of affecting their behaviour. Its primary role is to inform, persuade, and influence customers' purchase and adoption decisions. Promotion is made up of six elements: advertising, public relations, sales promotion, direct marketing, the Internet, and personal selling.

Increasingly, organizations and individuals are practising what is called integrated marketing communications or IMC. This, in fact, is what Michael did in the story we used to introduce this chapter. The idea behind IMC is to maximize impact, clarity, and effectiveness of all promotional activities by coordinating them to create and communicate a unified marketing message to all stakeholders. For most organizations and individuals, their most important stakeholders are their customers. Their other stakeholders could include employees, suppliers, shareholders, governments, the media, and the community at large.

> **IMC (integrated marketing communications)** — an approach that focuses on optimizing the impact of marketing communications by coordinating them to create a unified message to all stakeholders

Tim Penner, the president of Procter & Gamble Canada, summed up the notion of IMC perfectly in the following quotation from a 2003 article in the *National Post*:

> *Fifteen years ago, a young marketing employee might have worked six months almost exclusively on one new advertising campaign. Today in the same time period, a marketer will work on the ad campaign, a media sponsorship, a tie-in with a network, a direct-response email program, and a PR program targeting key outside stakeholders. Marketing in today's fragmented environment requires that we approach the consumer from many different angles concurrently.*

PROMOTION OBJECTIVES AND THE MARKETING MIX

A widely held misconception is that promotion, especially advertising, can make people buy things that they don't need. At the root of this notion is the assumption that people are easily manipulated and that marketing communication has the power to persuade them to make decisions that are not in their best interests. To test this notion, ask yourself the following question: when was the last time I bought something that I had no need for simply as a result of seeing an ad or commercial for it? (Buying that pair of designer jeans or shoes because you saw someone else wearing them doesn't count because that's not marketing communication.) When pressed, most people have a tough time identifying any occasion when they've purchased an unneeded product because of their exposure to marketing communications for it. There is no arguing, however, that advertising creates desire, but it rarely does so to the point of convincing consumers to purchase an unneeded or unwanted product.

Another common misconception is that marketing communications can persuade people to purchase poor products. There is actually some truth to this notion: marketing communications can in fact get people to buy an inferior product—but only once. After customers discover that a product is unsatisfactory, they'll never buy it again and will more than likely tell others about their bad experience. As many a marketer has exclaimed, nothing kills a bad product faster than great advertising.

A final misconception is that all by itself, marketing communication can generate sales. This is rarely the case. A sale is the culmination of all of the four Ps working together. So for a sale to occur, the product must satisfy the customer's needs or wants and must be of acceptable quality. Its price must be affordable. It has to be available in places that are accessible and convenient for the customer. So, where does marketing communications fit into the marketing mix? In fact it fulfills four essential roles. It informs. It persuades. It reminds. It forges relationships. Let's examine each of these roles.

1. MARKETING COMMUNICATION AS INFORMATION

As an information tool, marketing communication can:

- Tell customers about a new product or modifications to an existing one

- Let customers know where they can find your product
- Suggest new uses for an existing product
- Tell customers about a price change
- Correct false impressions or misconceptions
- Build an organization's or individual's image

2. MARKETING COMMUNICATION AS PERSUASION

Marketing communication can persuade by:

- Getting customers to prefer your brand over others
- Creating desire for your brand
- Getting customers to switch from a competing brand to yours
- Encouraging them to buy now instead of putting off their purchase decision
- Changing customers' perceptions of your brand

3. MARKETING COMMUNICATION AS A REMINDER

Marketing communication keeps products and brands in customers' minds by:

- Making it easy to remember your brand's name and identity
- Reminding customers that your product may be needed in the future and to keep it on hand
- Reminding customers where to buy your product
- Getting them to keep your product in mind during off-seasons

---

EXHIBIT 9.1 **Marketing Communications Inform**

The label for Old Orchard juice informs the audience that the product contains a low level of carbohydrates, is an apple-raspberry flavour, and contains Splenda sweetener.

PR NewsWire OLD ORCHARDS BRANDS.

EXHIBIT 9.2 Marketing Communications Persuade

Inhale.

Fresh Escapes™ from Dawn® Citrus Burst, Wildflower Medley and Apple Blossom scents.

This ad for Dawn dishwasher liquid introduces new fragrances and attempts to create desire for the product by inviting customers to experience the new scents.

Courtesy of Procter & Gamble Productions, Inc.

4. MARKETING COMMUNICATIONS AS A RELATIONSHIP BUILDER

Marketing communications can forge relationships by:

- Increasing customers' commitment and loyalty to your brand
- Giving them something to talk about and creating word-of-mouth and buzz
- Turning your satisfied customers into brand ambassadors
- Solidifying and expanding on the emotional bonds and commitment that customers have with your product and brand

MARKETING COMMUNICATION TOOLS: OVERVIEW

Here's a brief overview of the six marketing communications tools. We'll take a more in-depth look at the strategic use of each one later on.

1. ADVERTISING

advertising — any paid form of non-personal marketing communication for a product, organization, or person by an identified sponsor

Advertising is defined as any paid form of non-personal marketing communication for a product, brand, organization, idea, or person by an identified sponsor. An example of advertising is a 30-second commercial for Budweiser beer on the television broadcast of the Super Bowl.

EXHIBIT 9.3   Marketing Communications Remind

This ad attempts to remind consumers of the time-saving, fun benefits of Reynolds® Plastic Wrap, thereby facilitating recall of the brand's name and identity.

Reynolds® Plastic Wrap is a registered trademark of Alcoa Inc.

EXHIBIT 9.4   Marketing Communications Build Relationships

The clowns are from a series of cardboard cut-outs inserted in packages of Poulain chocolate bars in France in 1892. The company was among the first to use promotional gifts such as these and they bonded customers to the brand, helping make it one of the best-loved in France. (From "La magie du chocolat," by Marie Christine Clément and Didier Clément. [1998]. Éditions Albin Michel.)

Poulain Chocolat.

public relations — non-personal communication about a product, brand, organization, idea, or person not directly paid for or run under indentified sponsorship

sales promotion — catch-all term for those marketing activities that provide extra value or incentives to the ultimate consumer, sales force, or distributors to stimulate sales

direct marketing — any one-on-one communication with targeted individuals, such as direct mail (including direct email) and telemarketing

Advertisers pay for specific amounts of media space or time in which they place messages that they have created. This gives them complete control over what is said about them. Unlike public relations, advertising is easy to recognize because the sponsor is always identified in advertisements and commercials.

2. PUBLIC RELATIONS

Like advertising, public relations is non-personal communication about a product, brand, organization, idea, or person. Unlike advertising, it is not directly paid for or run under identified sponsorship. Consider an author who appears on a television talk show and speaks about his or her new book. He or she did not pay to be on the show. During the interview, neither the author nor the host announces that the reason why the author is appearing on the show is to create awareness and hopefully generate sales for the new book. In other words, the sponsor isn't identified.

Compared to advertising, public relations is relatively inexpensive; it can even be cost-free. However, unlike advertising, there is little or no control over the message or whether the message even gets communicated. What if the author asked to be on a number of talk shows and no producers agreed to have him or her on any of them?

Public relations includes the following:

- **Media relations:** Making sure the media have newsworthy information about the product
- **Corporate image advertising:** Creating a positive image of the organization, both internally and externally to stakeholders
- **Public affairs:** Maintaining positive relationships with the community whether at the local, provincial, state, or national level
- **Investor relations:** Maintaining positive relationships with investors
- **Crisis management:** Responding to unfavourable publicity or a negative event that threatens the image of the company

3. SALES PROMOTION

Sales promotion is a bit of a catch-all. It includes those marketing activities that provide extra value or incentives to the ultimate consumer, sales force, or distributors to stimulate sales. Contests, loyalty programs, coupons, sampling, event sponsorship, and discounts to retailers are all forms of sales promotion.

One of the major strengths of sales promotion is that its use can result in an immediate response. For example, almost immediately after receiving a $1-off coupon, a customer may head to the store to buy the product being couponed. Keep in mind that excessive use of sales promotion can cheapen a brand's image.

4. DIRECT MARKETING

Direct marketing is one-on-one communication with targeted individuals including customers and distribution channel members with the goal of generating an immediate response. Direct mail and mass email are examples, as is telemarketing.

The major strength of direct marketing is that it can result in a sale—instantaneously. One of its main disadvantages is that it can be perceived as intrusive and annoying by those people targeted by it.

5. THE INTERNET

The Internet has evolved from its original role as an information provider. It is now an entertainment and advertising medium. It's also a highly targeted direct marketing vehicle. In the introductory story to this chapter, Michael used the Internet to showcase his business, provide the before-and-after shots of projects his company completed, and get sales leads.

For many organizations and individuals, the Internet is the most efficient IMC tool of all because it can be used to reach very specific audiences at low cost. But competition for visitors is fierce, so driving traffic to particular websites can be challenging.

> **the Internet** — a highly targeted direct marketing vehicle that has evolved from its original role as an information provider

6. PERSONAL SELLING

Personal selling is person-to-person communication in which the seller attempts to assist or persuade prospective buyers to purchase his or her product or to act on an idea. There's no better example of personal selling than a job interview!

Personal selling is a two-way communication process in which the seller can adapt his or her message to changes in the amount and type of information provided by the buyer during the sales call. This makes it one of the most effective of all the IMC tools. It's also the most expensive tool of all, by far.

> **personal selling** — person-to-person communication in which the seller attempts to assist or persuade prospective buyers to purchase his or her product or to act on an idea

THE COMMUNICATION PROCESS

Exhibit 9.5 provides a simplified overview of how the communication process works. Let's examine each of the model's components from a marketing communications perspective. The source or sender is you or your organization. As the sender, you need to decide on a message to communicate. Typically, the purpose of the message is to influence your target market's attitudes and behaviour. For example, if you were looking for an entry-level software engineering position, the message that you might want to communicate is that your education and experience make you an ideal candidate. Then you would encode the message—that is, write the actual words that will communicate why you're perfect for the position. Next you would send the message via a channel. In this case it could be your cover letter and resume, which would be delivered by email or regular mail.

The receiver, let's say a human resources manager, must decode the message and hopefully understand what the sender intends to say. The clearer your message, the greater the chances are that it will be decoded and understood the way you intended it to be. At any time, noise or distractions can get in the way of the communication process. Examples of noise in this case would be the cover letters and resumes the human resources manager receives from other applicants. The telephone calls and emails he or she receives throughout the day are other sources of noise. By having an idea of the types and volume of noise that receivers experience, senders can

EXHIBIT 9.5 The Communication Process

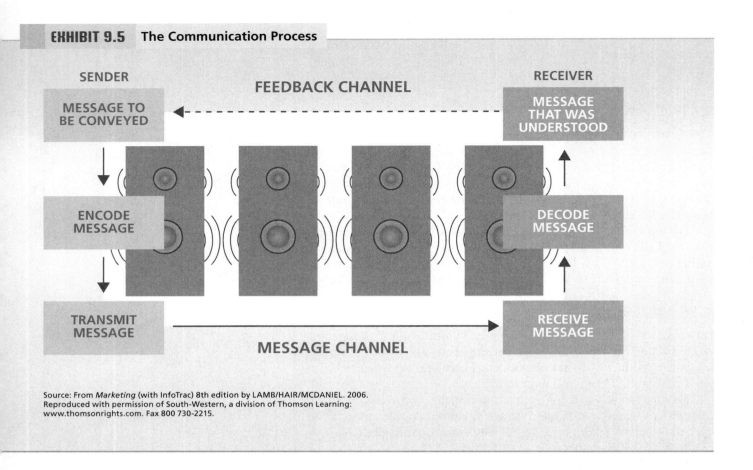

Source: From *Marketing* (with InfoTrac) 8th edition by LAMB/HAIR/MCDANIEL. 2006.
Reproduced with permission of South-Western, a division of Thomson Learning:
www.thomsonrights.com. Fax 800 730-2215.

gain valuable insight as to how they can formulate their messages so that they get noticed and acted upon.

Feedback helps senders determine if and to what extent receivers have decoded their messages in the intended manner. Getting a phone call to arrange an interview for the human resources position is one form of feedback. In a business context, feedback may consist of sales and market share data at the broadest level, and customer comments to 800 numbers or on web-forms at more specific levels. Exhibit 9.6 spells out the different steps in the communication process for three types of promotions.

Finally, to ensure that senders and receivers understand each other, they must have some shared frames of reference or fields of experience. These include vocabulary, attitudes, perceptions, and values. This is why it's so important to "talk the potential employer's language" when it comes to industry terminology and his or her corporate culture. For instance, a recent newspaper ad for a well-known hotel chain stated: "Businessman whose days consist of FYIs, OTs, ASAPs, and a little too much BS seeks TLC." Unless you were part of the target market or knew the meaning of all these acronyms, you most likely wouldn't have understood the ad.

BREAKDOWNS IN THE COMMUNICATION PROCESS AND HOW TO PREVENT THEM

For as simple as this basic model of communication is, there are a number of things that can get in the way of the communication process being successfully completed. These include the following:

EXHIBIT 9.6 The Communication Process for Three Types of Promotion

TYPE OF PROMOTION	Sender	Encoding by Sender	Channel	Decoding by Receiver	Response	Feedback
Personal Selling	IBM e-solutions networking	Sales presentation on new applications	IBM sales representative	Office manager and employees discuss sales presentation and those of competing suppliers.	Order is placed for IBM e-solutions system installation	Customer asks about a second system for subsidiary company.
Dollar-off coupon (sales promotion)	Kellogg's Special K cereal	Coupons prepared by Kellogg's marketing department and advertising agency	Coupon insert in Sunday newspaper	Newspaper reader sees coupon for Special K cereal and saves it.	Special K is purchased by consumer using coupon.	Kellogg researchers see increase in market share.
Television advertising	Paramount Canada's Wonderland	Advertisement developed by Wonderland's advertising agency featuring the new park rides	Network television ads air during program with high percentages of viewers under 20 years old.	Teens and young adults see ad and decide to try out the park	Wonderland tickets are purchased.	Customers purchase season ticket packages for Wonderland.

Source: From *Contemporary Marketing* 1/E by BOONE/KURTZ. 2007. Reproduced with permission of Nelson, a division of Thomson Learning: www.thomsonrights.com. Fax 800 730-2215.

- The sender—namely, you or your organization—is not clear on what it wants to say or tries to say too many things, some of which may be conflicting.
- The receiver is busy or noise prevents him or her from paying attention to or acting on your message.
- The receiver did not decode your message in the manner that you intended.
- The receiver decoded the message properly but did not take action.

So how can you prevent breakdowns in the communications process? Here are some suggestions.

- Be clear on what you want to say. The value of the situation analysis and the self-assessment tests you've taken on the Marketing Yourself website should be obvious in this regard.
- Think of the receiver's situation when sending your message. What level of noise or distraction is likely to be present? How can you adapt your message accordingly? For example, if you're applying for a position that has been advertised, it's likely that your resume and cover letter will be one of the many that the recipient will receive. What can you do to get yours to stand out and get read?

- Make decoding as easy as possible. While you can't entirely control how the receiver will decode your message, you can make your message as clear as possible. Eliminate ambiguity and the confusion it creates. Don't try to convey too many things. Take a lesson from the great advertisers such as Coke, Nike, BMW, L'Oréal, McDonald's, and Buckley's Mixture: less is more. The fewer the number of messages that you try to get across, the greater your likelihood of success-fully communicating them. The "great advertisers" we just named focus on one basic message in all of their marketing communications.

- Invite the receiver to take action and give him or her a reason to do so. In your written communications, you could include a postage-paid reply card that the receiver could use to confirm an appointment. In your verbal conversations, try using questions such as, "Can we schedule a phone call next week to discuss the opportunity? What times are good for you?"

GETTING CUSTOMERS TO ACT: THE ROLE OF MARKETING COMMUNICATIONS

The ultimate goal of virtually all marketing communications campaigns is to get one or more customers to act the way that you—as an entrepreneur, artist, professional, or prospective employee—want them to behave. Typical desired actions include the following:

- Getting a retailer to stock your product
- Getting the retailer's customers to buy your product
- Having potential clients call or visit your place of business
- Having customers buy your product or visit your place of business on a regular basis
- Having clients purchase your product directly from you
- Getting an employer to hire you

Actions such as these are usually the result of a complex decision-making process and, as part of this process, customers and potential employers typically go through a number of intervening stages before making purchase or hiring decisions. These stages are awareness, knowledge, liking and preference, purchase, and loyalty. Marketing communications can be used to influence customers and potential employers at each of these stages by informing them about a product's existence and availability, by communicating its bene-fits (particularly those that make the product more desirable than competitive offerings), by providing incentives to purchase, and by giving customers and employers reasons to continue purchasing or using the product.

PROMOTION OBJECTIVES AND STRATEGIES

SETTING PROMOTION OBJECTIVES

The first step in setting promotion objectives is to assess where customers and employers are in the decision-making process. So, for example, if they don't know what your product is or who you are, there is an obvious need to create awareness. If they are aware of your product (or you) but have little or no idea of how it or you will solve a problem for them or make them feel better, one goal will be to increase their knowledge about how your product can do this. If they know about your product's benefits but believe that your product is no better than your competitors' products, an objective will be to convince them of your product's superiority. If they are convinced that your product is better but remain *potential* customers and employers as opposed to *current* customers and employers, an objective could be to convert their attitudes and beliefs into action—namely, trying, buying, or hiring your product or yourself. If they are a current customer or employer, it's likely that you will want them to continue as such. As a result, the goal will be to maintain and strengthen their loyalty to you or your product.

Now let's examine the nature of promotion objectives for each stage, from awareness to loyalty, in a little more depth.

AWARENESS

Awareness is a necessary condition to create a sale, but it's not the only one. People won't buy a product that they don't know about. But just because they know about it doesn't necessarily mean that they will purchase it. Think about it: Each of us is aware of tens of thousands of products but we typically limit our actual purchases to a few hundred. That said, members of your target market need to be aware of your product before they will even consider buying it. Consequently, creating and increasing awareness are key promotion objectives.

So, for example, if you're launching a new product or putting yourself on the market for the first time, the awareness level among your target market is likely to be zero. In this case, the objective would be to create awareness with a certain number of potential customers (say, 100 000) or potential employers (say, 100). Keep in mind that it's important to quantify your promotion objectives at each stage. Doing so will guide your promotion strategy and provide you with benchmarks against which to evaluate how you are progressing with the promotion component of your marketing plan.

Marketers often break awareness down into the following three categories:

- **Aided awareness:** Here, target market members know about your product but need a memory jog—for example, an advertisement or commercial—to bring it to mind. On a piece of paper, write down all of the brands of cola that you're aware of. Is R.C. or Royal Crown brand one of them? If it's not on your list, but now, after having seen the brand mentioned here, you can recall it, this would be an example of aided awareness. Applying this notion to the workplace, consider the following situation: a vice-president is wondering who should be considered for a promotion to fill a recently created vacancy. Six people come to her mind, none of which is you. In a discussion with her management team about candidates for the position, the human resources manager brings up your name, which prompts the vice-president to recall you.

awareness — the first necessary (though not sufficient) step to create a sale; letting your target customers know of your existence, hopefully in a way that motivates them to seek further knowledge about your product, then develop a preference, and ultimately try and then keep purchasing your product

- **Unaided awareness:** If you had listed Royal Crown as one of the brands of cola that you are aware of—without any prompting whatsoever—this would be what is referred to as unaided awareness. Using our workplace example, if you were one of the six employees who came to the vice-president's mind when she was thinking about who to consider for the vacancy, you would have achieved unaided awareness.

- **Top-of-mind awareness:** Had you listed Royal Crown as the first cola brand that came to mind, this would be an example of top-of-mind awareness. If you had been the first person to come into the vice-president's mind, you too would have been in the enviable position of having attained top-of-mind awareness.

In addition to the number of target market members that you want to make aware of your product, what type of awareness—aided, unaided, or top-of-mind—do you want to achieve?

 Myth

*If potential employers or clients don't know of me or my product, the **only thing I need to do is to create awareness** among them in order to get them to agree to meet me.*

 **Reality Check**

Gaining awareness is **only the first step toward getting an interview** or the opportunity to pitch your product, but on its own it's far from enough. You need to communicate a clear and compelling reason why potential employers or clients should meet you in order for them to even think about agreeing to a meeting.

KNOWLEDGE

Once awareness has been achieved, the next step is to create knowledge among members of your target market. But knowledge of what? In a nutshell: product knowledge. To move potential buyers or employers closer to a purchase or hiring decision in your favour, it's crucial for them to know what your key product features and benefits are and how these will help them solve a problem, feel good, save money, or make money. As with any promotional objective, it is important to specify not only the exact knowledge about benefits and features you wish to communicate but also to how many target market members you want to communicate this knowledge. Here are two examples:

- To ensure that 70 000 target market members know that by using my company's cellular telephone service, they will be able to reduce their telephone expenses by up to 50 percent.

- To get 60 potential employers to know that I have the skills, education, and motivation needed to successfully fill the position of account manager.

PREFERENCE

Target market members are aware of your product and they know about its benefits to them. Now the goal is to make them like your product and to move them to the preference stage, where they're actually predisposed to liking your product more than your competitors'. One way to develop liking and preference for your product is to use a combination of words and visual imagery that instills desire for your product and its use. Potential employees can create desire among prospective employers by being thoroughly prepared and appropriately attired for job interviews. Sellers of goods and services can spark desire through image advertising and persuasive personal selling. Going through the process of setting preference goals usually results in entrepreneurs, artists, professionals, and job seekers challenging themselves to do a better job of promotion than their competitors. By establishing competitive promotion strategies and tactics as benchmarks to be surpassed, the chances of sales, revenue, or employment success are greatly enhanced.

Examples of preference goals are as follows:

- To ensure that 20 000 members of my target market perceive my company's cellular telephone service as being the best suited to their needs.

- To have ten potential employers like me so much better than other applicants that they want to interview me.

PURCHASE

Now that a significant number of target market members like your product more than they like your competitors', the next step is to move them to act. This can take two forms: trial and actual purchase.

Giving potential customers the opportunity to try your product before they commit to actually purchasing it or hiring you is an effective way to reduce the psychological and financial risks frequently involved in buying or hiring decisions. What if I buy the car and don't like the way it handles? A test drive will quickly resolve this doubt. What if I hire Kerry and she doesn't fit into our corporate culture? Think of an employment interview as a type of trial. The interviewer is trying to simulate what it would be like to have the interviewee as an employee. Many of his or her questions are designed to see how the interviewee would act in certain situations, including those involving corporate culture. That's why it's always a good idea to get to know as much as you can about an organization's culture before meeting with one of its interviewers. For an artist, trial could take different forms. Potential customers could rent the artwork prior to purchase. (Many art museum retail stores offer rental and appraisal services for potential buyers.) Trial could also be induced by mailing invitation cards to a gallery showing and having an actual painting reproduced on the cover. Posters, lithographs, even calendars are means of offering clients the chance to try a piece of art before investing in the actual work itself. An artist's website could offer screensaver downloads as a trial device.

Two examples of purchase goals are as follows:

- To achieve trial of my company's cellular phone service by 5000 potential customers and to convert 2000 of these into current customers.

FAVOURITES

JENNY HELLERS
http://www.jennyhellers.com

Jenny Hellers creates wall hangings using a unique enamel-on-copper technique. Her works have been shown in more than 100 countries and they can sell for thousands of dollars. She produces more affordable paper versions of her designs—prints, greeting cards, and calendars—to increase her popularity and visiblity.

- To secure six interviews from potential employers and to get an offer of employment from at least two of them.

LOYALTY

Potential customers and employers have become current customers and employers. Now the goal is to hold on to them and, in the case of customers, possibly to get them to buy more frequently from your company or, in the case of employers, to strengthen their bonds with you by assigning you increased levels of responsibility (with a higher salary, of course). Examples of marketing communication goals designed to create loyalty are as follows:

- To insulate my cellular phone company's customers from competitive offers and to upgrade 1000 of them to our premium package.

- To let my superiors know that I am ready and willing to take on projects that are more challenging than the ones that I have been working on since I joined the company six months ago.

PROMOTION STRATEGIES AND TACTICS

After promotion objectives have been set, the next step is to create an action plan—namely, how the integrated marketing communications tools (advertising, public relations, sales promotion, direct marketing, the Internet, and personal selling) will be used to achieve these goals. Before examining the roles of each of the IMC tools, let's take a look at two fundamental promotion strategies: push strategy and pull strategy.

When organizations or individuals use a push strategy, they focus their promotion efforts on distribution channel members such as distributors and retailers. The basic goal is to encourage them to stock and promote their products so that the final customer will be exposed to them and ultimately purchase them. For example, a manufacturer of Christmas gift wrapping paper could offer discounts and promotional allowances to outlets such as Costco and Sears to encourage them to buy their products, allocate prime shelf space to them, and prominently display them from mid-November to December 24th. Job seekers use push strategies too. If they need to go through intermediaries such as placement consultants or human resources managers in order to arrange an interview with, say, a director of clinical research, they'll need to push their cover letters, resumes, and themselves through the hiring chain.

Organizations and individuals use a pull strategy when they concentrate their promotions on appealing to the final customer directly. The objective here is to move their products through the distribution channel by having customers asking for or even insisting that they be available in retail stores. Advertising and public relations often play a major role here. For an idea of the ultimate power of a pull strategy, think of brands or products that you would actually switch retailers for if they weren't stocked where you usually shop. Do any of these come to mind? Apple's iPod, Heinz ketchup, Nike footwear, Tide detergent, Grey Goose vodka, and Sony televisions. Pull strategies can be employed by job seekers as well. For example, they can use networking to get the word out to potential

push strategy — promotion strategies and tactics (e.g., trade allowances) directed at members of a channel, such as distributors and retailers, to entice them to sell a product to the end consumer

pull strategy — concentrates on appealing to the end consumers directly so they in turn will request the product from members of the marketing channel

employers that they are or soon will be on the market, with the goal of piquing interest and even getting invited to an interview. In cases such as these, networks could be made up of parents, relatives, friends, former employers, and teachers.

Most organizations and individuals use a combination of push and pull strategies. Push to get their products into the pipeline and pull to move them out.

 ## Myth

*Great advertising can make up for the **shortfalls of a bad product**.*

 ## Reality Check

Nothing kills a bad product faster than great advertising. An effective ad campaign will quickly create high levels of awareness and expectations which, if they are not met, will only result in dissatisfied customers and fast-spreading negative word-of-mouth. If you advertise, you must have the goods to back it up. Likewise, when marketing yourself, **substance is just as important as presentation.**

MARKETING COMMUNICATION TOOLS: STRATEGIC ROLE

Let's now examine the roles that each of the IMC tools can play at both the strategic and tactical levels.

ADVERTISING

Advertising is particularly effective at creating product and brand awareness among large audiences. That's why it is often the IMC tool of choice for new product introductions and for making a large number of people quickly aware of your product. Advertising works particularly well at changing attitudes and perceptions. It's also one of the most efficient IMC tools. To illustrate, it costs approximately $30 to reach 1000 viewers of the Super Bowl with a 30-second spot, or 3 cents per person. Compare this with up to $5 for direct mail and more than $200 for a personal sales call.

Advertising is commonly used by marketers of consumer products as the main tool to establish and reinforce their IMC messages. It does this through the broadcast (television and radio), print (newspapers and magazines), and out-of-home (billboards and bus shelters) media. Unlike public relations and personal selling, advertising provides marketers with complete control over the message they want to communicate in terms of what is said and how, where it is said, and how often it is said. When marketing messages need to be repeated with high frequency, advertising is usually the most appropriate IMC tool of choice.

Despite its strengths, advertising has its share of weaknesses. By its very nature, it's intrusive. Advertising interrupts people while they are engaged in activities that they enjoy doing such as watching a sporting event or listening to relaxing music. As a result, audiences are often not in the most receptive frame of mind when an ad or commercial reaches them and, in ever-growing numbers, people are engaging in advertising-avoidance behaviour by using devices such as PVRs to remove commercials from television broadcasts and by subscribing to commercial-free satellite radio services.

It's becoming increasingly difficult for marketers to get their ads and commercials noticed and acted upon. Research clearly indicates that advertising recall is in a state of accelerating decline. One phenomenon that explains this is that the marketing communications environment is experiencing an unprecedented level of clutter. Not only is each of us exposed to more than 3000 ads and commercials every day through the traditional media, but also we're reached by hundreds more through our computers and cell phones, in movie theatres and public bathrooms, and in elevators and airport lounges. The overload consumers experience can result in advertising messages going unnoticed and unremembered.

While advertising is inexpensive and highly efficient relative to most other IMC tools, in an absolute sense it can be extremely costly. The 30 seconds of television network time to run a Super Bowl spot costs approximately $3 million. In addition, the cost of producing a Super Bowl–quality commercial typically exceeds $1 million. While the cost for reaching one person with a full-page black and white advertisement in a local city newspaper such as the *Toronto Star* is only 4 cents, the cost for the actual space in the paper is about $30 000.

PUBLIC RELATIONS

Public relations covers a broad range of activities, including getting positive media coverage for an organization or individual. When celebrities are featured in magazines or appear on talk shows, this is usually the result of successful public relations planning. When a product or movie is featured in a lifestyle magazine, it is usually the result of public relations. Public relations also includes being actively involved in various communities and causes. For example, McDonald's builds and maintains Ronald McDonald Houses, where parents stay while their children are in hospital. Tim Hortons sponsors local kids' hockey teams, and Starbucks supports community-based literacy programs. Many individuals volunteer their time to benefit certain causes as well as to expand their business and employment networks.

The tools of public relations are many and varied. Press releases can be sent to broadcast and print media editors to provide them with news with the goal of having them run a story about an organization or individual. These are often supported by press conferences. Lobbying can be used to influence politicians and legislators about an issue of concern. For example, Mothers Against Drunk Driving exerts constant pressure on governments to lower the legal blood alcohol level for drivers. Meetings can be held with specific stakeholder groups to sensitize them to a company's position on an important issue such as environmental protection. Social activities such as dinners, parties, and open houses can be used to build relationships with customers, distribution channel members, investors, and other stakeholders. Videos, sound files, custom magazines, and newsletters can be employed to communicate an organization's or individual's marketing message.

As an IMC tool, public relations has a number of major strengths. It can generate extensive media coverage at little or no cost. If sending a press release and following up with a phone call to pitch a story about your organization resulted in a front page newspaper article about you or your organization, the out-of-pocket expenses would be negligible. Public relations can create goodwill among organizations, individuals, and their stakeholders. The marketing messages that get communicated as a result of public relations can be strengthened by the media's stature and believability. Just having an individual's or organization's name mentioned in a positive context on a television network news broadcast can give a tremendous boost to their credibility. Messages delivered via public relations do not have to battle clutter the way ads and commercials do. Public relations–delivered messages do not need to be intrusive, as they are part of the media's actual content. As a result, audiences are typically more open to receive them than they are advertising messages. This can further enhance message credibility because the source of the message is not the organization or the individual— it's the medium, and as such will likely be perceived as being more objective. Public relations is an excellent image-building tool. It can be instrumental in creating buzz and word-of-mouth communication. As you'll see when you follow the link below, we've used public relations to get the word out on *Marketing Yourself*.

Public relations' one major weakness is that there is no guarantee that the marketing message will be delivered or that it will be delivered in the intended manner. After receiving the press release and attending the press conference, media outlets may decide not to run a story about you or your organization. Or they may have every intention of running it but a bigger news item hits their desks just prior to their deadline and they replace your story with that one. Finally, despite all of your best efforts, the media may run a negative story about you or your organization. Think of all the scathing restaurant and movie reviews you've ever read. The genesis of many of these was a press release and an invitation to a grand opening or screening.

SALES PROMOTION

Advertising and public relations efforts typically take a relatively long time to generate an actual sale compared to sales promotion. Advertising and public relations are particularly effective at the awareness and knowledge stages of the buying decision process. Most sales promotion tactics operate at the purchase and loyalty stages and can be categorized in two broad areas: those that are aimed at the ultimate customer or consumer and those targeted to distribution channel members.

CUSTOMER AND CONSUMER SALES PROMOTION TOOLS

These are usually employed as part of a pull strategy and include the following:

- **Sampling:** Considered the most effective way to generate trial, sampling is a means to give consumers or customers a quantity of product at no charge. For example, a manufacturer of laundry detergent could distribute packages containing just enough product for two or three loads on university campuses at the beginning of each academic term as a way to get students to try the product. Someone looking for a job at a radio or television station could offer to work for free for one month to give the potential employer the opportunity to test them out. Sampling is one of the most expensive forms of sales promotion, and to ensure the return on investment in it is maximized the sampled products should be demonstrably superior to the ones currently being used or considered by the target market.

- **Couponing:** This is the oldest and most widely used trial-inducing tool. Increasingly, it's being used to encourage repeat purchase and loyalty. Most coupons offer a discount off the retail selling price of an item. Some offer a free sample. There are myriad ways that coupons can be distributed, and the method of distribution can have a dramatic effect on actual redemptions. For example, coupons that are distributed as part of newspaper and magazine advertisements tend to have relatively low rates of redemption compared to those distributed in or on the packages of the products themselves or in-store. Redemption for coupons distributed through the mail tend to fall somewhere in between. Two examples of couponing: a restaurant could expand its market by distributing coupons for $5 off a main course in neighbourhoods just beyond those where the bulk of its current customers come from. After they have eaten at the restaurant and redeemed their coupons, these customers could be given a coupon for a free dessert on their next visit. As part of his or her cover letter and resume package, an individual looking for a position in a particular industry could include a coupon for a complimentary report on the results of a research project that he or she conducted on the industry while in college.

- **Premiums:** A premium is an offer of an item of merchandise or service as an extra incentive for purchasers. It can be free or low priced. Collectible premiums can be used to generate repeat purchases, for example Disney movie character toys included with a McDonald's Happy Meal. In addition to providing extra value to customers, premiums can be used to communicate and reinforce a brand's main IMC message. For example, if the objective for a brand of flour was to communicate that pies, cakes, and breads baked from it are healthy and nutritious, seeds to grow home herb gardens could be distributed at no charge in packages of the brand. Additionally, the packs could feature a mail-in offer of a set of six pots in which to plant the herbs for a purchase price of $9.99 plus two proofs of purchase.

- **Contests and sweepstakes:** These are excellent tools to attract attention to a product, to create a sense of excitement, to get customers involved with the brand or product, to reinforce an IMC message, and to build customer databases. By the way, the difference between the two terms is that contests are competitions based on skills or ability while sweepstakes winners are determined by pure chance. Using the previous flour example, a contest could be run with the prize of a one-week, all-expenses-paid stay at a European cooking school known for its emphasis on healthy meals. To enter, entrants would have to mail in their favourite family-pleasing and nutritious recipe (using the brand of flour, of course). The winner would be selected by a panel of expert judges made up of a nutritionist, family physician, personal fitness trainer, and renowned chef. Could a contest or sweepstakes be integrated into a promotional campaign for someone seeking a job? In certain industries—for example, entertainment, sales, event management, design, fundraising, and advertising—they could very well play an interesting role. Proceed with high levels of creativity, taste, and common sense!

- **Refunds, rebates, bonus packs, and price-off deals:** These tools offer the customer a tangible reward for making a purchase. Refunds and rebates are frequently used to provide consumers with financial incentives to buy without reducing the actual retail price of the product. This can serve to maintain a brand's price integrity. Bonus packs and price-off deals are typically aimed at current users of a product. As a result of tactics such as these, users stock up on the promoted products. Consequently, they are taken out of the market and away from competitive offers for extended periods of time, thereby fostering brand loyalty.

- **Frequency and loyalty programs:** These were pioneered by the airline industry and are now one of the fastest growing sales promotion tools. Today, they are being used by retailers in just about every field: building supply centres, supermarkets, automotive service facilities, coffee shops, car rentals, bookstores, and bakeries to name a few. Programs such as these not only strengthen customer loyalty, but also can be instrumental in enriching and expanding the relationships between marketers and their customers. Many frequency and loyalty programs require customers to provide information that is entered into retailers' databases, which in turn can be used to create personalized offers communicated by email, regular mail, telephone, or in person while the customer is at the retailer's checkout counter.

- **Event marketing:** This is the type of promotion where a company, brand, or individual is linked to an event or where a themed activity is developed for the purpose of creating experiences for customers and, of course, promoting the product or cause. As marketers become savvier in using IMC, event marketing is taking on an increasingly important role in communicating and reinforcing key brand messages and in strengthening customer relationships. BMW conducts winter driving schools to instruct owners how to safely get the most out of their vehicles' performance capability in snowy and icy conditions. Harley-Davidson organizes the week-long Sturgis Rally in the U.S., which, in the company's words, gives owners the opportunity to "experience breathtaking scenery and legendary revelry" and to test ride the brand's latest models. A related form of promotion is event sponsorship. Here an organization or individual develops sponsorship relations with a particular event, such as a concert, art exhibition, cultural activity, or sporting event, and provides sponsorship in return for the right to display a brand name, logo, or other IMC message and to be identified as the sponsor of the event. The NASCAR racing series is called the Nextel Cup. The Fiesta Bowl college football championship game is titled the Tostitos Fiesta Bowl. General Motors has been the lead sponsor of the annual Montreal Jazz Festival.

 **Myth**

People hate being sold to.

 **Reality Check**

People like to have their needs satisfied. Showing them how you or your product can satisfy one or more of their needs is at the heart of the selling process. And it can create a **win–win situation** for you and the person you're selling to. Haven't you ever bought something after seeing it advertised and thought "I'm glad I heard about this"? Same goes for customers and employers.

TRADE SALES PROMOTION TOOLS

Sales promotion programs targeted to members of the distribution channel are typically part of a push strategy. The most common objectives are to obtain distribution for new products, to maintain trade support for established products, to build retail inventories, and to encourage retailers to display the products they carry. Trade sales promotion tools include the following:

- **Trade allowances:** This is the most common form of trade promotion and it involves a discount or other financial incentive offered to retailers or wholesalers to encourage them to stock, promote, or display a manufacturer's products.

- **Displays and point-of-purchase materials:** These can help a manufacturer obtain more visibility in stores. They include posters, banners, end-of-aisle displays, stand-up racks, and shelf cards (some with blinking lights and animation to attract attention).

- **Sales training programs:** When a product requires or can benefit from in-depth product knowledge on the part of the retailer's salespeople, manufacturers and distributors often provide sales training programs to provide this knowledge. This is particularly the case in the cosmetics, computer, automotive, consumer electronics, wine, and sporting goods industries.

- **Trade shows:** Participating in trade shows is a targeted activity that allows organizations and individuals to display and sell their products to resellers and prospective buyers.

- **Trade events:** Marketers can leverage their consumer event sponsorship activities with trade members. For example, when a new brand of travellers' cheques was being introduced in Europe, the financial services company issuing the cheques sponsored a leading Formula One racing team to create mass consumer awareness of the brand. It arranged for hospitality suites to be built at each of the European racetracks in which senior executives from the countries where each race was being run would be hosted throughout the entire racing weekend. They were also introduced to the team's drivers and shared half an hour of face time with them. The goal? To strengthen the relationships with the people who had the power to decide whether or not to carry and promote the new brand of cheques at their banks.

DIRECT MARKETING

With this tool, direct marketing media are employed. These include telemarketing (still the most often used form), television (i.e., infomercials), print, the Internet, and, of course, direct mail. Job seekers typically use direct mail to communicate their availability and desirability to prospective employers by sending out their resumes and cover letters. They usually follow up by calling the people to whom they sent their employment packages, thereby using telemarketing. They also frequently use telemarketing to find prospective employers and to arrange interviews.

Businesses and other organizations, particularly not-for-profits, use direct marketing to communicate complex information, to provide purchase incentives, and to generate sales (or donations, in the case of not-for-profits). For example, a fashion retailer could mail catalogues to announce its spring collection to current customers. With the catalogue it could include a $10 coupon redeemable on purchases of $50 or more made within ten days of the mailing. The retailer might also include a form and website information so that recipients can order selected merchandise through return mail or online.

One of the unique features of direct marketing is its scalability. This is particularly attractive to organizations or individuals with very limited financial resources. To illustrate, let's use the example of a portrait artist who wants to increase her client base. We'll call her Jill. Using her creative talents, Jill puts together a postcard that features one of her paintings on one side, her contact information—including her website—on the other, and a limited-time offer of $50 off any portrait booked within 30 days of receipt of the coupon. Because the average price of her portraits is $500, Jill believes that her target market is made up of people living in the upscale neighbourhoods in the city where she lives. So she has 500 of her postcards printed at a cost of $100—the absolute maximum amount of money she can afford without missing meals—and delivers them herself to 500 houses in one of these neighbourhoods. She gets one $500 booking as a result of this campaign, which leaves her with $350—the $500 less the $50 discount less the $100 printing cost. Then she prints and personally delivers 1000 postcards at a cost of $200, from which she gets two bookings totalling $1000. She has now earned a net amount of $1050 from her direct marketing campaign—$1500 in sales less $150 for three $50 discounts less $300 in printing costs. From this she spends $400 to print 2000 postcards, which after being distributed result in four sales of $500 each and net income of $1400. Her total earnings are now $2450—and she not only can afford to scale her direct mail campaign up further, but also has the money to buy a new pair of shoes that are much-needed after all the walking she's been doing!

The key ingredients to a successful direct marketing campaign are a list of qualified prospective customers or donors, an offer (e.g., the $50 discount that Jill made on her postcards), a medium (in Jill's case it was direct mail), a message, and timing—namely, when to conduct the direct marketing campaign and how frequently to do it.

Direct marketing has its own set of strengths and weaknesses. Let's start with its strengths:

- **Selective reach:** Direct marketing allows marketers to communicate with specific audiences with a minimum of waste coverage.

- **Segmentation capabilities:** Marketers can use their own databases or purchase lists of product users, recent purchasers or donors, or prospective customers or contributors.

- **Personalization:** Direct marketing messages can be highly personalized. For example, cover letters include the name and address of the person or organization receiving them. They can also include text specific to recipients themselves or their companies.

- **Costs:** While mass direct marketing campaigns can cost in the millions of dollars, they can be produced and executed with very little money (as we saw in Jill's case).

- **Measuring effectiveness:** Unlike with other IMC tools, the results of direct marketing are immediate and virtually always accurate.

Direct marketing's weaknesses include the following:

- **Accuracy:** The mailing lists used for direct marketing purposes need to be updated regularly. If not, the message can go undelivered or delivered to the wrong people.

- **Image factors:** Many people perceive direct mail—especially unsolicited email—to be junk.

- **Cost:** While cost is one of direct marketing's strengths, on a cost-per-message-delivered basis, compared to advertising and public relations, it is significantly more expensive.

THE INTERNET

The Internet is the most versatile IMC tool of all, and with each passing day it becomes even more so. Marketers can sell products directly to businesses and consumers on the Internet. People looking for jobs can find potential employers on it. Additionally, entrepreneurs, artists, professionals, and job seekers can use the Internet to create awareness, disseminate information, and build a brand image through the following:

- **Advertising:** This can take many forms including banners, pop-ups, links, webcasting, and sponsorships of sections of websites or portals such as MSN and Yahoo. In fact, many websites are actually interactive advertisements. Online advertising can be purchased on a cost-per-thousand people exposed or on a pay-per-click basis as is the case with

Google's sponsored links. Advertising messages need not be limited to the 30-second format that is the norm for radio and television spots. As long as they maintain viewers' attention, they can be any length.

- **Sales promotion:** The Internet is an excellent medium for contests as it facilitates the collection of customer database information. It's also the most efficient medium through which to distribute coupons.

- **Public relations:** The Internet can be used to conduct public relations activities such as providing information about products, organizations, and individuals; strengthening relationships with governments, investors, and the community at large; and supporting philanthropic causes.

- **Personal selling:** The Internet can be employed to support and enhance personal selling efforts by communicating product and delivery information as well as by providing customized real-time online reporting.

- **Direct marketing:** Although spamming has dulled the overall effectiveness of email as an IMC tool, email is still a viable medium for communicating meaningful messages and offers to recipients who have opted-in to a list as a result of being a customer or subscriber to an online newsletter. Additionally, text messaging provides customers with the facility to immediately respond to relevant ads through their cell phones.

As an IMC tool the Internet has its own unique strengths and weaknesses. Among its many strengths are the following:

- **Target marketing:** No IMC tool is more effective at reaching specific customers or customer groups. For example, through Google's AdWords advertising program, sponsored pay-per-click links can be purchased so that they appear only when the results of specific search terms appear. So, if you were a seller of custom-made electric guitars, you could arrange for your sponsored link to be displayed only with the search results for keywords of your choosing, such as "custom-made guitars," "rock guitars," "folk guitars," "country guitars," and "classical guitars."

- **Message tailoring:** Messages can be created to appeal to the specific targets that are reached by the Internet. In our guitar example, you could design separate ads to appear when the results for each of the five keyword terms are displayed.

- **Interactive capabilities:** When customers have the opportunity to interact with your marketing messages, the more involved they become with your product. When it comes to interactivity, the Internet is unmatched. Continuing with our guitar example, visitors to the website could be offered the opportunity to hear how each of the different available models actually sounds.

- **Sales potential:** Unlike with most of the other IMC tools, the sales transactions can be completed on the Internet.

- **Creativity:** Not only can website design be highly creative, but also online ads have the full use of sight, sound, colour, and visitor involvement.

- **Cost and scalability:** Designing and building a professional-quality website can be done for less than $1000. As is the case with direct marketing, delivering messages on the Internet is highly efficient because of its extremely precise targeting; that is, there is minimal waste coverage. Marketers can start their Internet-based promotion campaigns with very small budgets, and as revenues from these efforts grow they can reinvest a portion of the returns to continuously increase the number of potential customers reached.

- **Measurability:** The ability to determine cost effectiveness of online marketing activities, especially those paid for on a cost-per-click basis, is unmatched by any other IMC tool.

The main weaknesses of the Internet as an IMC tool include low reach (because of its selectivity) and image problems (because of users' irritation and concerns with pop-up ads, spyware, fraud, and spam). Additionally, the Internet is becoming increasingly cluttered with ads as more and more marketers discover its unique IMC capabilities.

 **Myth**

The more I talk, the more likely I'll make the sale to my prospect.

 **Reality Check**

Effective selling and interviewing start with understanding prospects and gaining insight into what their needs and wants are. This can be achieved only by listening to them carefully. **The more you listen and the less you talk, the more successful your sales presentations and interviews will be.**

PERSONAL SELLING

This is a process of person-to-person presentation to a buyer or, in the case of job seekers, to a potential employer. It's used to sell products to distribution channel members (wholesalers, distributors, and retailers, for example) and to final users including businesses, not-for-profit organizations, and consumers. Personal selling can also be an invaluable tool in getting buy-in from investors and banks. Three guiding personal selling principles include:

- **Listen instead of talk:** The first order of business is to understand the customer or employer. The second step is for you to be understood. To solve the customer's or employer's problem you must first understand the problem.

- **Build trust and respect:** This is one of the reasons why the time from the first presentation to closing the sale can take so long. People buy from people whom they trust and respect. Trust and respect cannot be earned overnight.

- **Find solutions for your customers:** Recall that businesses buy products to make money or to save money. Consumers buy to solve a problem or to feel good. Sales presentations should focus how your product will satisfy these needs.

One of the greatest strengths of personal selling is that it involves two-way communication between buyers and sellers. Consequently, selling messages can be adapted during the selling process to respond to buyer reactions, concerns, and objections as they are raised. Plus, more than is the case with any of the other IMC tools, transactions (i.e., sales and hiring decisions) can actually be completed through personal selling.

As mentioned earlier in this chapter, personal selling is the most expensive IMC tool of all. The costs associated with keeping a salesperson on the road—salary, transportation expenses, accommodation, and entertainment—can be enormous. Personal selling is also the most time-consuming IMC tool. Additionally, the flexibility that salespeople have to adapt the message to their buyers' needs and wants can be a double-edged sword: on the one hand it can help to close the sale; on the other hand, when using personal selling organizations relinquish some control of the delivery of their IMC messages because salespeople can change messages based on their interpretation of buyers' needs and wants. These changes may not always be consistent with the organization's overall marketing communications strategy.

MY PROMOTIONAL MIX

Now that you're more familiar with the various IMC tools, you can start thinking about the various ones you may want to use as part of your promotional strategy. However, as you might suspect by now, such decisions should not be made in a vacuum: many factors bear upon your choice of promotional tools. Exhibit 9.7 lists the key factors influencing promotional mix decisions.

Naturally, the amount of funds available is a key concern; we'll discuss budgeting methods in the next section. Beyond funds, your choice of a push or pull strategy directly influences the tools chosen. Buying decisions that involve risk or are complex typically are better suited for personal selling. Products in the maturity or decline phase of their lifecycle tend to benefit the most from reminder advertising. The characteristics of your target market also bear a direct influence: for instance, higher income households are often less sensitive to sales promotions. As you begin to put your promotional mix together, ask yourself how the factors listed in Exhibit 9.7 might influence your choice of IMC tools.

HOW MUCH DO YOU SPEND ON IMC?

Whether you are an artist, entrepreneur, professional, or even a job seeker, you need to determine how much you're willing to invest in IMC. Notice we used the verb "invest." The reason is to underscore that money spent on IMC should be regarded as an investment rather than a cost. When you think of IMC expenses as investments, you focus on doing the right thing and on making sure that it produces a return. It also invites you to consider both short-term and longer-term payoffs on your investments. By contrast, if you

EXHIBIT 9.7   Influences on the Promotional Mix

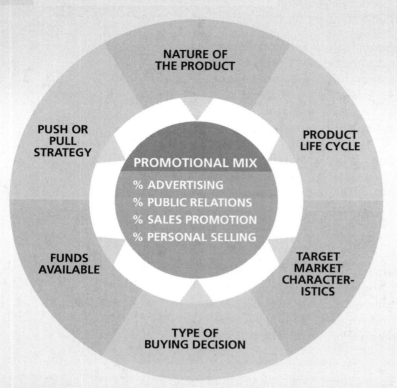

NATURE OF
THE PRODUCT

PUSH OR
PULL
STRATEGY

PRODUCT
LIFE CYCLE

PROMOTIONAL MIX
% ADVERTISING
% PUBLIC RELATIONS
% SALES PROMOTION
% PERSONAL SELLING

FUNDS
AVAILABLE

TARGET
MARKET
CHARACTER-
ISTICS

TYPE OF
BUYING DECISION

just think of IMC expenses as a cost of doing business, you're likely to miss worthwhile opportunities.

As you begin to think about how much to invest in your promotional activities, you may want to ask yourself how much you're willing to spend to acquire a new customer or to keep an existing one. Take, for example, the case of a local dental surgeon whose practice was doing well but was not functioning at peak capacity. He undertook a campaign to bring in new customers. When considering how much he should invest, he took into account that each new patient would generate approximately $125 on the first visit and would stay with him on average about three years, bringing in $225 per year on average. That's $800. How much was it worth to him to acquire an $800 source of revenue? To help you figure out the answer to this question, we've listed the four most common budgeting methods used in planning IMC campaigns. They are:

- **Percentage of sales:** With this method, your IMC spending is determined by using a specified percentage of either past or future sales. Restaurants, for example, typically spend between 2.5 and 5 percent of gross sales, depending on the segment they are in (e.g., fast food, midscale, family restaurant).

- **Fixed sum per unit:** With this method the IMC budget is set as a fixed and pre-determined dollar amount for each unit sold. So, for example, if you are a contractor or photographer you could decide to spend $45 per contract on IMC.

- **Competitive parity:** Here, you basically match what your competitors are spending on IMC. Pepsi and Coke are known to practise this type of budgeting. This results in stability in the market and helps avoid marketing warfare.
- **Objective–task method:** With this method, you begin by determining what needs to be done (the tasks) to achieve your objectives and then figuring out how much it will cost to perform these tasks. For example, assume you've set an objective of securing six interviews with potential employers in three different cities. How much will it cost to get and travel to the interviews?

objective–task method — a method of budgeting marketing communications expenses by first defining the objectives and then costing the tasks required to accomplish these objectives

DEVELOPING IMC MESSAGES: STRATEGIC ISSUES

One of the fundamental notions of IMC is that an organization or individual communicates the same basic marketing message to all of its stakeholders through all of its IMC tools. Over time, this creates synergy and maximum message impact. McDonald's consistently communicates wholesomeness and fun. Volvo stresses safety and Wal-Mart the lowest prices. The success of the IMC efforts of these brands can in large part be attributed to the fact that they follow one of the most basic principles of marketing communications: say one thing and say it well. As the marketing environment gets increasingly cluttered, this principle is even more poignant. So how do they come up with that one thing to say? While there are many ways to create a powerful and successful message, we've developed one that we believe is both simple and effective. It consists of answering the following seven questions.

1. **Why are we conducting integrated marketing communications?** The answer to this question identifies the problem that your IMC will address. Is it that your target market doesn't know about your product? Could it be that they aren't aware they need it, or that when the need arises they don't think of you? This question forces you to be crystal clear about your promotional objectives.

2. **Who must our marketing communications influence?** Here you identify and describe your stakeholders, including current and potential customers, clients, and employers. Try to be as specific and detailed as possible in your description and identify the stage of the buying process they're in. If you're a professional, artist, or entrepreneur, your stakeholders could include distribution channel members, your own employees, suppliers, and the community at large. If you're a job seeker, your stakeholders could include career placement staff, recruiting agents, interviewers, final decision makers on the employer side, and even your potential immediate supervisor.

3. **What do they think of us now?** The answer to this question should provide you with a snapshot of how your stakeholders perceive you. If you're a first-time job seeker, potential employers may think that, just like every other applicant, you're naive and inexperienced. If you're starting off as a professional, potential clients may doubt your expertise because you've just recently graduated. If you're an artist, an agent or gallery might be concerned about

how well your works will appeal to final customers. If you're an entrepreneur, it's important to determine how your current and potential customers perceive your products. You can collect this information through informal interviews and surveys.

4. **What do we want them to think and do?** Here you describe how you want stakeholders to perceive you and your product and the next step you would like them to take. As a job applicant, you would likely want prospective employers to think you're worth meeting and to arrange for an interview. As a freshly minted professional, you might want prospective clients to think that you are the most up-to-date in your field and, as a result, should be considered as more qualified than older professionals. As an artist, you could want to be seen as cutting-edge by agents and galleries and to be contacted by them for a portfolio review. If as an entrepreneur your product is thought to be too expensive, you could want prospective customers to see it as offering excellent value and to give it a try.

5. **What is the best thing we can say to affect their thinking and behaviour?** This is the heart of your message strategy. It is the single most persuasive thing that you can do or say to get stakeholders thinking and acting the way you would like. And it should be limited to one central and powerful claim. As a job seeker, you could claim that you bring an unusually high level of maturity to positions in your chosen industry. A professional could claim that your services will deliver the quickest, most cost-effective results. An as artist, your claim could be that your works will add a contemporary, avant-garde touch to homes and offices. In the case of the entrepreneur's product being perceived as being too expensive, you could claim that it requires less maintenance than competitive offerings.

6. **What is the support for our claim?** Supporting reasons for your central claim make it more convincing. A high level of maturity can be the result of your having had part-time and summer jobs that required an extraordinary level of responsibility on your part. Quicker, more cost-effective results can be delivered because you have access to the most innovative software in the industry. Your art will add an avant-garde touch to homes and offices because it's created with unexpected contemporary themes in mind. Your product needs less maintenance because it's made with the most durable materials available.

7. **What is the personality we want to communicate for our product or brand?** The final step in preparing your message strategy is to describe, in three or four words, the personality characteristics that you would like your stakeholders to remember about you or your product. Do you want prospective employers to recall you as being energetic, cool-headed, and resourceful? Potential professional services clients to remember you as knowledgeable, approachable, and thorough? Potential clients for your art to think of your works as daring, thought-provoking, and elegant? Current and prospective customers for your product to see it as being tough, reliable, and helpful?

While these seven questions are simple, coming up with clear, unambiguous, and meaningful answers can be a difficult process. But to successfully market yourself, you need to go through the process because your message strategy will help you respond to the single most important question of all: Why should we hire you? Why should we buy your product? Your answer should be the focal point of every IMC activity you engage in.

DEVELOPING IMC MESSAGES: CREATIVE EXECUTION ISSUES

These seven questions are intended to help you determine *what* you will say—that is, your message strategy. Once you determine the content of your IMC message, you need to figure out *how* you'll communicate it—that is, your message execution. Think of your strategy as the logic behind your message and the execution as the magic of your message. For example, the strategy or logic behind BMW's advertising is that BMW vehicles offer the best performance available. The execution or magic is contained in the brand's television commercials and magazine ads, which proclaim BMWs will deliver the "Ultimate driving experience." Before your mind races off and starts thinking about colour, type font, spokesperson, pictures, and musical background, you should first decide which type of appeal you'll be employing to persuade your target to think or behave the way you would like. Essentially, you need to choose from among the following: a rational appeal, an emotional appeal, or a combination of the two.

Rational appeals focus on your target's practical or functional needs. Messages that use rational appeals tend to be more informative, focusing on facts and using the logic of persuasion. Such messages typically attempt to persuade customers to buy a product because it is the best alternative on some functional dimension such as dependability, efficiency, and good health. For example, the ad in Exhibit 9.8 uses a rational appeal by stressing the functional benefits of drinking milk.

Rational appeals can take different forms. A *favourable price appeal* makes the price the dominant persuasive element in the message. Wal-Mart's messages typically use a favourable price appeal. A *feature appeal* focuses on the dominant or best feature of the product. For example, a car advertisement that cites "the roomiest interior in its class" is an example of a feature appeal. A *comparative appeal* entails comparing your product, implicitly or explicitly, to your competitor's. For instance, Arby's restaurants has used television messages that compared its grilled chicken sandwich to McDonald's chicken nuggets and heavily emphasized the additives found in the latter but not found in Arby's sandwiches. A *news appeal* highlights some recent news about the product, company, or issue that relates to the product. New product improvements or breakthroughs often use this type of appeal. A *popularity appeal* focuses on the popularity of the product by emphasizing how many customers already use it. For example, "the Number 1 dandruff shampoo" would be an example of a popularity appeal.

EXHIBIT 9.8   Example of a Rational Appeal

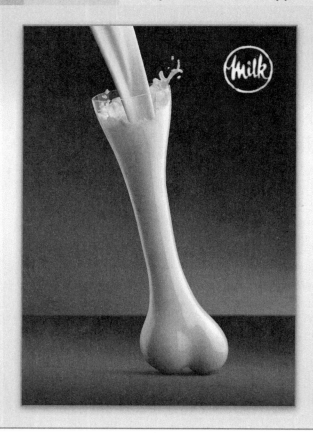

Courtesy of Dairy Farmers of Canada.
Photography: Philip Rostron—Instil Productions.

Emotional appeals, on the other hand, address customers' social and/or psychological needs. As was the case with rational appeals, they can take many forms and tap into a range of human emotions— from acceptance by loved ones and the hope of success to nationalism and respect. It is therefore essential to be clear on the precise emotion that will be associated with the product being promoted. Typically, marketers tend to focus on positive emotions. Exhibit 9.9, for example, contains an emotional-appeal ad for Blistex's SPA Effects line of lip care treatment that encourages customers to use the product to experience the emotional benefits of feeling uplifted, renewed, and relaxed.

Negative emotions can also be used, as is the case in *fear appeals.* These tend to work better when a moderate (as opposed to an extreme) level of fear is used. For example, Sure deodorant's campaign that stressed the social embarrassment that body odour can create is an example of a mild fear appeal.

Sex appeals and *humour appeals* are two special cases that need to be handled carefully. These appeals can certainly get your message noticed but they are not universally effective. Their effect depends both on the product being promoted and on the characteristics of the target market. Humour appeals can be used to promote the functional and emotional benefits of a product. For example, television commercials for Axe products for men promise that by using them guys will smell great (functional benefit) and will be swarmed by sexy young women who can't resist the fragrance (emotional benefit). The magazine ad shown in Exhibit 9.10 is another example of marketing communication that uses a humour appeal to build strong relationships with customers.

EXHIBIT 9.9 **Example of an Emotional Appeal**

Courtesy of Blistex Corporation.

EXHIBIT 9.10 **Humour Appeal by Virgin Atlantic**

Reproduced by permission of Virgin Atlantic Airways.

Combination appeals are used when customers' decisions involve both a strong rational and an equally powerful emotional component. For example, an ad for an SUV might emphasize its off-road handling, safety rating, and horsepower (feature appeals), while simultaneously using visual elements to connote the sense of power, status, and superiority that drivers will experience while driving such a vehicle (emotional appeals).

 Self Check

What type of appeal will you use to convey your message?

How will your target market likely react to

- a rational appeal?
- an emotional appeal?
- a humour appeal?
- a combination appeal?

 Myth

When networking, the question uppermost in my mind should be "What can this person do for me?"

 Reality Check

The first question you need to answer is "What can I do for them?" **Networking is not a one-way process** and is all about creating favourable exchanges for both parties. If your goal is to get people to help you, the surest way to achieve it is for you to demonstrate how you too can help them. You might know people who they could benefit from meeting. If you do, let them know. You could share some new industry information you've gathered that would be of interest to them. If you did a class project on their market or organization, you could give them a brief summary of the key outcomes of your project.

networking — the process of establishing relationships with people who can assist you with job search and customer acquisition strategies and particularly with finding job and sales leads

NETWORKING

Networking is actually a form of public relations, but it can be so crucial to employment and sales success that we're treating it as a separate topic. Networking is the process of establishing relationships with people who can assist you with job search and customer acquisition strategies and particularly with finding job and sales leads. The benefits of networking can't be overestimated, because networking can help you:

- Focus on your career direction
- Find out about jobs and sales opportunities you wouldn't otherwise know about. (Almost seven out of ten jobs are identified through networking.)
- Gain insider information about the industry, trends, job search, hiring, and buying processes in your field
- Get information about specific employers or buyers
- Create the opportunity to promote yourself or your product (and to deliver your message strategy to decision-makers)
- Sharpen your communication, interviewing, and sales presentation skills
- Get referrals to people who may help you

Your basic networking objectives should be:

- To make as many people as possible aware that you are searching for a job or have a product to offer
- To seek job and sales leads and referrals
- To make a good impression on potential employers and customers as well as on people who are connected to them

Every time you make a new contact, the network of people who can help you grows exponentially. Start your network with people you know and who can link you to others who in turn will help you discover job and sales prospects. Then build your network from some or all following sources:

- Friends, family, and neighbours
- Current and former customers, employers, and co-workers
- Current and former teachers and professors
- Career and job fairs
- Current and former classmates
- People you've met at conventions, trade shows, and networking events
- Fellow volunteers, websites, bulletin boards, and chat groups
- Industry and professional associations

You might be surprised at how quickly you can create a network of hundreds of people!

✓ Go out of your way to meet people.

✓ Treat everyone you meet with respect and courtesy.

✓ Respect your contact's time.

✓ Whenever someone helps you in any way, thank them. A hand-written note or a telephone call says a lot more than an email.

✓ Ask people in your network for advice about how to find customers or the job you want. Ask for referrals.

✓ While in school, participate in extracurricular activities.

✓ Join and actively participate in industry, trade, or professional associations and attend their events even if you only do so as a volunteer.

✓ Even if you don't have a job or a business, have professionally designed business cards so that you can give them to new members of your network.

✓ Help others and they in turn will help you.

✓ Remember that networking is a two-way street. Asking if you can provide assistance to someone who has helped you is an excellent approach to marketing yourself and strengthening your network relationships.

✓ Let your contacts know when you get a job or land a customer from their referral.

🖐 *Myth*

*Only people who are naturally outgoing and **extroverts are good at networking.***

☑ *Reality Check*

If at first it feels awkward to walk up to someone at a cocktail reception or conference, tell yourself that the other person is probably interested in expanding his or her network as much as you are in expanding yours. Approach this exercise from a win–win perspective and **if you're stuck or shy, try to strike a conversation by talking about something you know the other person is interested in.** A simple compliment might often be enough to get the ball rolling ("I really enjoyed your presentation"), and before you know it you'll be chatting away and expanding your network. Then follow up by email with a simple "it was nice to meet you."

	artist	*employee*	*entrepreneur*	*professional*
MY PROMOTION OBJECTIVES	Communicate to target clientele and influencers that I am a serious artist whose works will give homes and offices a fresh, contemporary touch	Communicate to potential employers and influencers (e.g., university placement office personnel, executive search consultants, former professors) that I am a desirable candidate for long-term employment and advancement	1) Create awareness and excitement about the magazine among potential readers with the ultimate goal of building readership to levels that will be attractive to advertisers 2) Introduce the magazine to potential advertisers and persuade them to allocate a portion of their budgets to the magazine	1) Create awareness among residents within a 5-kilometre radius of my office 2) Induce 250 potential clients to come in for a free examination 3) Generate 100 new account openings
MY PROMOTION STRATEGY	Communicate my positioning and brand identity to the target market using direct marketing, Internet, and public relations	Communicate my positioning and brand identity to the target market using direct marketing and public relations (especially networking)	1) Create high levels of word-of-mouth prior to and during the launch; obtain links with related websites 2) Reach potential advertisers using telephone, email, and regular mail; make personal sales calls when time and money permit	Use direct mail and advertising in community newspapers
MY PROMOTION TACTICS	1) Drive traffic to my website via online advertising and link exchanges 2) Build a database of potential customers via a contest on my website and then use direct marketing to communicate with them about my new works 3) Get at least one article published about my work in local newspaper	1) Create a resume and cover letter that communicate my unique characteristics and value to the target market. Mail these to a qualified list of potential employers and follow up by telephone 2) Create opportunities to network with influencers 3) Secure at least one radio interview about the not-for-profit organization I volunteer with	1) Create a compelling story about the magazine, prepare a press release and distribute it electronically to the general and skiing/snowboarding media; provide radio stations in Vancouver, Calgary, and Montreal with contest prizes (for example, ski hill passes for two) to give away to listeners who call in to enter a contest sponsored by the magazine 2) Have teams dressed in colourful clothing with the magazine's logo and URL on the front and back to visit ski hills and hand out promotional material; exchange links with related websites 3) Identify key potential advertisers and create a call/mail list; prepare and send out introductory promotional material and rate card; follow up systematically with potential advertisers	1) Design a compelling quarter-page ad and run it 12 times in the appropriate local community newspapers 2) Design and print direct mail postcard to be distributed by a reliable direct marketing company

MY Promotion Objectives

Typical objectives include creating:

- awareness
- knowledge
- liking and preference
- trial
- purchase
- loyalty

MY Promotion Strategy: How Will I Achieve My Promotion Objectives?

What are your specific, quantified goals for each IMC tool?

Which promotion tools—public relations, direct marketing, advertising, personal selling, sales promotion, word-of-mouth, and the Internet—will you employ?

What role will networking play?

MY Promotion Tactics: How Will I Execute My Promotion Strategy?

What specific promotion activities will you use, when, and at what cost?

KEY TERMS

advertising — any paid, non-personal form of communication by an identified sponsor

awareness — the first necessary (though not sufficient) step to create a sale; letting your target customers know of your existence, hopefully in a way that motivates them to seek further knowledge about your product, then develop a preference, and ultimately try and then keep purchasing your product

direct marketing — any one-on-one communication with targeted individuals, such as direct mail (including direct email) and telemarketing

IMC (integrated marketing communications) — an approach that focuses on optimizing the impact of marketing communications by coordinating them to create a unified message to all stakeholders

the Internet — a highly targeted direct marketing vehicle that has evolved from its original role as an information provider

networking — the process of establishing relationships with people who can assist you with job search and customer acquisition strategies and particularly with finding job and sales leads

objective–task method — a method of budgeting marketing communications expenses by first defining the objectives and then costing the tasks required to accomplish these objectives

personal selling — person-to-person communication in which the seller attempts to assist or persuade prospective buyers to purchase his or her product or to act on an idea

public relations — non-personal communication about a product, brand, organization, idea, or person not directly paid for or run under direct sponsorship

pull strategy — concentrates on appealing to the end consumers directly so they in turn will request the product from members of the marketing channel

push strategy — promotion strategies and tactics (e.g., trade allowances) directed at members of a channel, such as distributors and retailers, to entice them to sell a product to the end consumer

sales promotion — catch-all term for those marketing activities that provide extra value or incentives to the ultimate consumer, sales force, or distributors to stimulate sales

How Marketing-Savvy Have You Become?

1. It's been said that rational appeals can change people's minds, but emotional appeals can change their behaviour. In fact, most advertising campaigns appeal to both the brain and the heart. Identify three television commercials you've recently seen and discuss how each of them uses both types of appeals. In each of the spots that you have chosen, which type of appeal is the most prominent?

2. Assume you're a painter and you would like a particular gallery in your city to carry your works. What types of public relations and sales promotion programs could you propose to the gallery's owners to convince them that your paintings draw potential clients to the gallery?

3. You're an entrepreneur who is just about to launch your own line of premium cat and dog food supplements to be sold through pet food stores, pet shops, and veterinarians' offices. How could you use sales promotion as part of both a push and a pull strategy?

4. If you met someone at a party and had only 30 seconds to tell them why they should consider hiring or referring you to someone they know who is hiring, what would you say?

5. "Nothing kills a bad product faster than great advertising." What does this statement imply?

NOW WHAT?

You've now completed the four steps required to create your marketing strategy. Well, almost. In the next chapter we'll cover promotion tools that are unique to marketing yourself, including resume and cover letter writing and interviewing skills. With your appreciation of the importance of all of the four Ps, especially product, and the knowledge you've gained about the area you want to work in and about yourself, you're well positioned to take maximum advantage of the potential that these tools offer.

When marketing yourself is part of your everyday life

Meet Aline Massouh. Aline is a brand manager for Mega Bloks, a leading toy manufacturer. She gathers and analyzes competitive intelligence, follows up on the product development process, and develops the positioning and marketing strategies for new and existing products. To move forward on the various mandates that she is entrusted with, Aline works with many individuals from different divisions within the company. This often requires tact and diplomacy.

While still in university Aline realized that reaching her career objectives was going to entail more than just crafting an attractive resume. At school and in her part-time jobs, she made a point of becoming known as a reliable "go-to" person. In every group project she worked on, Aline made sure it was completed on time and she consistently was a helpful and enthusiastic team member. She knew that a reputation takes time to build, and, as she puts it, "You never know how the person you are sitting next to in a classroom could be the catalyst in your career!"

Upon graduation, Aline turned down an offer for what looked like a very good job but one that she was not passionate about. Although she had no other offers on the table, she waited and ultimately accepted a lower paying position with Mega Bloks. In effect, she used a penetration pricing strategy, and this was a key to helping Aline secure a job in an industry that interested and excited her. While not the highest paying, her new position held the promise of fast advancement. So, true to her personality and work ethic, Aline became a "go-to" person at Mega Bloks, forging relationships with co-workers and individuals across departmental lines. To be sure, Aline used more than a smile to reach her objectives. She constantly provided more than her supervisor and co-workers expected. As she had done at school, she became known as a resourceful, productive, and friendly colleague. After only six months, Aline received a promotion to the position of assistant brand manager, and within less than a year was promoted again to her current position.

We asked Aline what three tips she would like to share with readers of *Marketing Yourself*. Here are her thoughts:

1. *Know yourself.* Knowing what you don't like is just as important as knowing what you do like. Know your strengths and how to leverage them. There is no reason why you should accept a job that you are not truly excited about, but in order to find that job, you must first know yourself.

2. *Know what is available.* Research companies and entire industries. This way you will be able to make better decisions when the job offers come in.

3. *Learn to sell yourself.* Every day, every contact is a selling opportunity. Developing relationships takes time and effort, but it is well worth it. Seize every opportunity to forge ties with people in your classroom, at the gym, at work. If people don't know that you are looking for a job or what your talents are, you may be missing out on opportunities.

Imagine being the human resources manager for a company that placed the following advertisement in the employment section of a local newspaper in a major city:

National Advertising Agency Needs an Account Coordinator—Now!

We have landed a major new client in the computer gaming industry creating an immediate opening for an account coordinator to work with a team of account managers and planners for this new client. This is an entry-level position and while no agency or industry experience is required, candidates who have worked in business-to-business customer service will be given preferential consideration. An undergraduate university degree in communications or business and excellent written and oral communication skills are essential. If you meet these requirements, are a team player, and enjoy working in a fast-paced environment, send your resume to Box 7777 within the next four business days. A competitive salary and benefits package are offered.

Response levels to ads such as this is typically very strong, especially if they are run in spring—just before the end of the academic year, when fresh graduates begin to flood the job market. It wouldn't be unusual for you, as the human resources manager, to receive more than 250 resumes to this ad. If your goal is to narrow down the number of interested and qualified candidates to ten, you'll have to filter out 96 percent of the resumes you've received. Eliminating the first 200 will likely be fairly easy. Up to 20 percent, or 50 of the 250 applicants, will not meet the requirements set out in your ad or will confuse the job title with a position in the field of accounting. The resumes of the remaining 75 percent, or 150 applicants, will likely have one or more of the following flaws:

- No accomplishments listed

- Negative visual impact

- Poorly written or no cover letter

- Lack of a statement of objective

- Format problems
- Inclusion of irrelevant information
- Unexplained time gaps
- Excessive length

So, now you have 50 resumes remaining and you need to eliminate 40 of them. How might you go about this? Well, first you'd probably rank the applicants on certain "hard" criteria, such as how strongly their work experience relates to the job as well as the extent of their involvement in extracurricular activities and how these relate to the job. A list and description of their academic, work, and extracurricular accomplishments would enhance an applicant's position, as would a cover letter that focuses on how the applicant can meet or exceed the requirements for the job (and in the process make you look good!). Next, you'd rank the applicants on the "soft" criteria, including the quality of the language and grammar used in the resumes and cover letters, how the writing tone and manner connect with you, and the overall appearance and reader-friendliness of the documents.

After much ranking and re-ranking, you and the future coordinator's supervisor choose the ten applicants to interview. After every interview, you both evaluate each candidate on a number of criteria including their appearance, attitude, job qualifications, verbal communication, nonverbal communication, listening skills, and enthusiasm. If, after an interview, one or more candidates send a note thanking you or the supervisor for the time spent with them, all other things being equal, you might rank them higher than candidates who didn't send a thank-you note.

At the end of all of this, if more than one candidate remains, second and even third interviews could be conducted. And, finally, an offer will be made to one or two of them.

Now let's reverse your role from that of the employer to that of you being one of the applicants. The principles you've covered so far in this book can go a long way to helping you make the final ten and ultimately being made an offer. You've researched potential employers with the goal of determining what they look for in employees and the problems they need solved. You've assessed your aptitudes, strengths, and weaknesses and have made the product improvements necessary to satisfy their hiring criteria. You've created a message strategy that answers the potential employer's question: Of all the other candidates out there, why should we hire you? As a result of all this, you have a real advantage over most, if not all, of the other candidates. To turn this advantage into an interview opportunity and an offer, you'll need a competitive, professional, and compelling resume and cover letter. And you'll need to convincingly present the product that is you in employment interviews. These are among the final all-important steps in marketing yourself.

Myth

*The job search process **starts** with the preparation of a professional resume and a killer cover letter.*

Reality Check

The job search process **ends** with the writing of resumes and cover letters. Preparation of these documents is the final step of your personal marketing plan.

CREATING COMPELLING RESUMES

A resume is a document that communicates your qualifications for a particular job. Many people believe that its primary purpose is to inform. They're dead wrong. A resume is a marketing tool that is written to impress, and it does this by communicating the most impressive information about you.

Compelling resumes have four basic objectives:

1. *To quickly show that you have the qualifications for the job.* This can be achieved by including a clear job objective and by listing your qualifications and capabilities at the top of your resume.

2. *To demonstrate that you can meet or exceed the employer's needs.* To achieve this, include examples of work-related accomplishments in your resume.

3. *To communicate that you are likable and can work well with others.* Emphasize that you are enthusiastic, cooperative, and dependable. Stress activities, teamwork, and leadership.

4. *To appeal to the reader—both human and electronic.* Use action words to describe what you have accomplished. Include keywords throughout to catch readers' attention and pass electronic reviews. Format your resume so that it is compatible with most scanners.

With these goals in mind, we suggest that you begin writing your resume using the following four-step process.

STEP 1: WRITE YOUR JOB OBJECTIVE STATEMENT

You've decided on your objective and your message strategy; now it's time to write them in a format that's appropriate for your resume. Your job objective should be expressed as a job title or the type of work you wish to do. Based on your research, it should reflect the needs of the potential employer. It should also include one or more of your most important job-related skills.

If you have more than one objective, write a separate resume for each of your goals. And, as much as possible, customize your objective statement to each potential employer.

To give you an idea of what constitutes a good objective statement, here are few examples.

> To be an analyst with a global financial services company where knowledge of derivatives and Asian equity markets is an asset.

> To work as an editorial assistant with a medium-sized textbook publisher where my experience in electronic publishing will be an added value.

> To teach in a rural private high school where my fluency in English, French, and Spanish will be put to full use.

> To start my career in human resources management with a Fortune 1000 company with which I can build on my leadership and team-building skills.

> To secure an entry-level position with a medium- to large-sized information technology consulting firm where my education and training as a software engineer will be put to use on leading-edge product development projects.

STEP 2: DECIDE ON THE TYPE OF RESUME

The three most common resume types are chronological, functional, and combination. Let's examine each of them.

CHRONOLOGICAL

chronological resume — a type of resume organization that places the emphasis on employment history and career progression in a way that directly relates to the job the candidate is applying for

This layout style is the one most people are familiar with and is the most appropriate for large, traditional organizations. It documents your skills, work experience, and career progression in a way that is directly related to the job you are applying for. Chronological resumes place the emphasis on steady, work-related experience.

Start the resume with your objective followed by the information category—education or employment history—that best supports your objective. (List your employment history in reverse chronological order, with the most recent position first.) Stress your major responsibilities and accomplishments for each job.

See Exhibit 10.1 on page 250 for an example of a chronological resume.

FUNCTIONAL

functional resume — a type of resume organization that highlights the skills, knowledge, and other qualifications a job seeker brings to the job. Useful for individuals who lack work experience or have gaps in their employment history

This style is particularly appropriate for people who lack work experience that is directly related to the jobs they are applying for and for those who have gaps in their employment histories. Functional resumes highlight the skills, knowledge, and other qualifications you bring to the job. As much as possible, back these up with related accomplishments. Use separate paragraphs to emphasize each qualification and arrange these in order of importance to the job.

See Exhibit 10.2 on page 251 for an example of a functional resume.

COMBINATION

Resumes using this style emphasize the match between your qualifications and the requirements for the position. If you want to emphasize your qualifications or have limited experience, combination resumes may be the most appropriate for you.

List your skills immediately after your objective. Then document your accomplishments in a reverse chronological list of your job experiences. Linking these with specific employers and time periods can add credibility. Insert your education information where it best supports your objective.

See Exhibit 10.3 on page 252 for an example of a combination resume.

STEP 3: ORGANIZE YOUR RESUME AND WRITE CONVINCINGLY

Using the resume style that you've chosen as a framework, prepare a simple and complete outline for it. Then introduce each major section and subsection with a headline followed by a sentence or short paragraph. For example:

> **RELATED EXPERIENCE**
>
> **Leadership:** As vice-president of the university Geography Students' Association, organized three field trips and initiated a successful recruitment campaign.

Communicate your qualifications and experience clearly and concisely. Make sure you don't leave out any information that may be relevant to the employer or the position. Avoid clichés, outdated expressions, and unnecessarily complex terms. Where appropriate, use numbers and specific examples of accomplishments. "Reduced shipping costs by 25 percent" is much more persuasive than "Significantly reduced shipping costs."

Your resume will be much more convincing if you use action verbs and omit "I" and "my." "Conducted telephone and personal interviews to assess customer satisfaction; analyzed the data collected and reported on major findings" is more convincing than "My duties included interviewing customers on the telephone and in person and reporting on the results."

Keywords are words and phrases that employers look for when reviewing resumes personally or electronically. They typically represent or describe the skills, knowledge, and capabilities required for the position. In effect, keywords name the attributes that qualified applicants must have. You can find the keywords for the jobs you want by reading employers' job descriptions and reviewing industry and professional association websites and magazines.

Many employers scan resumes and rely on resume-tracking software to accelerate this portion of the recruitment process. This is particularly important when it comes to resume-tracking software: the more keywords it identifies, the greater the likelihood that your resume will be among those chosen. Here are some of the keywords this type of software could search for the position of an advertising agency media buyer:

> radio, television, magazines, newspaper, out-of-home, media strategy, media planning, negotiating skills, AC Nielsen, Internet, network, creative, attention to detail, media research, budgeting, team player, analysis, gross rating points, efficiency, presentation skills

Two final points: First, customize your resume to each specific opening you're applying for. Targeted resumes connect with readers much more effectively than do generic ones. Second, limit the length of your resume to one or two pages. For many positions, employers receive hundreds of resumes and for that reason alone they prefer those that are brief and to the point. Remember to emphasize how you can meet employers' needs and that every word in your resume is important. Make them all count.

STEP 4: DRAFT EACH SECTION OF YOUR RESUME

Choose sections that are the most appropriate for your resume and the positions you are applying for. Present them in the order you believe will best address the employer's needs. Following are section-by-section guidelines that you can use to fine-tune your resume.

CONTACT INFORMATION

This appears at the top of your resume and it's where you provide your name, mailing address, telephone number, and email address. Make sure that your voicemail greeting and your email address present you in the best light possible. Don't lose an interview opportunity because either of these is crude or unprofessional.

JOB OBJECTIVE

Place this directly below your contact information; it should be customized for each position you're applying for.

QUALIFICATIONS

Here, you highlight why you should be considered for the position. Employers focus on this section, so use it to emphasize your relevant skills, capabilities, and accomplishments, including the following:

- Your skills and knowledge of software
- Your credentials and degrees
- Your years of experience in a specific field or the specialized skills you possess
- Your work and volunteer accomplishments

Draw attention to each of your qualifications by using bullet points presented in order of the importance of each of them to your objective. For example:

- MA in Education Technology with extensive experience in instructional design for web-based college and university courses
- Four years of experience in client acquisition and customer relations management in the mutual fund industry
- Proven skills as a team player during three successful co-op work terms
- Helped raise funds and secure sponsorships that covered six months of the operating budget for a local Big Brothers and Big Sisters chapter
- Consistently among the top ten percent of salespeople during two years of selling with a retailer of home entertainment electronics

WORK EXPERIENCE

If you're using a reverse chronological layout, list your most recent job experience first and finish with the first relevant job you held. For each job, list the month and year of your employment (e.g., November 2005 to May 2006); the job title (e.g., Laboratory Technician); the employer's company or organization name, city, and province or state; and a short description of the job focusing on results and accomplishments. As mentioned earlier, the more you can quantify the results of your work, the more powerful your resume will be.

If you have held jobs with increasing levels of responsibility with one employer, communicate this to demonstrate that you are reliable and that you have proven growth potential. List only the new responsibilities and accomplishments for each promotion.

If you have little or no full-time work experience, list your part-time and summer jobs as well as any volunteer or community work you have performed including positions held in student organizations. Identify and communicate all of your accomplishments and the skills you developed through these experiences. So, for example, if you earned enough money to support yourself while in college or university, one of your accomplishments could be as follows:

> While studying, earned enough money to pay for rent, food, and other expenses by working part-time during the school year and full-time during summers.

This type of initiative, discipline, and resourcefulness is highly regarded by employers, especially for entry-level positions.

EDUCATION

As was the case with your work experience, list your education in reverse chronological order. List the names of universities, colleges, and technical schools you have attended, the years you attended them, and the degrees and certificates you earned. If you have relevant certifications or specialized training or if you have attended relevant seminars, include them too.

Recent graduates with limited work experience should highlight school activities, internships, and any notable education achievements. If you have a major or minor that supports your job objective, list it. For example, a psychology major with a minor in biology who wants to work in pharmaceutical sales could benefit by listing the specific biology courses he or she has taken.

PERSONAL DATA

Leave out information about height, weight, age, gender, marital status, race, and nationality on your resume. It is against the law in most countries for employers to ask for such data. Don't include a photograph, because employers wishing to avoid discrimination will not consider a resume with an enclosed photo.

If your pastimes and interests are relevant to your job objective, include them and make sure to highlight any notable accomplishments. Being on a championship sports team makes a statement about how well you work with others in pursuing a goal. Reading and writing interests—particularly those that relate to the position you're applying for—can be used to show that you are curious and that you act on your curiosity. And that you're highly literate!

REFERENCES

Most employers do not expect applicants to include references in their resumes, so omit them unless they're specifically requested. However, at some point in the hiring process, you may be asked to provide references. To be prepared for this request, it's a good idea to prepare a separate sheet that includes the names, titles, addresses, phone numbers, and email addresses of your references. Ideally, you should have at least one reference in each of the following categories: employment, academic, and personal. It's important to let your referees know ahead of time that a potential employer may be calling.

STEP 5: FORMAT YOUR RESUME LIKE A PROFESSIONAL

Now it's time to turn your draft into your final resume. Formatting is the first step in this process.

FORMATTING YOUR RESUME

Your resume should be customized for each employer using language that addresses the needs they've identified in their job opening advertisements and notices. Since some employers scan the hard copy resumes they receive, as mentioned earlier, you should ensure your resume is scannable by formatting it so it's appealing to the human eye and easily scanned by electronic eyes.

Here are some formatting tips that will help make your resume reader-friendly to both people and computers.

- Use a simple layout to maximize visual legibility.
- Employ a standard font. Since Times New Roman is overused, consider Arial as an alternative. Body text should be 12 point and headings no bigger than 14 point.
- Use only one space after periods and at the end of sentences.
- Print your resume on laser or inkjet paper in black ink on one side of white or light-coloured 8½ inch by 11 inch paper. Photocopiers typically produce copies that are not of sufficient quality to ensure they are scannable.

Also make sure that you:

- Do not use a highly formatted style, especially one with columns.
- Avoid using underlining, italics, shadows, or coloured text.
- Don't use parentheses.
- Avoid using graphic images and boxes.
- Don't fold or staple your resume.

As the old cliché goes, you have only one chance to make a first impression. That's why it's crucial that your resume instantly communicates credibility and professionalism. To achieve this:

- Don't use the heading "Resume" or "Curriculum Vitae" on your resume.
- Single-space the body of your resume and double- or triple-space between sections.
- Use thick, high-quality white or light-coloured 8½ inch by 11 inch paper.

- Use 1 inch margins on all sides of your resume.
- Use white space to draw attention to important parts of your resume.
- Use bold capital letters for your headings.

After you've drafted your resume, review it carefully and thoroughly with the idea of finding areas that can be improved. Rewrite it as often as is necessary to make sure your resume is as strong as it can be. Edit out unnecessary words and replace weak terms with clear and powerful ones. Then proofread your resume and correct any errors. Finally, have two or three people who have excellent writing skills go over your resume and provide you with feedback. If they have experience in the field you would like to work in, so much the better.

 Myth

*The best way to promote my art is **through email and the Internet**.*

 **Reality Check**

According to John Dawes, president of MusicHosting.net, artists have a tendency to abuse email and Internet promotion by using it to replace human interaction when dealing with venues, the press, retailers, and other industry professionals or to avoid talking with potential customers or fans. He argues that too often music artists tend to follow the latest online promotion fad (like uploading songs on iTunes). Instead, he suggests that **music artists should build and nurture relationships with their fans and industry professionals.** If you're an artist, he suggests, people want to learn about your story and ongoing successes.

SAMPLE RESUMES

On the following pages you'll find samples of the three types of resumes: chronological, functional, and combination.

EXHIBIT 10.1 Sample Chronological Resume

ROBIN K. METZ

127 Mackay Street, Montreal, QC H3G 1M8
514-555-7277   rkmetz@valmail.ca

OBJECTIVE

To start my marketing career with a global consumer products company where I can build on my selling and creative skills.

EDUCATION

Bachelor of Commerce, 2008, John Molson School of Business, Concordia University, Montreal, QC
- Major in Marketing

Related Courses and Skills:

- Proven Personal and Telephone Sales Capabilities
- Advertising and Sales Promotion
- Sales Management
- Marketing Research
- Business Writing (Word and WordPerfect)
- Presentation Software (PowerPoint)
- Website Software (Flash and Macromedia)
- Database Management Software (Access)
- Fundraising
- Fluent in English and French

EXPERIENCE

- **Inter-Canada Bank, Montreal, QC**   January 2006 to present
  Customer Service Representative, part-time during school year and full-time during summers of 2005 and 2006. Processed banking transactions. Offered lines of credit and other debt instruments as well as the bank's investment products. Led all part-time staff in successful mutual fund account openings in 2005.

- **National Telemarketing, Montreal, QC**   Summer 2005
  Conducted outbound telemarketing campaign selling add-on services to subscribers of a major cable company. Attained a closing rate among the top 10 percent of all employees.

- **Share the Warmth, Montreal, QC, Volunteer**   January 2004 to present
  Member of three event planning and fundraising teams, which have raised more than $100 000 in charitable donations to date. Wrote text for website and donation solicitation letters. Revise and update donor database on a regular basis.

EXHIBIT 10.2 Sample Functional Resume

ROBIN K. METZ

127 Mackay Street, Montreal, QC H3G 1M8

514-555-7277   rkmetz@valmail.ca

OBJECTIVE

To start my marketing career with a global consumer products company where I can build on my selling and creative skills.

EDUCATION

Bachelor of Commerce, 2008, John Molson School of Business, Concordia University, Montreal, QC
* Major in Marketing

PROFESSIONAL SKILLS

Personal and Telephone Selling: Trained in selling services to English- and French-speaking consumers as well as in corporate and individual fundraising.
* Opened lines of credit and mutual fund accounts.
* Sold add-on cable television services.
* Solicit charitable donations through personal and telephone appeals.

Business Writing and Website Creation: Expert in using English and French versions of Word, WordPerfect, Flash, and Macromedia. Write professional-quality reports, websites, and promotional material.
* Prepared top-graded advertising, marketing research, and marketing strategy papers for university courses.
* Designed website and wrote text and donation solicitation letters for Share the Warmth, a not-for-profit organization.

Presentations: Proficient with PowerPoint.
* Created and delivered individual and team presentations that were consistently graded among the highest in my business classes.

Database Management: Design, maintain, and generate reports with Access.
* Assisted in the design of a database to track and report on individual and corporate donations for Share the Warmth. Revise and update database on a regular basis.

EXPERIENCE

Inter-Bank Canada, Montreal, QC

January 2006 to present

Share the Warmth

January 2004 to present

National Telemarketing, Montreal, QC

Summer 2005

EXHIBIT 10.3 Sample Combination Resume

ROBIN K. METZ

127 Mackay Street, Montreal, QC H3G 1M8

514-555-7277   rkmetz@valmail.ca

OBJECTIVE

To start my marketing career with a global consumer products company where I can build on my selling and creative skills.

RELATED QUALIFICATIONS

- Trained and experienced in personal and telephone selling of financial and entertainment products
- Create and write business reports and promotional material using Word and WordPerfect
- Design websites using Flash and Macromedia
- Create professional-quality presentations using PowerPoint
- Build and maintain databases using Access
- Fundraising for not-for-profit organization
- Fluent in English and French

EDUCATION

Bachelor of Commerce, 2008, John Molson School of Business, Concordia University, Montreal, QC

- Major in Marketing

EXPERIENCE

Inter-Canada Bank, Montreal, QC   January 2006 to present
- Customer Service Representative, part-time during school year and full-time summers of 2005 and 2006. Processed banking transactions. Offered lines of credit and other debt instruments as well as the bank's investment products. Led all part-time staff in successful mutual fund account openings in 2005.

National Telemarketing, Montreal, QC   Summer 2005
- Conducted outbound telemarketing campaign selling add-on services to subscribers of a major cable company. Attained a closing rate among the top ten percent of all employees.

Share the Warmth, Montreal, QC, Volunteer   January 2004 to present
- Member of three event planning and fundraising teams that have raised more than $100 000 in charitable donations to date. Wrote text for website and donation solicitation letters. Revise and update donor database on a regular basis.

✓ Is your resume customized to the position (and organization) you are applying for?

✓ Have you included a compelling objective statement?

✓ Does your resume speak to your target customers?

✓ Does it address their needs?

✓ Are you using the appropriate keywords?

✓ Does your resume convey the brand that is YOU?

✓ What three key benefits about your brand does it convey?

✓ Type:
Chronological? Functional? Combination?

✓ Format & Presentation:
Have you included key section headings?

✓ Is your resume reader-friendly to humans and scanners?

✓ Does it have a professional and clean appearance?

✓ Are the print quality and font clearly legible?

✓ Have you limited the number of font types to one or two?

✓ Content:
Have you excluded irrelevant information?

✓ For each of your past jobs, have you listed the month and year of its duration, the job title, employer identification, summary of duties, and achievements?

✓ Have you avoided unexplained time gaps?

✓ Did you use convincing language?

✓ Have you provided your contact information?

Myth

In preparing my resume and cover letter, I should use formats that are recommended in popular books on this subject.

Reality Check

While these are an excellent place to start the writing process, on their own they're insufficient. Many, if not most, of your competitors will be using these books to guide them in preparing their resumes and cover letters. As a result, they will likely all look the same. Do you want yours to get lost in this crowd? If not, think of yourself as a brand and then **communicate your brand in every piece of communication you send out about yourself.**

WRITING WINNING COVER LETTERS

Cover letters, like resumes, are marketing tools. You are the brand that your cover letter is selling and, as you know by now, successful selling begins with a focus on the buyer (i.e., the person who will be reading the letter) and not the seller (i.e., you). Keep this uppermost in your mind when composing your cover letters by emphasizing what you can do for the organization, not what it can do for you. See Exhibit 10.4 for a sample cover letter.

Typically, cover letters contain four paragraphs. Each has a specific purpose.

- Paragraph 1 identifies who you are and why you are writing. Mention the specific position you're applying for. Explain how you learned about it. Express your desire to be considered for the position.

- Paragraph 2 demonstrates your understanding of the job requirements, why you are interested in the organization or field of work, and what you have to offer.

- Paragraph 3 shows how you specifically meet or exceed the requirements for the position. Refer the reader to your resume and key skills. Emphasize the strongest features that you have to offer as they relate to the position or field.

- Paragraph 4 asks for an interview. Include your phone number. State that you will call on a specific date—approximately five business days after mailing your resume and cover letter—to determine the reader's availability. Thank the reader for taking the time to consider your application.

EXHIBIT 10.4 Sample Cover Letter

127 Mackay Street
Montreal, QC
H3G 1M8
514-555-7277
rkmetz@valmail.ca

March 5, 2007

Ms. Anne Martin
Vice President of Marketing
L'Oréal Paris Inc.
567 University St.
Montreal, QC
H4T 2L2

Dear Ms. Martin,

I will be graduating this May from the John Molson School of Business with a Bachelor of Commerce. My major is marketing. As a result of speaking with two L'Oréal product managers at a recent job fair at my university, I'm keenly interested in an entry-level position with your marketing team.

As a global leader in the beauty products industry, L'Oréal expects its people to perform at the highest levels. I have a passion for consumer products marketing and a strong desire to work in this area domestically and, ultimately, internationally. With the support of your company's world-class training programs, I believe that my levels of energy and motivation will develop me into the type of employee that will contribute to L'Oréal's continued success.

As you will see in the enclosed resume, in addition to the advertising, sales management, marketing research, and business communications courses that I have completed, I am highly proficient with PowerPoint, Access, and Macromedia. My part-time and summer work as a customer service representative with a major financial institution and my volunteer activities have taught me how to thrive in a team environment and have sharpened my sales skills. As a copywriter, I have created text for a variety of promotional materials. I believe that my education, work experience, and attitude make me an excellent prospect for your marketing department.

May I meet with you to discuss employment opportunities at L'Oréal? I will call you next week to request an appointment or you can reach me at the contact information above. I look forward to talking with you.

Yours truly,

Robin Metz

Enclosure: Resume

1	Avoid using a seeking approach, such as "I am looking for a challenging opportunity in software engineering." Instead, take a reader-oriented approach such as "You have the opportunity to hire an energetic, creative problem-solver with a proven track record in developing process control software."
2	Personalize your cover letters by addressing them to the appropriate person and by using his or her correct full name and title.
3	As was the case with your resume, create an immediate positive first impression with your cover letter.
4	Project an approachable and professional image in your writing style.
5	Exude confidence in your qualifications. Show interest and enthusiasm for the position.
6	If there is the possibility that the position will require you to move, state your willingness to relocate
7	Print your letter on the best quality paper you can buy and format it in acceptable business style.
8	Hand-sign your letters with a blue ink pen.
9	Make sure your letter is perfect, with no spelling or grammatical errors whatsoever. After you've proofread it at least twice, have someone who has excellent language skills proofread your letter as well.

REMEMBER TO SAY THANK YOU

Immediately after an information gathering or job interview, you should send a thank-you letter to the key people with whom you talked. While email is an increasingly popular medium, letters sent by regular mail are more likely to stand out and get noticed. If you'll be using regular mail, try to send out your thank-you letters the same day as the interview. Hand-write or type them based on your assessment of the organization's culture. If in doubt, type it. As with your cover letter, use the best quality paper you can afford. Your thank-you letter should be warm, personal, and professional. Most of all, it should be sincere.

Thank-you letters show that you are mature and understand business etiquette. They should express your appreciation for the interviewer's time and reaffirm your interest in the position and organization. Your thank-you letter can also be used to clarify things discussed during the interview and add any information that you believe will strengthen your candidacy. See Exhibit 10.5 for a sample thank-you letter.

EXHIBIT 10.5 **Sample Thank-You Letter**

127 Mackay Street
Montreal, QC
H3G 1M8
514-555-7277
rkmetz@valmail.ca

March 5, 2008

Ms. Anne Martin
Vice President of Marketing
L'Oréal Paris Inc.
567 University St.
Montreal, QC
H4T 2L2

Dear Ms. Martin,

Thank you for taking the time to see me on Monday and for giving me a tour of your marketing department. I thoroughly enjoyed talking with the four team members to whom you introduced me. Their levels of excitement and energy are impressive and speaking with them reaffirmed my desire to work for a market leader such as L'Oréal.

Needless to say, I am still very interested in the assistant product management position that you mentioned will become available at the end of April. I believe that my education combined with my previous customer service experience at Inter-Canada Bank and my marketing work with Share the Warmth qualifies me for the position. I very much appreciate your invitation to include me in the interview process.

Until then, if you have any questions whatsoever or if there is any information that you would like me to send to you, please let me know. I look forward to meeting you again.

Yours truly,

Robin Metz

Myth

If my resume is attractive, potential employers will read it in its entirety.

Reality Check

In most cases, employers will spend less than 30 seconds reviewing your resume *if* it catches their eyes, and even less otherwise. They frequently have hundreds of resumes to go over in a day or less and don't have the time to read every one thoroughly. The lesson? **In addition to making your resume reader-friendly and attractive, make every word count**: from the very first section, give employers a compelling reason to keep reading your resume. Use attention-grabbing keywords, and highlight your key qualifications and accomplishments where appropriate. Most of all, let employers quickly identify what need(s) you can fulfill for them or their organizations.

INTERVIEW LIKE A PROFESSIONAL

The interview is crucial for both you and the potential employer. It is the best opportunity for you to sell yourself and for employers to assess your qualifications relative to their needs. At the end of the interview both of you should have a clear idea of the extent to which you meet each other's expectations and how well you fit together. In this section, we'll give you an idea of what to expect from interviews and how to prepare for them.

INTERVIEW PREPARATION

After you secure an interview, the next order of business is to prepare for it. Here are the key preparatory steps you need to consider.

REHEARSE

Your situation analysis and the self-assessment tests you have completed using the Marketing Yourself website have given you insight into what your strengths and aptitudes are. You have set short- and long-term goals for yourself. You've created your personal positioning statement and message strategy. Review these and write answers to sample interview questions, including the following:

- What are your greatest strengths?
- In what areas could you improve?
- Where do you see yourself five years from now?
- What are the things that attract you to this industry and our organization?
- Why do you believe you're a good candidate for this position?

Rehearse your answers with someone whose knowledge and experience you have confidence in.

UNDERSTAND THE ORGANIZATION

As part of your situation analysis, you conducted an in-depth review of the area you want to work in and the dynamics of it. You may have even analyzed some of the key players in it, including the ones whom you would like to work for. Go over this part of your marketing plan and do whatever is necessary to learn as much as you can about the organization you'll be interviewing with. Talk to your contacts, search the Internet, visit your school's library, get copies of annual reports, read every magazine and newspaper article about the organization that you can find. This alone could give you an enormous competitive advantage, as only a minority of interviewees conduct any background research on potential employers before actually going to interviews.

Here are the main aspects about the organization with which you should try to familiarize yourself.

1. **The Industry and Environment in Which the Organization Operates**
   - Is the organization in a stable, cyclical, or rapidly changing industry or environment?
   - What is the current and potential growth of the industry or area of activity that the organization is in?
   - What is the short- and long-term outlook for the industry or environment?

2. **The Organization Itself**
   - In the case of a company, is it public or privately owned? What is its level of sales and how are they trending?
   - How many people does the organization employ?
   - Is the organization's scope local, regional, national, or international?
   - How stable is the organization?
   - What are its economic and social goals? Its mission?
   - Has the organization been recognized for any recent achievements? If so, what are they?

3. **The Organization's Values**
   - One of the most critical factors to your success with an employer is how well your core values fit with theirs. A good fit typically results in satisfaction for both parties. A bad fit almost always creates dissatisfaction for at least one of you. During the interview process, organizations will try to determine how their core values relate to yours. Information about an organization's values can be in its mission and value statements.

Getting answers to the following questions will give you a clear sense of the organization's values.
   - To what extent are employees part of a team?
   - Do employees seem to enjoy themselves on the job?
   - Does the organization have clear goals? Does it live by them?

- How does the organization compensate employees? Does it offer profit sharing? Is extraordinary performance rewarded? How?

- Does the organization seem open to change and are individual employees encouraged to make a difference?

- How does the organization develop its employees?

If you can't find answers to all of these, keep a note of the questions and ask them during the interview. Interviewers are generally impressed by candidates who prepare and ask good questions. Asking poorly thought-out questions or none at all can make the difference between a successful interview and one that's a failure.

 Myth

As long as I'm sending out cover letters and resumes, I'll get interviews.

 **Reality Check**

This might be the case in very tight job markets or for those of you who are applying to very specific jobs for which you're perfectly qualified. For the most part, however, **you need to be more proactive in your job search.** Network. Follow up on every job lead. Call potential employers and request interviews. Even if you are not fully qualified for a particular position, ask for an interview anyway. The employer might just have or know about other openings that require someone with your qualifications.

TYPES OF INTERVIEWS

There are many types of employment interviews, the most common ones being the screening interview, the behavioural interview, the assignment interview, and the stress interview. Let's take a look at each of them.

THE SCREENING INTERVIEW

The screening interview is used by organizations to identify qualified applicants for the next level of interviews and to screen out those who are judged not to meet the basic criteria for the job. Your prime objective in a screening interview is to make your qualifications clear and, of course, to leave a good impression. If you're successful in this interview you may be asked to return for a second interview, where you will likely meet one or more members of the management team, including the person responsible for making the hiring decision.

THE BEHAVIOURAL INTERVIEW

In this type of interview, the interviewer asks questions aimed at getting you to provide specific examples of how you have successfully applied the skills required to do the job. So while your personality and some clever answers may have gotten you through the screening interview, you'll need much more than these to be successful in a behavioural interview.

In behavioural interviews, potential employers are looking for hard evidence of skills in each of these areas:

- *Content skills:* Work-specific skills such as knowledge of particular types of software or hardware, research processes, financial reporting, and scientific equipment.

- *Functional or transferable skills:* These are applicable to any number of jobs and include people skills, communication skills, math skills, and analytical skills.

- *Adaptive or self-management skills:* These include personal characteristics such as being dependable, self-directed, a leader, a team player, a problem solver, and a decision maker.

Here are some examples of the types of questions you might be asked in a behavioural interview.

- Can you give me an example of a job situation where you felt you were in over your head? What made you feel that way? How did you handle the situation?

- Tell me how you have put your leadership traits to work in job, sports, or school situations.

- Talk to me about a job-related conflict that you were confronted with and how you resolved it.

- Have you ever been in situations where you had to deal with difficult co-workers or supervisors? How did you manage these situations?

- What is the most challenging situation that you have experienced with a customer? How did you handle it?

- Describe how you used Access to create and maintain the database of current and potential donors.

- Give me three examples of when you went above and beyond the call of duty to get a job done.

THE ASSIGNMENT INTERVIEW

The purpose of the assignment interview is to test how you will perform in a job-related situation. During the interview you could be asked to solve an accounting problem, recommend a solution to a sticky human resources situation, prepare and give a sales presentation, or analyze a technical problem. Alternatively, you could be asked to read a case study, identify the problem in it, and propose one or more solutions to the problem.

In interviews such as these, the key is to be clear-headed by remaining as cool and collected as you can. Don't rush, and cooperate with all of the other participants in the interview.

assignment interview — a type of interview designed to create a situation or scenario similar to the job being applied for in order to test how the candidate will respond

THE STRESS INTERVIEW

The stress interview is usually designed and structured to test your behaviour, logic, and emotional control under pressure and is typically used only for jobs that involve high and constant levels of pressure. Examples of jobs of this nature include air traffic controllers, emergency room physicians and nurses, social workers, lawyers, advertising agency executives, and sales managers.

stress interview — a type of interview where the interviewer puts the candidate in a stress situation to test the candidate's behaviour, logic, and emotional response under pressure

Some of the techniques used by interviewers in stress interviews include the following:

- Staying silent after you've answered an interviewer's question
- Asking questions in rapid succession
- Trying to put you on the defensive by asking irritating questions and making off-handed remarks
- Being highly critical of your responses

To be successful in stress interviews you need to respond with courtesy and to show that you can keep your emotions under control and remain poised. This is not always easy to do. So, to prepare for a stress interview you should rehearse by having someone ask you questions that will test your ability to respond appropriately and, in the process, improve your ability to perform under stress interview situations.

Here are some sample questions asked in a stress interview:

- Your grades aren't as high as I expected. How can I be sure you'll be able to do the job well?
- We've seen many candidates with similar qualifications to yours; why should we choose you?
- Take a look at the desk I'm sitting at. Now sell it to me.
- Why have you held so many jobs in the past?
- Of all the weaknesses that you have, what is the greatest one?

 Myth

If I get nervous during an interview, I should just go through with it and hope for the best.

 *Reality Check*

Letting an interviewer know you are nervous can sometimes play to your advantage. It shows humility and an ability to acknowledge your shortcomings. There is however a fine line between whining and admitting to your nervousness. A forthright approach such as "I'm sorry, that was not my best answer, I'm very nervous because I really want this job. May I take a second crack at answering your question?" might very well help you land a second interview, if not the job itself.

INTERVIEW QUESTIONS YOU CAN EXPECT

We can't predict with 100 percent certainty that you will be asked any of the interview questions that follow. But there's an excellent chance you'll be asked some of them. To ensure you respond in the most compelling way possible, prepare by developing answers to these frequently asked questions.

- How did you choose your career path?
- Why do you want to work for our organization?
- How would you describe yourself?
- What motivates you?
- What are your core values?
- What's more important to you: the money or the opportunity?
- What are your three greatest strengths?
- What are your three greatest weaknesses?
- How would your friends describe you?
- Are you a team player?
- Where do you see yourself in five years?
- Are you willing to move to another city?
- Have you ever been fired from a job? Why?
- Why do you want to leave your current job?
- As they relate to the job you're applying for, what are the accomplishments that you're most proud of?
- Why should we hire you?

Rehearse your answers with someone whose judgment you trust and ask for honest feedback. Then repeat the process until you feel you've developed the best answers you possibly can.

QUESTIONS FOR YOU TO ASK

In most interviews you will be asked if you have any questions. This is a test of your interest and confidence. From your standpoint, asking questions allows you to take on a more active role in the interview. To get you thinking about the questions you might ask, here are some examples. Using these as thought-starters, come up with four or five questions of your own.

- Do you have a training program for this position? Can you tell me about it?
- How would you describe the tasks and duties of this position in a typical workday?
- How will the responsibilities of this position expand with time and experience on the job?
- Can you tell me about the people with whom I will be working?
- Is there any additional information that you need about my qualifications and experience?
- May I ask when you'll be making your hiring decision?

MANAGING INTERVIEW STRESS

Job interviews are among life's most stressful experiences for a number of reasons. Going to interviews means that we'll be subjecting ourselves to evaluation by people we don't know. Typically, these people are in a much more powerful position than we are. Most of us are shy. The fear of rejection, failure, and the unknown plague all

Chapter 10 — Promotion Tools for Marketing Yourself

of us to some degree. Very few of us are comfortable with the idea of selling ourselves. Plus, interviewers frequently turn up the stress level with their tough questions and hard-to-read reactions. As you know by now, the interview is not just about you, it's about what you can do for the employer.

Managing stress is essential to your success and, when it comes to job interviews, you've come a long way in improving your ability to manage it. You've prepared yourself by researching the fields you want to work in and the organizations that particularly interest you. You've learned about yourself by taking a number of self-assessment tests. You've set clear goals and created the strategies to achieve them and you've prepared professional resumes and cover letters. Here are some additional actions you can take to manage the stress that's part of the job interview package.

- *Rehearse:* We've mentioned rehearsing plenty of times in this chapter, but one more repetition is warranted. By practising for the interview, you'll build confidence—and the more confidence you have, the less stress you'll feel. Conduct mock interviews and have the interviewer ask you tough questions and give you honest feedback. Repeat until you are sure you're doing the best you can. If you're able to, videotape yourself in a practice interview. Then watch the tape with a close friend and ask him or her to critique (constructively!) your performance. As you watch yourself (never an easy exercise!) you'll undoubtedly see areas for improvement. Try to correct those behaviours you feel might send the wrong message during an interview.

- *Plan ahead:* Minimize anxiety by being organized and punctual. Don't leave seemingly little things—such as printing your resume, compiling any necessary documentation, selecting your wardrobe, and arranging transportation—to the last minute. Arrive for the interview ten minutes early so that you have time to collect yourself and enjoy a few moments of relative relaxation.

- *Take care of your body:* Get a good night's sleep before the interview. Physical activity is a proven stress-reducer, so go for a workout, a swim, a run, or a power walk on the day of the interview. Not only will this make you feel calmer, you'll also look healthier and more alert.

- *Stay positive:* Remind yourself that the thorough preparation and the effort you've put into the interview opportunity give you every reason to be confident. Remember that interviewers want you to do well, because if you succeed in the interview and are made an offer, they succeed. Finally, keep in mind that no matter what the outcome of the interview is, you'll have taken another important step in moving your career forward. Even if an offer isn't forthcoming, you've had the opportunity to learn about an organization, to sharpen your interview skills, and to make a good and lasting impression.

EVALUATING AND RESPONDING TO JOB OFFERS

The interview has been a success and has resulted in you being made an offer. It's time to evaluate the offer and to put to work the nego-

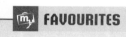

tiation strategies you learned in Chapter 7. To ensure the job meets your needs and objectives, ask yourself the following questions.

- How well does the job fit into my long-term career goals?
- Are there opportunities for career growth?
- Are the values and philosophies of the organization compatible with mine?
- Am I comfortable with the organization's structure and people?
- Is the job itself acceptable to me? Will the work be interesting and challenging?

If the answers to these questions are satisfactory to you and you've negotiated an acceptable salary and benefits package, you'll likely accept the offer. If they're not, you probably won't.

If the offer is made over the telephone or in person, ask for a day to think it over but make sure that this will not inconvenience the interviewer. (If it will, and you're convinced the job is for you, accept the offer on the spot.) The extra 24 hours will give you the opportunity to evaluate the pros and cons of the job. If the offer is made by letter, it may contain a deadline by which to respond. Otherwise, respond within two days of receiving it.

If you accept the offer verbally, confirm your acceptance in writing. Use a positive and enthusiastic tone in your acceptance letter. If you have had interviews with other organizations, advise them in writing about your having accepted a job elsewhere. Call or write all of the people who helped you in your job search, including your referees, to thank them.

If you decide to reject the offer, let the employer know by telephone first. Be prepared to answer questions about why you are declining it. Follow this up with a polite letter confirming your decision and thanking the employer for having made the offer.

KEY TERMS

assignment interview — a type of interview designed to create a situation or scenario similar to the job being applied for in order to test how the candidate will respond

chronological resume — a type of resume organization that places the emphasis on employment history and career progression in a way that directly relates to the job the candidate is applying for

functional resume — a type of resume organization that highlights the skills, knowledge, and other qualifications a job seeker brings to the job. Useful for individuals who lack work experience or have gaps in their employment history

stress interview — a type of interview where the interviewer puts the candidate in a stress situation to test the candidate's behaviour, logic, and emotional response under pressure

How Marketing-Savvy Have You Become?

1. Identify and briefly describe five ways that cover letters and resumes written by people who have gone through the process of preparing their personal marketing plans will likely stand out from the cover letters and resumes written by people who haven't.

2. Why is it highly recommended that you prepare individual cover letters and resumes for each employer you are applying to?

3. For most people, one-page resumes are much more difficult to write than multi-page resumes. Why is this so?

4. How are job interview skills similar to those required for sales calls? How do they differ?

5. What are five things you can do to make that all-important good first impression in an interview?

NOW WHAT?

You've completed almost all of the steps involved in creating your marketing plan. You've conducted a situation analysis and a self-assessment. You've set objectives and identified the strategies to achieve them. You know how to write compelling cover letters and resumes and how to prepare for and conduct yourself in interviews. There's just one step remaining: to put all of this into action by setting out the tactics and timetable for your marketing plan. That's what we'll cover in the next and final chapter of *Marketing Yourself*.

When marketing yourself is in your everyday actions

Meet Robert Roach. Rob is a technology sales manager for Oracle Corporation, where he is responsible for selling Oracle's software to the Canadian federal government. After finishing his undergraduate degree, Rob wanted to go into advertising. However, after a long and unproductive search, he revised his objective. Ultimately, Rob's habit of keeping in touch with people and maintaining his list of contacts paid off and led to an opportunity in the sales department of NCR. He has been working in sales ever since and loves the interaction with clients and the variety of challenges that each new selling opportunity brings.

A position in sales, as Rob knows too well, is fraught with ups and downs: the personal satisfaction of closing a sale and helping a client one day versus the disappointment of losing a contract the next. Rob's most important key to success: keep a positive attitude even when others don't share your enthusiasm. Keeping a positive outlook has helped him to successfully deal with the many details and juggle the often stressful tasks involved in sales. However, mistakes do happen. But as Rob puts it: "I'm glad I made the mistakes I did. You only regret the ones you repeat because you haven't learned anything from them. Most employers will forgive mistakes if you correct things and continue to add value to the organization."

Rob found that one way to add value to the organization is by joining something, anything. Volunteering with a charitable organization, joining an exercise class, being part of a book club, anything that extends your network. Naturally, it takes time to build and maintain your contacts, but in the end it usually benefits you personally and your employer as well. Rob also stresses that you should never be embarrassed or reluctant to talk about your successes—without sounding arrogant, of course. As he puts it, "People want to associate with a winner."

We asked Rob what three tips he would like to share with readers of *Marketing Yourself*. Here are his thoughts:

1. *Fight off the temptation to burn your bridges.* All too often we let our temper get the better of us and decide to cut people out of our lives for whatever reasons. You never know where someone's path might cross yours…again!

2. *Don't be afraid to use your contacts.* People like to hear from you, even if it's to pick their brains or ask for advice or a favour. Naturally, you should reciprocate when asked. Start telling people what you are looking for; you never know where help will come.

3. *Make sure your resume and cover letter are top notch.* Work on it early on, polish it, have others read it, and have different versions ready to go.

BY THE END OF THIS CHAPTER...

YOU WILL:

- know how to put your marketing plan together

- know how to implement your marketing plan

- understand your marketing plan is a life-long project

- know what an actual marketing plan looks like

Consider the case of a young man who, at the beginning of his second year at university, decided that he wanted to pursue a career in industrial relations. So he enrolled in as many courses as he could find that were in any way related to the field, including management, industrial psychology, and the history of organized labour. Between his third and fourth years of study he secured a summer job in the industrial relations department of a global packaging company. He initiated the publication of a daily newsletter to keep the 600 plant employees informed about the company's activities. He recruited workers, handled employee insurance claims, and did research to help his supervisor deal with union grievances. This experience strengthened his desire to work in his chosen area, and upon graduation he was hired by the company as the plant's assistant industrial relations supervisor. Marketing objective number one achieved!

After he'd been with the company for three months he was invited to attend his first monthly union/management meeting. The afternoon before the meeting, his supervisor gave him a copy of the agenda—which contained 36 items, all of them related to unresolved contentious issues including the procedure for selecting employees for overtime work, travel and meal allowances for employees who from time to time were asked to work at one of the company's other plants in the city, and the amount of soap management allotted to the factory's washrooms. His supervisor told him that the meeting would last exactly two hours and that his role was to observe and record the proceedings. Under no circumstances was he to say anything.

The four union representatives arrived at the meeting room at the same time as the four members of management. Pleasantries were exchanged and discussion of the first agenda got underway. Within minutes the atmosphere in the room became poisonous as the union accused management of cheating certain employees in the way it allocated overtime hours and management responded that the union representatives were only interested in getting special treatment for their cronies. Each side questioned the other's integrity. Insults were exchanged, some of them personal. The discussion of the first item went on for one and a half hours when both sides agreed that it couldn't be resolved at this meeting and would be discussed at next month's meeting. The discussion of the second item was no less acrimonious and it too went unresolved. With five minutes remaining, the meeting was adjourned and each side tabled three additional items for the next meeting, thereby swelling its agenda to 42 items.

The assistant industrial relations supervisor was more than a bit shocked by the meeting and he asked his supervisor what went wrong. "Wrong?" the supervisor replied. "The meeting went exactly as planned." "But nothing was resolved and the list of contentious issues grew by six. How will we possibly resolve everything next time?" asked the assistant. "We won't resolve any of them. We've had the same meeting 14 times and we'll have it another 22 times and we'll never get past that first item. You see, these meetings are just a warm-up for the major company-wide union/management contract negotiations that take place every three years. They're sparring sessions. Each side is testing the other to see who'll be the first to back down. Neither will, and we're both saving our best shots for the negotiation of the really important contract issues such as wages, management rights, and employee benefits. That's when you'll get to take part in non-stop negotiating sessions that can last up to 72 hours. And for most of that time, all the management and union representatives will be doing is staring at each other waiting for the other side to be the first to blink."

The idea of taking part in such prolonged, tedious, and acrimonious negotiations and at some point becoming the leader of the company's negotiating team held no appeal for the young assistant. He was an outgoing young man who thrived on teamwork, collaboration, and achievement. Plus, he was far from what could be called patient. Disappointed, he realized that the real work of industrial relations was not for him. After a 30-day period of feeling sorry for himself and regretting his first career, he put his Plan B into action: to work in marketing. After spending five educational and productive years in marketing management (during which time he began part-time study for his MBA), he moved into the advertising agency business. After 10 exhilarating years in that industry, with MBA in hand, he decided to investigate one of his passions—teaching. He became a part-time university professor and enjoyed teaching so much that when he was offered a full-time teaching contract, he resigned from his ad agency position and embarked on a new career path. Since then, he has expanded his product offering to include some of his many other passions: consulting, student coaching, volunteering, course development, and book writing. And if you haven't guessed who "he" is by now, he's Harold Simpkins, co-author of *Marketing Yourself*!

The point of this story? There are a few. First, cut your losses early. If you discover you've put yourself in a career situation that's not for you, and in all likelihood will never be for you, move on fast but make sure to learn from the experience. Second, understand that there will inevitably be bumps along your career path. Some will be small and others may throw you right off track. It's a good idea to have a contingency plan just in case your original plan doesn't work out. Third, your marketing plan shouldn't be static. Think of it as being a living document, one that you should adapt to your constantly changing circumstances, your evolving tastes and passions, and your ever-increasing knowledge about yourself.

Myth

Marketing plans take so much time to complete. **They're not worth it.**

Reality Check

Say your marketing plan took you 80 hours to complete. On one hand, that certainly is a lot of time. On the other, it represents about two weeks of full-time work. Compared to the many hundreds—even thousands—of weeks that lie ahead in your career, is two weeks really so much?

PUTTING YOUR MARKETING PLAN TOGETHER

To get you thinking about assembling your complete marketing plan, let's begin with a brief review of the marketing planning process, which we discussed in Chapter 2. Exhibit 11.1 should look familiar to you, especially since you have completed almost all the steps.

EXHIBIT 11.1 The Marketing Planning Process

GATHER INFORMATION, RESEARCH, AND ANALYZE THE MARKETING SITUATION

▼

FORMULATE MARKETING OBJECTIVES

▼

SELECT ONE OR MORE TARGET MARKETS

▼

DEVELOP MARKETING STRATEGIES AND TACTICS

▼

PREPARE A MARKETING PLAN DOCUMENT

▼

IMPLEMENT MARKETING ACTIVITIES

▼

EVALUATE PROGRESS IN ACHIEVING OBJECTIVES

▼

MAKE STRATEGIC AND IMPLEMENTATION ADJUSTMENTS AS REQUIRED

Using Exhibit 11.1 as a backdrop, let's now examine where we've been and what still needs to be done in order to finalize your marketing plan.

SITUATION ANALYSIS

Here you examined the external and internal influences that are most likely to have an impact on how you define and ultimately attain your career goals. This included an in-depth self-assessment that hopefully confirmed some of your self-knowledge and revealed undiscovered aspects of your personality.

GOALS, TARGET MARKET, AND MARKETING MIX DECISIONS

At this stage, you set your career objectives, defined your target markets, and set out the strategies and tactics for each of the four Ps—product, price, place, and promotion. You may have even prepared your resume and cover letter as part of your promotional mix.

IMPLEMENTATION

This step involves identifying how you'll be putting your tactics into action, when you'll be doing this, and then, to paraphrase that famous Nike slogan, "just doing it."

CONTROL

If life were perfect, the implementation of the tactics you identified in your marketing plan would result in the attainment of all of the goals and objectives you had established. But life is far from perfect, and it's more than likely your plan will need to be adapted to the ever-changing and unexpected realities you'll encounter as time goes on. This is where control comes in. At the control stage, you ask and answer the following questions:

- Am I on track to achieve what I set out to achieve?
- If I get off track, what went wrong?
- Why did it go wrong?
- What do I have to do to get back on track?

Your marketing plan is just two relatively short steps away from completion—namely, how you will implement it, and how you will control its progress. To get these steps underway, start by revisiting each section of your marketing plan and ask yourself the following questions:

- Are my analyses still valid? If they're not, you should revise them.
- Have there been any changes in my personal situation or in that of my chosen field that need to be addressed? If so, determine if these will require modifications to your analyses and make any necessary changes.
- Do I still agree with the conclusions that I came to and documented as a result of my analyses? If not, change them.
- Are the goals and objectives that I have set still the ones that I want and need to achieve? If not, modify them.

Chapter 11 — Your Complete Marketing Plan

- Have I identified one or more target markets whose needs I can satisfy with the resources I currently possess or will possess when I put my marketing plan into action? If not, you need to do this.
- Will my marketing mix give me the best shot at attaining my goals and objectives? Review the product, price, place, and promotion strategies and tactics that you've developed and make any adjustments you believe are necessary.

After you've made any necessary changes to your marketing objectives, strategies, and tactics, the next order of business is to set out how and when you will implement the tactics you've decided to undertake.

Myth

Planning will limit my flexibility.

Reality Check

Having a plan is more likely to increase the amount of flexibility you have. A plan sets out your goals and the strategies you'll use to achieve them. With these in mind, you have unlimited flexibility in deciding when and how you'll implement your strategies. In the absence of a plan, **what seems like flexibility is usually aimlessness and an inability or unwillingness to make crucial decisions.**

IMPLEMENTATION

Strategy without tactics is the slowest route to victory. Tactics without strategy is the noise before defeat.

—Sun Tzu (author of The Art of War, 6th century B.C.)

Sun Tzu recorded these powerful insights more than 2600 years ago and they're as valid today as they were then. Implicit in the first part of his statement is that for a strategy to be effective, tactics need to be more than just expressions of intent—they must be implemented. Brilliant strategies and clever tactics are of little value unless they're executed with a constant focus on the objectives they're intended to achieve.

Implementation is the nuts and bolts of your marketing plan, since it involves the actual execution of your strategies and tactics. Implementation starts with identifying the specific activities to be performed in order to put your tactics into action and assigning a timetable for their completion.

Implementation efforts can be derailed by a number of factors. Some of these are under your control, while others are unpredictable and uncontrollable. A typing error, a poorly chosen word, or an overlooked detail can turn an excellent strategy into a fiasco. So can an unforeseen change in the market, an unexpected competitive activity, or failure to deliver by a supplier. How do you prevent a fiasco from happening or at least minimize its impact? By carefully setting out the key implementation steps needed to put your strategy and tactics into action. To do this, break down each tactic into its constituent activities, identifying the controllable events and making contingencies for the uncontrollable ones. This will enable you to anticipate potential breakdowns in your implementation plan and enable you to put in the safety checks to catch mistakes before they occur (knowing full well that Murphy's law—"whatever can go wrong will go wrong"—will eventually apply! When was the last time your printer's ink cartridge went dry ten minutes before the deadline for submitting a 20-page report?).

Carefully listing individual implementation activities and specifying the timeframe for their execution has a way of mobilizing and focusing your energies and efforts. Have you ever wanted to get a project done but delayed its completion for what seemed like valid reasons? "Oh I'm waiting for my teammate to call me back with some missing information." Or "My co-worker was supposed to bring me the graphics this Tuesday but he won't be able to until next week." And then other obstacles (or the sheer power of procrastination) get in the way and you end up never completing the project. Well, once you've spelled out what needs to be done and by when, you'll be less accepting of delays and excuses.

Table 11.1 contains a detailed implementation plan for a fairly simple promotional tactic: getting a one-page flyer printed and distributed. Did you think that getting a simple flyer printed and distributed could involve so many steps? Now, consider that the tactic being implemented in Table 11.1 involves just one flyer to be distributed in a rather small geographic area. Imagine the implementation of a more complex promotional tactic, like when a food manufacturer such as Kraft introduces a new salad dressing and uses a promotional contest where television and print advertisements invite consumers to log on to a promotion-specific website (e.g., www.CoolRanchDelights.com) to enter a sweepstakes for a chance to win a dream kitchen renovation, to get recipes, and to print a cents-off coupon redeemable at their supermarket. Successful implementation would require a complex plan that would involve coordination among many departments, people, retail outlets, and suppliers (including lawyers, to ensure that the contest rules and regulations conform to local legal requirements). The coordination challenge is enormous—one missed detail could sink the whole promotion.

TABLE 11.1   Sample Implementation Plan for a Promotional Tactic

1. Call post office to determine size and other requirements for direct mailings as well as cost (Answer: 15 cents/flyer; oversize gets charged extra; must pick specific postal delivery routes; minimum of 500; must bring flyers in packets of 100 bound with elastic bands).

2. Ask post office when the best time is to mail for maximum impact (Answer: mailing on Tuesday guarantees delivery Thursday). Determine how far in advance I must bring flyers (Answer: two days before mailing date).

3. Determine optimal size. Check flyers I get in the mail and determine which one fits best in mailbox and attracts my attention (Answer: 4 in. x 7 in. seems appropriate).

4. Determine content of flyer. What do I want people to remember and do after seeing the flyer? Come up with draft of content with logo and artwork.

5. Call on printers to find best price. Visit three printers and bring draft to ask for advice on quality of paper. Get quotes. Ask printer to bundle flyers in packets of 100 with elastic bands. What is lead time? How far in advance must I bring material? When can flyers be delivered?

6. Finalize visual and text content of flyer.

7. Get two friends to proof final content. What do they think of the font? Graphics?

8. Make corrections as needed and suggested.

9. Get final material to chosen printer. Ask printer to make sure flyers are ready for Friday morning, June 14.

10. Pick up material from printer no later than noon on Friday, June 14.

11. Take flyers to post office on Friday, June 14. Pick specific routes.

12. Ask for Tuesday, June 18 mailout.

 **Myth**

Successful organizations and people fail less than relatively unsuccessful organizations and people.

 **Reality Check**

In fact, the opposite is true. **Success is typically the result of trying many things, learning and adapting quickly, and keeping what works.** As the old cliché goes: the difference between losers and winners is that losers don't fail as much.

IMPLEMENTATION ACTIONS YOU NEED TO TAKE

In addition to defining the tasks and due dates for each of your tactics, there are three actions that need to be part of your implementation plan. They are as follows:

- If you're the person responsible for implementing the plan (and if you're a job seeker or one-person enterprise, you are that person), take complete responsibility for its implementation. Take responsibility not only for initiating the tasks set out in your marketing plan but also for reaching the plan's objectives.

- Track all tasks, tactics, and strategies and measure what is planned compared to what actually occurs. Make any required adjustments and, most importantly, don't continue any unproductive action "because it is in the plan."

- As the implementation of your plan progresses, track changes in the key environments in which you operate (i.e., social and cultural, economic, technological, political and legal, competitive). Changes may indicate that certain actions you have planned should be changed, revised, or not taken at all.

EVALUATION AND CONTROL

The purpose of evaluation and control is to track the progress of your implementation process and monitor the extent to which your objectives are being met within the timeframe you've established. Evaluation and control should be ongoing since, as we just noted, changes in the marketing environment may require corrective action and changes to your strategies, tactics, and implementation.

The idea of control is to put in place a system of checks and balances to monitor whether you're on track and to learn from your progress so that you can realign your objectives, strategies, tactics, and implementation as needed. The three main components of control are as follows:

- **Setting the standards and defining the timing of your assessment:** List the criteria you'll be using to evaluate your performance—for example, new skills learned, number of job interviews scheduled, sales calls made, and works completed. Then set the specific times you will be evaluating your performance against these benchmarks.

- **Monitoring the results:** Identify what went right and what went wrong. Get to the heart of your successes and failures. Understand the reasons for each. Learn from them and move forward.

- **Taking corrective action:** Decide what to do when your actual performance doesn't meet your planned performance. Set a timetable to take corrective actions. Alternatively, redefine your standards by changing your objectives, strategies, and/or tactics. Your corrective actions or redefinition of standards is input for the setting or re-evaluation of objectives for the next planning cycle.

Perhaps the most widely used control mechanism is the **marketing audit**. The marketing audit is a thorough, systematic, and periodic evaluation of your marketing goals, strategies, tactics, and implementation activities. It can be conducted either by an external

> **marketing audit** — a thorough, systematic, and periodic evaluation of marketing goals, strategies, tactics, and implementation activities

or independent evaluator, and it's intended to comprehensively cover all the major marketing issues facing an organization or individual. A marketing audit tracks the implementation of a firm's marketing plan and helps managers and individuals allocate resources more efficiently for the next phase or period.

While you may not need to conduct a full marketing audit for yourself, you need to decide on the controls you'll use to monitor your progress. To get you thinking about your control mechanisms, you may want to consider the behaviours and activities to be performed before and during implementation as well as the desired outcomes of the implementation process. These are referred to as input controls, process controls, and output controls, respectively.

Input controls include activities to be performed before the actual implementation of your marketing plan, such as securing financing or the selection and training of employees. The idea here is to ensure that you have the tools and resources you need to implement your strategy at your disposal.

Process controls include activities needed during implementation and include issues such as commitment to the marketing strategy, motivation and compensation of employees, and internal communications. For example, an insurance company could create a customer service strategy with the goal of faster turnaround of customer claims. One process control could be to examine the systems and procedures put in place to empower front-line employees to receive claims via email or the Internet. Practising how you handle yourself in interviews with a friend or family member on an ongoing basis and getting their feedback is another example of a process control.

Output controls ensure that marketing outcomes are as expected. Performance standards are typically used as output controls and may include the number of interviews arranged, offers received, sales, number of customers served, market share, profitability, number of referrals, and number of repeat customers. Performance standards need to be linked to your marketing objectives. For instance, if one of your product objectives is to establish yourself as an innovative graphic artist who delivers on time, then your performance standards should reflect this goal. You may decide, for example, to monitor how fast you turn around material for your clients and how far in advance of the due date you deliver. Or you could survey your customers to determine what their perceptions of your turnaround time are. Performance standards may also be set using industry benchmarks. Industry benchmarks are standards that reflect the performance of industry leaders. For example, in the hospitality industry, Ritz-Carlton is often regarded as a benchmark in terms of personalized service. Observing and learning from leaders in your and other industries can produce valuable insights. How do they do it? How have they achieved their success, and what performance standards are they using?

To help you put marketing objectives, strategies, tactics, implementation, and control into perspective and to give you an idea of how they relate to and flow from one another, we've provided the following examples for artists, employees, entrepreneurs, and professionals.

input controls — activities to be performed before the actual implementation of a marketing plan, such as securing financing or the selection and training of employees

process controls — activities and behaviour needed during implementation of a marketing plan, including issues such as commitment to the marketing strategy, motivation and compensation of employees, and internal communications

output controls — activities to ensure that marketing outcomes are as expected

You as an Artist

MY Goal	To have a career as a solo alternative music guitarist and singer
MY Promotion Objective	To expand the audience for my music by securing performance dates in clubs and by making it available in recorded form.
MY Promotion Strategy	Use public relations to create a buzz in the media and among alternative music opinion leaders. Employ the Internet to facilitate sampling of my work. Communicate to club owners that I can help increase their customer counts and revenues.
MY Promotion Tactics	Secure interviews with local weekly entertainment newspapers as well as with college and university papers. Play at low or no cost at selected college and university events. Design an attractive, easy-to-navigate website from which a limited selection of my works can be downloaded. Use direct marketing and personal selling to get club dates.
MY Implementation Steps	Prepare individualized press releases for each newspaper. Contact college and university event organizers and choose which ones to offer my services to. Hire a design student to create my website and get my tech-savvy younger brother to do the programming for it. Write and design a mailer to be sent to clubs. Prepare a contact list of club managers and telephone or visit them after the mailer has been sent out.
MY Timing	Finalize press releases one week before contacting newspapers. Finalize website by February 15. Contact organizers by March 1. Send out mailers by April 30. Visit or call managers by May 30
MY Control Measures	Finished newspaper press releases. Event organizer contact list finalized and calls made. Website design and programming completed. Mailers sent and club managers contacted.

You as an Employee

MY Goal	To secure an entry-level position in human resources at the head office of a major chain retail fashion store within three months of graduating with a bachelor's degree
MY Product Objective	To become knowledgeable about the major types of psychological tests that are used to screen potential employees and those being considered for promotion
MY Product Strategy	To take at least one course in psychological testing and to conduct online and library research on the subject
My Product Tactics	Investigate which course on psychological testing are offered at my university. If there are inadequate courses available at my school, find out where they can be taken at nearby universities or online.
MY Implementation Steps	Register for one course in the upcoming school term
MY Timing	Register for the course as soon as the registration period begins
MY Control Measures	Successful completion of the registration process and obtaining a grade of at least a B in the course

You as an Entrepreneur

MY Goal	To own and operate a successful online wedding planning business within six months of graduating from university
MY Price Objective	To generate at least $35 000 in advertising revenue during the first 12 months of operations
MY Price Strategy	Research how much participants in the wedding industry (e.g., reception halls, invitation designers and printers, wedding dress retailers, jewellery stores, travel agencies, and limousine companies) are currently paying to advertise in magazines and online. Set my prices at comparable levels but offer a one-time 20 percent discount to first-time advertisers on their first order
MY Price Tactics	Design and write an advertising rate card as well as a promotional flyer announcing the 20 percent discount
MY Implementation Steps	Produce online versions of the rate card and flyer. Print 100 copies of each of the rate card and the flyer.
MY Timing	Complete the production of each version one week before launching the website
MY Control Measures	Uploading error-free rate card to website. Delivery of error-free printed rate cards from supplier on time.

You as a Professional

MY Goal	To secure a position with a global management consulting firm with the ultimate objective of becoming an independent management consultant within 10 years of obtaining my MBA
MY Place Objective	To work in a city where the quality of consulting services is regarded as being among the highest in the world and where I can develop an international network of successful consultants and potential clients. These cities include New York, London, and Hong Kong.
MY Place Strategy	Find people who have worked in the consulting field in these cities. Ask about the pros and cons of living in these cities and about any of their peculiarities
MY Place Tactics	Get interviews with the local offices of consulting companies that have branches in each of these cities. If any of them express an interest in hiring me, determine if they will cover the cost of travelling to their offices for interviews. If none are willing to pick up my travel expenses, investigate what these costs will be and decide to go to the city whose travel costs will be the most affordable for me.
MY Implementation Steps	If one or more potential employers are willing to cover my travel expenses, take them up on it! If not, line up interviews in the city I've chosen and make travel and accommodation arrangements.
MY Timing Steps	Begin local interviews during the first month of my last university semester. Arrange for interviews in other cities to take place immediately after the end of my last semester.
MY Control Measures	Did I interview with the local offices of all of the consulting firms that have offices in New York, London, and Hong Kong? If these did not lead to a successful conclusion, did I arrange interviews in the city that is the most affordable for me?

YOUR MARKETING PLAN AS A LIFE-LONG PROJECT

Whether in your personal or professional life, change will always be a major factor. And—as you've probably heard one too many times for your liking—change is occurring at a quicker pace than ever before in history. And the rate of change is actually accelerating! Expect to experience more changes, more often. For the most part, you can't control the changes that will be occurring but you can manage how you control yourself in the face of change. That's where having a personal marketing plan comes in. One of its many benefits is that it will help you deal with the changes that you'll be experiencing throughout your life. You'll be less likely to be taken by surprise by unexpected events and, if you adjust and adapt your marketing plan as you and your circumstances change, you'll be able to take advantage of the opportunities that changes create. The old cliché just might be true: luck is where preparation meets opportunity.

The marketing planning process can be broken down into five questions, the answers to which comprise the plan itself.

1. **Where Am I?**   The answer is your situation analysis.

2. **Where Do I Want to Be?**   The answers are your goals and objectives.

3. **How Do I Get There?**   Your answers make up your strategies, tactics, and implementation.

4. **Am I Getting There?**   The answer to this question comes from the diagnosis that you conducted as part of your control.

5. **Where Am I?**   Now that your plan has been implemented for some time and you've evaluated your progress, where are you now? What do you think the next question is? If you answered, "Where do I want to be?" you're absolutely right. The next cycle of your planning process has begun.

The frequency with which you revise or redo your marketing plan depends on your plan's performance as well as changes in your circumstances and yourself. And since change will be a major force in shaping your future and how you respond to it, we recommend that you review your plan no less frequently than every 90 days. (The first Mondays of January, April, July, and October are easy-to-remember times for your regular review.) Update your plan as often as you judge necessary. Some plans may continue to be appropriate and effective for years; others for months. When you've finished reading this book and completed all of the recommended planning steps, you'll have created a comprehensive marketing plan that should act as a guide for the short and medium terms and a foundation to build on for the long term. You'll have invested your precious time, energy, intelligence, and emotion in preparing your personal marketing plan. Make this investment work for you for the rest of your life.

EXAMPLES OF PERSONAL MARKETING PLANS

We'd like to leave you with a clear idea of what a complete personal marketing plan looks like. So, from the hundreds of marketing plans that have been submitted by students of our online Marketing Yourself course, we've chosen one outstanding example from each of the four career groups: job seekers, entrepreneurs, professionals, and artists. (You'll recognize some of the writers from the Marketing in Action profiles that appeared at the beginning of each chapter of this book.) The marketing plans for a job seeker and an artist are included in this book and begin on page 288 and 304, respectively. The rest are available for you to read at www.MarketingYourself.ca.

KEY TERMS

input controls — activities to be performed before the actual implementation of a marketing plan, such as securing financing or the selection and training of employees

marketing audit — a thorough, systematic, and periodic evaluation of marketing goals, strategies, tactics, and implementation activities

output controls — activities to ensure that marketing outcomes are as expected

process controls — activities and behaviour needed during implementation of a marketing plan, including issues such as commitment to the marketing strategy, motivation and compensation of employees, and internal communications

NOW WHAT?

It's all up to you! We wish you every success in marketing yourself and in finding the job you love.

SOME CONCLUDING THOUGHTS AND A BRIEF REVIEW OF MARKETING YOURSELF

As the saying goes, "Theory without practice is meaningless, but practice without theory is blind." With this book, our goal was to acquaint you with the basic theories from the field of marketing and to show you how you can put them into practice by applying them to your career. Until about 20 years ago, most people (and many scholars) held the belief that marketing was primarily a tool to help big business get into consumers' hearts, minds, and wallets. Since then, non-profit organizations—including museums, educational institutions, hospitals, political parties, and even countries—have adopted marketing to help them achieve their objectives. In 2003, as we brainstormed the idea of putting together a full-fledged online university-level course to teach students how to apply the concepts of marketing to their careers, we became increasingly convinced of the benefits that marketing concepts could deliver to budding job seekers, entrepreneurs, professionals, and artists. Up to that point in time, no one was actually teaching students how to do this. Yes, there were books on resume writing, interview skills, and networking, but precious little on the big picture of career planning and how to use the principles of marketing to help set and achieve career goals. As you've come to appreciate by now (we hope), successful career planning involves much more than promotion. Product, price, and place all play enormous roles. So do other fundamental marketing concepts such as pricing, positioning, and segmentation. With that in mind, we arrived at the following conclusion: by using critical marketing notions we could introduce (or reintroduce) the field of marketing to students by showing them how to apply marketing concepts to themselves. And by having them relate marketing to themselves, we believed that we could make these concepts resonate more strongly and ultimately become more fully assimilated into their day-to-day lives.

Marketing is an enormous field, and we had to make our own strategic choices in deciding what not to cover, what to cover, and how to cover it. For instance, as in the online version of our course, we used the framework of the four Ps. Now, you may be aware of alternative frameworks: some authors have argued that the four Ps are outdated and that there should be a fifth P, even a sixth or seventh. Still others have proposed entirely non-P models. We decided to use the four Ps because they represent a simple, elegant means to help you appreciate the power of marketing and how it can be applied to your career. We also made choices about the concepts to cover and how far down to drill into each one. To be sure, there is much more to be said about segmentation and the various techniques that can be used to paint a complete picture of customers' lifestyles and demographic profiles. Distribution and channel management could have had their own separate chapters. Same for consumer behaviour. It is our hope, however, that through our discussion of the application of the four Ps and the other material we covered provided you with a solid foundation in marketing and stimulated your thinking to explore and implement ways to market yourself, and perhaps to further your marketing education.

Over the years, the marketing concept has been broadened beyond the traditional notions of goods and services. For example, it's now being applied to causes, ideas, and fundraising. If your experience in reading this book is anything like those of our online students and others we've taught over the years, chances are that you are now seeing the influence of marketing in places where you previously didn't notice it. In 1969,[1] in what has now become a classic article in the marketing literature, authors Philip Kotler and Sidney Levy described what they termed "organizational marketing." They argued that non-business organizations can benefit from the same marketing tools used by traditional business enterprises. Political parties, labour unions, social cause advocates, and even public schools can all benefit from the power of marketing. For these organizations, the term "consumers" takes on a new meaning and includes all their various stakeholders—including, but not limited to, the general public, governments, opinion leaders, the media, and the community at large. And, just like traditional businesses, these organizations need to keep their fingers on the pulse of the needs and perceptions of their stakeholders by soliciting continuous feedback from them.

Today, we're all used to seeing organizations such as these taking leadership roles in the area of marketing, and you may want to consider the employment opportunities they offer. Think of campaigns you have been exposed to for MADD, PETA, the Jane Goodall Institute, the Salvation Army, politicians and their parties, and entire cities and countries, which put themselves on the map by actively marketing to tourists and convention organizers. Even publicly owned museums are now marketing themselves with growing sophistication. They're actively trying to attract new visitors and patrons by using marketing to move museums away from their previous high-brow, unapproachable images. If you're not convinced of the value of marketing for not-for-profit organizations such as these, visit the online store for the New York Metropolitan Museum of Art at http://www.metmuseum.org/store to get an idea of just how complex and marketing-intensive its product offering and promotion have become. And let's not forget government-owned corporations, which for decades had very constrained and often poorly executed approaches to marketing relying largely on public relations to react to customers' complaints. Today, these organizations have multifaceted marketing strategies that run the gamut from product innovation to store design, from ad campaigns to event sponsorships designed to establish a corporate presence and a more consumer-focused positioning within their communities. For example, over the past 15 years, the LCBO (Liquor Control Board of Ontario—http://www.lcbo.com) has become one of the largest wine and spirits distributors in the world. Constant tracking of beverage trends and consumer preferences, innovative store design and layout, a sales staff trained to provide recommendations (for which it won more than 200 industry awards), and a sophisticated magazine called *Food & Drink* (http://www.lcbo.com/fooddrink) that could easily rival *Gourmet* and other newsstand publications are all marketing tactics that have contributed to the LCBO's success. In fact, results of a survey published in the June 2005 issue of *Canadian Business* showed that the LCBO was perceived as one of the top ten best managed brands in Canada.

Professional and amateur sports are yet other areas where marketing has made enormous inroads. Remember the 2004/2005 National Hockey League lock-out? Many experts offered up dire predictions about the future of the league during the 12-month stoppage in play—especially in the United States, where hockey ranks well below football, baseball, and basketball in terms of fan support. But attendance in the year immediately after the lock-out hit record levels in most NHL markets. One of the key contributors to the league's successful return was product improvement. During the stoppage, the NHL initiated one of the most sweeping rule changes in its history. The change made the game more exciting by dramatically cutting down on the previously rampant clutching and grabbing that slowed the game and made star skaters and scorers the victims of relentless and frustrating (and not much fun to watch) checking. Only since the 1990s have Major League Baseball teams come to fully embrace marketing. Where in the past their most commonly used marketing tool was media relations, today many have senior executives responsible for branding and fan experience. (Remember Darcy Raymond of the Tampa Bay Devil Rays in Chapter 1? That's what he does.) In the recent past, not only have major professional sports organizations such as NASCAR and Formula One greatly expanded their marketing efforts—and markets—so too have organizations representing such niche sports as ultimate Frisbee, skateboarding, beach volleyball, and skeleton sledding. Competition for sports fans' time and money is becoming increasingly intense. This is great news for any of you considering a career in this field.

 ## Myth

My philosophy is to "go with the flow." It's worked for me up until now so I'm pretty sure it will continue to work for me in the future.

 **Reality Check**

Going with the flow can work in the short term, but over the longer haul it is very likely to take you somewhere you don't want to go. **If you don't control your future, your future will control you**.

In writing this book we tried to create each chapter with the content, tone, and general perspective that would leave you with lasting and useful take-aways. Five years from now you probably won't remember most of the definitions, tables, and statistics that we've covered, but there are a number of important concepts that will serve you well and that you should refer to as your career plan unfolds. They're central to marketing and, whether you're marketing yourself or anything (or anyone!) else, applying them will greatly enhance your chances of success. With that in mind, let's briefly review the key take-aways from each chapter of *Marketing Yourself*.

- In Chapter 1, we began by going over the definition of marketing and exploring the evolution of marketing. Can you remember the definition and central idea of marketing? (*Hint:* it focuses on exchange and meeting customer needs.) We presented the point of view that as career planning is becoming more complex, marketing could be extremely useful in helping you choose and succeed at the job you love.

- In Chapter 2, we focused on marketing planning, which starts with analyzing the marketing situation. We also introduced the notion of the marketing mix, or the four Ps— product, place, price, and promotion.

- In Chapter 3, we went over the importance and content of situation analysis and stressed the importance of knowing yourself. Can you list the various environments you should scan and attend to in your situation analysis? Have you zeroed in on the key environmental factors that will impact your chosen field and, as a result, your career opportunities in it?

- In Chapter 4, we discussed the importance of goals and objectives and the characteristics that good objectives should possess. We also encouraged you to identify your personal needs and take various self-assessment tests to help you do that. Looking back on your needs and your marketing objectives, do they still make sense?

- In Chapter 5, we discussed target marketing, product positioning, and buyer behaviour. We emphasized the importance of having a clear picture of the prime prospects you'll be targeting and to understand the needs they wish to fulfill. If there is one dominant idea you should retain from this entire book it would come from this chapter: whether creating your product strategy, giving a presentation, or networking at a gathering, always start with the needs of your audience and ask yourself how you can fulfill those needs or help the audience you're addressing fulfill them.

- In Chapter 6, we discussed product strategy and explained the goods–services continuum. An important notion from this chapter was the distinction between core and augmented product. We also covered the product lifecycle and a number of basic branding concepts. Have you figured out how you can augment your product and what your brand will stand for?

- In Chapter 7, we outlined different approaches to pricing, some basic negotiation principles, and ways to add value to your product. We suggested that you complete a monthly budget worksheet. Were you surprised at the totals you arrived at?

- In Chapter 8, we discussed different distribution strategies and described some of the issues and challenges in opening a retail space. Have you identified which side of the street might be the better place to be?

- In Chapter 9, we stressed the importance and benefits of integrated marketing communications. We provided you with an overview of various marketing communications tools and again stressed that it starts by addressing the needs of your market and what they may or may not already know about you and/or your product. Have you determined which tools are best suited to your situation? Have you found how to integrate them to leverage their individual contributions?

- In Chapter 10, we focused on resumes, cover letters, and interviews as promotional tools to communicate what your brand stands for. Can you now appreciate why resume writing shouldn't be the first step in the job search process, but rather its culmination?

- In Chapter 11, we underscored the importance of implementation and control. We stressed the need to carefully map out and attend to the executional details of your plan. A great plan with poor implementation is almost certain to fail. We also emphasized the benefits of having clear standards and evaluation mechanisms. How else will you know if you are going forward or not?

At the beginning of this book, when introducing the marketing planning process, we pointed out that what matters is not really the plan itself, as in the physical final product or 20-something-page document you'll end up with. Rather, it's the process of planning and what it teaches you about yourself and your environment that matters. Success often depends on being on the right side of the street at the right time. And it is true that life has its own unique way of taking care of you by putting what you'll need to succeed on your path. And yet, you're most likely to succeed if you see, interpret, and seize the opportunities that life throws your way.

When we developed the online course Marketing Yourself, we designed it with the hope that students and recent and not-so-recent graduates in a variety of fields and domains would benefit from learning basic marketing concepts. You've already met some of our students who have applied those concepts to launch or relaunch their careers—from Kim Tien's Shanghai adventure to Harvey's reorientation to start his own company. Let's follow up with some of these individuals to see how they're doing.

- Erica Horn, who you met in Chapter 3, was spotlighted in the Career section of *The Montreal Gazette* by journalist Stephanie Whittaker (July 16, 2005), who wrote about Erica's career path and success in finding a job she is passionate about. Recently, Erica was promoted to senior analyst and was given more autonomy to make decisions, and she's being given more complex projects to work on. She still thoroughly enjoys her job at Ad Hoc Research since, as she puts it, she is "always in problem-solving mode and no two days are the same."

- In Chapter 4, you were introduced to Julie-Anne Arsenault. She's made two big moves. First she and her husband packed their bags and headed to Seattle, Washington, to seek their fortunes. After five interviews, Julie-Anne was hired by Microsoft as a marketing specialist and is responsible for content promotion and distribution, product awareness–raising events, and the company's travelling information technology labs.

- After building a successful coaching practice and enrolling in a sports psychology degree program, Marc-Olivier Bossé received and accepted an unexpected offer. He joined the cast of a multimedia figure-skating show onboard one of the world's largest cruise ships, the *Liberty of the Seas*. Four nights each week, he headlines a state-of-the-art extravaganza before an audience of 800 people. The company that produces the show has expressed interest in retaining Marc-Olivier's services at the end of his current contract to assist in the development of new shows in pre-production at their headquarters in Santa Monica, California.

- In Chapter 7, we introduced you to Mark Gentile. While he continues to provide personal fitness training to a select number of clients, Mark has taken on a full-time marketing job with Ice.com, the world's biggest online jewellery retailer. Ice.com was actually part of Mark's network, as he had previously worked there on a work term as a co-op student.

- Kim Tien Huynh, who we introduced in Chapter 8, has experienced more than her fair share of ups and downs in her China sojourn. She has confronted her needs for safety, security, stability, and structure. As she put it in a recent email, "I broke my record by moving five times in the past two months. As a result, my creativity and productivity decreased." With a partner she has started her own consulting business, and to make ends meet during the start-up phase Kim Tien has taken on a job teaching creative arts and cooking classes to young children. She is enjoying this new role and the opportunity to reflect on her career: "Stuff happens and things happen for a reason...It is only when you step back that you fully appreciate why."

So, after 12 chapters, here you are. We sincerely hope that the marketing concepts we've covered in this book have inspired you to create strategies and tactics to effectively market yourself and, in the process, to appreciate the power of marketing in your life. Hopefully you're more comfortable with the idea of thinking of yourself as a product and that by doing so you'll ensure your product does not become a commodity and your personal brand continuously increases in value. We wish you every success in finding the career you love—so that you'll never have to work another day of your life.

Harold J. Simpkins   *Jordan L. Le Bel*

 Myth

At the end of the day, it's all about finding a career that will provide me with the financial security I need.

Reality Check

At the risk of being repetitive, we'll leave the last word to Confucius: **"Find a job you love, and you'll never work another day in your life."**

Note
1. *Journal of Marketing*, vol. 33 (January), pp. 10–15.

August 12, 2011

Dr. Linda Grommit
Department of Sociology
Simon Fraser University
8888 University Drive
Burnaby, B.C.V5A 1S6

Dear Dr. Grommit,

The time has come! I first visited Vancouver in the fall of 2007 for the IAC conference and I fell in love with the city. When we met there, you told me that I needed to work on my publications and continue my presentations at conferences. If you look over my CV now, you'll see I have followed through on your advice. I am about to finish my doctoral studies at UC Berkeley and take my place as an accredited researcher and professor. How appropriate for me, then, that you are about to launch a new Digital Culture department at Simon Fraser! I want to be part of your new team. I am writing to you to ask that you consider me for the position of assistant professor.

While you are aware that I have presented a few dozen conference papers on diverse topics, from digital interaction to research methods and from feminist theory to discourse deconstructions of fear and risk, you may not be aware of my upcoming book, *Getting Pixelled*, co-authored with acclaimed digital games researcher, Kelly Bantham. You also may not know that, in 2011, I was recognized by the American Sociological Association as their most promising scholar for the next decade. I have also held the title of senior researcher on Canadian Research Chair Dr. Vinko's Feminist Political Economy project. Other achievements have included creating and managing a variety of undergraduate courses at York and Berkeley and writing an award-winning journal article for New Media & Culture.

Given my professional background, scholarly and research achievements, and our longstanding professional relationship, I know we could collaborate well together as you move ahead with this new Digital Culture department. I hope you will consider me for one of the open faculty positions. Your leadership has been invaluable to me thus far, and I would like to continue working with you at Simon Fraser University.

With deepest respect,

Tamara Paradis

*In the pages that follow, you'll find sample marketing plans prepared by students who have taken the Marketing Yourself online course. We have left their submissions as they were handed in without any changes whatsoever.

CURRICULUM VITAE

Education

Doctor of Philosophy – Culture & Digital Interaction University of California Berkeley, CA	September 2008 – Forthcoming
Master of Arts – Communications & Culture York University, Toronto, ON • Joint program with Ryerson University	September 2006 – May 2008
Bachelor of Arts – Sociology Concordia University, Montreal, QC	September 2001 – April 2006

Areas of Interest

- Digital culture
- Material culture, popular and mass culture
- Fear and risk
- Media effects and biopower
- Ethnographies, discourse analysis, feminist qualitative methods

Awards & Scholarships

American Sociological Association Promising Scholar Award	August 2010
University of California Graduate Fellowship ($40 000)	September 2009
Government of Ontario Scholar	December 2007
York University Dean's Honour	May 2007
York University Entering Master Scholarship ($10 000)	September 2006
York University Entrance Scholarship ($5000)	September 2006
Concordia University Scholar's Award ($250)	October 2003
Concordia University Dean's List	October 2003 & October 2005

Publications

[Books – Edited

Getting Pixelled: Digital qualitative research methods (with Kelly Bantham). Sage Publications. (Forthcoming.)

Blogging boundaries, digital divides (with Louisa Larchmar). Cambridge, MA: Harvard University Press. 2011.

Doing it digital: Space, place and interaction online. Toronto: University of Toronto Press. 2009.

[Chapters in Edited Books

"Let's chat about cyberspace: Ruminating on social theory in the digital context." In Anna Dostevki, Ed., *Logging, lagging, lurking: Examining life online.* Thousand Oaks, CA: Sage Publications. 2011. (Submitted.)

"Representing the past: emerging postmodern theory" (with Leslie Marcuse). In David Mitchell & Sonja Grassa, Eds., *Social and Cultural Theory for the 21st Century.* Boston: Harvard University Press. (Forthcoming.)

"Where am I? How'd I get here?" In Lucinda Larsen, Joanne Weber, and Claude Bussiere, Eds., *Digital Hobos, Net Wanderers and Cyberutopias: Narratives of Naturalization in Digital Space.* Cambridge, MA: MIT Press. 2009. 25–69.

"Working while playing: Space management issues in digital domains" In R. Carter and K. Bantham, *Play & Digital Interaction.* Toronto: Sumach Press. 2007. 256–272.

[Refereed Journal Articles

"Going grrrly: Feminism, activism and political action on the net." *Third Space: Journal of Digital Feminism.* (Forthcoming.)

"Managing multiplicity: A digital field guide to doing feminist research online." *Journal of Qualitative Research Methods.* Volume 22, Issue 2 (2009).

"What's the matter with 'using cyberspace'? Recontextualizing digital experience." *Journal of Sociology.* Volume 43, Volume 1 (2007).

"Grabbing on, letting go: Digital fear and risky behaviour." *New Media & Culture.* Volume 9, Issue 3 (2006) 42–50.

"Feminism and digital space: Connecting the dots." *Canadian Woman Studies/les cahiers de la femmes* (CWS/cf). Volume 36/21, Number 10/1 (Winter/Spring 2006) 6–14.

[Book Reviews

"Understanding digital risk." *Journal of Fear and Risk Studies.* (Forthcoming.)

"Action and adventure in the digital wild west." *Canadian Journal of Communication.* (Forthcoming.)

"European social thought, 1700–1950: A cultural history" (with Kelly Bantham). *Journal of European Theory.* Volume 48, Issue 3 (December 2008) 542–546.

"Exploding the digital divide: Equality and experience in the online context." *Canadian Woman Studies/ les cahiers de la femmes* (CWS/cf). Volume 22, Number 4 (Winter 2007) 153–154.

[Theses

Moving ahead, moving beyond: Towards an interactional digital model of space and place. PhD Dissertation. University of California Berkley, Culture and Digital Interaction Doctoral Program. (In progress.)

From use to interaction: Restructuring statistical reporting of digital activity. MA Thesis. York University, April 2008.

Use of space? Female digital interaction versus statistical reporting. BA Thesis. Concordia University, 2006.

Conference Experience

[Refereed Conferences

"Foucauldian feminism and digital activism." *Power & Potentialities.* Annual conference for the American Sociological Association. Anchorage, AK. August 2011.

Learning in the lines: E-learning and websites." At *Children, Technology and the Future* conference. University of Chicago. Chicago, IL. March 2011.

"Show & Tell: Visual images and digital research." At *Technological Transfer.* Annual conference for the American Sociological Association. New York, NY. August 2010.

"Baubles, bubbles and babble: Internet devices as identity accessories." At *Internet Generations 11.0.* Annual conference for the Association of Internet Researchers. Budapest, Hungary. October, 2009.

"Clashing traditions: Norway and the EU at a crossroads." At *Banal Borders: Transnationalism & Globalization.* Annual conference for the American Sociological Association. San Juan, Puerto Rico. September 2009.

"Wondering women, wandering women: Fidelity and marriage in the 21st century." At *Internet Generations 10.0.* Annual conference for the Association of Internet Researchers. Seattle, WA. October 2008.

"Studying women in the digital context." At *Internet Generations 9.0.* Annual conference for the Association of Internet Researchers. Bath, UK September 2008.

"Foucault & webspace: Power and politics for everyday people." At *Totalities & Authorities*. Annual conference for the American Sociological Association. Hamilton, Bermuda. August 2008.

"Getting a piece of it: URLs as i-Space identity presentation." At *Internet Generations 8.0*. Annual conference for the Association of Internet Researchers. Vancouver, BC. October 2007.

"Being female, doing digital: Feminist postmodernist methods in Internet interactions." At *Grafting*. Annual graduate students conference for Communications & Culture at York & Ryerson Universities. Toronto, ON. March 2007.

"Rapping Adorno: Moving beyond negativity through the revelatory character of the German-Turkish youth rapper." At *Great Divides: Transgressing Boundaries*. Annual conference for the American Sociological Association. Montreal, QC. August 2006.

"Conceiving digital fear and risk." At *The City: A Festival of Knowledge*. Annual conference for the Canadian Sociology & Anthropology Association. Canadian Federation for the Humanities and Social Sciences annual conference. York University. Toronto, ON. May 2006.

"Bodies, bedrooms and bytes: Female digital youth practices." At *The City: A Festival of Knowledge*. Annual conference for the Canadian Sociology & Anthropology Association. Canadian Federation for the Humanities and Social Sciences annual conference. York University. Toronto, ON. May 2006.

"Buying youth culture: Theory and rap music." At *The City: A Festival of Knowledge*. Annual conference for the Canadian Sociology & Anthropology Association. Canadian Federation for the Humanities and Social Sciences annual conference. York University. Toronto, ON. May 2006.

"Why the worry? Fear & risk in the digital anomaly." At *Technology, Performance & Identity: Mediation, Remediation and the Politics of Self*. Eighth annual conference for Buckinghamshire Chilterns University College Department of Arts and Media. Buckinghamshire, UK. April 2006.

"Bling is the thing: A material culture analysis of the right hand diamond ring." At *Cultural Artefacts Symposium* for the Society for the Study of Symbolic Artefacts annual conference. Canther, GA. February 2006.

"Fear, risk in the digital anomaly." At *Internet Generations 6.0*. Annual conference for the Association of Internet Researchers. Chicago, IL. October 2005.

[Conference Chairs
"Identity management online." Panel at *Internet Generations 11.0*. Annual conference for the Association of Internet Researchers. Budapest, Hungary. October 2009.

"Women & relationships in the digital age." Round table session at *Internet Generations 10.0*. Annual conference for the Association of Internet Researchers. Seattle, WA. October 2008.

Memberships

North America Association of Digital Culture Researchers	2008 – Present
Canadian Association of Cultural Studies (CACS)	2005 – Present
Canadian Sociology and Anthropology Association	2003 – Present
Association of Internet Researchers	2003 – Present
American Sociological Association	2005 – Present
Canadian Association of Communications	2005 – Present
International Association of Business Communications (Past member)	1995–2001
Association of Internet Marketing & Sales	1996–2005

Teaching Experience

Qualitative research methods
Faculty of Sociology, University of California Berkeley

September 2011 – May 2012
September 2010 – May 2011

Feminism and social theory (BSFT 552.9)
Faculty of Women's Studies, University of California Berkeley

September 2009 – May 2010
September 2008 – May 2009

Introduction to Sociological Theory (BSST 543.2)
Faculty of Sociology, University of California Berkeley

September 2009 – May 2010
September 2008 – May 2009

Qualitative Research Methods for Social Scientists (SOCI 4642)
Sociology, Atkinson College, York University

January 2008 – May 2008

Socio-cultural theories I (SOCI 2612)
Sociology, Atkinson College, York University

September 2007 – December 2007
May 2007 – July 2007

Writing as a cultural activity (ENGL 3645)
Department of English, Ryerson University

September 2006 – December 2006
January 2007 – May 2007

Research Project Experience

Researcher, Berkeley Women's Center "Women go online" project
University of California Berkeley

January 2011 – Present

Research Director, Urban Culture & Digital Space (SSHRC funded)
University of California Berkeley

September 2009 – Present

Researcher, Feminist Political Economy Phase II
Canadian Research Chair project headed by Dr. Laura Vinko
York University

November 2006 – March 2008

Research Assistant
CODE research group (SSHRC funded)

September 2005 – April 2006

Other Professional Experience

Systems Analyst
Jersey Inc.

June 2001 – May 2005

Senior Technical Consultant
Pelletier Consulting Group

December 2000 – May 2001

Strategist
Match Inc.

February 2000 – December 2000

Portals Manager
Connections

August 1997 – February 2000

Solutions Strategist
New Net Technologies

November 1996 – June 1997
(Contract)

Internet Specialist
Computers Canada Ltd.

April 1995 – November 1996
(Contract)

Manager
Online Services International

February 1993 – June 1995

Systems Specialist
Tech Tutors Inc.

April 1991 – February 1999

SITUATION ANALYSIS

I am working towards a second career in academia as a tenured professor and digital culture researcher within the disciplines of sociology, cultural studies, communications, or philosophy.

EXTERNAL INFLUENCES

The global market economy is expected to intensify the interconnected global telematic interactions (Sassen, 2000, pp. 2–4), which require a transition to a 24/7 business model (Sassen, 2000, pp. 2–4; Kanter, 2001). A corresponding decline in the North American production of raw resources and manufacturing is intensifying the knowledge-based economy (Sassen, 2000, p. 3). The trickle-down social effect of these macro-economic factors is that North Americans are transitioning away from the old single-path life-course. In order to manage multiple roles, jobs, or even careers in a human lifespan, the average North American adult is adopting a commitment to lifelong learning. Therefore, the existing annual increase in students undertaking post-secondary studies, either in degree programs or in continuing education, will continue and educational institutions will have to ramp up their offerings in order to meet the demand. Given the wide-reaching applicability of the social sciences to all levels of business, I anticipate that this will correlate to an increase in demand for social sciences and humanities training.

Canadian and US statistical data suggest that the cohort of baby boomers is expected to start retiring en masse in the next 5–15 years, causing a possible glut in opportunities for those able to replace them (Statistics Canada, 2005b; US Department of Labor, 2006a). In the university system in North America alone, it is estimated that one in four faculty members will be at retirement age during that period (Statistics Canada, 2005a; US Department of Labor,

2006b). When the impact of that that retiring exodus is combined with the influx of their university-aged children, the increase in adult learners taking courses throughout their lifespan, and an expected immigration increase (Schmidt, 1999), it is reasonable to expect a mini-hiring boom in universities (ibid; Lindholm, 2004, p. 604). As the social and economic impacts of technology systems and networks continue to intensify (Kanter, 2001, p. 287; Tapscott, Ticoll & Lowy, 2000, p. 170), there will be an increased demand on universities. As has already started happening, digital culture as an academic discipline is therefore on the rise in North American universities (York University, 2006) and universities are seeking individuals trained and researching in this emerging discipline.

MARKET SIZE

In North America alone, there are almost 4500 post-secondary institutions, with most having some sort of humanities or social sciences department, due to the popularity of such programs. In 2005, Canadian universities and colleges reported over $27 billion in revenues (Statistics Canada, 2005c), an increase of more than 21 percent from 2001. The annual average Canadian increase in revenues is 5.36 percent (Statistics Canada, 2005c). While there is no data available that allow for a reduced compiled figure for humanities and social sciences professors, aggregate data suggest that in 2004, there were 33 908 full-time professors at all levels in Canada (Statistics Canada, 2004). US data for the same period indicates a substantially larger market, at 1.6 million. (US Department of Labor, 2006c).

GEOGRAPHIC REGIONS OF IMPORTANCE

It is difficult to know if there is a specific geographic region in North America in which the market for a social scientist is significantly stronger. Concentration in any specific geographic area depends largely on the curriculum strategy and research focus intent of any department in any given scholastic year. Also, a social scientist could be hired to instruct students and do research in a wide variety of disciplines within the humanities and social sciences. There is some research, however, that indicates that general academic hiring across all disciplines will be strongest in the Western US states, Ontario, Alberta, and British Columbia, and weakest in the Atlantic provinces and North-Central US states (Schmidt, 1999). There is no particular prejudice between urban and rural areas within this breakdown.

COMPETITIVE ANALYSIS

My primary competition for positions in this market will be other PhD graduates from the fields of political science, sociology, anthropology, communications, cultural studies, philosophy, and possibly computer science or history. These graduates may graduate in the same year I anticipate finishing my own studies (which is 2012). However, they may have already graduated and have already done two to four years of post-doctoral work as research fellows or assistants. I would not expect the majority of these graduates to have had prior careers or professional experience outside academia at the time of their graduation. Each will probably have published at least two scholarly articles in peer-reviewed journals and each will have amassed experience presenting papers and research at academic conferences. If they have not yet published their Doctoral thesis as a book, most will be striving towards that goal.

My secondary competition for positions will be individuals who have graduated more than five years before myself and who have been amassing teaching experience through part-time or adjunct professorships or sessional instructor roles at colleges and universities. These individuals may have had prior careers or professional experience in non-academic fields prior to their involvement in the academic job market.

SELF-ASSESSMENT

(FOR THE SCORE RESULTS TABLE, PLEASE SEE APPENDIX 1)

I value intelligence, creativity, reason and possibility. I am able to deal with change and speed using creativity and intuition. I am an idea person who works well with intellectual pursuits but is comfortable being the centre of attention and directing the action. I can produce quality work even when juggling multiple responsibilities in a fluid and unstructured environment. Given my comfort and flair for language and verbalization, I enjoy reading and expressing ideas in writing and talking about concepts with others. I am adaptable, persistent, goal-oriented, inquisitive about the world, and apt to use my intellect and ingenuity to ethically solve problems as I strive towards defined goals. I like helping others to achieve their potential and I have the listening and communication skills needed to do this effectively.

I am comfortable in social situations where I need to present and promote myself and my ideas, but I am equally comfortable working on self-directed solitary tasks for long periods. I tend to pick the work style that best suits my needs according to the requirements of my goals or desires. My capacity to self-monitor both my own performance and the opinions and feelings of those around me coupled with my ability to exercise intuition and empathy permit me to adjust my self-presentations as required throughout the lifespan of a situation. I like some structure in my work environment but generally prefer a less authoritative, more organic organization.

SWOT ANALYSIS

My chief strength is my flexible and analytic mind. I demonstrate strong ability for lateral independent and innovative thinking and my intelligence has been tested and proven through my high GPA, exceptional GRE scores, strong written and verbal skills, and demonstrated ability to produce publishable-quality work. My facility with analyzing disparate information and combining it into a novel conceptual theory is well demonstrated and I am able to adjust my level of information communication to match my audience. I have a marked ease and flair for classroom leadership and information presentation, where I am able to break down complex concepts into easily understood lessons, using an everyday vernacular and common metaphors. I have received much inter-disciplinary training and I have developed a deep expertise in social theory and qualitative methods. I have practical experience from a 15-year professional background in project management, web services management, corporate communications, and team leadership. This gives me visionary capacities, a realistic outlook, seasoned problem-solving capabilities and well-honed financial and project management expertise. Finally, I possess extensive experience in digital culture management, analysis, and research, giving me a differentiating marketable edge.

I do not yet have any published works to my name. I do not have academic conference leadership experience, nor have I acted as an editor for a journal or a book. I have also not yet had the opportunity to participate in a peer-review process for publishing selection nor have I officially taught a class for university students. The various funding application and award processes are unfamiliar to me. I have a shallow network of academic contacts and colleagues, which is somewhat exacerbated by my slight tendency towards introversion and preference. I also am not comfortable working with numbers, which, in the absence of a collaborator, limits my research possibilities to qualitative research only.

As I am about to enter graduate school in a large and prestigious Canadian university, my new environment will present me with many opportunities to work towards minimizing or eliminating my weaknesses. If I use my mind and time wisely in this upcoming period, I should exit with an expanded academic network, as well as a greater body of published work, volunteer editorialships and peer-review positions, and a solid history of participation and leadership in research projects. I should also have a stronger understanding of the Canadian grants and funding process (preferably as an award recipient myself) and I should possess demonstrated expertise in classroom instruction, mentoring, and grading. Building upon these opportunities in post-graduate work should allow me to create a solid and compelling portfolio that will position me very competitively in the market upon graduation with my PhD.

The two primary threats to my career goal is North American universities' increasing disinclination towards the hire of full-time salaried faculty due to funding reductions and the current push in the US to eliminate tenure-track positions. A secondary threat would be my own potential to keep my focus and not lose track of the goal that is driving my studies. I need to avoid the pitfalls and detours that waylay many good graduate and post-graduate students, causing them to prolong their studies.

MARKETING OBJECTIVES

Within 12 months of graduation with my PhD in 2012, I will be a North American or European university lecturer, researcher, and assistant professor, earning $40 000–$55 000 annually. Within three years, I intend to be on the tenure track towards at least an associate professor position, earning a salary of $50 000–$75 000 annually and starting to earn small dividends from book revenues and speaking engagements. I would anticipate having two or three PhD students and one or two MA students under my supervision, along with the directorship of a funded mid-term research project.

TARGET MARKET

Given my preference for deep social analysis and theory, my prime employer targets in 2012 are expected to be the 651 US universities and 47 Canadian English universities with sociology departments (Dierke, 2004). Of particular interest to me in 2012 will be any university that has started to develop a specialty in digital culture within sociology. A nascent field, it is not yet possible to quantify where or how many digital culture departments may emerge out of existing sociology or communications departments, or out of existing interdisciplinary programs. Currently, digital culture teaching and research takes place mainly in these inter-disciplinary program, such as York University's Communications and Culture, University of Calgary's Communications and Culture group, or Georgetown University's Communication, Culture and Technology department. These departments are virtual, in that they are an administrative and educational construct only—they do not have their own faculty members and instead draw on faculty from across the university. I foresee this changing in the next five years, putting me in an excellent position for employment in 2012 in any such new discipline at any North American university, given my pre-existing market differentiation in digital culture.

When seeking new faculty, sociology departments look for individuals with a strong analytical and inquisitive intelligence slanted towards examination of abstract and concrete social problems. They seek someone whose approach to knowledge can be as a fellow collaborator or as a mentor. They demand a demonstrated track record in academic research and publishing, along with excellent written, verbal, and social communication skills in one of the official languages and strong organizational and multi-tasking abilities (Manitoba Job Futures, n.d.). For the digital culture specialization, there is the added need for candidates to demonstrate through publications and conference presentations that they deeply understand the interplay between digital technologies, society, and individuals.

PRODUCT

In order to have maximum marketability at execution of this plan in 2012, my primary objective is to polish my strengths and overcome my weaknesses so that I excel at all of the required and optional elements defined by the key employers in my target market. Those elements fall within teaching, research methods, and execution in a specialty, publishing, and business administration. As I have a strong background in professional business, I can therefore focus my attention on the other three elements. To align, I will need dedication, drive, vision, discipline, leadership, a sense of autonomy, excellence in writing and presentation, and the willingness to work hard. I will also require expertise in a humanities or social sciences area that is a growing concern in academia. For me, given my pre-existing expertise, that specialty area is digital culture.

I need to work carefully with this objective in mind during the upcoming 6-year product development stage that is my MA and PhD studies. This entails careful course selection, with an eye towards a breadth of knowledge in sociology, communications, and cultural studies, and a depth of expertise and analysis in digital culture. I need to careful pick my activity scope and supervisors for my teaching and research assistantships. I also need to ensure that my activities within peer-review and editorial boards strategically align with my marketability objectives.

Tactically, it is crucial during this upcoming development stage that I keep my eye on learning, research, publishing, and teaching. I need to seek out a Canadian Research Chair at York University, where I will be doing my graduate work, and secure a research assistantship with that person. I need to find and win a teaching assistantship in one of my core areas with a well-known faculty member at York or Ryerson. Continuing on my careful choice of the digital culture-oriented joint MA program at York and Ryerson, I will need to pick a prestigious university for my PhD work, where opportunities for learning and experience are plentiful. At both levels, I need to pick my courses wisely, skewing them towards areas in which I am currently weak and underdeveloped, such as media analysis, discourse analysis, and deconstruction and the sociology of knowledge. This will give me opportunities to create new written work that showcases the understandings I will obtain in such courses.

PLACE

In the three to five years following the completion of my PhD thesis, I would accept academic teaching/research work anywhere in the world. As such, place is a relatively unimportant objective to my overall strategy. I do have mildly preferred regions, however. In Canada, I am particularly interested in Ontario, Alberta, and the Atlantic provinces. In the US, I am particularly interested in the Eastern Seaboard and the Northern Midwest. In Europe, I would target the Northern quadrant, particularly the UK and Scandinavian regions, with a special emphasis on Norway and the south of Britain. To secure employment in Canada, the strategies and tactics outlined herein for my Product and Promotion strategies will allow me to achieve my Place strategy. Recruitment for North American university academic positions typically takes place at a North American level, and so no special tactics would be necessary over top of those outlined in the Product and Placement sections herein. A small boost to my European place objectives might be obtained, however, if I am able to pursue my PhD in Britain or Norway. It might also be beneficial to present at a conference, attend a summer study program in my desired area of expertise, or pursue a summer research internship in one of those countries.

PRICE

Collective bargaining agreements and policies by organizations such as the Canadian Association of University Teachers (2006) stringently control and dictate North American academic remuneration for teaching and research professionals. These agreements fix salaries at specific levels and set out exactly how much someone can be paid at the three-tier faculty experience and positional levels. With this in mind, my objective to achieve a better market price in the 2012–2017 time period will be to accelerate my promotion path. I will do this by executing a research and publishing strategy. I understand that university departments are largely directed by their purse strings, and that the more senior positions go to those faculty members capable of bringing research and infrastructure funding into the university. Therefore, I will work towards bringing in larger amount of research funding into innovative or new and emerging category research projects that align with my career needs and publishing the results of my research findings. Tactically, this will involve educating myself on funding avenues, both known and obscure, learning how to write effective grant funding proposals, networking with other successfully funded researchers, and writing compelling research reports and papers.

PROMOTION

My promotion objective is to raise my profile in the minds of prospective employers. My promotion strategy is three-pronged approach of strategies and tactics, centring around the objectives of informing my potential market of my existence, persuading them to see me as a desirable hiring choice for their institution and forging relationships with key decision-makers and market influencers at each institution.

Tied equally to my product objectives, my promotion strategies involve raising my profile, enhancing my reputation as a solid researcher and strong intellectual. I therefore need to work at strategically inserting myself into where the purchases go to investigate possible choices and select appropriate candidates. To raise awareness of my abilities and potential, I have to become part of the informal network of contacts and referrals within my chosen disciplines and within my research specialty and I have to make it my own. Being well-placed in that network will allow other people to work for me, by prompting them to suggest my name to potential departments with a vacancy. They will be able to bring to my attention possible employers or departments who are expressing problems or interests in my key areas of specialization. These key contacts within this network need to understand my qualifications and differentiators, along with the benefits I offer to a prospective hiring committee. This network involves not just the people hiring individuals know, however, but also the journals they read, the conferences they attend and the websites they visit. Key tactics in this, then, are word-of-mouth referrals, building a strong reputation, and participating in events, associations, and research consortiums. For those opportunities that require a direct contact in a formal hiring process, I need to polish my CV and interview skills, have an exemplary portfolio of research papers and work available as proof of my abilities and a deep list of possible references to pull from to back up my claims of knowledge and expertise.

IMPLEMENTATION AND CONTROL

While many controls are built-in to the actual tactics, such as getting my degrees or getting something published, I have devised an implementation schedule and controls instrument that acts as an overview of strategies and tactics. Please see Appendix II for this.

TEST	RESULT	CONCLUSION
Basic Personality	Conscientiousness 13 Openness 12 Emotional Stability 12 Extraversion 10 Agreeableness 9	High marks in top three indicate excellent choice as an employee due to demonstrated flexibility, adaptability, and stability
Type A Personality?	Marginal type A	Expect to juggle many things
Jungian Type	ENTP	Conceptualizer; innovative problem solver; marginally extroverted, analytical, rely on intelligence and perception
Emotional Intelligence	37	Moderately high; able to perform publicly; excellent interpersonal skill; demonstrate empathy towards others
Entrepreneur	86	Average score; no particular inclination towards entrepreneurship
Pro-activity	92	Highly proactive, positively correlates to leadership qualities
Flexibility	36	Average score
Decision-making Style	Conceptual (C)	Big picture creative thinker
Intuitiveness	12 (Highest possible)	Able to handle uncertainty; thrive on spontaneity and creativity
Multiple Intelligences	Combination of: • Verbal/Linguistic • Interpersonal • Intrapersonal	Excel at tasks require spoken and written language/communication skills; collaborative; take others needs into account in decisions
Ethics		Showed negative view of business ethics and positive view of strong personal ethics
Turbulent Change	87	Above average; open and responsive to change but not in environments with constant turbulence;
Impression Management	Self-promotion 3.75 Ingratiation 4.75 Exemplification 3.50 Intimidation 2.00 Supplication 1.20	Well suited for academia, where self-promotion is key and there is a need to give of yourself to students.
Organization Structure Preference	45	Slightly into the no-preference zone, with a leaning towards a more organic structure
Listening Skills	49	High average range
Preferred Organizational Culture	20	Cusp score indicates a desire for structure with a humanistic bent

	START DATE	END DATE
Phase 1: Undergraduate (BA) – Development stage I		
• Course completion	September 2001	April 2006
• Convocation	June 2006	—
Phase 2: Graduate (MA) – Development stage II		
• Choose school	November 2005	April 2006
• Find adviser & committee	April 2006	October 2006
• Find & secure teaching assistantship	August 2006	September 2006
• Write & publish thesis	July 2007	June 2008
Phase 3: Post-graduate (PhD) – Development stage III		
• Choose school	September 2007	April 2008
• Find adviser & committee	February 2008	October 2008
• Find & secure teaching assistantship	August 2008	October 2008
• Find & secure research assistantship	October 2008	January 2009
• Do independent digital culture research	January 2009	January 2010
• Write/publish thesis & research findings	June 2009	December 2011
Phase 4: Job Search – Implementation		
• Identify potential employers	December 2010	September 2011
• Put CV out to contact network	September 2011	December 2011
• Attend key academic events	July 2010	April 2012
• Start cold-calling & informal meetings	August 2011	January 2012
• Interviews & followups	January 2012	May 2012
• Selection & closing	May 2012	July 2012
Phase 5: Junior Professor – Execution stage I		
• New course development & delivery	July 2012	September 2012
• Supervision of MA/PhD students	December 2012	December 2016
• Funding proposals & grant selections	September 2012	December 2013
• Research & publishing	January 2013	December 2016
• Secure junior Canadian Research Chair	January 2015	—
Phase 6: Senior Professor – Execution stage II		
• Secure senior position	October 2016	January 2017
• Augment funding & grants	October 2016	May 2017
• Expand research & publishing activities	January 2017	December 2018
• Add additional student supervisions	March 2017	December 2018
• Obtain tenure	January 2019	June 2019

BIBLIOGRAPHY

Canadian Association of University Teachers. (2006).General CAUT policy. Retrieved March 10, 2006 from https://www.caut.ca/en/policies/general.asp

Dierke, J. (2004). U.S. Sociology Departments. Sociolog: Comprehensive guide to sociology online. Retrieved April 2, 2006 from http://www.sociolog.com/us_links/

Kanter, R.M. (2001). *Evolve: Succeeding in the digital culture of tomorrow*. Boston: Harvard Business School Press.

Lindholm, J. (2004). Pathways to the professoriate: The role of self, others, and environment in shaping academic career aspirations. *The Journal of Higher Education, 75(6)*.

Manitoba Job Futures. (n.d.). University professors (NOC 4121). Retrieved April 2, 2006 from http://mb.jobfutures.org/profiles/profile.cfm?noc=4121&lang=en&site=graphic

Sassen, S. (2000). *Cities in a world economy*. Thousand Oaks, CA: Pine Forge Press.

Schmidt, K. (1999). Will the job market ever get better? *Science, 285(5433)*.

Statistics Canada. (2004). Salaries and salary scales of full-time teaching staff at Canadian universities, 2003–2004: Final report. Catalogue no. 81-595-MIE — No. 031. Retrieved February 1, 2006 from http://www.statcan.ca/bsolc/english/bsolc?catno=81-595-MIE2005031

Statistics Canada. (2005a). The Daily, Study: The rising profile of women academics. Retrieved February 4, 2006 from http://www.statcan.ca/Daily/English/050224/d050224c.htm

Statistics Canada. (2005b). Analytical Series: Mandatory retirement rules and the retirement decisions of university professors in Canada, Report 11F0019MIE, no 271. Retrieved February 3, 2006 from http://www.statcan.ca/bsolc/english/bsolc?catno=11F0019M2005271

Statistics Canada. (2005c). University and college revenue and expenditures, for fiscal year ending March 31 annual. CANSIM Table 385-0007. Retrieved April 2, 2006 from http://cansim2.statcan.ca/cgi-win/CNSMCGI.EXE

Tapscott, D., Ticoll, D, & Lowy, A. (2000). *Digital capital: Harnessing the power of business webs*. Boston: Harvard Business School Press.

US Department of Labor. (2006a). National Center for Education Statistics, NSOPF:04. Retrieved February 4, 2006 from http://nces.ed.gov/pubs2006/2006176.pdf

US Department of Labor. (2006b).Occupational outlook handbook, 2006–07 Edition, Teachers Postsecondary. Retrieved February 2, 2006 from http://www.bls.gov/oco/ocos066.htm

U.S. Department of Labor (2006c). Occupational Outlook Handbook, 2006-07 Edition, Teachers—Postsecondary. Retrieved February 4, 2006 from http://www.bls.gov/oco/ocos066.htm

York University – Department of Communications and Culture (2006). Departmental website content. Retrieved April 2, 2006 from http://comcult.yorku.ca/

LETTER OF INTRODUCTION

I have researched your organization and contend that my art would be an excellent addition to your already stellar, reputable collection. Having already had exhibitions and a great deal of experience, I now urgently require representation to further my career.

Knowing the level of quality and distinction that you require, my art would be an invaluable asset to your respectable organization. I believe that we could both benefit from the creation of a contract. My skills are developed and exemplary, and I have a personal style that intrigues and fascinates. I possess a strong work ethic that, with aid from you, will denote much success in my field.

I believe in an art with an insistence upon avant-garde thought, opinionated minds, and a diverse mentality and emotionality to prove that I seek not only to reveal universal truths, record the world, or give tangible form to feelings but that I combine all aspects to be an inventor and a scientist of the world.

I strive for a common image that all can understand to remove the "elitist idiom" that the viewer may feel. The realist portraits that I paint formalize a serene ideal of beauty and elegance that has undergone a radical transformation; one can circumscribe to the social consciousness of today while being attuned to the visionary symbolism that creates one's dreams. I desire the theme of symbolism and surrealism because it is a mutation of and a development of realism.

I seek to figuratively exemplify iconography through appearances. I appropriate the human as a symbol; the face can so effortlessly denote and connote various implicit values that structure the hierarchy of thinking for each individual consciousness. There is an unconscious nature to return to the specific motif of women, elegant and seemingly pure. I enjoy the traditional and the contemporary dovetailed with one another: elements of classicism, the femme fatale, and delusory, arbitrary colour. The contrast of hyper-real features with aspects of fiction endorses the academic tradition in realism with an amalgamation of flamboyance.

My art reflects a placating, artistic delectation that is self-indulgent because I brazenly involve myself with the exotic. My art is charged with a ferocious wit, elegance, solitude, disillusionment, hostility, and surrealism. To me they are not imagery; they are equations of my personality.

CURRICULUM VITAE

Summer Geraghty

392 Fairfield St.
Greenfield Park, Quebec
J4V 1Z9
Canada

Date of Birth: November 9, 1979
Telephone: (450) 672-9698
E-mail: cyposia@gmail.com

Career Objective

- Independent or gallery-employed visual artist

Skills Profile

- Oil (specialty), acrylic, watercolour paints
- Oil and dry pastels, charcoal
- Clay, wood, plaster casting, mold, and amateur metal sculpture
- Copper etching, linoleum prints
- Video art, theatre, music, amateur photography, D.J. experience
- Microsoft Word and PowerPoint

Education

- Champlain College, 900 Riverside Drive, St. Lambert, Quebec, J4P 3P2
  - Diplome d'études collegiales (DEC) in Fine Arts, honours
  - 1997–2001
- Concordia University, 1455 de Maisonneuve Blvd. West, Montreal, Quebec, H3G 1M8
  - Interdisciplinary Arts Program
  - 2002–2008 (projected year of graduation)
- Saidye Bronfman Centre for the Arts
  - Summer 2001, painting course

Qualifications

- Olympic Coca-Cola Bottle Competition, Feb. 1996, Canadian submission, 1st place prize (Centennial Regional High School)
- Scholarship to Champlain College, Fine Arts
- Chambly Regional Art Contest, Nov. 1997, Jury Mention
- Solo Exhibition: Champlain College, St. Lambert, Sept. 2000
- Group Exhibition: Foufounes Electriques, Montreal, Sept. 2001, Feb. 2002
- Solo Exhibition: Café Chaos, Montreal, Aug. 2003
- Group Exhibition: le locale, Montreal, Apr. 2005

MARKETING PLAN

SITUATION ANALYSIS

EXTERNAL INFLUENCES

Macro-economic factors will affect my career as an artist with results varying from affliction to opportunity. Statistics Canada revealed in July 2005 that the gross domestic product in Canada rose 0.3 percent monthly and that it had matured 2.8 percent from the previous year (infotrac-college.com, *FWN Select*, July 29, 2005). The rising GDP could prove difficult since it may suggest that others in my career path have been able to establish themselves during this period.

Globalization is a trend that could hinder or administer an opportunity. As local art often depicts particulars of community identity and variations of culture, globalization could demote these qualities, reducing the appeal of local artists. Interest and demand for other cultures' art reduces the market for local/national artists. However, this could work to my advantage if I market myself to other countries (infotrac-college.com, *Art Journal*, winter 1998).

Unemployment in Canada improved in June 2005 by 0.1 percent from May's 6.8 percent, which had already been at its lowest since June 2000 (infotrac-college.com, *Xinhua News Agency*, July 8, 2005). This rise of employment is unfavourable to my prospect of finding work. However, it may suggest that markets are more willing to hire as of late.

There are social and demographic trends that can influence and impinge my opportunities. Rising immigration will promote fiercer competition, especially around the metropolitan areas such as Montreal, which are the centre of concentration for arts organizations and individual artists. There are also many grants that are reserved for aboriginal arts and minority artists that divide the arts' national budget even further, creating more difficulty for local artists to earn grants and endorsements. There is one demographic trend that is favourable for the arts. The aging population in Canada works to the arts' advantage. An increase of average income for Canadian seniors, who in 1995 represented 12 percent of the population, with the combination of a greater leisure time, resulted in seniors attending and promoting art (www.canadacouncil.ca, May 2002). It is reasonable to assume that these reliable audiences will not be affected by fluctuations in the economy or a lack of leisure time.

Most exposure to art occurs during one's free time. Since the 1990s, leisure time has decreased, affecting cultural activities. Statistics Canada studies exhibit correlations between one's leisure time and one's schooling. A survey conducted demonstrated that a larger proportion of the audience at art events consisted of Canadians with a portion of or a completed post-secondary education (www.canadacouncil.ca, May 2002).

Even though education has increased in Canada, a possible threat to art is the change in technology. With the population becoming more computer literate, leisure time dwindles and attention is directed away from social and cultural activities. Home entertainment systems do the same; Statistics Canada illustrated that in 1998, Canadians spent 2.2 hours a day watching television of their 3.4 hours of leisure time (www.canadacouncil.ca, May 2002).

The visual arts market is large. There is a decent percentage of the population with the resources to purchase the services and/or product of an artist; however, there are far more artists than there are people with a need for the service/product. The cultural sector in Canada's economy contributes close to $40 billion to the Gross Domestic Product, while the Federal Government invests $3.4 billion (www.canadacouncil.ca, November 2005). Canadian consumers spent $530 million on works of art, carvings, and vases in 2003; a 48 percent increase since 1997 (info@hillstrategies.com, May 2005).

There are approximately 13 770 organizations in Canada involved with arts and culture (info@hillstrategies.com, May 2005); however, the organization that holds the most lofty and prestigious position is the Canadian Council for the Arts. Awarding over 70 fellowships and prizes to nearly 100 artists and scholars a year, in addition to a multitude of grants and services available to professional Canadian artists, the Council is considered the most illustrious organization in Canada (www.canadacouncil.ca).

There are regions where the markets are more commanding than Montreal. New York City is considered to be the centre of the art world and the strongest marketplace for contemporary arts (ttcc/market/publications/visArtsVis/index_e.cfm, no date). The concentration of commerce and wealth in New York has provided finance for art movements and is the home to the majority of buyers and sellers of art (ttcc/market/publications/visArtsVis/index_e.cfm, no date). Europe has an established art market and a history of exhibiting, supporting and collecting art. "… European art, strength in traditional painting and decorative arts and antiques are still valid and contribute to shaping the current market" (ttcc/market/publications/visArtsVis/index_e.cfm, no date). Berlin and Frankfurt are considered new hotspots for art since the fall of the Berlin wall. Paris is known for its art, especially the area of Montmartre that already has an influx of painters joining the scene. A large revival of attention in the 1990s once again began focusing on the UK (ttcc/market/publications/visArtsVis/index_e.cfm, no date).

COMPETITIVE ANALYSIS

The number of artists in Canada is 131 000 (www.canadacouncil.ca, November 2005). Between 1971 and 2001, the number of artists more than tripled, and between 1991 and 2001, there was an increase of 29 percent (info@hillstrategies.com, May 2005). There are approximately 13 770 organizations in Canada involved with arts and culture (info@hillstrategies.com, May 2005).

I will be encountering competition from professional and non-professional visual artists. As an unestablished and low-income student artist, there are many factors working against me: galleries and dealers that only exhibit recognized artists; art advisors that are looking for work for their artist clients; galleries that must be purchased for exhibition; grants and prizes that can be won by only professionals; and artists with an established and exclusive clientele, those with a higher level of education, and those with years of expertise. Professional or non-professional competing artists will also offer an array of genres to potential clients and it then simply becomes what the buyer prefers. With globalization, I will not only be competing against local artists, but with international ones. Since immigration is on the rise, aboriginal and minority art also diverts the focus from other artists. The advances in technology and the novelty of various mediums of art present competition; computer graphics and the like are quite en vogue and can provide an original piece of art occasionally for a lesser price.

While a competitor's skill in art can vary substantially, it does not equate one's success or failure, although one's skill ought to be apparent. One may have a superb designing skill, but not the ability to bring it to fruition. While one's artistic skill is definitely in question when a client is proposing to buy a piece, an artist needs a solid marketing skill—something that many artists sadly lack. They are often too focused on the creative aspect of art and not the business side of it. Education levels of artists vary greatly as well. Some artists have never been scholastically taught and still have the ability/expertise to become known. Art does not have to be a learned and schooled process, although it can be more greatly developed that way. Although over 40 percent of artists have a university degree, they earn only slightly more than labour workers with a high school diploma (info@hillstrategies.com, May 2005).

SELF-ASSESSMENT

PERSONALITY TESTS	RESULTS
1. What Do I Value?	- Most valued terminal values: knowledge and wisdom - Most valued instrumental values: education and intellectual pursuits
2. Am I Type A?	- Score: 105, type A
3. What Is My Jungian 16 Type Personality?	- Score: INTP
4. What's My Emotional Intelligence Score?	- Score: 40/high EI
5. Am I Likely To Be an Entrepreneur?	- Score: 110/high proactive personality
6. How Well Do I Handle Ambiguity?	- Score: 50/average
7. How Flexible Am I?	- Score: 55/high self-monitor
8. What's My Basic Personality?	- Score: extraversion: 12, agreeableness: 11, conscientiousness: 13, emotional stability: 8, openness to experience: 15
9. How Proactive Am I?	- Score: 111/high proactive personality
10. What's My Decision-Making Style?	- Score: c/conceptual
11. How Intuitive Am I?	- Score: 10/high intuition
12. What Motivates Me?	- Score: growth needs: 19/most important
13. How Involved Am I in My Job?	- Score: 38/average
14. What's My Attitude Toward Achievement?	- Score: - favour seeing successful people rewarded: 59 - favour seeing successful people fall: 22
15. What Rewards Do I Value Most?	- Score: most desired: prestigious title, job security, recognition, interesting work, pleasant conditions, chances to succeed

PERSONALITY TESTS	RESULTS
16. How Well Do I Manage Impressions?	- Score: - ingratiation: 5, self promotion: 4.75, exemplification: 4, intimidation: 3.8
17. How Well Do I Respond to Turbulent Change?	- Score: 98/above average
18. How Stressful Is My Life?	- Score: 182/low stress
19. How Do My Ethics Rate?	- Score: quite ethical comparatively
20. What Type of Organization Structure Do I Prefer?	- Score: 37/preference for organic structure
21. What's the Right Organizational Culture for Me?	- Score: 18/more comfortable in a formal, mechanistic, rule-oriented, and structured culture
22. What's My Face-to-Face Communication Style?	- Score: contentious, impression leaving and attentive
23. How Good Are My Listening Skills?	- Score: 42/average to good

Achievement is extremely imperative, not only on a personal level but to sustain an existence as an artist. I am persistent, organized, thorough, reliable, and able to take initiative in directing either myself or others. I am eager to begin my career and often feel impatient with all the goals I must achieve in order to get there. I can sometimes develop stress due to my impatience and need for perfection. I prefer to take charge of situations, but am also able to take orders and thoroughly complete a task required of me. I have a wide variety of interests and am fascinated with innovation, whether it is new and exploratory projects or original approaches to a trusted way of completing an assignment. I am imaginative, artistically inclined, intuitive, and open to new experiences. I do, however, prefer a project's objectives and criteria to be direct. I favour a straightforward approach as to what is required and sought after by an employer; I am not emotional in my undertaking of a job because I appreciate that most business necessitates logic and rationale. While I do prefer structure, I am proficient at handling spontaneity and uncertainness since my behaviour and attitude is consistent. I am adept at assessing a situation and adjusting my behaviour as well as my appearance accordingly. I am motivated and have no fear of speaking to a group to get a job done or for a sales presentation. I identify opportunities and strive to finalize them. I am dedicated to my work and persevere until it is appropriately accomplished. I am very ethically inclined and respond well to virtually any change. I leave superior and enduring impressions because my people and interview skills are developed and I listen well, thus affording me plenty of necessary information for communication and for realizing what my employer wants and needs.

SWOT ANALYSIS

STRENGTHS

I am fortunate to have a skill for my profession that many cannot duplicate. My main expertise is portraiture, and while there could be numerous people doing it, the quality of my work is possibly superior. I have a passion for my work and am very involved in it; I am never satisfied to complete an assignment without inserting personal connotations. I have assorted interests that allow me to create intelligent, diversified art that can pertain to many people on various levels. I have clear goals and direction and am very committed to achieving status as an artist; therefore, my work can appreciate in value. I have good presentation skills and an awareness of the marketing process that gives me an advantage. I am constantly challenging myself to develop my skills, knowledge, and accomplishments. I am determined to complete my Bachelors, my Masters, extracurricular projects, and to continue the exploration of marketing.

WEAKNESSES

A major weakness that can affect the beginning of my career is the fact that I have no experience as a professional. Although proficiency often graduates after one begins one's career, there is a possibility that because galleries focus on professionals that I will never be granted the opportunity to exhibit. Production is often a problem for me; I must begin a stricter regiment as to how many hours I paint/produce a day/week/month. I do not have any contacts in the art world other than my professors nor am I aware of the structure or hierarchy that I am sure exists. I have not participated in any competitions lately and must launch that process again. My skill level is not as developed as I need it to be, nor is it consistent enough for my liking.

OPPORTUNITIES

Various competitions, awards, and grants are available for applications that are favourable in gaining notoriety. I am able to donate works to foundations to popularize my style and name. I can join organizations in order to immerse myself in the culture and to create contacts. I can apply for a job in an art gallery to introduce myself to the structure of a gallery. I can apply for a job in an art supplies store since it could be possible to make contacts. I have the opportunity to continue marketing and gallery-concentrated courses to further my knowledge. Living in Montreal is an opportunity in itself. Although one may never sell a work, there are many clubs and bars that will exhibit one's work for free (without safety insurance). Another opportunity is that I am still in university, which will assist in honing my skills, making contacts, and furthering my education.

THREATS

There often appear to be overwhelming threats menacing the survival of an artist. Art departments graduate a multitude of students. Even though most of these people will not go on to become artists, it makes the first step of attaining recognition very difficult because of the sheer number of people attempting the same objective. The competition also comes from minority groups, aboriginal arts, and globalization or international artists. Salaries for artists, especially non-professionals, are extremely low even though the profession is monetarily demanding. The average income of an artist is $23 500 per year (www.canadacouncil.ca, November 2005). Without any present funding, I am unable to rent a gallery or even update my portfolio. I must rely on free venues, which often return one's work damaged. Many galleries only accept volunteers and do not actually hire. Art can be unrewarding when having to change one's style, price, etc., for a gallery/client, and that customer still has the choice to not select one's work after it has been altered. Cutbacks are also inevitable in the arts community if the economy deteriorates. Since art is a luxury, it is one of the first services/products to be disregarded.

MARKETING OBJECTIVES

Within one to three years of graduation, I want to be earning the average Canadian artist's salary of $23 500 (www.canadacouncil.ca, November 2005). This average income would cover the cost of living and artist material expenses. I will also be applying for grants, most notably the Elizabeth Greenshield's grant of $10 000.

"One-half of artists... earn about $10 000 or less." (www.canada council.ca, November 2005) This is almost definitely the salary that I will be making the first year. Within three years, assuming I have experience in the field and with gallery renting prices in mind (approximately $500 a week), an ideal salary would be $40 000 or more. This would facilitate spending the $6000–12 000 a year for rent, supplies, advertising, and living.

Within 12 months of graduation, I hope to be routinely exhibiting and making a profit of $2000 a year from my art. I will need to be employed in an art-related job, even if it is in an art supplies store. Within three years of graduation, I hope to be exhibiting three or more times a year and making a profit of $5000. It would be ideal to have a full- or part-time position in an art gallery. This would provide contacts, a salary, a sense of achievement, recognition, and a possible outlet for me to exhibit my work. A part-time position would specifically allow me to create art to market in my spare time.

I will stay in Montreal after graduation to see if I can make an imprint here. I will consider moving to Toronto or Ottawa for a gallery position, purely based on the fact that I could concentrate on selling my art in English. I will consider moving to any city, province/state, or country if I recognize a large potential target market and demand for my work, providing that I can afford to do so.

TARGET MARKET

Prime customers will be looking for several factors when purchasing art: its quality, its price, its historical value, its personal value, its aesthetic value, its popularity, the artist's curriculum, the material used, and/or even its size.

Appendix A — Sample Marketing Plans

Collectors habitually keep themselves up to date on trends in art, but while they are often looking for specific pieces, they are also willing to expose themselves to new artists (ttcc/market/publications/visArtsVis/index_e.cfm, no date) There are business-to-business clients who are looking for art to sell and market. They will often engage in negotiations with specific wants and set budgets (ttcc/market/publications/visArtsVis/index_e.cfm, no date). High-end clients are not considered collectors, but have often bought art in the past. They have a high disposable income, are open to a variety of prices and trends, and are interested in the most promising piece/artist in any field (ttcc/market/publications/visArtsVis/index_e.cfm, no date). First-time buyers are infrequently looking for a specific item, but are prone to impulse purchases that are affordable (ttcc/market/publications/visArtsVis/index_e.cfm, no date). There is no specified time of year to buy art; however, due to more leisure time in the summer, it is possible that more art is sold in the summer. As all consumers' spending rises around Christmas, art is probably purchased more frequently around that season.

Seniors, with an increase in an average income and more leisure time, are a potential and reliable target market since economic fluctuations and a lack of leisure time do not apply to them.

Income is a major factor in clientele since art is considered a luxury. Although most potential customers will have a solid career, some clients may come from below the average income if they want to acquire a specific commission.

Education, occupation, marital status, household formation, and ethnic or religious diversity do not have a specified bearing on who a client may be. A person interested in art may have a higher education or one particular to arts and a family with children may have no use or place for art, but they may also want to decorate their home.

Gender economics could affect my prospects; women having their own careers and budgets could aid my product since much of my art involves a form of feminism.

Psychographic segmentation is practical in conveying a target market. As my art is non-traditional, it could appeal to joiner activists, bold achievers, and self-indulgent people whom comprise 45 percent of Canadians (adapted from studies of Millward Brown, lesson 8 reading, page 25). Since my art celebrates diversity, atheism, and women, these would be key factors to search for in a community.

Purchase behaviour can be as dissimilar as one's clients; one may be loyal and order many works, while another may be a single-time purchaser. One may prefer acrylic paint to oil, or wood to canvas, and these attributes affect the price. Commissions often involve precise details that must be followed in accordance to the client's inclination.

Owning a piece of art can be viewed as having achieved success. Since it is considered a luxury item and can frequently only be afforded by those with a high income, a piece may represent the owner's accomplishment and status. Admirers and owners of art are often considered intellectual and cultured, so it may exemplify one's prestige.

The need for power and uniqueness will be satisfied. Possessing art can empower an individual by providing resources of stature and class. Also, if clients receive a good deal with the opportunity to negotiate, then they experience a sense of mastery over their environment. The power of choice invokes them with a sense of control as well. The choice they make for a particular piece of art gratifies a need for uniqueness since art preferences assert their individual identity through the product and selection.

Financially, clients may benefit from investing in art since it may appreciate in value. They can also take pride from knowing that they aided in supporting cultural activities.

PRODUCT

I insist on improving my art through developing my technique, having a personalized style, learning how to personally document my work, and securing a position in the art market. To attain suitable product objectives, I must first complete my university education. I will create a collection of paintings that will appeal to my target audience. I will be taking a photography course, so that I can document my work for my portfolio more efficiently, as well as a portfolio course, in order to produce an exemplary one. I will achieve more success in taking future marketing courses. I will volunteer at a gallery in order to promote my art and possibly secure a position in that gallery.

Product strategies will include improving the product, analyzing the packaging of the product, and extending product development. Continuous improvement will incorporate the completion of my degree in art and taking photography, portfolio, and marketing courses. It involves creating a routine to paint regularly to create a collection of more than 40 works and developing a personal style. I will be involved in dynamic improvement by assessing whether I need to develop new skills so as not to fall behind the competition. I will analyze whether the packaging of my product is effective (framing, advertising, and price can aid or hinder an artist). I will attempt to continually enhance product development through attaining the aforementioned factors. I will prepare for my introduction into the market after graduation by exhibiting now and also by volunteering in a gallery.

Tactics will include the constant re-examining and revising of my objectives and strategies. I will incorporate the development of product management into my everyday routine since I will need to improve my product daily and to have a large collection of work. I will identify themes that I am comfortable painting. To find a gallery to volunteer for will necessitate my involvement in regularly investigating all possibilities around Montreal. Also, to keep up to date with popular styles, I will visit museums and galleries to improve my knowledge. I will research galleries, clubs, and restaurants where I can exhibit my work now without any financial backing.

All these factors ought to contribute to personalizing my brand. I will be establishing a brand by building a reputation and name in the field. By setting expectations of excellence and providing evidence that my art can/will appreciate in value could easily support brand loyalty.

PLACE

My place objectives involve exhibiting in Montreal for the next few years, since I prefer to finish my education at Concordia. Montreal provides many opportunities for an artist due to its extensive amount of galleries, festivals, art organizations, and events that bring in tourism and because it is a populated urban area. I wish to expose at least 400 potential clients to my work; I will be researching exhibition areas as well as any prestigious company/restaurant/club where I may expose my work to a target audience.

Strategically, I must situate the best places to exhibit that will promote status and sales. Before submitting my portfolio to these places that have fees, I must sell work to attain revenue. I will have to first exhibit in any available space and promote word-of-mouth advertisement. Montreal provides opportunities for struggling artists by means of co-ops and organizations; the Artothèque de Montréal provides a popular venue for a minimal cost. I will send my portfolio to as many Montreal galleries as possible, as well as participating in competitions to further my status and achievements as an artist. I must develop a website promoting my work since popularity is central to an artist; if I can obtain notoriety in other regions as well as this one, it augments my chances of a better career. Business cards will be essential. Since one may consider personal promotion key to my place objectives, I must also formulate involving hypothesizes about my art and art in general and be able to do so in French and English.

Tactically, I will be purchasing the *Montreal Artist's Handbook*, which provides essential information. "Topics covered include marketing... employment & business basics, and funding for artists" (www.yesmontreal.ca, no date). I will apply for several grants in hopes that I can obtain superior venues to promote my work. I must assemble a commendable portfolio for any prestigious gallery or grant organization to consider it. I must expand my French-speaking skills by taking a course. I must complete art history lessons. I will be required to establish potential connections, and could do so through seeking advice from professors at Concordia. I will also build a personal homepage on the Internet to showcase my work and to communicate with potential clients.

PRICE

Within the next three to five years, I would prefer to be earning the average Canadian artist's salary of $23 500 (www.canadacouncil.ca, November 2005). Although not extravagant, this salary could prove accurate if not exaggerated, especially considering that I have at least two more years of university. This average income would cover the cost of living and artist material expenses. I will also be applying for grants, most notably the Elizabeth Greenshield's grant of $10 000. From my art, I wish to earn $2000 a year from now until graduation in 2008.

In order to position myself now to earn this salary in the future, I will price my work with a market penetration and value pricing strategies, but they will have a minimum price of $250. This will encourage those who are aware of me being unprofessional to still buy since my work is high quality and thus a bargain. A product line strategy will be utilized to finalize pricing for the market penetration strategy since art materials and mediums vary in price and art varies in size and subject matter. There will be a chance for negotiation and I may employ some preferential treatment or customer segmented pricing; I would charge a gallery more for the same piece since they would have more money. There will be periods when I will employ promotional pricing, such as immediately before or at an exhibit. I may utilize a psychological pricing strategy if the subject matter is profound and deeply involving. Buyers may be less price-sensitive when purchasing art since the product is unique; however, prestige, quality, and exclusivity can profit one greatly.

Applied tactics for price strategies will include convincing my audience that my product is worth the asking price by providing an artist's profile: all exhibits that I have participated in, prizes and awards that I have collected, grants that I have been awarded, commentary from reliable sources, the level of education completed, and any prestigious, relevant activities. I will also explain to each customer why the pricing is what it is to promote knowledge and awareness about the work and the cost (the cost of specific paint, canvas, framing, subject matter, and quality).

PROMOTION

Promotional objectives will include awareness, knowledge, creating preference, and trial. To generate awareness, I will exhibit my work, donate pieces to high-traffic spaces, find sponsorships, and produce and distribute business cards. To encourage knowledge about my work/genre, I will provide pamphlets about me as an artist to buyers or potential clients and essays about certain pieces of my work. I will communicate to my target customers how I vow to be a serious artist and how I am an artist that is worth supporting. To build preference, I will retain quality, deliver prompt service, provide discounts, allow selected clientele to view new works before they are exhibited, and inform them of any past and future prizes and grants that I may obtain. I may allow trusted potential clients to borrow a piece to see how they feel about it for a short period of time as a means of trial. A customer can also commission a work that could be considered a trial.

There will be several strategies that I will utilize. I will confirm a unique selling proposition in which I will distinguish what I have to offer that the competition does not, and focus on the rewards/ benefits of purchasing art. I will assemble a data collection of clients and galleries from networking, and execute data mining so that I may situate where the clients are located and what is purchased. I will advertise on the Internet and telephone clients when I have new paintings or upcoming exhibits. There are free websites that I can advertise on, such as www.myspace.com, and distribute flyers, such as www.canadapost.ca. Providing preference to potential clients will consist of providing testimonials from former customers and a personal guarantee that I will attempt to build status as an artist, thereby increasing the value of my work.

Personal selling will be my primary strategy to publicize my work since I represent myself and can do so well through presentations.

Word of mouth is the most valuable method of promoting the awareness and knowledge of an unprofessional artist since it is free of charge.

My brand positioning will become distinguished the further I continue the study of art, thus creating my own discernible style.

Promotional tactics will include the donation of works, persuasive approaches alluding to the value, the advertisement of grants and prizes won, profile pamphlets, a website, and press releases. I will promote my website and attempt to drive up traffic. I will make an effort to have an article about myself and my expertise written about me in as many local newspapers as possible.

I have created a functional resume to highlight my talents and strengths. This C.V. proves more impressive than a combination or chronological one due to my lack of work experience and instead focuses attention on my accomplishments.

IMPLEMENTATION AND CONTROL

IMPLEMENTATION CONTROL

PRODUCT	PRICE	PLACE	PROMOTION
1. Investigation of museums and art magazines to focus on new potential themes that would expand my repertoire and enhance my technique.	1. Write a summary of the work explaining topics, title, and inspiration. Add photo of work for customers to keep. Include with painting a certificate of authenticity.	1. Research restaurants, bars, clubs, and free venues that are popular with my target market; arrange appointment with manager to discuss insurance for work, advertisement, price, and commission policies.	1. Promote Internet site by adding address on emails, direct marketing material.
2. Paint every day, no exceptions	2. Publicize a suggested price next to work in portfolio, with a 10 percent margin for negotiation over preferred price. I will imply that special prices can be arranged for institutional buyers.	2. Prepare and distribute business cards.	2. Strengthen database of contacts; research galleries, collect business cards, use Canada Post free mail service of sending out flyers.
3. Ask for honest feedback from artist peers and professors.		3. Find free Internet service provider to launch site; upload and design site; include contact information and encourage comments.	3. Send press releases to local newspapers, galleries and all contacts; include a representation of best work.
4. Buy supplies with any extra money, so that I always have stock.	3. Review all past work and re-price on sale to sell easily and quickly.	4. Ask for advice from professors as to where to exhibit.	4. Send out regular emails with photo of every new work to all contacts.
5. Document all past work and translate into slides, 8" x 11" photographs, and onto CD/DVD.		5. Take short trips to Ottawa and Toronto; collect local newspapers and business cards of galleries.	5. Send emails to friends and family with photos of past work and new sales' prices.
6. Research possible courses in photography, marketing and portfolio making to ensure good representation of product.		6. Research any out-of-province gallery or festival where I could exhibit.	6. Research addresses and contacts for galleries/ organizations; send out resumes and cover letters.
			7. Represent quality depictions of work in portfolio and in all advertising.

PRODUCT	PRICE	PLACE	PROMOTION
1. Keep and develop research on explored themes to help formulate essays and how it appeals to target markets.	1. Keep sales record.	1. Arrange three exhibitions for the coming year.	1. Have potential clients updated on work continually.
2. Have two works accomplished to my standards every month, complete with summary.	2. Accumulate clients' feedback.	2. Put one to three works in clubs, bars, and restaurants in the next two months.	2. Monitor hits and comments on website and be involved and responsive.
3. Examine any progress or deterioration of skill after each completed painting.	3. Keep records of price reduction from negotiations.	3. Have one work placed in a company within three months.	3. Have article in press before graduation.
4. Compare my work to competitors to ensure a unique style and an exemplary quality.	4. Augment price accordingly if sales are good and often within the next four months.	4. Monitor number of hits and comments on website.	4. Evaluate how I have been managing the marketing (advertising) communications twice a year.
5. Receive a minimum GPA of 3.8, thereby having evidence of product quality.	5. Examine effect of prices on sales every time I negotiate, sell, or do not sell.	5. Examine progress, or lack thereof, of finding new venues.	
	6. Compare my prices to competitors to appraise my work properly.	6. Evaluate which venues sell better and with which themes.	

PRODUCT	PRICE	PLACE	PROMOTION
1. Brainstorm themes and begin projects immediately. Have two or more finished every month.	1. Begin summaries of work, develop packaging of certificates of authenticity and photos immediately for previous works and complete these packages as paintings are completed.	1. Research areas for exhibition immediately; meet with managers.	1. Add website address to my contact information as soon as webpage is functional.
2. Have a collection of at least 40 new works within two years.		2. Approach three companies within the next two months.	2. Begin assembling direct mail campaign immediately; send press releases immediately.
3. When preparing for an exhibit, have all inclusive work finished two weeks prior to opening.	2. Set base and suggested prices for work upon completion.	3. Begin organizing website; have it launched within three months.	
4. Document all past work immediately.		4. When organizing an exhibit, have all arrangements done two weeks or more prior to its opening.	
5. Have my university education (and therefore my product development) done by 2008, my Masters by 2010.			

GENERAL

TEST SUPERSITES WITH INTERACTIVE SELF-ASSESSMENTS

http://www.testcafe.com

http://www.queendom.com

http://www.outofservice.com

http://www.psychtests.com

http://assessment.monster.ca

http://www.workingresources.com

http://www.iqtest.com

http://www.adv-leadership-grp.com

GROUPS AND INTERPERSONAL RELATIONS

Are You a Team Player?
http://content.monster.com/tools/quizzes/teamplayer/

Leader Personality
http://www.similarminds.com/leader.html

Conflict Style and Conflict Management
http://www.cios.org/encyclopedia/conflict/selftest.htm

http://www.conversationswithoutconflict.com/test.html

Stress
http://stress-management.net/stress-test.htm

http://www.adv-leadership-grp.com/programs/
evaluations/stress.htm

Change Resiliency
http://www.workingresources.com/changeresiliency/

How Culturally Aware Are You?
http://www.kwintessential.co.uk/resources/culture-
tests.html

artists

PHOTOGRAPHERS

Photo Life Magazine
> http://www.photolife.com/
>> Articles and portfolios from photographers

Profotos.com
> http://www.profotos.com/
>> Online resource centre that promotes photography and photographers

The Canadian Association for Photographic Art
> http://www.capacanada.ca/
>> Connects Canadian photographers for peer support

Online Portfolio Postings
> http://www.portfolios.com/
>> Post and view online portfolios of photographers, animators, designers, and more

MUSICIANS/SINGERS

The Society of Composers, Authors and Music Publishers of Canada
> http://www.socan.ca/
>> Links Canadian musicians to listeners around the world

Fekda Fonik
> http://www.fekdafonik.com/
>> Production and publishing company that favours local talent

Canada's Entertainment Source
> http://www.canehdian.com/industry.html
>> Links to relevant industry resources

CIRPA—Canadian Independent Record Production Association
> http://www.cirpa.ca/
>> Supports independent Canadian music

FILMMAKERS

Filmmaker

http://www.filmmakermagazine.com/

Monthly news on independent filmmaking, actors, and festivals

Cineworks

http://www.cineworks.ca/

Good place to find workshops and rent filmmaking equipment

Qui Fait Quoi

http://www.qfq.com

Portrait of news in the communication industry (French)

Association des Producteurs de Films et de Télévision du Québec

http://www.apftq.qc.ca/en/index.asp

Represents the independent film and television production companies

Canadian Film & Television Production Association

http://www.cftpa.ca/

Represents television, film, and interactive production in the country

FASHION DESIGNERS

YES—Youth Employment Services

http://www.yesmontreal.ca/yes.php

Delivers English-language job-search and self-employment services to Quebeckers

Style Career

http://www.stylecareer.com/

Tips on the fashion and image industry and how to promote yourself within it

514 Connexion

http://www.514connexion.com/

Corporate site of a fashion designer who established herself

PAINTERS

Canada Council for the Arts

http://www.canadacouncil.ca/

Promotes arts and culture in Canada

Coop St-Laurent

http://www.coopstlaurent.org/

Helps artists get affordable studios or equipment

Café Graffiti
> http://www.cafegraffiti.net/
>> Promotes urban art and artists

PERFORMANCE ARTISTS

Quebec Drama Federation
> http://www.quebecdrama.org/
>> Resources for the performing arts

ACTRA (Alliance of Canadian Cinema, Television and Radio Artists)
> http://www.actra.ca
>> National organization of Canadian performers working in the English-language recorded media

Women Artists' Mentoring Program
> http://www.mawa.ca/
>> Puts mentors together with people who wish to gain experience in the visual arts

WRITERS

Association of Canadian Publishers
> http://www.publishers.ca/CNM_Index.wws
>> Promotes Canadian books

Association of English-Language Publishers of Quebec
> http://www.aelaq.org/
>> Promotes the publication of English books from Quebec

Writers Guild of Canada
> http://www.wgc.ca/sign_producers/
>> National association representing writers working in film, television, radio, and multimedia production in Canada

Job Seekers

RESUME WRITING

JobStar Central
> http://jobstar.org/tools/resume/index.cfm
>> Tools for all the important details of looking for a job

BakosGroup
> http://bakosgroup.com/
>> Professional and executive resume writing service from which you can receive free feedback

Broadcast a Resume

http://www.broadcastaresume.com/job_seekers/video_resume.html

Helps in the preparation of video resumes

INTERVIEW TIPS

Canadian Association of Career Educators and Employers

http://www.cacee.com/

Non-profit partnership of employer recruiters and career services professionals

Job.Interview.net

http://www.job-interview.net/Bank/QuestionBankInDepth.htm

Complete resource centre to adequately prepare for a good interview

Monster.ca

http://interview.monster.com/archives/tips/

Tips on interview FAQs

JOB POSTINGS

Human Resources and Social Development Canada

http://www.hrsdc.gc.ca/en/home.shtml

Government site that lets you research careers

Monster.ca

http://www.monster.ca

Search engine for anything that involves employment

CareerBuilder.ca

http://www.careerbuilder.ca

A resource centre to help you excel in your chosen career

CollegeGrad.com

http://www.collegegrad.com/

Geared for recently graduated job seekers

Montreal Jobs

http://www.jobsmontreal.com

Online source for finding a job in Montreal

FabJob.com

http://www.fabjob.com/

Insider information on how to get yourself your dream job

INTERNSHIPS

CareerEdge

> http://overview.careeredge.ca/index.asp?FirstTime=True
> &context=0&FromContext=1&language=1

> Canada's internship organization for the business
community

Federal Public Sector Youth Internship Program

> http://www.youth.gc.ca/yip-psj/

> Program for Canadian youth from Service Canada

Experience Canada

> http://www.experiencecanada.com/en_html/index.html

> Internship programs to get experience abroad

CAREERS IN FINANCE

Careers in Finance

> http://www.careers-in-finance.com/

> Information about pursuing a career in finance; discusses
in detail careers in commercial banking, corporate finance,
financial planning, insurance, investment banking, money
management, and real estate

Jobs in the Money

> http://www.jobsinthemoney.com/

> Dedicated to the financial services industry; job postings
section, resume writing help, and career news and advice

Career Voyages

> http://www.careervoyages.gov/

> Created by the U.S. Dept. of Education and U.S. Dept.
of Labor; information on pursuing careers in finance, healthcare,
transportation, construction, retail, information technology, and
others

Insurance and Financial Services Jobs

> http://www.ifsjobs.com/

> A place to view job listings and post resumes for those
interested in a career in insurance or financial services.

Entrepreneurs

ENTREPRENEURSHIP

Industry Canada

> http://www.strategis.ic.gc.ca/

> Canadian directory of all registered companies

Statistics Canada

> http://www.statcan.ca/

> Canadian directory of statistics in a variety of fields

Human Resources and Social Development Canada
http://www.hrsdc.gc.ca/en/home.shtml

Can help you with questions related to human resources in Canada

Entrepreneurship Magazine
http://www.entrepreneur.com

Magazine that enables you to keep in contact with the news relevant to entrepreneurs

FRANCHISING

Canadian Franchise Association
http://www.cfa.ca/

Resource centre for both franchises and franchisees

ADVERTISING

Advertising Principles
http://fourps.wharton.upenn.edu/advertising/

Ideas about how to create an effective advertising campaign

Hoover Web Design
http://www.hooverwebdesign.com/business/index.php

About design and development for small businesses

LEGAL SERVICES

Canada Legal
http://www.canadalegal.com/

Canadian legal resource directory

Legal Services
http://www.entrepreneurship.com/consultations/
zoomConsultation.asp?ID=13

The Entrepreneurship Centre; provides a 30-minute consultation on specific entrepreneur issues for $25

GRANTS

Government Grants
http://www.businessguide.net/

Business guide to government grants and loans available in Canada

Small Business Funding Centre
http://cdn-grants.grants-loans.org/

Tips on how to fund your small business for training, staff, equipment, etc.

Professionals

NETWORKING

Career Journal

http://www.careerjournal.com/jobhunting/networking/

Articles on how to network and different ways to do it

Networking for Professionals

http://www.networkingforprofessionals.com/index.php

Devoted to help professionals network

MindTools

http://www.mindtools.com/page5.html

Essential time management skills

LAWYERS

Quebec Bar Association

http://www.barreau.qc.ca/

The association of Quebec lawyers

Canadian Bar Association

http://www.cba.org/CBA/Home.asp

Information service of the Canadian Bar Association

ENGINEERS

Engineering.com

http://www.engineering.com/

Trade publication for all engineers that features news, technology, and events

Canadian Society for Civil Engineering

http://www.csce.ca/

Society intended to develop and maintain high standards of civil engineering practice

RESTAURATEURS/CHEFS

Wired Hotelier

http://www.wiredhotelier.com/index.html

Industry site with news and events

Baking, Pastry & Chef Schools

http://www.chef-schools-baking-pastry.org/

Directory of cooking schools

Restaurant Owner

http://www.restaurantowner.com/

Industry guide magazine to help improve the business end of a restaurant

HUMAN RESOURCES

Human Resources Professionals Association of Ontario
   http://www.hrpao.org/hrpao
      Professional association advocating for the human resources profession

HEALTH SERVICES

Canadian Nurses Association
   http://www.cna-nurses.ca/cna/
      Association with the goal to advance the quality of nursing in the country

Canadian Medical Association
   http://www.cma.ca/index.cfm/ci_id/121/la_id/1.htm
      Association of physicians who recognize the need for a national medical body

Canadian Chiropractic Association
   http://www.ccachiro.org/
      National organization that advocates on behalf of the chiropractic profession and chiropractic patients

Canadian Dental Association
   http://www.cda-adc.ca/
      Online link to news and information on dentistry and oral health in Canada

Canadian Psychological Association
   http://www.cpa.ca/
      Association for psychologists in Canada

Canadian Pharmacists Association
   http://www.pharmacists.ca/flash.cfm
      Leadership for the profession of pharmacy

TEACHERS

Canadian Association of Second Language Teachers
   http://www.caslt.org/
      For teachers who wish to teach English as a second language

JOURNALISTS

Canadian Association of Journalists
   http://www.caj.ca/
      Promotes excellence in investigative journalism in Canada

Canadian Newspaper Association
   http://www.cna-acj.ca/
      The voice of Canada's daily newspaper industry

Concordia University Department of Journalism
   http://journalism.concordia.ca/
      The Faculty of Arts & Sciences, a unique department of
journalism

ADVERTISING

Canadian Marketing Association
   http://www.the-cma.org/
      Canada's largest marketing association

AdvertisingAge
   http://www.adage.com/
      Latest news on the advertising industry

BCP
   http://www.bcp.ca/
      Leading Quebec advertising agency

ACCOUNTANTS

Chartered Accountants of Canada
   http://www.cica.ca/index.cfm/ci_id/17150/la_id/1.htm
      Association that wishes to uphold the professional
integrity, standards, and pre-eminence of the accounting
profession

Certified General Accountants Association of Canada
   http://www.cga-online.org/servlet/custom/
      publicView?region=ca
      Self-regulating, professional association of CGAs

Society of Management Accountants of Canada
   http://www.cma-canada.org/index.cfm/ci_id/45/la_id/1.htm
      Careers, publications, and more for certified management
accountants

PHYSIOTHERAPISTS

Canadian Physiotherapy Association
   http://www.physiotherapy.ca/
      Resource centre for Canadian physiotherapists

Canadian Kinesiology Alliance
   http://www.cka.ca/home.php
      Not-for-profit corporation that promotes the advancement
of and advocates the profession of kinesiology in Canada

advertising — any paid, non-personal form of communication by an identified sponsor

assignment interview — a type of interview designed to create a situation or scenario similar to the job being applied for in order to test how the candidate will respond

augmented product — the entire bundle of benefits or features in the core product

awareness — the first necessary (though not sufficient) step to create a sale; letting your target customers know of your existence, hopefully in a way that motivates them to seek further knowledge about your product, then develop a preference, and ultimately try and then keep purchasing your product

benefits — the positive consequences of using a product; benefits may be functional or psycho-social

brand — any combination of characteristics that uniquely identifies the product of one seller

brand advocates or brand ambassadors — consumers who spread positive word-of-mouth, adding to and becoming part of the buzz around a brand

brand commitment — when a customer experiences such a deeply rooted and emotional connection with a brand that he or she is willing to exert extraordinary effort to buy the brand

bundling — combining two or more items in a single package at a set price

ceiling price — the maximum price at which a customer will decide to either postpone the buying decision or seek ways to fulfill needs with substitute products

chronological resume — a type of resume organization that places the emphasis on employment history and career progression in a way that directly relates to the job the candidate is applying for

compatibility — the degree to which a new product is consistent with customers' values, knowledge, past experiences, and needs; also influences adoption

competitive pricing (also known as *pricing parity* and *status quo pricing*) — reducing the emphasis on price by matching competitors' prices and concentrating marketing efforts on the other three elements of the marketing mix

complexity — the level of difficulty in understanding and using a new product

consumer adoption process — the process through which consumers eventually adopt or reject a product, from becoming aware of the product's existence, to interest, evaluation, trial, and eventually adoption

consumer innovators — people who purchase new products as soon as they reach the market

convenience products — goods and services that consumers purchase frequently, immediately, and with little effort

core product — the basic benefit or key feature at the heart of what an organization offers to its customers

CRM — customer relationship management, a business philosophy that focuses on the long-term value of a customer and attempts to nurture relationships with consumers

customer satisfaction — a confirmation or disconfirmation of expectations

decline stage — period when innovations or changes in customer preferences result in declining industry sales

diffusion process — concentrates on all members of a community or social system in making purchase decisions

direct channel — channel that carries products directly from a producer to the business user or consumer

direct marketing — any one-on-one communication with targeted individuals, such as direct mail (including direct email) and telemarketing

direct selling — a marketing strategy in which the producer establishes direct sales contact with the product's final users

distribution intensity — the number of intermediaries through which a producer distributes its products in a particular market

early adopters — people who often look to the innovators for advice in making purchase decisions

early majority — people who follow the early adopters in making purchase decisions

emergency products — products purchased in response to unexpected and urgent needs

environmental analysis — part of the broader situation analysis, it includes a detailed analysis of the socio-cultural, economic, as well as political and legal environment in which you will compete

exclusive distribution — strategy where a producer may decide to give the exclusive rights to a wholesaler or retailer to sell its products in a geographic region or country

expectations — set in part by marketers by advertising, promotions, brand names, distribution, and product packaging

flexible pricing — different customers pay different prices for the same product

floor price — a price below which the quality will become suspicious and the customer might decide to look elsewhere

functional resume — a type of resume organization that highlights the skills, knowledge, and other qualifications a job seeker brings to the job. Useful for individuals who lack work experience or have gaps in their employment history

goals — meaningful things you truly want to accomplish

growth stage — period when new customers make their first purchases and early buyers repurchase the product

IMC (integrated marketing communications) — an approach that focuses on optimizing the impact of marketing communications by coordinating them to create a unified message to all stakeholders

impulse products — products that are purchased on the spur of the moment

input controls — activities to be performed before the actual implementation of a marketing plan, such as securing financing or the selection and training of employees

intensive distribution — a strategy that aims to have a product distributed through all available channels in a trade area

the Internet — a highly targeted direct marketing vehicle that has evolved from its original role as an information provider

introductory stage — period when organizations and individuals focus their marketing efforts on stimulating demand for their new product

laggards — people who are among the last to adopt new products

late majority — people who follow the early majority in making purchase decisions

market segmentation — the process of dividing a market into distinct groups of customers (or organizations) that share certain characteristics and react in a similar way to a marketing offer

marketing — planning and executing the conception, pricing, promotion, and distribution of ideas, goods, services, organizations, and events to create and maintain relationships that will satisfy individual and organizational objectives

marketing audit — a thorough, systematic, and periodic evaluation of marketing goals, strategies, tactics, and implementation activities

marketing channel — a set of intermediaries organized to ensure the movement of goods from producer to end-consumers

marketing intermediaries — organizations along the distribution channel that ensure the movement of goods from producer to end-consumers; can include import agents, wholesalers, brokers, retailers, and others

marketing objectives — short-term destinations along the path toward longer-term organizational or personal goals

marketing orientation — implies that achieving organizational and individual goals starts with determining the needs and wants of target markets and delivering the desired satisfactions more effectively and efficiently than competitors do

marketing plan — document assembled at the outcome of the planning process that details each of its steps

marketing planning process — the process of researching the marketing environment, establishing objectives, formulating strategies and tactics to achieve these objectives, and implementing and evaluating the impact of activities used to execute the strategies

marketing strategy — long term plan of action designed to achieve the marketing objectives

maturity stage — period when sales and profits continue to grow but then reach a plateau as the number of potential customers declines

needs — the reason, purpose of underlying actions. May be physiological or psychological in nature

networking — the process of establishing relationships with people who can assist you with job search and customer acquisition strategies and particularly with finding job and sales leads

objective–task method — a method of budgeting marketing communications expenses by first defining the objectives and then costing the tasks required to accomplish these objectives

observability — the extent to which the benefits of a new product can be observed by potential customers

odd pricing — the most commonly used psychological pricing tactic, where prices are set at odd numbers just below round numbers

output controls — activities to ensure that marketing outcomes are as expected

penetration pricing strategy — a strategy whereby low prices are used as a major marketing tool to enter a new market

personal selling — person-to-person communication in which the seller attempts to assist or persuade prospective buyers to purchase his or her product or to act on an idea

place — one of the four Ps of marketing; concerned with issues of distribution, channel management, and location selection

positioning — teaching your customers to think (or feel) about your product as a solution to a need (broadly defined) and in a way that is superior to the competition's offering

price elasticity — the fact that different customers will react differently to changes in price

price skimming — a pricing strategy that involves setting relatively high prices compared to your competitors; often used to enter a market for products with little or no competition

process controls — activities and behaviour needed during implementation of a marketing plan, including issues such as commitment to the marketing strategy, motivation and compensation of employees, and internal communications

product lifecycle — the various stages a product goes through as it ages; typically marked by different levels of sales

product line pricing — a tactic whereby several items within a product line are offered at specific price points

production orientation — focuses on the product, on what an organization can produce and control, as opposed to consumers' needs and desires

profits — whatever is left from revenues after all expenses have been paid

promotional pricing — temporarily reducing regular prices

psychographic data — information concerned with consumers' lifestyles, usually described in terms of preferred activities, interests, and opinions

psychological pricing — based on the belief that certain prices or price ranges make products appealing

public relations — non-personal communication about a product, brand, organization, idea, or person not directly paid for or run under identified sponsorsip

pull strategy — concentrates on appealing to the end consumers directly so they in turn will request the product from members of the marketing channel

push strategy — promotion strategies and tactics (e.g., trade allowances) directed at members of a channel, such as distributors and retailers, to entice them to sell a product to the end consumer

quality assurance — intended to identify and solve, even before they occur, potential problems or breakdowns that could jeopardize quality

quality control — implementing the necessary inspection checks to make sure that no defective product ever leaves the factory

relative advantage — a new product's clear and meaningful advantage over substitutes and competing products

sales orientation — invests heavily in advertising, sales promotion, and personal selling

sales promotion — catch-all term for those marketing activities that provide extra value or incentives to the ultimate consumer, sales force, or distributors to stimulate sales

selective distribution strategy — strategy where organizations and individuals choose a limited number of outlets in a market area to sell its products

shopping products — products that consumers buy only after comparing competing offerings on such criteria as price, quality, style, colour, and fit

single-price pricing — occurs when a retailer or professional sells all its goods and services at the same price

situation analysis — detailed research and analysis of the environment you will be competing in, designed to provide you with vital information to formulate other key portions of your marketing plan (such as objectives, strategies, and tactics)

societal marketing orientation (also sometimes called *social marketing*) — takes the marketing orientation one step further by including the idea that satisfying customers should be done in ways that maintain or improve the well-being of both customers and society

specialty products — products that offer unique features and benefits that result in consumers placing high value on them and their brands

staples — convenience products that consumers constantly replenish so they'll always have them on hand

stress interview — a type of interview where the interviewer puts the candidate in a stress situation to test the candidate's behaviour, logic, and emotional response under pressure

SWOT analysis — a type of analysis designed to examine internal (strengths, weaknesses) and external (threats, opportunities) factors that can influence your ability to achieve your objectives

tactics — short- to mid-term activities that will be carried out to put the strategy into action

target marketing — a marketing approach designed to focus on key groups of consumers and tailor the marketing mix to their needs and wants

total quality management (TQM) — continually improving products and processes with the goal of achieving ever-increasing levels of customer satisfaction

trialability — a product's ability to be tried on a limited basis

unbundling — the practice opposite to bundling; limits the number of goods or services that come with a basic offer

unsought products — products marketed to consumers who may not yet realize any need for them

values — central beliefs that guide your actions and decisions. Values may be instrumental (modes of conduct; "to be or to act") or terminal (desired end states; "to have")

p. iv: Courtesy Jordan L. Le Bel.

p. v: Ryan Blau/PBL Photography.

p. 1: Photo courtesy of Darcy Raymond.

p. 19: Photo courtesy of Mike Owen.

p. 32: Photo courtesy of Erica Horn.

p. 56: Photo courtesy of Julie-Anne Arsenault.

p. 78: Photo courtesy of Harvey Schwartz.

p. 112: Photo courtesy of Marc-Olivier Bossé.

p. 153: Photo courtesy of Mark Gentile.

p. 180: Photo of Kim Tien Huynh courtesy of Tandy Sean Arnold.

p. 198: Photo courtesy of Peter J. Loyello.

p. 240: Photo courtesy of Aline Massouh.

p. 267: Photo courtesy of Robert Roach.

pp. 288–303: Courtesy of Tamara Paradis.

pp. 304–317: Courtesy of Summer Geraghty.